Collecting American Presidential Autographs

In memory of Kent Taber

Collecting American Presidential Autographs

Paul C. Richards'
The Presidents of the United States of America

Edited and Introduced by
Paul Rich

WESTPHALIA PRESS
An imprint of Policy Studies Organization

Collecting American Presidential Autographs:
Paul C. Richards'
The Presidents of the United States of America

Westphalia Press
An imprint of Policy Studies Organization
dgutierrezs@ipsonet.org

For information:
Westphalia Press
1527 New Hampshire Ave., N.W.
Washington, D.C. 20036

ISBN-13: 978-0944285756
ISBN-10: 0944285759

Updated material and comments on this edition can be found at the Policy Studies Organization website:
http://www.ipsonet.org/

INTRODUCTION TO NEW EDITION

The autograph dealer Paul C. Richards was a 1961 graduate of Boston University, to which he gave massive collections of valuable manuscript material. There are very few important collections of original documents in American libraries that do not have some items, which passed through Richards' hands. Along with Charles Hamilton and Kenneth Rendell (still very active and now the doyen American dealers), he ranks as one of the most authoritative autograph experts of the last part of the twentieth century. Rendell was a friend of Richards and so from his website (ironic for an autograph dealer!) it is appropriate to quote his own views on collecting:

"Historical document and autograph collecting, and collecting historical memorabilia is a virtual time machine that takes us into the lives of those persons in culture and history whose genius has touched us, whose lives and accomplishments have inspired us, whose efforts have created our heritage and influenced our present. History and the people who made it are the keys to who we are today and who we may be tomorrow. Autograph letters and documents are the most direct link we can have to the heroes and heroines, villains, and ordinary people of the past. They show these men and women as human beings, dealing with matters on a scale that all of us can relate to. We begin to appreciate that their lives may not be all that different from our own—that people of the past confronted the same feelings and fears that we all do, that they preserved to achieve the goals—both great and small—of their lives. Perhaps the greatest emotion elicited by collecting autographs, historical letters and documents is inspiration. While many may think of collecting historical memorabilia as an intellectual pursuit, it is an emotional one as well. Many collectors have told me of their being overwhelmed with emotion sitting in a room at home with the "presence" of those they admire. One told me that he walked through the rooms of his home every night in awe of those whose letters and documents he had displayed on his walls. Another described how during moments, when inspiration escaped her in her work, she sat gazing at her collection and reflecting on the highs and lows of these people's lives and how they had overcome the difficult times and persevered to attain greatness."

Certainly this is the spirit in which to remember Richards, a sometimes controversial and immensely active figure, both generous and eccentric. His comments on Presidential autographs are well worth preserving.

THE PRESIDENTS OF THE UNITED STATES OF AMERICA

AUTOGRAPH LETTERS
HISTORICAL DOCUMENTS

PAUL C. RICHARDS — AUTOGRAPHS

FIVE DOLLARS

Toll-Free 1-800-637-7711
617-939-8981
(Mass. & Outside U.S.A.)

Paul C. Richards Autographs

High Acres
TEMPLETON, MASS. 01468

MANUSCRIPTS AND BOOKS
POLITICAL AMERICANA

ABAA ANTIQUARIAN BOOKSELLERS ASSOCIATION of AMERICA

CATALOGUE 179

TERMS: Material may be ordered on a one-day approval basis; all items guaranteed genuine and as described; accounts payable in 30 days for those who have established credit; postage payable on all orders including approvals. Credit available to responsible persons upon request. For telegrams and cables the code word for this catalogue is " CENTURY ". Massachusetts residents must add 5% State Sales Tax.

Foreword

Collecting the autographs of the men who have held the office of President of the United States continues to be the single most popular area of concentration for American collectors. No other category of autograph collecting has such a broad-based appeal. Whether it is the specialist who seeks the letters and other autographic materials of his "hero", or the history buff who aspires to assemble a complete set of the thirty-nine men who have held the highest elected office in the land, the gathering of Presidential Autographs is a way to bring the colorful panorama of American history before our eyes.

Not only does the collecting of Presidential Autographs appeal to a larger percentage of collectors than autographs in other areas, they have, as a group, out-performed most other autographs, and for that matter collectibles in general, from the standpoint of investment and financial growth. While we do not share with some of our colleagues the point of view that Presidential Autographs, or any other autographs, should be collected solely as an investment, still it is hard to ignore the history of their past performance as a collectible that has increased in value ahead of the rate of inflation. I believe that a collector should build his collection for the love, enjoyment, fascination, and yes pride, in what he has been able to accomplish.

We have assembled in this Catalogue a wide variety of autograph material from all of our Chief Executives. Letters, documents (official and unofficial), checks, signed photographs, inscribed books, franked address-leaves, White House and Executive Mansion cards, vignette cards and cut signatures may be found in these pages. It is our objective to offer material of the highest quality in all price ranges. All material offered in this Catalogue is unconditionally guaranteed authentic.

As you read the personal thoughts of these thirty-nine men, some great figures with a flare for flamboyance, some profound and scholarly, some reserved in the dignity of their office, and others near failures, do-nothings or persons of questionable character, let us remember that each, with the single exception of Gerald Ford, was popularly elected to the office of President or Vice President by the people, and as a group they reflect the true character of the electorate who voted them into office.

Come, we beckon you, travel back through the years of our past, and share with these special men their thoughts, their dreams, their schemes, their aspirations, and yes, even a glimpse of their personal character.

PAUL C. RICHARDS

TOLL-FREE CALLING

PS. As a convenience to our customers we have had installed a toll-free number. If you live outside of Massachusetts and within the United States, we will welcome your call at 1-800-637-7711.

1. MADISON, JAMES. President. Handsome, partly-engraved Document Signed, as President. Tall folio, vellum. Washington, April 22, 1816. Countersigned by BENJAMIN W. CROWNINSHIELD, Secretary of the Navy. Embossed white wafer seal of the Navy Department affixed with red wax at bottom center. President Madison commissions SAMUEL L BREESE to serve as a Lieutenant in the U.S. Navy. Breese was a distinguished naval officer who later achieved prominence in the Mexican War, and retired with the rank of Admiral. Handsome engraved vignette of a large spread-eagle at top center, and another of military accoutrements at bottom. Extremely fine condition with Madison's signature particularly choice. Crowninshield's signature is light. Very striking appearance, and a wonderful wall decoration for the naval buff. 1250.00

P.M.G.

Are all these selected in accordance with the executive order of the summer?

FDR

2. ROOSEVELT, FRANKLIN D. President. Highly unusual Autograph Endorsement Signed "F.D.R.", as President, penned in bright blue ink at the bottom of a typed document headed "Memorandum for the Postmaster General", on the imprinted stationery of the First Assistant Postmaster General. 1 page, 4to. Washington, January 7, 1937. The subject is nominations for local postmasters, and the memorandum reads: "This list contains 341 nominations. There are two large offices: Boston, Massachusetts / Elizabeth, New Jersey - recommended by Sen. Moore". In his note, addressed to "P.M.G." [James A. Farley, Postmaster General], FDR enquires: "Are all these selected in accordance with the executive order of the summer? FDR" Fascinating in-house communication between the President and his Postmaster General concerning the appointments of local postmasters, traditionally a matter of patronage, until "reformed" by Civil Service regulations. Excellent condition. 950.00

3. LINCOLN, ABRAHAM. President. Handsome partly engraved Document Signed "Abraham Lincoln", as President. Tall folio, vellum. Washington, July 2, 1862. Countersigned by EDWIN M. STANTON Secretary of War. Embossed blue wafer seal of the War Department. Lincoln commissions John J. Bowen an Assistant Quartermaster of Volunteers, with the rank of Captain, in the U.S. Army Ornate document, with large spread-eagle vignette at top center, and another military vignette featuring flags, swords, lances, rifles and bayonets at bottom. Fine condition, with a nice full signature of the lamented president. 2500.00

4. HAYES, RUTHERFORD B. President. Handsome partly printed Document Signed, as President. Full page, 4to. Washington, May 12, 1880. President Hayes authorizes the Secretary of State to affix the Seal of the United States to "warrants for the pardon of J. W. Mattingly and Thomas McGue." Pristine condition. With portrait. 425.00

5. REAGAN, RONALD. President. Handsome, full-face, smiling bust photograph, boldly inscribed in bright blue ink on the lower white margin: "To Howard Lee - With warmest wishes & Best Regards / Ronald Reagan". Quarto. Imprint of photographer, Harry Langdon, Los Angeles, on verso. Probably dates from the late 1970's. Striking pose! Choice!! 175.00

TWO-VOLUME UNIFORMLY BOUND SET OF CLEVELAND'S PRESIDENTIAL PAPERS FOR BOTH ADMINISTRATIONS, INSCRIBED TO THE SAME INDIVIDUAL

6. CLEVELAND, GROVER. President. Printed books: The Public Papers of Grover Cleveland...March 4, 1885, to March 4, 1889. Original deep magenta cloth, gilt-lettered spine. Government Printing Office: Washington, 1889. First edition. AND: The Public Papers of Grover Cleveland... March 4, 1893, to March 4, 1897. Original deep magenta cloth, gilt-lettered spine. Government Printing Office: Washington, 1897. First edition. Both volumes bear identical presentation inscriptions by the former president: "Miss Mary G. Desmond / from / Grover Cleveland / Oct. 20, 1898". Extremely fine condition, identically bound, and rarely found as a match set with both volumes inscribed to the same party. 1000.00

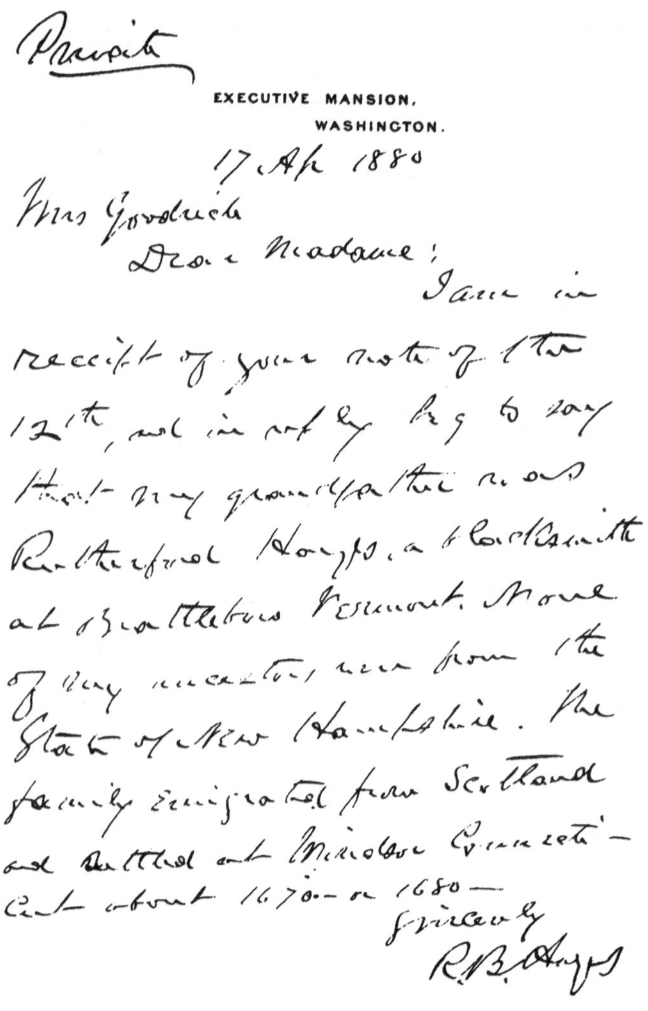
Private

EXECUTIVE MANSION,
WASHINGTON.

17 Ap 1880

Mrs Goodrich
Dear Madame:
I am in receipt of your note of the 12th, and in reply beg to say that my grandfather was Rutherford Hayes, a blacksmith at Brattleboro Vermont. None of my ancestors were from the State of New Hampshire. The family emigrated from Scotland and settled at Windsor Connecticut about 1670 or 1680—
Sincerely
R.B. Hayes

PRESIDENT HAYES SUPPLIES GENEALOGICAL INFORMATION ABOUT HIS FAMILY

7. HAYES, RUTHERFORD B. President. Choice Autograph Letter Signed, as President, on imprinted Executive Mansion stationery. Full page, 8vo. Washington, April 17, 1880. To Mrs. [J. B.] Goodrich, Maxfield, Maine. Original postmarked envelope (stamp removed), addressed by Hayes. Headed Private. In responding to his correspondent's note, Hayes begs "...to say that my grandfather was Rutherford Hayes, a blacksmith at Brattleboro, Vermont. None of my ancestors were from the State of New Hampshire. The family emigrated from Scotland and settled at Windsor, Connecticut about 1670 or 1680...." Fine condition. 1500.00

SCARCE EARLY FORM OF HIS SIGNATURE

8. HOOVER, HERBERT. President. Typed Letter Signed "H. C. Hoover", on his imprinted stationery, while in business as a mining engineer. 1 1/2 separate pages, 4to. London, September 3, 1913. To John A. Stewart, New York City. Hoover has penned "Confidential" at the top of the first page. In part: "...I have simply lost all heart in the San Francisco position. I have on three occasions, after most careful consideration and discussion with prominent Englishmen and Officials, outlined definite courses of action to the Exposition people in San Francisco. On all these occasions...they refused to follow my advice, and I have now come to the firm resolve that my connection shall hereafter be nil. On each of the two previous occasions I have been proved absolutely right...and I have not the slightest doubt that I shall prove right in the more recent instance. San Francisco looks mighty diminutive when looked at from the West End of London, whereas it probably looks very large from the Exposition buildings in San Francisco. The whole of the difficulties arise out of the inability ...to put the opposite end of this line of vision in the proper perspective...." Excellent condition, and a very early letter bearing the scarce form of his signature. 350.00

A VOLUME FROM THE PRESIDENT'S LIBRARY

9. BUCHANAN, JAMES. President. Volume VI of Edward Gibbon's The History of the Decline and Fall of the Roman Empire. Second American edition. Philadelphia, 1816. Original decorated calf binding (worn); front and rear hinges very weak (should, and could be professionally restored). Signed in full by Buchanan at the top of the title-page; also signed by HARRIET LANE JOHNSTON, the president's niece and White House hostess, who has added "Wheatland, October 1868". Books from Buchanan's library are seldom encountered. 350.00

10. CLEVELAND, GROVER. President. Autograph Letter Signed, as President, on imprinted Executive Mansion stationery. 2 pages, 8vo. Washington, March 22, 1886. To [William H.] Villas, his Postmaster General. Cleveland writes a note of introduction for Francis W. Bird of East Walpole, Mass. "The bearer of this is Mr. F. W. Bird of Mass. who is of the good kind and knows a great deal about Dedham and some other places. He wants to talk a very little and I want him to see the Dedham papers. He can tell about the Democratic support of Cummings. I have held his nomination until tomorrow to hear what Mr. Bird will say after seeing the papers..." Excellent condition, and an interesting political letter pertaining to the appointment of a postmaster at Dedham. 750.00

11. JACKSON, ANDREW. President. Partly printed Document Signed, as President. Oblong folio, vellum. Washington, November 2, 1830. Countersigned by ELIJAH HAYWARD, Commissioner of the General Land Office. Remnant of wafer seal. Grant of 124 and 56/100 acres of land in the area of Zanesville, Ohio, as authorized by "by Acts of Congress, entitled An Act providing for the sale of the Lands of the United States in the Territory north west of the OHIO, and above the mouth of Kentucky River..." Fine condition, save for the seal defect as noted, with a good long signature of Jackson. With engraved portrait. 695.00

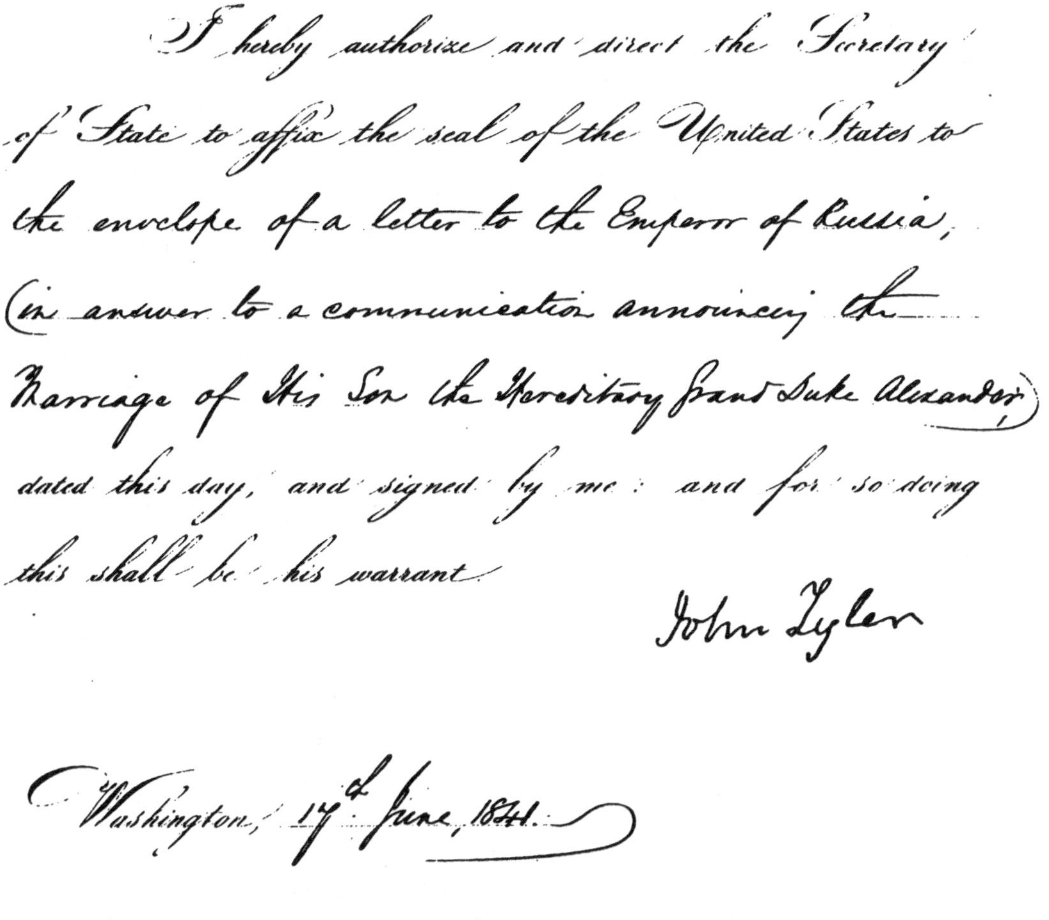

I hereby authorize and direct the Secretary of State to affix the seal of the United States to the envelope of a letter to the Emperor of Russia, (in answer to a communication announcing the Marriage of His Son the Hereditary Grand Duke Alexander) dated this day, and signed by me: and for so doing this shall be his warrant

John Tyler

Washington, 17th June, 1841.

CONGRATULATIONS FOR THE RUSSIAN EMPEROR

12. TYLER, JOHN. President and Vice President. Handsome partly printed Document Signed, as President. Full page, 4to. Washington, June 17, 1841. President Tyler authorizes the Secretary of State to affix the Seal of the United States to "the envelope of a letter to the Emperor of Russia, (in answer to a communication announcing the Marriage of His Son the Hereditary Grand Duke Alexander)..." Attractive document, boldly signed, in fresh condition. 750.00

13. DAVIS, JEFFERSON. President, Confederate States of America. Attractive Autograph Letter Signed, as a Senator from Mississippi. 1 page, 4to. Senate Chamber [Washington], April 11, 1850. To General Thomas Jessup, Quarter Master General. Davis writes: "I some time since directed the papers in the case of Geo. Poindexter claiming compensation for damages done to his property by cavalry in service of U.S., to be sent to your office. Please inform me whether you have received those papers and if any decision has been made thereon...." In the first session of the Thirty-first Congress, Davis served as chairman of the important Committee on Military Affairs. After the death of John C. Calhoun, not long before this letter was written, he assumed leadership of the Southern Democrats in their opposition to the Compromise of 1850. Fine condition. With engraved portrait. 495.00

14. JOHNSON, ANDREW. President and Vice President; Governor of Tenn. Attractive albumin carte de visit showing the bust profile of the president. Boldly signed on the lower white margin of the mount. Very fine condition, and quite scarce in this format. 2000.00

15. EISENHOWER, DWIGHT D. President and General. Strikingly handsome quarto photograph depicting a 3/4 length, full-face, seated image of the President, holding his eyeglasses in his right hand. Photo by J. Anthony Wills, Houston, Texas. Beneath a neatly lettered secretarial inscription for Richard Rendell, Ike has penned in jet-black ink: "with best wishes / Dwight D. Eisenhower". Pristine condition, and a really handsome photograph! 250.00

16. CLEVELAND, GROVER. President. Lower half of a partly printed Document Signed, as President. 1 page, oblong folio. Washington, August 25, 1893. Countersigned by W. Q. GRESHAM, Secretary of State. Large white, embossed wafer seal of the Department of State at left. Although a fragment, complete in itself. Excellent condition. 150.00

17. HARDING, WARREN G. AND FLORENCE K. President and First Lady. Unusual partly printed Document Signed by both. 1 page, small 4to. Probate Court, Marion County, Ohio, April 29, 1914. Headed "Waiver of Summons, on Petition to Sell Real Estate". Signed by the future president who was acting as Administrator of the Estate of Mary Harding. Also signed by his wife, his

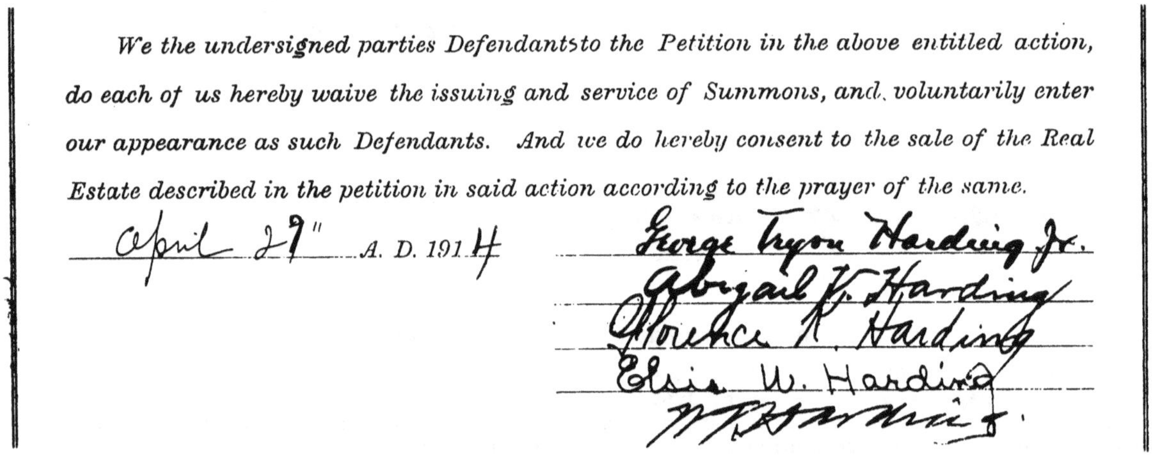
We the undersigned parties Defendants to the Petition in the above entitled action, do each of us hereby waive the issuing and service of Summons, and voluntarily enter our appearance as such Defendants. And we do hereby consent to the sale of the Real Estate described in the petition in said action according to the prayer of the same.

April 29" A. D. 1914

George Tryon Harding Jr.
Abigail V. Harding
Florence K. Harding
Elsie W. Harding
W. G. Harding

brother George, and other members of the Harding family. Seldom do such personal presidential documents come on the market. Fine condition. [Bottom half of document illustrated above]. 395.00

18. ROOSEVELT, FRANKLIN D. President. Handsome oblong quarto photograph depicting a beaming FDR seated at his desk, wearing a bow tie but no jacket. A very large globe of the world is behind him. There are two other men in the photograph, one of whom is Paul Wooton, the journalist. Inscribed on the wide white margin at the bottom: "To Paul Wooton from his old friend / Franklin D. Roosevelt". Mounted. Fine. 250.00

REDECORATING THE WHITE HOUSE

19. COOLIDGE, GRACE GOODHUE. First Lady. Autograph Letter Signed, as First Lady, on the gilt-crested stationery of The White House. 2 full separate pages, 8vo. Washington, Tuesday [November 17, 1925]. To the wife of Coolidge's Postmaster General, Mrs. Harry S. New. Original imprinted White House envelope, postmarked, and addressed by Mrs. Coolidge, with the two-cent black Harding commemorative postage stamp. Mrs. Coolidge writes: "I do not know about Riley and that which may have moved him to write as he did but I do know something about painters for they have been working here ever since we came back and are taking their ladders and brushes away to-day. May I come out Friday afternoon to see your home?...I want you to come and have dinner with me on Gridiron night this time. It will not be a party but we will try to have a good time. Dinner at seven. Sincerely your friend...." Fine and scarce! With printed portrait. 225.00

20. MADISON, JAMES. President. Handsome, partly-engraved Document Signed, as President. Tall folio, vellum. Washington, April 1, 1811. Countersigned by WILLIAM EUSTIS, Secretary of War. Embossed, perforated, white wafer seal of the War Department at upper left. Madison appoints Josiah Bacon, Jr., Second Lieutenant in the Fourth Regiment of Infantry in the U.S. Army. Wonderful spread-eagle (with shield and talons) vignette at top center, and a huge vignette of flags and military accoutrements (by I. Draper, Sculp.) covering the entire lower portion of this splendid document. Very fine condition. A sight to behold!! 950.00

21. ROOSEVELT, THEODORE. President and Vice President. Typed Letter Signed, as President, on imprinted White House stationery. 1 page, 4to. Washington, February 10, 1908. To Hon. Curtis Guild, Jr., Governor of Massachusetts, Boston. Roosevelt writes: "I think that is very interesting. I always feel about such adherents just the way that you do. Will you give Mr. Fitzwilliams my warm regards, and tell him that I appreciate both the song and the letter and value his friendship and goodwill, and that I shall try to continue to deserve them by my public actions? I look forward to seeing you ten days hence...." Two small punch-file holes in top blank margin, otherwise fine. Bold signature! 595.00

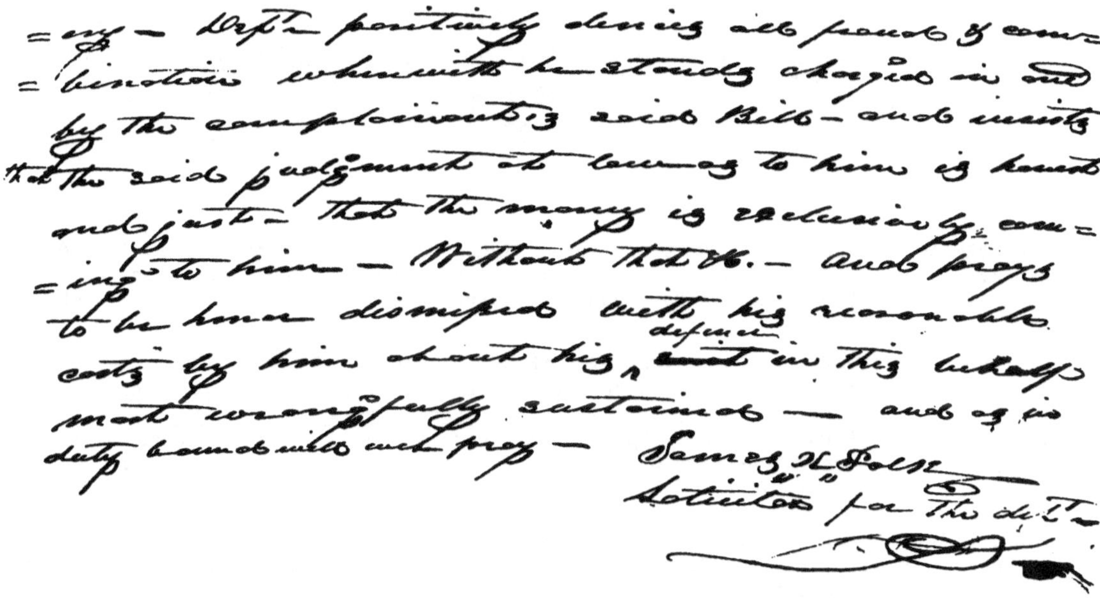
=ing - Deft positively denies all frauds & com-
=binations wherewith he stands charged in and
by the complainants said Bill - and insists
that the said judgment at law as to him is honest
and just - that the money is exclusively com-
=ing to him - Without that &c. - and prays
to be hence dismissed with his reasonable
costs by him about his defence in this behalf
most wrongfully sustained - and as in
duty bound will ever pray - James K. Polk
Solicitor for the deft.

RARE HOLOGRAPH LEGAL BRIEF BY THE FUTURE PRESIDENT

22. POLK, JAMES K. President. Excessively rare Autograph Document Signed, as a young attorney in Tennessee. 2 full pages, legal folio. Maury Circuit Court, Tennessee, December 31, 1824. As attorney for the defense in a legal action, Polk prays for the dismissal of the charges, explaining in some detail his reason. On the integral leaf there is a document in another hand signed by the defendant (Polk's client) swearing that the facts contained in the adjoining document are true. There is also a six-line docket in Polk's hand on the verso of the integral leaf. We have never before seen a legal brief in Polk's holograph, and for those collectors who desire presidential documents in this format, this might well be a once-in-a-lifetime opportunity. Extremely fine condition. 950.00

23. TRUMAN, HARRY S. President and Vice President. Typed Letter Signed, as President, on imprinted White House stationery. 1 page, 4to. Washington, March 16, 1946. To Bishop G. Bromley Oxnam, New York City. Original stamped, postmarked envelope. Truman writes: "I appreciated very much your courtesy in sending me a copy of your book, BEHOLD THY MOTHER. I am particularly pleased with the inscription. The meeting at Columbus was a very fine one, I think, and will do this country and the world some good. I enjoyed the visit with you and the people of Columbus very much...." Pristine condition. A real gem!! 475.00

PIERCE WRITES PRESIDENT POLK FROM MEXICO

24. PIERCE, FRANKLIN. President; General in Mexican War. Choice Autograph Letter Signed. 1 2/3 pages, 4to. Head Quarters, 3rd Division, Calle de Cadina, Mexico, October 25, 1847. To His Excy. James K. Polk, President of the United States, Washington. Docketed integral address-leaf bearing circular OLD POINT COMFORT, VA. / FREE postmark. Fine letter of recommendation for Lieutenant William H. French, who had been serving as Pierce's aid de camp. He writes: "...Lieut. French took his degree with high reputation at West Point in 1837 and from that time has been constantly on duty, having never been absent a day on leave. He served in the Commissary Department in charge of the principal Depot of the Army at Brazos...[until] relieved at his own request to participate in the active operations on this line. He was at the siege of Vera Cruz, at Cerro Gordo. From the siege of Vera Cruz he served as Chief of Major General Patterson's Staff until that officer left the Country. From that time until he became my aid de Camp since we took possession of this City, he has served with high reputation as second in command in Taylor's battery, and had an active participation in all the battles of this Valley....If pure character, high attainments, distinguished conduct on the field and superior qualifications can insure success, Lt. French's friends may certainly indulge sanguine hopes of a result which...would subserve the best interests of the service and be a just reward of long and meritorious services...." French gained the Captaincy, and later during the Civil War, in the Army of the Potomac, commanded a division at Fredricksburg, Chancellorsville and Harpers Ferry. He was relieved by Meade from command of the Third Corps in 1863, for the failure of the Mine Run campaign which was blamed solely on French. 1500.00

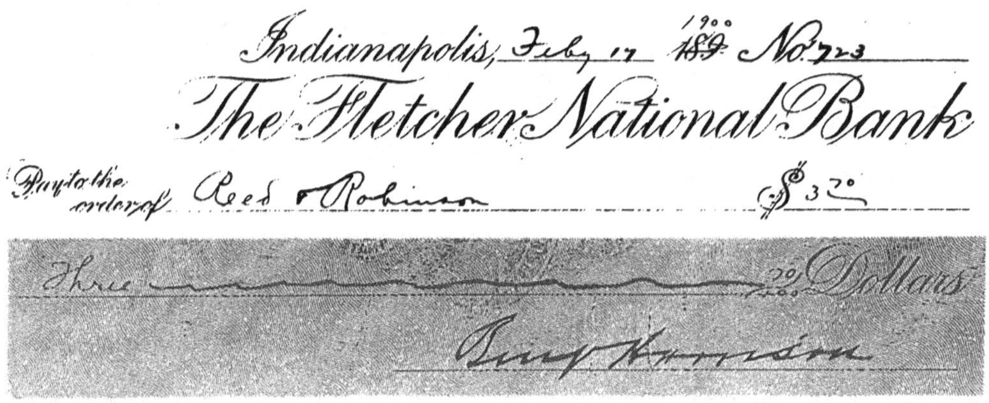
Indianapolis, Feby 17 1900 No. 723
The Fletcher National Bank
Pay to the order of Reed & Robinson $3 70/100
Three 70/100 Dollars
Benj Harrison

25. HARRISON, BENJAMIN. President. Partly printed Signed Bank Check, accomplished in the hand of a secretary. Oblong 12mo. Indianapolis, Indiana, February 17, 1900. Drawn on the Fletcher National Bank. Payable to Reed & Robinson. Cut-cancelled (nothing missing). 495.00

HOOVER'S AUTOBIOGRAPHY -- THREE VOLUME SET -- EACH VOLUME INSCRIBED

26. HOOVER, HERBERT. President. The three-volume set of his Memoirs: Years of Adventure 1874 - 1920; The Cabinet & The Presidency 1920-1933; The Great Depression 1929-1941. Cloth. New York, 1951-52. All First Editions. Each volume bears a signed inscription on the front endpapers by Hoover to the Womens City Club of San Francisco. Original dust-jackets. Very fine set of this important chronicle. 350.00

27. ROOSEVELT, ELEANOR. First Lady. Very scarce Autograph Letter Signed "E. R.", on her imprinted New York City stationery, as First Lady of New York State. 3 pages, 8vo. New York, September 13 [1932]. To "Dearest children" [Corporal Earl R. Miller, FDR's bodyguard, and his new bride]. She writes: "This will I hope reach you on your return steamer to tell you that I hope every moment has been pleasant but I'm going to be glad when I feel you a little nearer to me again. You were good to wireless, but I want to know how you are! Ruth dear, your Mother sounded happy over the telephone & Earl she said she loved you and your wire has made them both so happy. You know you are dears to all us elders! Anna started with a bad cold last night but Malvina wires all well on the train. Maine going Democratic has let every one up here! F. Jr. & I will motor to Groton Sunday & Louis may come there to drive back with me Monday. I'll be here for dinner Monday night to take you both & Elliott & Bevy I hope to the play. It will be good to see your faces & hug you again. A world of love to you both...." The Millers were married at a private ceremony at Val Kill Cottage in Hyde Park, New York, and went on a cruise for their honeymoon. This letter of Mrs. Roosevelt, penned during the presidential campaign of 1932, shows her affection for the couple. Fine. 175.00

FULL SHEET OF AL SMITH COMEMMORATIVE POSTAGE STAMPS

28. TRUMAN, HARRY S. President and Vice President. Full sheet of 100 three-cent postage stamps issued by the U.S. Post Office in 1945, in honor of Al Smith, former Governor of New York and presidential candidate. Signed on the left selvage by Truman, probably as President since the stamps were issued during his incumbency, and also by HAROLD L. ICKES, Secretary of the Interior. The sheet is in mint condition. Very rare in this format! 225.00

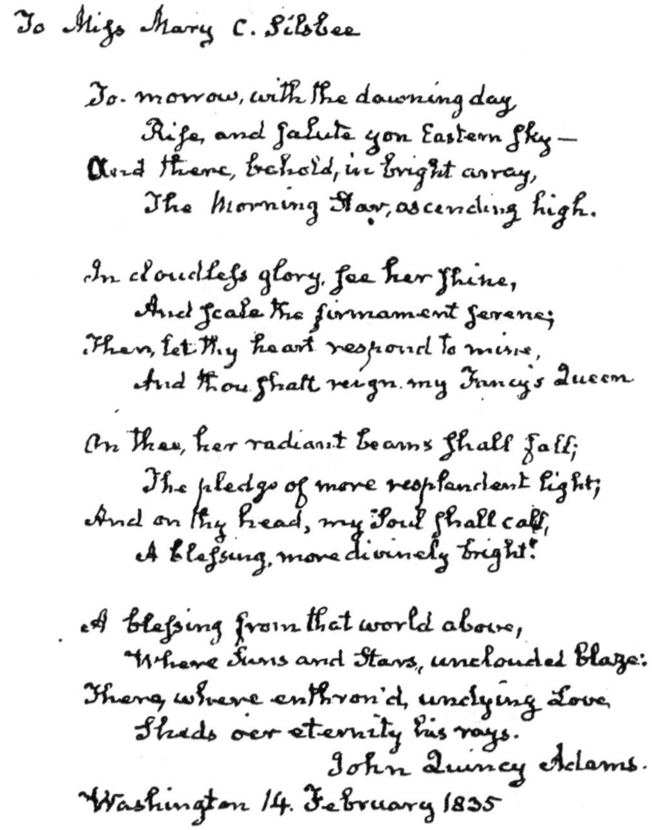

To Miss Mary C. Silsbee

To-morrow, with the dawning day
Rise, and salute yon Eastern Sky—
And there, behold, in bright array,
The Morning Star, ascending high.

In cloudless glory, see her shine,
And scale the firmament serene;
Then, let thy heart respond to mine,
And thou shalt reign my Fancy's Queen

On thee, her radiant beams shall fall;
The pledge of more resplendent light;
And on thy head, my Soul shall call,
A blessing, more divinely bright!

A blessing from that world above,
Where Suns and Stars, unclouded blaze:
There, where enthron'd, undying Love,
Sheds o'er eternity his rays.
John Quincy Adams.
Washington 14. February 1835

A POEM FOR SENATOR SILSBEE'S DAUGHTER

29. ADAMS, JOHN QUINCY. President. Autograph Manuscript Poem Signed, penned after his presidency while representing Massachusetts in Congress. Full page, 8vo. Washington, February 14, 1835. Touching four-stanza poem penned for Miss Mary C. Silsbee, the daughter of U.S. Senator Nathaniel Silsbee of Salem, Mass.

To-morrow, with the dawning day
Rise, and salute yon Eastern Sky --
And there, behold, in bright array,
The Morning Star, ascending high.

In cloudless glory, see her shine,
And scale the firmament serene;
Then, let thy heart respond to mine,
And thou shalt reign, my Fancy's Queen.

On thee, her radiant beams shall fall;
The pledge of more resplendent light;
And on thy head, my Soul shall çall,
A blessing more divinely bright.

A blessing from that world above,
Where Suns and Stars, unclouded blaze:
There, where enthron'd, undying Love,
Sheds oer eternity his rays.

Adams is the only American president who is also a published poet. He penned these sweet verses for the daughter of his colleague on Valentine's Day. Choice condition. 2500.00

FOOD ADMINISTRATION CERTIFICATE OF APPRECIATION

30. HOOVER, HERBERT. President. Very scarce, and highly attractive, partly engraved Document Signed, as United States Food Administrator. 1 page, small oblong folio. No place or date. [Washington, 1919]. Text reads: "The United States Food Administration to L. G. Dawson in appreciation of efficient and patriotic service during the Great War, 1917-1918." Hoover's signature is at bottom center. Handsome engraved vignette at head showing a bounty of produce coming forth from two cornucopias. The first document of this type we have seen. 225.00

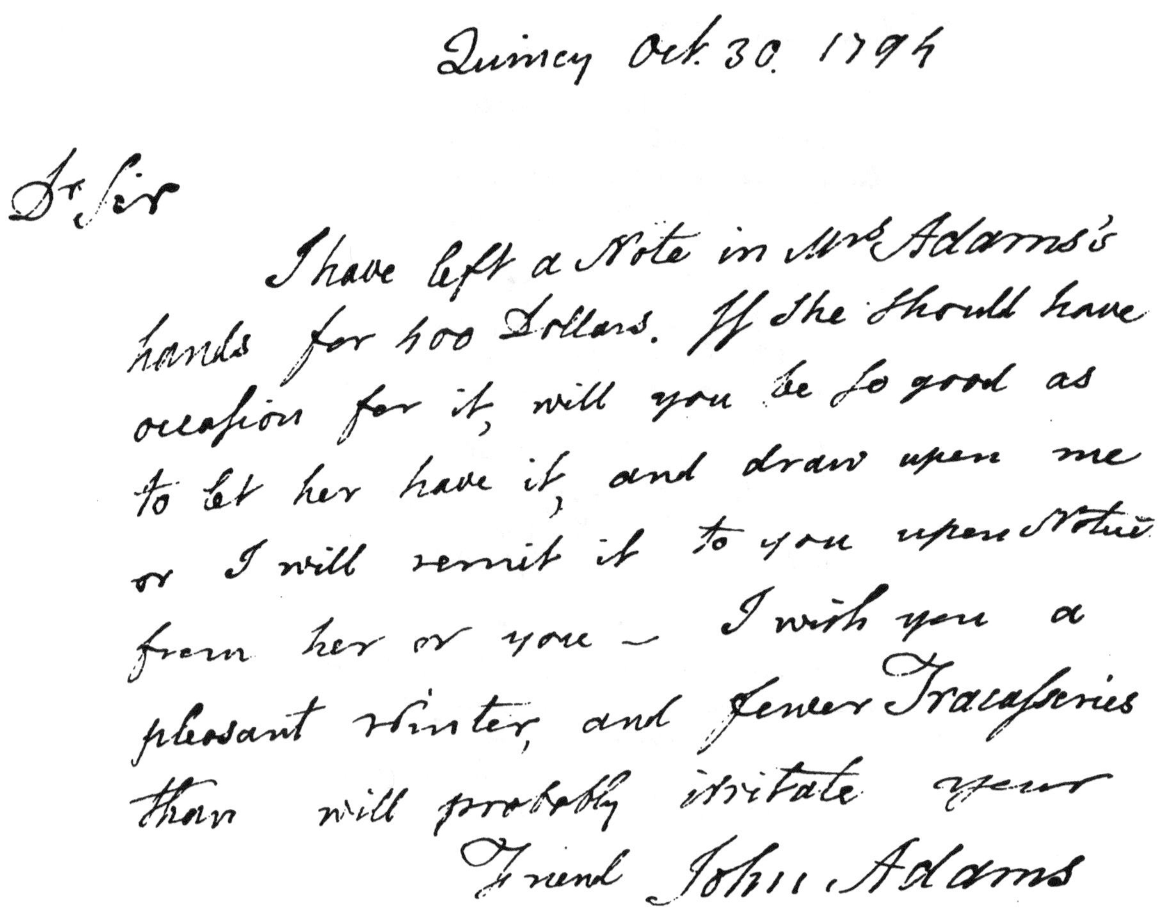
Quincy Oct. 30. 1794

Dr Sir

I have left a Note in Mrs Adams's hands for 400 Dollars. If She Should have occasion for it, will you be so good as to let her have it, and draw upon me or I will remit it to you upon Notice from her or you — I wish you a pleasant Winter, and fewer Tracasseries than will probably irritate your Friend John Adams

31. ADAMS, JOHN. President and Vice President. Superb Autograph Letter Signed, as Vice President. 1 page, 4to. Quincy, October 30, 1794. To General [Benjamin] Lincoln. Integral leaf addresed in Adams' hand. Interesting letter showing the Vice President's concern that his wife, Abigail, have enough money for her needs. "I have left a Note in Mrs. Adams's hands for 400 Dollars. If she should have occasion for it, will you be so good as to let her have it, and draw upon me or I will remit it to you upon Notice from her or you. I wish you a pleasant Winter, and fewer Tracasseries than will probably irritate your Friend / John Adams". A neat note penned at the foot of this letter by J. G. Morris in 1853 tells of the provenance. Handsomely preserved. With steel-engraved portrait. 4500.00

APPOINTMENT OF A SECRETARY FOR THE U.S. MISSION TO CHILE

32. JOHNSON, ANDREW. President and Vice President. Attractive partly printed Document Signed, as President. Oblong folio. Washington, November 11, 1865. Countersigned by WILLIAM H. SEWARD, Secretary of State. Unusual embossed lavender seal of the State Department affixed at lower left. Johnson appoints Edwin F. Cook, of New Jersey, to serve as Secretary of the Legation of the United States of America to Chile. Folds reinforced with tissue on verso, else quite fine. Nice appearing document for framing or display. 650.00

33. FILLMORE, MILLARD. President and Vice President. Autograph Letter Signed. 1 page, 8vo. Buffalo, N.Y., April 11, 1872. To E. Burrows, regretting that "I have no manuscripts of mine worth sending, as you requested..." Fine example. With portrait. 225.00

VICE PRESIDENT JOHNSON DENIES DISCRIMINATION EXISTS IN THE SECRET SERVICE OR ON THE DOMESTIC STAFF AT THE WHITE HOUSE

34. JOHNSON, LYNDON B. President and Vice President. Remarkable Typed Letter Signed, as Vice President, on imprinted blue-crested stationery. Full page, 4to. Washington, March 17, 1961. To D. Temple, Huntington Station, New York. Johnson appreciates his correspondent writing about his concern for "discrimination in government employment." He continues: "...The President [Kennedy] has established by Executive Order the President's Committee on Equal Employment Opportunity to carry out the Government's policy that there will be no discrimination on account of race, creed, color or national origin in governmental employment or employment on Government contracts. With respect to your specific question, I am informed by the Department of the Treasury that there are negroes employed by the Secret Service. Employment as domestic staff or attendants of the White House is certainly not limited to any race, creed, or color...." An important statement of President Kennedy's policy. Choice! 750.00

CATALOGUING GENERAL GARFIELD'S PAPERS

35. GARFIELD, LUCRETIA R. First Lady. Autograph Letter Signed, on her crested monogrammed mourning stationery. 2 1/2 pages, 12mo. Cleveland, Ohio, January 26, 1883. To W. H. Treadway. The widow of President Garfield writes: "...My secretary is now in Washington arranging and cataloguing General Garfield's papers. This work as most important must be done first. In time we shall reach these later accumulations but until then it will derange our method of work to undertake to make such [a] list as you desire especially since they have never yet been collected in one place. When we are able to do this it will give me pleasure to furnish you with our list...." Fine. 250.00

"OUR MASSACHUSETTS PEOPLE HAVE A REAL ENTHUSIASM, EVEN THOUGH IT BE NOT EXPRESSED ALL THE TIME"

36. COOLIDGE, CALVIN. President and Vice President. Typed Letter Signed, as Governor of Massachusetts and Vice President-elect, on the gilt and blue imprinted stationery of the governorship. Full page, 4to. State House, Boston, November 11, 1920. To Hon. Everett J. Lake, Governor of Connecticut, Hartford, saying that he tried to call on him, but found him out. Coolidge continues: "I want to take this occasion to tell you what a pleasure it was to meet you and express my appreciation of your exceedingly gracious reference to me at the Chamber of Commerce dinner. I hope that you will keep in mind that our Massachusetts people have a real enthusiasm. Even though it be not expressed all the time it is none the less real and I am sure from the reports that come to me the Chamber of Commerce has a real enthusiasm for you ...." Coolidge had been elected Vice President just days before writing this letter. Fine condition. 325.00

SIGNED PRESIDENTIAL MESSAGE

37. HAYES, RUTHERFORD B. President; Governor of Ohio; Union officer in Civil War. Printed: Message of the President...returning to the House of Representatives the Bill Entitled 'An Act Making Appropriations for the Support of the Army'..April 29, 1879. Tall 8vo. Government Printing Office: Washington, 1879. Printed wrappers. At the top of the front wrapper the President has penned: "With Compliments of / R. B. Hayes". This veto of the Army Appropriation was one of the many reasons Hayes had a falling-out with his fellow Republicans, and was not renominated in 1880. Fine. 450.00

38. TAFT, WILLIAM H. President; Chief Justice, U.S. Supreme Court. Typed Letter Signed, on his imprinted stationery. 1 page, 4to. New Haven, January 21, 1917. To Albert B. Kerr, Wall St., New York. Original stamped envelope. The former president acknowledges Kerr's "interesting suggestion to secure peace by depositing gold...." He comments: "I am afraid that it would be less easy to secure the consent of the great powers to this than to some other method, which might be equally effective...." Taft was president of the League to Enforce Peace. Certainly an interesting theory for bringing about world peace! Fine. 295.00

39. EISENHOWER, MAMIE D. First Lady. Typed Letter Signed, as First Lady, on gilt-imprinted White House stationery. 1 page, small 4to. Washington, February 24, 1958. To Miss Mary Barker, Rock Creek, Ohio, congratulating her on the completion of sixty years of service as Church Clerk of the Rock Creek Congregational Church. Nice warm letter. With envelope. 50.00

40. ROOSEVELT, THEODORE. President and Vice President. Autograph Letter Signed, with initials "T. R.", to a relative, whom he addresses as "Darling Pussie". Full page, 8vo. [1893]. Penned on the verso of a Typed Letter Signed from J. B. Gilder to Roosevelt, on stationery of The Critic, dated April 13, 1893. Gilder writes: "We are very glad to get the notice of Mrs. Dana's Wild Flowers, and will tack the last half of it on to our regular reviewer's account of the book...." Roosevelt writes: "This is not very satisfactory, as I don't think one can do much with a multilated review, and I suppose the half he doesn't tack on will be the part I liked best and considered the best tribute to Fanny's book. Still, I suppose it is all that can be done. If you see Fanny, tell her. Love to Douglas. I must have a fearfully gloomy talk with him over my finances...." Probably written to TR's sister, who married Douglas Robinson. Fine. 575.00

41. HOOVER, HERBERT. President. Superb studio photograph by Underwood & Underwood showing the full-face bust image of Hoover. Signed on the wide lower white margin: "The Kind Regards of / Herbert Hoover". Not inscribed to a named person. Handsome, and pristine! 250.00

WITH A FINE HOLOGRAPH POSTSCRIPT

42. TRUMAN, HARRY S. President and Vice President. Typed Letter Signed, as U.S. Senator from Missouri, on imprinted stationery of the United States Senate. Full page, large 4to. Washington, October 31, 1943. To Lt. Fred Whitaker, Camp Cooke, California. With a three-line holograph postscript in Truman's hand. Truman writes: "Dear Fred: I am certainly sorry I was out of town when you were at Camp Lee because I was extremely anxious to see you, but it looks as if we just cant (sic) get together. I had quite a visit in Missouri and you should have been with me. I was in Caruthersville, Joplin, Springfield, and Kirksville, and had a session all the way around. Politics are really picking up in Missouri and I am going to be sorry I dont (sic) have you to ride around with me in the next campaign...." In the postscript Truman adds: "I was counting on seeing you while you were here. I'm extremely sorry we didn't get together." Fine condition. 575.00

THE WHITE HOUSE
WASHINGTON

July 13, 1946

Dear Bishop Oxnam:

As veterans return to college by the hundreds of thousands, the institutions of higher education face a period of trial which is taxing their resources and their resourcefulness to the utmost. The Federal Government is taking all practicable steps to assist the institutions to meet this challenge and to assure that all qualified veterans desirous of continuing their education have the opportunity to do so. I am confident that the combined efforts of the educational institutions, the States, and the Federal Government will succeed in solving these immediate problems.

It seems particularly important, therefore, that we should now re-examine our system of higher education in terms of its objectives, methods, and facilities; and in the light of the social role it has to play.

These matters are of such far-reaching national importance that I have decided to appoint a Presidential Commission on Higher Education. This Commission will be composed of outstanding civic and educational leaders and will be charged with an examination of the functions of higher education in our democracy and of the means by which they can best be performed. I should like you to serve on this body.

Among the more specific questions with which I hope the Commission will concern itself are: ways and means of expanding educational opportunities for all able young people; the adequacy of curricula, particularly in the fields of international affairs and social understanding; the desirability of establishing a series of intermediate technical institutes; the financial structure of higher education with particular reference to the requirements for the rapid expansion of physical facilities. These topics of inquiry are merely suggestive and not intended to limit in any way the scope of the Commission's work.

I hope that you will find it possible to serve on this Commission.

Very sincerely yours,

Harry Truman

Bishop G. Bromley Oxnam,
President,
Federal Council of Churches of
Christ in America,
581 Boylston Street,
Boston,
Massachusetts.

TRUMAN ORDERS A PRESIDENTIAL COMMISSION TO EXAMINE HIGHER EDUCATION

43. TRUMAN, HARRY S. President and Vice President. Important, lengthy Typed Letter Signed, as President, on imprinted White House Stationery. Full page, large 4to. Washington, July 13, 1946. To Bishop G. Bromley Oxnam, President, Federal Council of Churches of Christ in America, Boston, Mass. Truman explains in detail the need for a Presidential Commission to examine the needs of higher education in America and the strain placed on these institutions by veterans returning to college under the GI Bill. He asks Bishop Oxnam to serve on this Commission. Text reproduced in full above. Fascinating presidential letter! 875.00

44. ROOSEVELT, FRANKLIN D. President. Typed Letter Signed, as President, on imprinted White House stationery. Full page, 4to. Washington, July 30, 1937. To Alexander G. Grant, Jr., Baltimore, Maryland. Original stamped, addressed White House envelope. In this curious letter to a close friend, Roosevelt writes: "Dear Zee:- Thank you much for your letter. I had no idea that Bill was coming out in the Senate. I hope you will read the debate that took place on it. The difficulty in the Senate lay, I think, in the fact that the proponents of the Bill seemed to have most of the arguments and there was little answer given on the other side of the case. The Bill has not been reported out by the House Committee. I do hope to see you one of these days. Affectionately..." It would be interesting to learn what the Bill was all about. Perhaps it was his attempt to pack the Supreme Court. Choice!! 650.00

"G[REAT] B[RITAIN] IS BEGINNING TO RELAX IN HER INJURIOUS POLICY TOWARDS THIS COUNTRY"

45. MADISON, JAMES. President; signer of U.S. Constitution and one of its authors and champions; co-author of The Federalist Papers; Secretary of State. Interesting Autograph Letter Signed, while representing Virginia in the U.S. Congress. 2 full pages, 4to. Philadelphia, November 15, 1794. To Major Lee. Madison writes:

> "My last requested the favor of you to give me such information as you might be able on the subject of my brother's & my joint interest in Kentucky. I wrote at the same time and made the same request to our friend Mr. H. Taylor. I write again to him as well as to you...and hope thro' your material and friendly assistance, to be able to understand and arrange every thing necessary to do justice to my brother's estate, as well as to myself....
>
> I have not yet rec'd any draught for the last payment due for the land; nor do I know whether you wish me to wait for one, or to make the remittance to you. Whatever your choice may be, you will please to let me know. In case a draught on me is preferred, I must request the favor of you to make it payable at 20 or 30 days sight if it be not inconvenient, as it might possibly find me in a place or at a moment not suited to discharge it.
>
> This will be forwarded by Col. James Innes who is charged I understand with explanations for your country on the measures & prospects relating to the Mississippi. It appears from the last acc'ts from Europe that G[reat] B[ritain] is beginning to relax in her injurious policy towards this country, and that some favorable issue may be expected to the mission of Mr. Jay. As far as this change may be the effect of misfortunes to the combined arms, the cause is increasing every moment. The French have signalized themselves more of late than at any period of the war. They have penetrated considerably into Spain, as well as regained their lost towns and overrun much of the territory of their enemies in the Netherlands. It is not improbable that they are before this in Amsterdam. In Poland also events are taking place which increase the alarm of all the sovereigns of Europe; of the K. of Prussia in particular who finds himself not only embarrassed there, but threatened with serious commotions in his own Dominions. I refer to the quicker and fuller acc'ts you will have from Fort Pitt of what has past in that quarter...."

Important, relatively early letter from Madison's career showing some insight into his personal finances and land dealings in Kentucky, and his concern for European politics. Some slight wear to the folds which have been partially strengthened with tissue, else in very good condition. 3500.00

46. FILLMORE, MILLARD. President and Vice President. Handsome Autograph Sentiment Signed: "For Mr. Sam'l L. Avery / With the Respects of / Millard Fillmore / Buffalo, N.Y. / Feby. 10th 1865." 16mo. With attractive steel-engraved portrait. Ideal for framing. 150.00

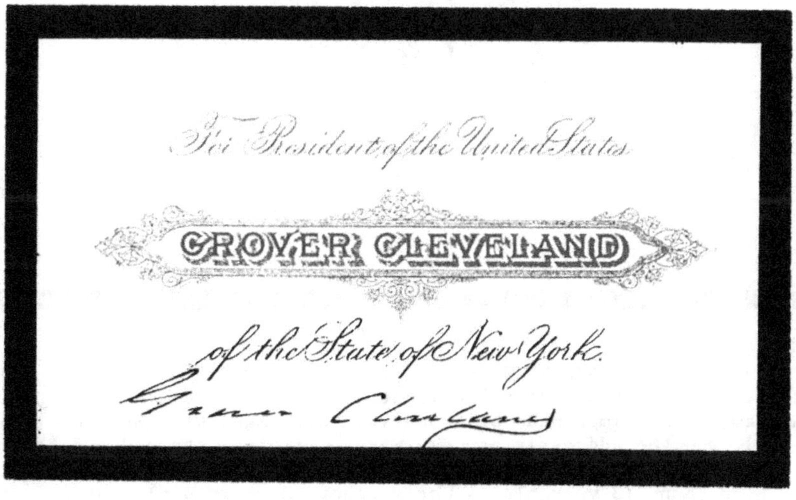

47. CLEVELAND, GROVER. President. Rare printed Electoral College voting ticket, reading "For President of the United States / GROVER CLEVELAND / of the State of New York." Signed in full by Cleveland beneath the last line of type. Rare, and most unusual! 250.00

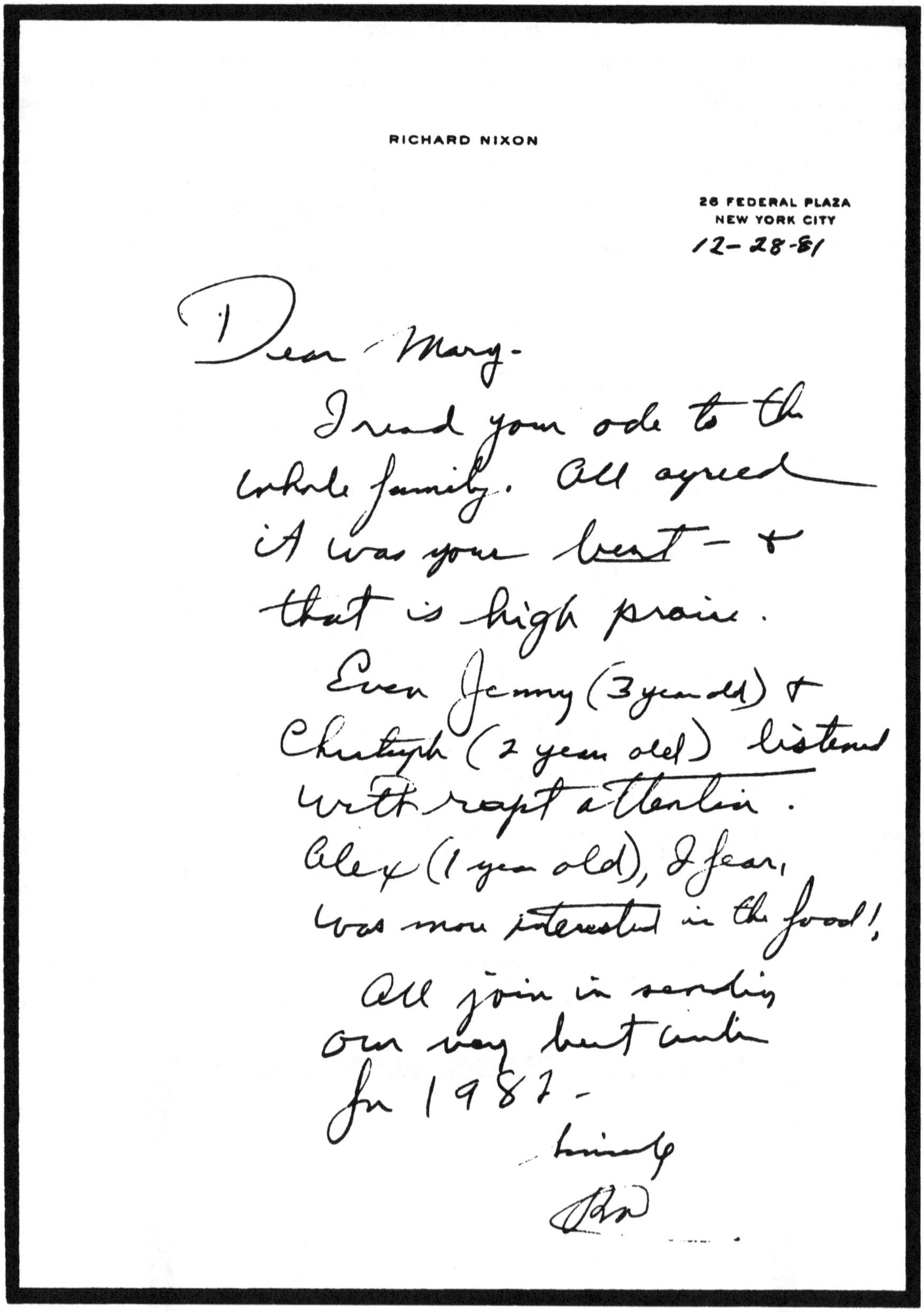
RICHARD NIXON

26 FEDERAL PLAZA
NEW YORK CITY

12-28-81

Dear Mary-

I read your ode to the whole family. All agreed it was your best - & that is high praise.

Even Jenny (3 year old) & Christoph (2 year old) listened with rapt attention. Alex (1 year old), I fear, was more interested in the food!

All join in sending our very best wishes for 1982-

Sincerely

RN

RARE NIXON LETTER IN FULL HOLOGRAPH

48. NIXON, RICHARD M. President and Vice President. Extremely rare Autograph Letter Signed with his "RN" monogram, on his imprinted stationery. Full page, 4to. New York, December 28, 1981. To Mary [Fenton], whom he addresses as Dear Mary. Original stamped and postmarked envelope. Nixon writes: "I read your ode to the whole family. All agreed it was your best -- & that is high praise. Even Jenny (3 year old) & Christopher (2 years old) listened with rapt attention. Alex (1 year old), I fear was more interested in the food! All join in sending our very best wishes for 1982...." Fine condition. This is the first ALS of Nixon that we have offered for sale, and needless to say they are quite rare. The young children are of course Nixon's grandchildren. 2500.00

"...BY MARRYING THE TWO FINEST GIRLS IN NEW YORK, [YOU] ARE IN A WAY TO MAKE FEDERAL IDEAS GROW..."

49. ADAMS, JOHN. Second President of the United States; Signer of Declaration of Independence; American Minister to Holland, France and England. Magnificent Autograph Letter Signed "John Adams", written while serving as Minister to England. 4 full pages, legal folio. Grosvener Square [London], May 24, 1786. To Elbridge Gerry, Massachusetts patriot and a fellow Signer, whose three-line docket appears in the margin of the fourth page. In part:

"...The Issue of all my 'Negotiations respecting the Interest of British Debts, during the war', and respecting every Thing else, is just nothing at all. I have done all in my Power to do to no purpose, and I tell you freely, that the British Ministry will do nothing about this or any Thing else untill the States shall support their Credit, and regulate their own trade, in a manner that shall shew that it is not left to British Merchants and Politicians to manage as they please. Nor then, in my opinion, will they ever intermeddle, or agree to relinquish the Interest. It will finally be left to every Debtor to make the best Agreement he can with his Creditors, or to dispute it at law, and avoid the payment of the Interest by the Verdict of a Jury. If the Juries give it against our Merchants, they will never find any other Remedy. As to any Clamour that may be raised by my concealed Competitors, it will do them no good nor me any harm. If they want my Place, and Congress give it them it will be with my hearty Consent, without any Clamour at all. A more disagreeable situation than mine no Man ever held in Life and whoever succeeds me, will not find it more pleasant.

If any one thinks he can do better in mercy, let him put up, and if any body thinks of any other man who can do more let him vote for him in the name of freedom. Old as I am, I had rather draw Writs and Pleas in Abatement than to suffer what is now my Lot. Making brick without straw, which has been my employment ever since I have been in Europe, and is more so now than ever, was never reckoned an easy, or pleasant Task, from the Days of the Israelites in Egypt to this moment. Untill I came to England I was as little apprised as you of the relent of this evil of Interest. It was too carefully concealed, by American Debtors, untill it was past a Remedy. The time is long since perfectly past, for doing any Thing in this Country, and another opportunity will never arrive, untill after a long and arduous Struggle.

You and our Friend [Rufus] King, by marrying the two finest Girls in New York, are in a Way to make federal Ideas grow, and may they prosper untill Congress shall have the Power and the Will, to form a System, which shall bring this Country to think. You may depend upon it, every man who expects any Thing from my Negotiations will be disappointed. I am not an Idler. My whole Time is employed to the Utmost of my Strength and Capacity, and to no more purpose, than if I were at Horse Races or Stage Plays....If it is not thought worth while to continue me here...I am myself fully of that mind, and am quite prepared to be recalled.

With great Esteem and Affection, your Friend

John Adams

Somehow it is impossible to follow the description of an Adams letter with comment, so it will suffice to say, that it is in choice condition. 7,500.00

50. [HARRISON, WILLIAM HENRY]. ATWATER, CALEB. 1778-1867. Ohio lawyer, state legislator, postmaster, Indian Commissioner, historian and author. Highly interesting Autograph Letter Signed. 3 full pages, legal folio. Circleville [Ohio], December 30, 1837. To General William H. Harrison, North Bend, Ohio. Docketed, postmarked integral address-leaf. Writing the defeated presidential candidate (1836), Atwater states: "...During the last few weeks, I have written over again, many parts of my History, especially that part devoted to a history of the War of 1812, in Ohio. At its conclusion, I have devoted several pages to a biographical sketch of Wm. H. Harrison. Want of money now prevents my getting out the Work. That difficulty removed I shall proceed to publish it. You have seen...the accounts of the drunken frolicks in the East, called, by the revellers Whig celebrations. Six millions of people living now in the great Whig states of the West, were placed at the tail end of all the states, and you were forgotten among those drunkards. So be it. The eastern revellers have uncovered the gulph before our feet, and we will avoid it. Away with a national convention; where we stand no chance. Let us have state nominations in Ohio, Indiana, Kentucky, and Pennsylvania, and go ahead. Now is the day and now is the hour. What do we care for the East, whose shameless treatment of us, shows where we stand in their estimation?...While you were suffering hunger, cold, and every privation -- travassing...swamps...where was Daniel Webster? In congress opposing all appropriations of men and money to support the War....I have prepared myself for a political campaign, for you...." With much more political content. Choice! 225.00

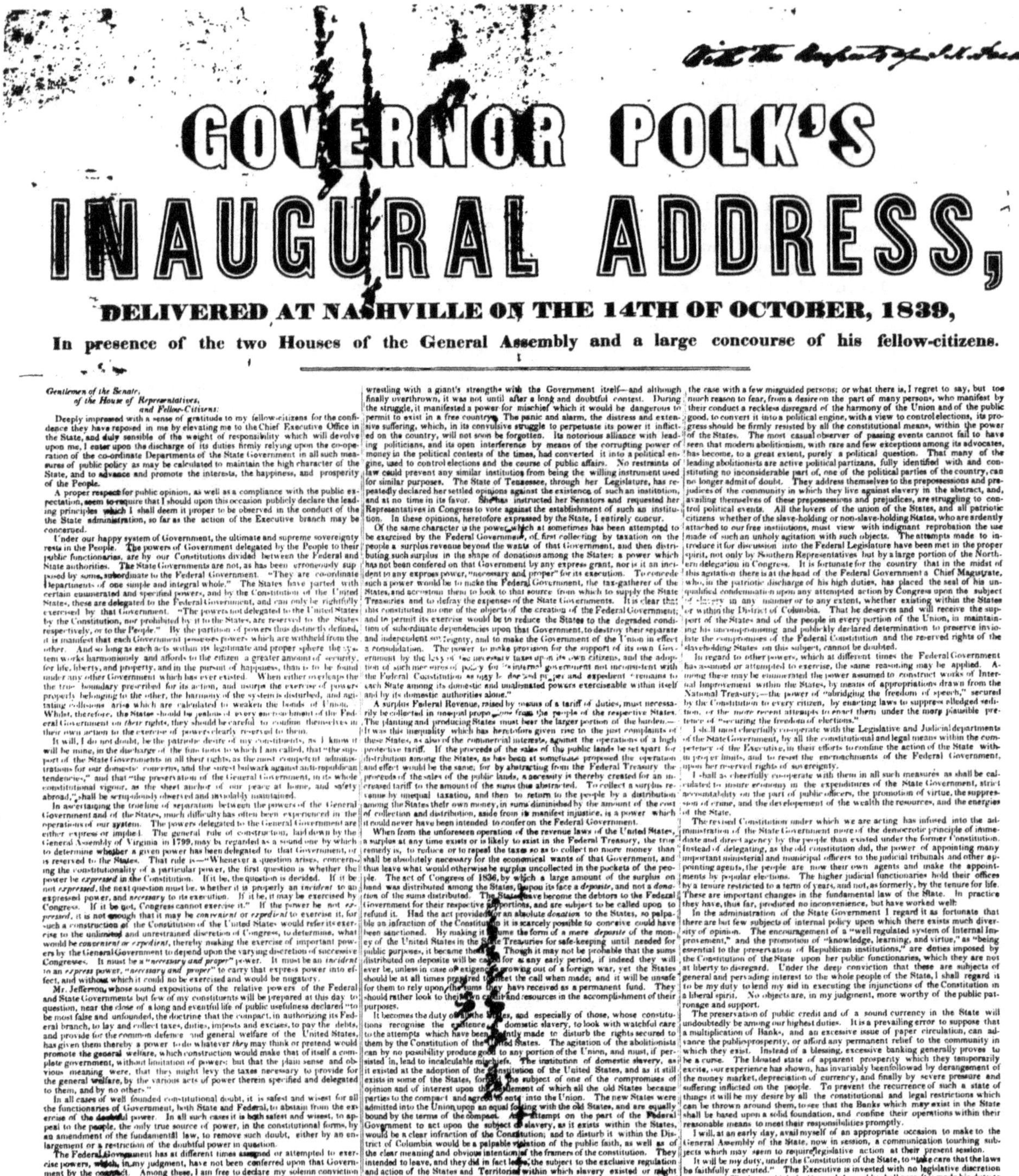
With the Respects of J. K. Polk

GOVERNOR POLK'S INAUGURAL ADDRESS,

DELIVERED AT NASHVILLE ON THE 14TH OF OCTOBER, 1839,

In presence of the two Houses of the General Assembly and a large concourse of his fellow-citizens.

SIGNED BROADSIDE PRINTING OF GOVERNOR POLK'S INAUGURAL ADDRESS

51. POLK, JAMES K. President; Governor of Tennessee; Speaker of U.S. House. Broadside headed: "Governor Polk's Inaugural Address, Delivered at Nashville on the 14th of October, 1839, in Presence of the two Houses of the General Assembly and a large concourse of his fellow-citizens." Large folio. [Nashville, 1839]. Boldly signed by the future President in the upper right corner "With the Respects of J. K. Polk". Originally folded to be sent thru the mail, Polk has penned the following address on the verso: "Hon. John H. Howe / Philadelphia" and there is also a "25" manuscript postal marking. The recipient has also placed his docket on the verso: "Gov. Polk's Inaugural / 1839." Other than some show-through from the address and docket on the verso, this very rare broadside is in fine condition. Polk is among the rarest of the Presidents to obtain in signed books or pamphlets, and while oversize, should be a welcome acquisition, indeed, to such a collection. We have never seen anything like it in our twenty years of dealing. 2,750.00

"YOU CANNOT BE TRUE TO THE PRINCIPLES OF THE REPUBLICANS OF THE DAYS OF LINCOLN...UNLESS YOU TURN AND SMITE DOWN THE BOSSES OF THE PARTY AND BREAK UP THE EVIL ALLIANCE BETWEEN COMMERCIALISM AND POLITICS"

52. ROOSEVELT, THEODORE. President and Vice President. Magnificent, lengthy Typed Letter Signed, on the imprinted stationery of The Outlook. 6 full separate pages, 4to. New York, September 18, 1913. To Hon. Charles S. Bird, Boston, Mass. Having lost his Presidential bid as the Progressive Party candidate in November, 1912, Roosevelt in writing to gubernatorial hopeful Bird, extols the virtues of the party, making a strong plea for thinking men of both traditional parties to work against the corrupt Republican and Democratic machines. In part:

"...Over a year has passed since we founded the Progressive Party, and what has happened since has served to make immeasurably clearer the vital need of our action. Massachusetts has always taken the lead for the right in every great crisis of our history, and I trust and believe that she will justify her ancient place of leadership at the present time. I make my appeal for your election not only to all the honest men who supported the Progressive ticket last year, but to all...men who...felt there was hope of salvation within the two old parties to which they had so long paid allegiance....

In the first place I appeal to all the good and honest men and women who make up the rank and file of the Republican party. I appeal to every Republican who is loyal to the principles of Abraham Lincoln, who is loyal to the great memories of Sumner and Andrew. Last year the bosses of the Republican Party stole from the rank and file of the Republican Party their right to nominate their own ticket and to enunciate their own platform. They turned the Republican Party with its back squarely to the principles of Abraham Lincoln and delivered it bound and shackled into the hands of those who are the enemies of every principle that Lincoln professed and practiced. These men have the Republican Party absolutely in their grip today....At this moment the Republican Party is the party of Lorimerism, and you can break Lorimerism only...by smashing the unprincipled machine which now has control of the party. It has this control as absolutely in Massachuetts as in New York and Illinois. Your men who control the Republican organization in your State work hand in glove with Mr. Barnes and Mr. Lorimer, with Mr. Penrose and Mr. Smoot; and you cannot be true to the principles of the Republicans of the days of Lincoln, you the rank and file of the Republican Party, unless you turn and smite down the bosses of the party, and break up the evil alliance between commercialism and politics for which those bosses stand; and you can do this only by supporting the Progressive Party.

As for the good and honest men and women who make up the rank and file of the Democratic Party, I ask them in their turn to consider what has been done by the Democratic machines in all the States of the Union...since their triumph last year. In New York State, Tammany has decreed the impeachment of the Governor, whom they themselves elected, because that Governor [Sulzer] has stood by the cause of the people, has championed direct primaries, and has endeavored to keep the pledges his party made before election. One main cause of the impeachment proceedings against him is the fact that he has endeavored to put into jail certain of the prominent Tammany politicians for misfeasance or malfeasance in office. In your own State half of the Democratic legislators have gone back upon their solemn pre-election promises with shameless effrontery, and the solidarity between these men is shown by the fact that the Democratic Candidate for Governor refuses to repudiate these men although they are running for re-election.

Finally, to all independent citizens, and to all party men who put country above party, I make this appeal. The bosses have long counted upon the fact that revolt against boss domination in one party could only find expression in seating in power the boss-controlled opposition party. In the last analysis, the bosses of the two old parties work together. Here in New York Mr. Murphy and Mr. Barnes desire nothing so much as a spirit of ironclad loyalty to the Republican and Democratic parties, so that dissatisfaction with either will result merely in its replacement by the other... At this moment Mr. Barnes in New York is trusting that he will regain power for his machine by taking advantage of the discontent with Mr. Murphy. Doubtless Mr. Murphy and Mr. Barnes would each of them like to control the State all the time; but they are entirely satisfied with the working compromise of having each of them control the State half the time....You can crush the boss system. You can put in effective fashion the stamp of your disapproval on the union of commercialism and politics. You can express your abhorrence of the politicians who win power and position through promises which with cynical indifference they repudiate as soon as elected. You can work for far-reaching measures of social and industrial reform, for genuine popular rule, and for the exercise of this rule in a spirit of justice to all our people, business men, farmers and wageworkers alike. All this you can do; but you can do it only by supporting the Progressive Party....We believe in having our practices square with our promises....If you are elected, it will be a magnificent thing for the splendid old Commonwealth of Massachusetts, and it will lift the heart of every struggler for good government, for fair play in the business and industrial world, throughout this Union...."

There are numerous corrections and additions in TR's hand throughout. Superb!! 4500.00

53. ROOSEVELT, THEODORE. President and Vice President. Interesting Typed Letter Signed, on his green imprinted "Oyster Bay" stationery. 1 page, 4to. Oyster Bay, October 7, 1915. To William Riis, son of Jacob Riis (1849-1914), in Williamstown, Mass. Original stamped envelope. The former President writes: "If you will turn to my last article in the Metropolitan magazine, you will see the full quotations from those treaties. Either they meant something or they did not. If they did not mean something, it was silly to have signed them. If they did, then of course it is impossible not to believe that we should have acted in some fashion or other...." Roosevelt suggests where copies of the treaties may be obtained. He has supplied two words in his own hand to the text. At this time Roosevelt was campaigning for American preparedness, in anticipation of war with Germany. Fine condition. 450.00

SIGNED LIMITED MINIATURE BOOK BY PRESIDENT FORD

54. FORD, GERALD R. President and Vice President. His book: <u>Global Stability</u>. Cloth. Lord John Press, 1981. A miniature book, measuring less than three inches. One of 400 numbered copies signed by the former President. Unopened, mint, as issued. 95.00

55. FORD, GERALD R. Same as above. Deluxe edition, bound in leather with marbled endpapers. One of 100 numbered copies. Cloth slipcase. Unopened, mint, as issued. 150.00

56. TAFT, WILLIAM H. President; Chief Justice, U.S. Supreme Court. Typed Letter Signed, while Chief Justice, on imprinted Supreme Court stationery. Full page, 4to. Pointe-au-Pic, Canada (Taft's summer home), July 27, 1926. To his friend Clarence H. Kelsey, New York City. In part: "...I am getting along but not as fast as I had hoped for. When I came up here the Doctor here thought I ought to undertake another period of rest cure and digitalis, which I have just completed. He thinks that...I have made progress, so that my pulse is more regular, but the readjustment and restoration to normal have not yet come. However, in every other respect I seem to be doing very well. This is a most recuperative air. I haven't been doing any work and am just existing in a most delightful way...." Then in reference to his house in Washington: "My own improvements are going on, and I hope to have them all done when I reach Washington the latter part of September. Helen's family are here and are occupying the new house which I built for her in the same inclosure with ours. Next month we look for Bob and his family and Charlie and his family, and hope that we may have all the grandchildren and all the children here..." Nice personal family letter. 350.00

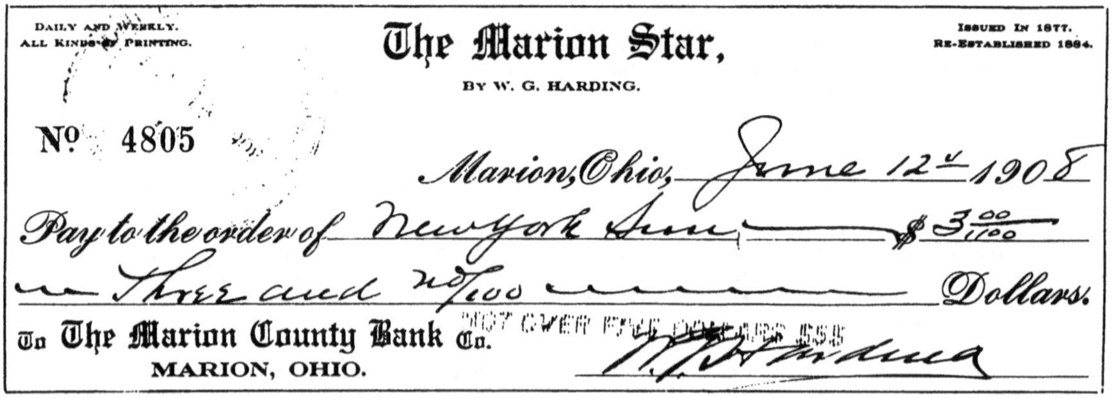
DAILY AND WEEKLY.
ALL KINDS OF PRINTING.
The Marion Star,
BY W. G. HARDING.
ISSUED IN 1877.
RE-ESTABLISHED 1884.
No 4805
Marion, Ohio, June 12th 1908
Pay to the order of New York Sun $3 00/100
Three and no/100 Dollars.
To The Marion County Bank Co.
MARION, OHIO.
W G Harding

57. HARDING, WARREN G. President; Governor and Ohio Senator; publisher. Partly printed Signed Bank Check, accomplished in his hand. Oblong 8vo. Marion, Ohio, June 12, 1908. Drawn on the account of his newspaper, <u>The Marion Star</u>, on the Marion County Bank, in favor of <u>The New York Sun</u>, the well known New York newspaper. Probably a subscription. Stamped bank cancellation in top left corner. Fine condition. Harding is relatively scarce in checks. 575.00

PRESIDENT CLEVELAND SENDS A POLITICAL CONTRIBUTION

58. CLEVELAND, GROVER. President. Autograph Letter Signed, as President, on imprinted Executive Mansion stationery. 1 1/2 pages, 8vo. Washington, March 5, 1888. To H. L. Bissal, Treasurer. Cleveland writes: "Upon inquiry I find that you are the Treasurer of an organization located here, having for its object the distribution of political information in the interest of Democratic doctrines. I desire to make a contribution to a cause so legitimate and useful. Enclosed please find my check for one hundred dollars...." Horizontal fold repaired with "magic mending tape" (newly applied), else fine. Unusual content for a president! 350.00

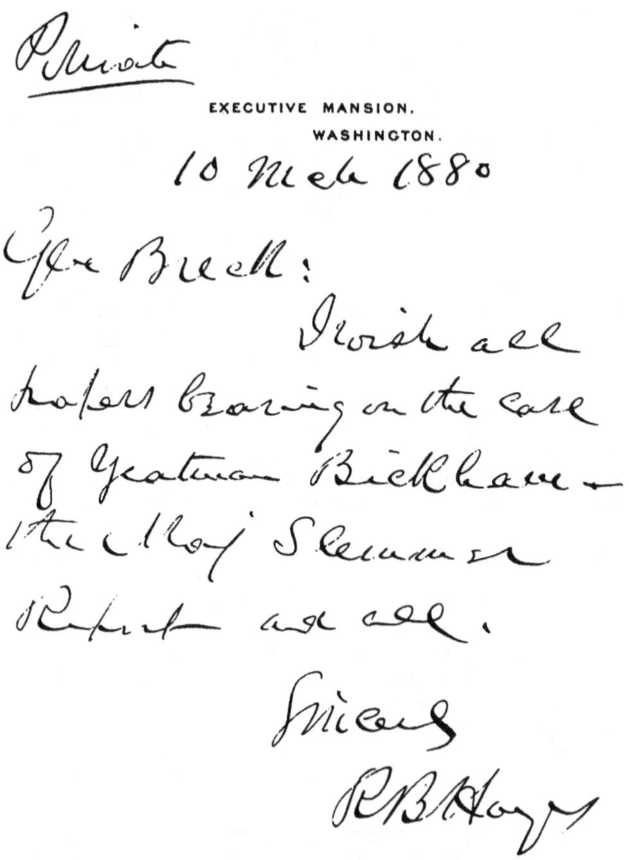
Private

EXECUTIVE MANSION,
WASHINGTON.

10 Mch 1880

Gen Breck:
I wish all papers bearing on the case of Yeatman Bickham — the Maj Slemmer Report and all.

Sincerely
R.B. Hayes

59. HAYES, RUTHERFORD B. President. Autograph Letter Signed, as President, on imprinted Executive Mansion stationery. 1 page, 8vo. Washington, March 10, 1880. To General Breck. Headed Private. Full text reads: "I wish all papers bearing on the case of Yeatman Bickham -- the Maj. Slemmer Report and all...." Boldly penned, and a handsome specimen. 750.00

60. MC KINLEY, WILLIAM. President; assassinated. Typed Letter Signed, as Governor of Ohio, on imprinted Executive Department stationery. ½ page, 4to. Columbus, February 19, 1895. To John Bell Bouton, Cambridge, Mass. Full message reads: "I have read your little production Uncle Sam's Church, and I take occasion to give expression to the pleasure it gave me in reading it...." Attractive specimen, with very bold signature. 195.00

61. ROOSEVELT, THEODORE. President and Vice President. Superb studio-size photo-gravure of the John Singer Sargent standing portrait of Roosevelt. Inscribed at top left against the light background: "Good luck to / Senator Joseph S. Frelinghuysen / from his friend / Theodore Roosevelt / May 11th 1917". Sargent painted the president's likeness from life in 1903, and the painting hangs in the White House today. We have not seen this gravure likeness before and believe it to be quite rare. A stunning 3/4 image of Roosevelt. Choice!! 575.00

62. TYLER, JOHN. President and Vice President. Partly printed Document Signed, as Governor of Virginia. 1 page, 4to. Richmond, December 8, 1826. Countersigned. Embossed wafer seal affixed with red wax at lower left. Governor Tyler appoints John Miller, "Lieutenant Colonel of the thirty-fifth Regiment, in the nineteenth Brigade and fifth Division of the...Militia, to rank as such agreeably to the number and date hereof." Unusual form of document which we have not seen before. With engraved portrait. Excellent condition. 325.00

BEEF AND FLOUR FOR THE OTTAWA INDIANS

63. HARRISON, WILLIAM HENRY. 1773-1841. President; General in War of 1812. Choice, early Autograph Document Signed "Wm. H. Harrison / a.d.c." 1 page, narrow oblong 8vo. Greeneville, August 7, 1794. Full text reads: "For the Ottawas thirty seven pounds of beef and flour..." Excellent condition. Attractively mounted and framed with a handsome steel-engraved portrait of Harrison. The matt is sage-green, and the frame 1/2 inch antique-gilt. A striking ensemble, newly framed, and ready for your den or office. 575.00

EXTRAORDINARY PRESIDENTIAL DOCUMENT BY WHICH PRESIDENT VAN BUREN SELLS TWO LOTS OF THE FORMER MILITARY SITE AT FORT DEARBORN IN CHICAGO

64. VAN BUREN, MARTIN. President and Vice President. Remarkable partly printed Document Signed, as President. One page, small square folio, vellum. Washington, November 1, 1839. Countersigned by JOEL R. POINSETT, Secretary of War. Embossed white wafer seal of the War Department affixed with red wax at lower left. The text commences: "WHEREAS, The Military Site of FORT DEARBORN belonging to the UNITED STATES, situate upon the South West fractional quarter of Section ten, in Township thirty-nine, North, of Range fourteen, East of the third principal Meridian, in the State of Illinois, having become useless for military purposes, the SECRETARY OF WAR, under the direction of the PRESIDENT OF THE UNITED STATES, appointed and authorized MATTHEW BIRCHARD, Solicitor of the General Land Office...to survey and sell the same in Town Lots, according to an act of Congress of the 3rd March, 1819, entitled An act authorising the sale of certain Military Sites...as the FORT DEARBORN -- ADDITION TO CHICAGO...." President Van Buren sells to Silas B. Cobb, of Chicago, for the sum of $516.00, Lots 10 and 11 of Block number Ten. This location is now the southwest corner of Michigan Avenue and Lake Street. The official Cook County, Illinois registration of this property appears on the verso of the document. In our over twenty years in the autograph business, and some seven years prior as a collector, we have never seen another document of this type. Land grants bearing the actual signature of Van Buren are practically non-existent, making this very special format all the more rare and desirable. Fine condition. 2000.00

BUSINESS LETTER TO HIS LAW PARTNER WHILE ON VACATION

65. ROOSEVELT, FRANKLIN D. President. Typed Letter Signed, as Vice President of the Fidelity and Deposit Company of Maryland, on their imprinted letterhead. 1 page, 4to. Long Key, Florida, February 21, 1925. To Basil O'Connor, his law partner, New York City. Roosevelt hopes that O'Connor will be able to see him in Florida while on route to Mexico, and continues: "Julian Goldman writes me that he has given you a case to handle in Pennsylvania under the old contract clause. Send him a bill for $1250 sometime in March. The $5,000 retainer started January 1st and is payable quarterly. Louis Howe wrote me about a man who claimed to know me -- he may, but I don't know him!..." Three pencil dockets, and stamped docket at top right; two small punch-file holes in blank left margin. Interesting and unusual!! 325.00

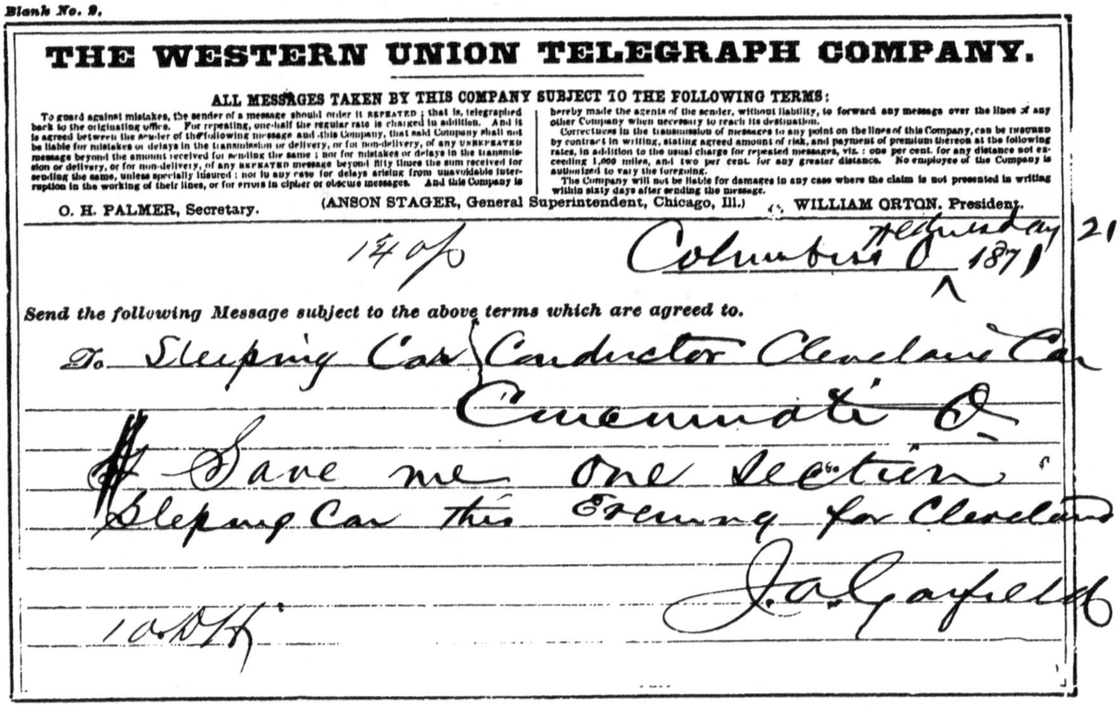
Blank No. 9.

THE WESTERN UNION TELEGRAPH COMPANY.

ALL MESSAGES TAKEN BY THIS COMPANY SUBJECT TO THE FOLLOWING TERMS:

To guard against mistakes, the sender of a message should order it REPEATED; that is, telegraphed back to the originating office. For repeating, one-half the regular rate is charged in addition. And it is agreed between the sender of the following message and this Company, that said Company shall not be liable for mistakes or delays in the transmission or delivery, or for non-delivery, of any UNREPEATED message beyond the amount received for sending the same; nor for mistakes or delays in the transmission or delivery, or for non-delivery, of any REPEATED message beyond fifty times the sum received for sending the same, unless specially insured; nor in any case for delays arising from unavoidable interruption in the working of their lines, or for errors in cipher or obscure messages. And this Company is hereby made the agents of the sender, without liability, to forward any message over the lines of any other Company when necessary to reach its destination.

Correctness in the transmission of messages to any point on the lines of this Company, can be INSURED by contract in writing, stating agreed amount of risk, and payment of premium thereon at the following rates, in addition to the usual charge for repeated messages, viz.: one per cent. for any distance not exceeding 1,000 miles, and two per cent. for any greater distance. No employee of the Company is authorized to vary the foregoing.

The Company will not be liable for damages in any case where the claim is not presented in writing within sixty days after sending the message.

O. H. PALMER, Secretary. (ANSON STAGER, General Superintendent, Chicago, Ill.) WILLIAM ORTON, President.

140/0 Columbus O Wednesday 21 1871

Send the following Message subject to the above terms which are agreed to.

To Sleeping Car Conductor Cleveland Car
Cincinnati O
Save me one Section
Sleeping Car this Evening for Cleveland
J. A. Garfield
10 DH

66. GARFIELD, JAMES A. President. Autograph Message Signed, penned on an imprinted form of The Western Union Telegraph Company. 1 page, oblong 8vo. Columbus, Ohio, Wednesday 21, 1871. To the Sleeping Car Conductor, Cleveland Car, Cincinnati, Ohio. Congressman Garfield directs: "Save me one Section Sleeping Car this evening for Cleveland..." Fine specimen! 450.00

APPOINTMENT OF AN ATTORNEY FOR NEBRASKA

67. JOHNSON, ANDREW. President and Vice President. Choice partly printed Document Signed, as President. Oblong folio. Washington, April 10, 1867. Countersigned by WILLIAM H. SEWARD, Secretary of State. Embossed white wafer seal of the State Department. President Johnson appoints S. A. Strickland an Attorney of the United States for the District of Nebraska. On the blank verso Strickland has signed an Oath for performing his duties as Attorney. Folds reinforced with tissue on verso, else fine. Unusual form of appointment. 650.00

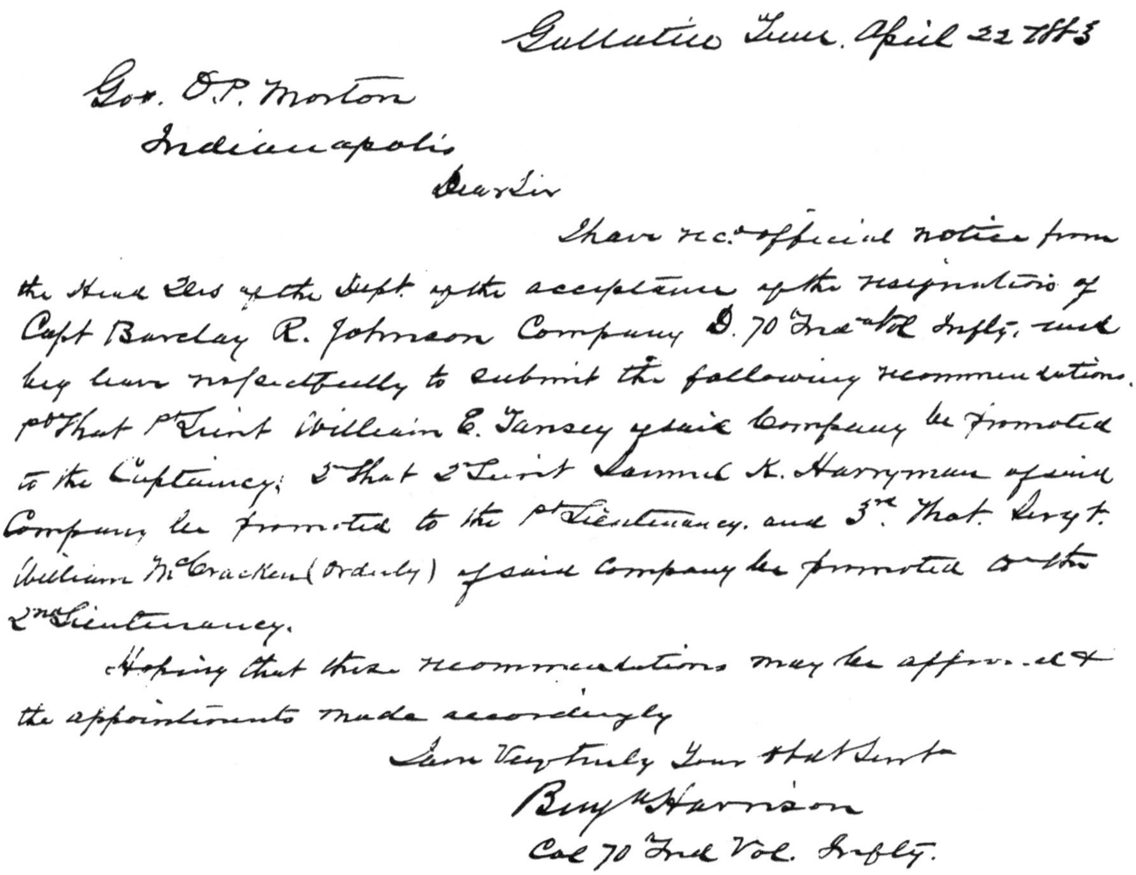
Gallatin Tenn. April 22 1863

Gov. O.P. Morton
Indianapolis
Dear Sir

I have rec^d official notice from the Head Qrs of the Dept. of the acceptance of the resignation of Capt Barclay R. Johnson Company D. 70 Ind^a Vol Infty, and beg leave respectfully to submit the following recommendations. 1st That 1st Lieut William E. Tansey of said Company be promoted to the Captaincy; 2nd That 2 Lieut Samuel K. Harryman of said Company be promoted to the 1st Lieutenancy, and 3rd That Sergt. William McCracken (Orderly) of said Company be promoted to the 2nd Lieutenancy.

Hoping that these recommendations may be approved & the appointments made accordingly

I am Very truly Your obt Servt
Benjn Harrison
Col 70 Ind Vol. Infty.

FINE MILITARY LETTER PENNED DURING THE CIVIL WAR

68. **HARRISON, BENJAMIN.** President. Scarce, early Autograph Letter Signed, as Colonel of the 70th Indiana Volunteer Infantry. 1 page, 4to. Gallatin, Tennessee, April 22, 1863. To Oliver P. Morton, Governor of Indiana, Indianapolis. The future president writes: "I have rec'd official notice from the Head Qtrs. of the Dept. of the acceptance of the resignation of Capt. Barclay R. Johnson, Company D 70 Ind. Vol. Infty, and beg leave respectfully to submit the following recommendations...." Harrison then gives the names of the three men with his suggestions for promoting them. He closes: "Hoping that these recommendations may be approved and the appointments made accordingly...." Excellent condition. Letters of Harrison written during the Civil War are seldom obtainable. 750.00

69. **EISENHOWER, DWIGHT D.** President and General; planned Allied invasion of Europe. Typed Letter Signed "Ike", on his gilt-lettered five-star stationery. 1 page, 4to. No place, December 11, 1950. To Robert W. Woodruff, President, Coca Cola Co., Atlanta, Georgia. In this "Dear Bob" letter, Eisenhower writes: "I have had to cancel my proposed trip to Pasadena. You are familiar with the circumstances that makes the decision necessary....I thought you may want to drop [Mr. T. Carl Thompson] a note to tell him of my appreciation for his offer to provide tickets to the Santa Anita Race Track. It is just one more thing I will have to place on my hope to do soon list...." Fine example. 250.00

70. **PIERCE, FRANKLIN.** President. Autograph Letter Signed. 2 full pages, 8vo. Concord, N.H., May 15, 1867, penned on his embossed-initialed stationery. To Hon. J. Glancey Jones, Reading, Penn. Original envelope front addressed by Pierce. Pierce acknowledges Jones' letter, saying: "...We could not satisfactorily discuss matters to which you particularly refer in letters. I expect to pass the summer at a bluff called Little Boars Head in North Hampton on the Sea. I can meet you in Boston at any time after the middle of July or perhaps in New York, if that would be more agreeable to you...." Fine condition. 395.00

BOTH VOLUMES INSCRIBED TO HILDEGARDE!!

71. **TRUMAN, HARRY S** President and Vice President. Two-volume set of his Memoirs: Year of Decisions and Years of Trial and Hope 1946-1952. Printed black cloth. Garden City, N.Y., 1955-56. Each volume inscribed by the former president to the popular entertainer on the half-titles: "To Hildegarde / From / Harry S Truman". Colorful red, white and blue dust-jackets present. Handsome set, and an interesting association!! 325.00

THE PAINTING OF THE COOLIDGE PORTRAIT FOR THE WHITE HOUSE

72. COOLIDGE, GRACE GOODHUE. First Lady. Magnificent Autograph Letter Signed. 4 full pages, small 4to. Northampton, Mass., February 3, 1932. To Mrs. [Harry S.] New, wife of Coolidge's Postmaster General. She writes:

> "For the first time, we are having a wintry picture painted for us in about three inches of snow, yesterday. To-day, a misty rain is wiping it away. Mr. Coolidge said that he dreaded the winter which sounded funny on the second of February..
>
> Your letter gave us a good laugh. You wrote it the day after the Cabinet dinner and it sounded as though the cook had sent up something which hadn't agreed with you -- or was it that your husband couldn't cut the ice cream? I cannot understand what is the trouble and my sympathy is working over time. It all seems awfully pathetic...
>
> Do you ever attend the Senate Ladies luncheons? Does Mrs. Hoover sometimes go? Does Mrs. Smoot attend? Tell me something about her -- and what do you know about the woman Will Hays married? Alas, I want to know how you like the new Memorial bridge and what is being done to the tomb of the unknown soldier. Did you see De Lazelo's portrait of Mrs. Hoover? I have not seen a photograph of it and have been watching the papers. Did he paint a portrait of the President? We are expecting a portrait painter as house guest, to-day. I hope that he will paint a portrait of Mr. Coolidge which we should like enough to have in the White House. It is a great advantage to have him stay with us so that he can see his subject when not making a grim business of sitting. It goes without saying that the man is an American painter...."

Wonderful post-presidential letter by the former First Lady. Fine condition. 250.00

GRANT OF LAND TO A REVOLUTIONARY WAR SOLDIER

73. JACKSON, ANDREW. President. Unusual Manuscript Document Signed, as President. 1 1/3 pages, small folio, vellum. Washington, August 1, 1832. Countersigned by Elijah Hayward, Commissioner of the General Land Office. Embossed white wafer seal of the Land Office affixed with red wax to the left of Jackson's bold signature on the second side. Grant of 24 acres of land to John Cockrell "three years a Sergeant to the United States in the Virginia Line on Continental Establishment..." The land was situated in Ohio, and is fully described as to location. The unusual feature about this land grant is that it is not the usual partly printed form used for Virginia Line veterans, but is totally in holograph. Fine condition, and exceptionally nice signature of Jackson measuring six inches in length! 850.00

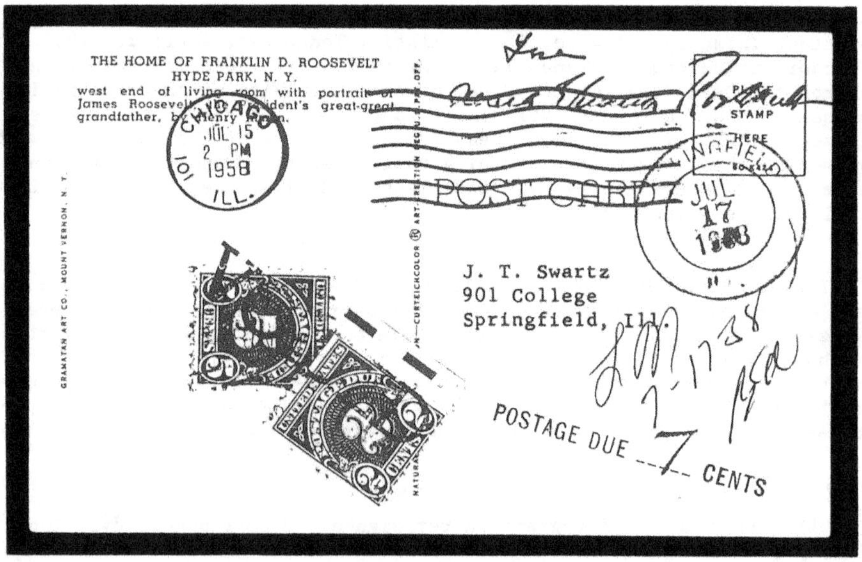

HIGHLY UNUSUAL WIDOW'S FRANK

74. ROOSEVELT, ELEANOR. First Lady. Colorful picture postcard featuring the view of the Living Room at the Roosevelt's family home in Hyde Park. On the verso (address side), the former First Lady has placed her franking signature "Free / Anna Eleanor Roosevelt" in the top right corner. The postmark reads "Chicago, Ill., July 15, 1958" and the card is addressed to a party in Springfield, Illinois. Apparently on reaching the post office in Springfield, the postal clerk did not notice or recognize the franking signature, so he surcharged the card "POSTAGE DUE 7 CENTS" and affixed two postage due stamps. When the recipient was asked to pay the postage due, he pointed out to the clerk that the card had been franked by the former First Lady, and that there was no money due, whereupon the clerk stamped "VOIDED" across the stamps, adding his initials and a Springfield postmark. Very rare postal item! 225.00

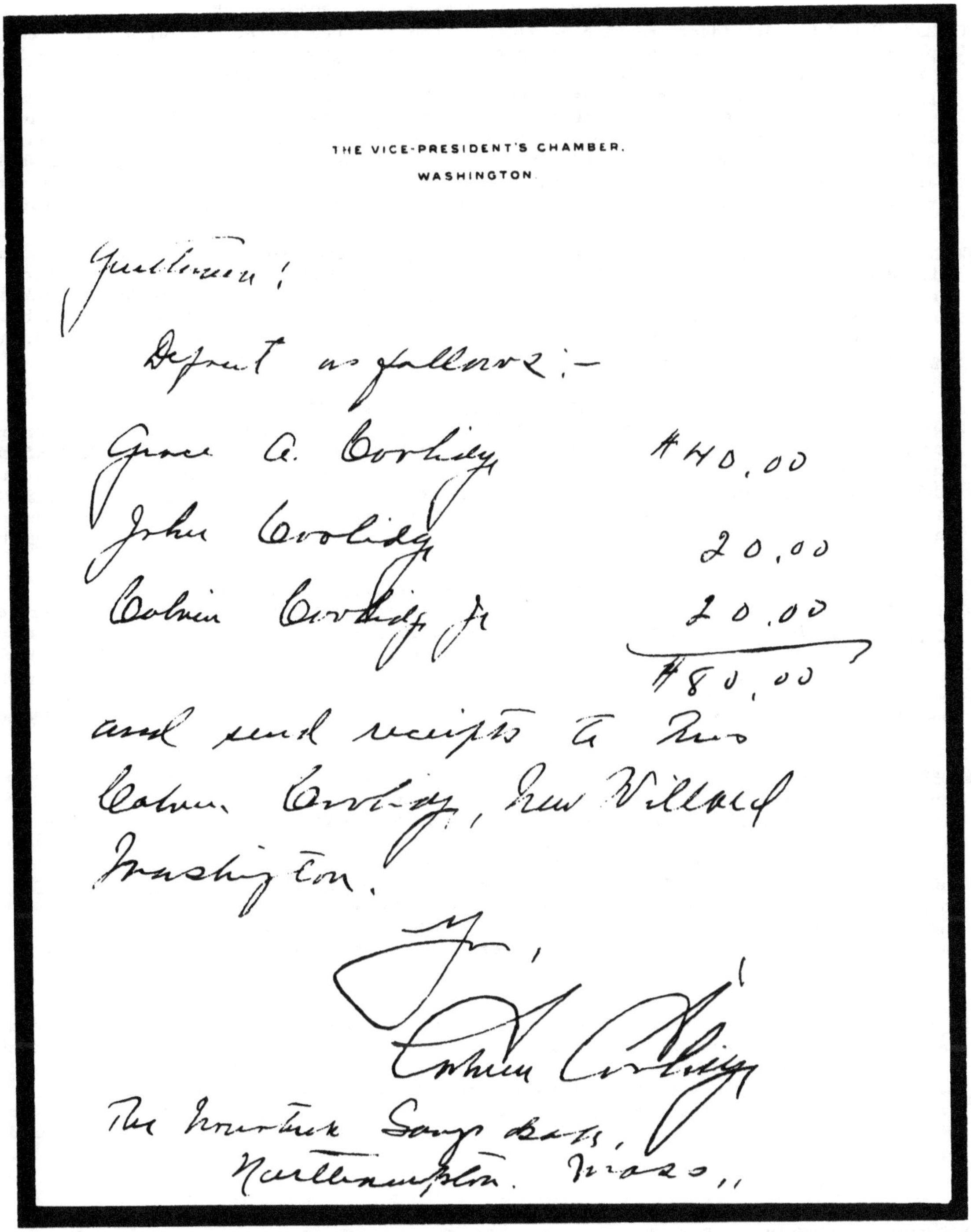

THE VICE-PRESIDENT'S CHAMBER,
WASHINGTON

Gentlemen:

Deposit as follows:-

Grace A. Coolidge	$40.00
John Coolidge	20.00
Calvin Coolidge Jr	20.00
	$80.00

and send receipts to Mrs Calvin Coolidge, New Willard Washington.

Yours,

Calvin Coolidge

The Nourtuck Savings Bank,
Northampton, Mass.,

75. COOLIDGE, CALVIN. President and Vice President. Autograph Letter Signed, as Vice President, on imprinted stationery of The Vice-President's Chamber. Full page, 4to. Washington, no date To the Nourtuck Savings Bank, Northampton, Mass. Coolidge sends eighty dollars to be deposited in the savings accounts of his wife and two sons, requesting that the receipts be sent to Mrs. Calvin Coolidge, New Willard [Hotel], Washington. Coolidge is very rare in full holograph, particularly as Vice President and President. Pristine condition. 2500.00

76. ROOSEVELT, ELEANOR. First Lady. Imprinted White House card, fully signed. Nice! 75.00

77. HAYES, RUTHERFORD B. President. Signature on verso of his imprinted visiting card. 125.00

78. HAYES, LUCY WEBB. First Lady; known as "Lemonade Lucy". Attractive full signature. 75.00

79. GARFIELD, JAMES A. President. Attractive signature "J. A. Garfield", as a Congressman. With engraved portrait. Nice pair for framing or display. 125.00

"THE DEMOCRATIC PARTY MUST GO FORWARD..."

80. TRUMAN, HARRY S. President and Vice President. Choice Typed Letter Signed, as President, on imprinted White House stationery. Full page, 4to. Washington, November 12, 1948. To Justin G. Turner, noted autograph collector and Lincoln specialist, Los Angeles, California. Important letter written by Truman just days after his unexpected re-election to the Presidency. He writes: "I have heard of the generous way in which you expressed confidence in my leadership and want you to know of my heartfelt appreciation. I am more grateful than I can say. The Democratic Party must go forward with progress and the support which you gave so wholeheartedly gives me strength and courage and renewed faith in the principles for which our party must always stand...." Fine condition, and a wonderful Truman letter!! 750.00

81. COOLIDGE, CALVIN. President and Vice President. Typed Letter Signed, as President, on imprinted White House stationery. 1 page, 4to. Washington, March 31, 1925. To Hon. Myron T. Herrick, The American Embassy, Paris, France. Coolidge acknowledges Ambassador Herrick's letter, saying: "...I am glad to have these matters, which you present so interestingly, brought in this way to my personal attention. What you say about the debt question is both interesting and important...." Pressure-mounted, else fine. Nice association. 350.00

THE REPUBLICAN PRESIDENTIAL TICKET FOR 1928

82. HOOVER, HERBERT. President. Choice small oblong quarto sepia photograph depicting Herbert Hoover and CHARLES G. DAWES, Republican candidates for President and Vice President of the United States, seated in high-back lawn chairs engrossed in conversation, with smiles on both their faces [obviously from the 1928 campaign!]. Signed on the lower white margin by by Hoover and Dawes. This is the first jugate photograph of the candidates we have encountered bearing both their signatures. Choice campaign souvenir!! 395.00

WITH AN ORIGINAL PHOTOGRAPH OF THE SUMMER WHITE HOUSE

83. CLEVELAND, GROVER. President. Autograph Letter Signed, on the blind-stamped stationery of Gray Gables, his home on Cape Cod, which was used as the Summer White House during his second term. Full page, 8vo. Buzzards Bay, Mass., October 8, 1899. To George F. Klack. Cleveland writes: "I received from you a short time ago a remarkably clear and well taken photograph of my Summer home -- for which I desire to return my sincere thanks...." Mounted on the integral leaf is the photograph of Gray Gables mentioned in this letter. Fine. 275.00

84. ROOSEVELT, ELEANOR. First Lady. Choice Typed Letter Signed, with two holograph sentences, penned on her imprinted stationery. 1 page, 4to. New York, November 17, 1955. To Miss Cunningham, thanking her for her letter and interest. She continues: "I have never been to Russia so I cannot tell you that I have seen the women work in the streets through I believe they share the burden with the men. Hyde Park house now belongs to the government and is not occupied by any member of my family. My husband did travel by plane but he liked the Sea. I do not mind sea or air travel. Sometimes when the weather is rough I feel a little uncomfortable but I have never been really ill. My husband was taller and heavier than I. I write every month for McCall's...." The two underlined sentences are in Mrs. R's hand. 225.00

85. MC KINLEY, WILLIAM. President. Handsome, ornately engraved Document Signed, as President. Tall folio, vellum. Washington, December 24, 1898. Countersigned by R. A. ALGER, Secretary of War. Vivid embossed blue seal of the War Department affixed at bottom left. President Mc Kinley appoints Samuel M. Mansfield a Colonel in the Corps of Engineers. Engraved and printed by the Bureau of Engraving & Printing. Superb spread-eagle vignette at top, and another vignette of military accoutrements at bottom. Wonderful document for framing or display. Clean and fresh!! 450.00

"EYES FOR THE NAVY"

86. ROOSEVELT, FRANKLIN D. President. Interesting Typed Letter Signed, as Assistant Secretary of the Navy, on imprinted letterhead. Full page, 4to. Washington, April 18, 1918. To George W. Campbell, Ilion, Illinois. The future president writes: "Your prompt and patriotic response to the NAVY'S call for binoculars, telescopes, and spy-glasses, is most appreciated. The glasses will be very useful in the prosecution of Naval Operations until victory is won. At the termination of the war, if possible, every effort will be made to return them to you, when it is hoped that you will feel compensated for any evidence of wear, by the knowledge that you have supplied Eyes for the NAVY during a very trying period...." Fine letter dating from the Great War when the Navy appealed to the public for the loan of equipment as stated above. Fine. 325.00

87. MONROE, JAMES. President. Attractive partly printed Document Signed, as President. Oblong legal folio, vellum. Washington, September 13, 1820. Countersigned by JOSIAH MEIGS, Commissioner of the General Land Office. Embossed white wafer seal of the General Land Office affixed with red wax at lower left. President Monroe grants 160 acres of land in the area of Vincennes, Indiana, under his authority as granted by "the Act of Congress, entitled An Act providing for the sale of the Lands of the United States, in the Territory north west of the Ohio, and above the mouth of Kentucky River..." Choice condition, with a handsome, bold signature of Monroe. Engraved portrait. 450.00

Farewell Address of President Jimmy Carter

January 14, 1981

PRESIDENT CARTER'S "FAREWELL ADDRESS" ** SIGNED LIMITED EDITION

88. CARTER, JIMMY. President. Printed book: Farewell Address of President Jimmy Carter. Royal blue cloth, gilt-lettered spine. Palaemon Press, 1981. Signed by Carter on the title-page beneath the Presidential Seal. First and only separate edition. Limited to 300 numbered copies, of which 150 were reserved for Mr. Carter, and 50 reserved for hors-commerce distribution by the publisher to his friends, thus leaving only 100 copies available for public distribution. Mint, unopened, in blue cloth case with tipped-on paper label. Destined to become one of the rarest of signed presidential books. Only a few copies left. Order yours now! 225.00

AUTHORIZING PAYMENT FOR A FREE COLORED WASHWOMAN

89. JACKSON, ANDREW. President; General in War of 1812, and hero of Battle of New Orleans. Manuscript Document Signed "Andrew Jackson / Major Gen'l Comdg." Full page, legal folio. Hospital N. Orleans, March 3, 1815. As commanding general Jackson signed a certification of the one-month employment of Rosina, a free girl of color, whose services as a washwoman at the "hospital for General Coffee's brigade" were worth ten dollars, "the lowest price at which, under existing circumstances, washwomen could be procured." The document is also signed by David C. Kerr, Hospital Surgeon and Director, and has been receipted by Rosina with her "X". The Battle of New Orleans was won by General Jackson and his motley collection of troops which contained frontiersmen, Creoles, Negroes and pirates (January 8, 1815). The saving of New Orleans made Jackson the major hero of the war as well as a national figure to be considered as a presidential possibility. Documents dating from the New Orleans period are rare. Fine. 1500.00

REFERRING TO ATOMIC ENERGY: "I BELIEVE WE ARE ON THE ROAD TO A CONSTRUCTIVE RESULT."

90. TRUMAN, HARRY S. President and Vice President. Typed Letter Signed, as President, on imprinted White House stationery. 1 page, 4to. Washington, January 9, 1946. To Sir John Anderson, G.C.B., Chairman of the Advisory Committee to the Government on Atomic Energy, London. Original addressed White House envelope. Truman acknowledges receipt of his correspondent's letter "and the beautiful calendar", adding "I shall keep it before me and think of your every day." In the concluding paragraph Truman makes reference to a White House visit by the English Advisory Committee on Atomic Energy: "I enjoyed the visit of Mr. Attlee, Mr. King and yourself very much. I believe we are on the road to a constructive result...." It was Truman who authorized the first use of atomic energy in warfare, and any reference to this subject is most uncommon. Pristine condition. Also present is a draft ALS by the recipient to Truman, dated December 21, 1945. 650.00

91. EISENHOWER, DWIGHT D. President and General. Typed Letter Signed "Ike", on his gilt-monogrammed stationery. 1 page, 4to. Gettysburg, Penn., October 18, 1967. To Hon. Robert Cutler, Boston, Mass., whom he greets as "Dear Bobby". Ike acknowledges a book about quail which he read without stopping. "It was indeed a touching story." He continues: "Of course I am glad you are enjoying your visit to the University of Kansas and have had an opportunity to see some of the beauty of my home-state. At the moment, the doctors have me in their clutches but if all goes well Mamie and I shall go to Augusta on Friday for a stay of about ten days...." Cutler served Eisenhower during his Presidency as a Security Council aide. Letters signed with the familiar "Ike" are scarce, as he did this only when writing close friends. Fine. 250.00

"THE WORK AHEAD OF ME DAUNTS ME..."

92. WILSON, WOODROW. President of the United States. Typed Letter Signed, as President of Princeton University, during the period he was campaigning for the governorship of New Jersey. Full page, 8vo., on imprinted "President's Room" stationery. Princeton, September 19, 1910. To Rev. Dr. A. W. Hazen. "It was very delightful to see your handwriting again and your letter has stirred my heart. We think of Mrs. Hazen and you so often and nothing cheers me more than approving messages and proofs of your continued friendship. The work ahead of me daunts me somewhat but it can be done so long as men like yourself believe in me...." Fine. 295.00

A.

B.

93. CLEVELAND, GROVER. President. Two engraved vignettes of the Executive Mansion, both signed and dated as President. 12mo. Printed by the Bureau of Engraving and Printing. Pristine.

A. Front approach to the Executive Mansion showing much activity in the wide drive. Signed and dated "1888" during Cleveland's first term. 395.00

B. Back yard at the Executive Mansion showing children at play. Signed and dated "March 1896" during the President's second term. 395.00

94. ROOSEVELT, THEODORE. President and Vice President. Autograph Letter Signed, on his wife's monogrammed "EKR" stationery. 2 full separate pages, 8vo. [Washington, March 7, 1890]. To the American writer and editor, Charles Dudley Warner. Original postmarked envelope addressed by Roosevelt to Warner at Welcher's Hotel, Washington. Roosevelt, who was then serving on the U. S. Civil Service Commission, writes: "I have been so driven that I could not get round to see you; and every evening, to my sorrow, we have been engaged, and I could not break the engagements. Adams, when I told him you were here, was much interested and said he would call on you at once. Remember, you are due here next Sunday evening at 7.30..." Attractive early example. 650.00

95. CLEVELAND, FRANCES FOLSOM. First Lady. Autograph Letter Signed, as First Lady, on her imprinted monogrammed Executive Mansion stationery. 3 full pages, 12mo. Washington, June 3, 1896. To Mrs. D. Lathrop. Original envelope. "I might really first as well have given you my answer when you first spoke to me of this honor you wished to confer upon me, because it was all thought out as clearly, then, as now....I do not think it is best to do what you ask. All the reasons which operated against my accepting the Presidency of the Daughters are quite as strong in the case of the Children's Society, - with the added one of having refused that. I appreciate the honor intended me, & I am glad that you wanted me...." Fine. 125.00

SEEKING THE "ADVICE AND CONSENT" OF THE SENATE TO A CONVENTION

96. ROOSEVELT, FRANKLIN D. President. Typewritten Message Signed, as President, on stationery embossed with the Presidential Seal at upper left. 1 1/2 separate pages, legal folio. The White House [Washington], April 20, 1939. To "The Senate of the United States", transmitting "...a convention between the United States of America and Sweden for the avoidance of double taxation and the establishment of rules of reciprocal administrative assistance in the case of income and other taxation, signed at Washington on March 23, 1939." Roosevelt continues: "The convention was negotiated and signed under full powers issued by me. It has the approval of the Department of State and the Treasury Department. It also has my approval, and I ask the advice and consent of the Senate to its ratification, together with the protocol attached thereto and made an integral part of the convention, which defines certain terms used in the convention and contains provisions to govern the administration of the convention...." Very scarce form of presidential document. Pristine condition. Newly framed under glass with a handsome photograph of FDR by Pach Brothers. The frame is moulded one-inch, antiqued-gilt. Overall size of the ensemble: 28 x 17 1/2 inches. [Upon request, we will remove the document from the frame, but at the same time we stress the beauty of the ensemble]. 1200.00

OUTSPOKEN LETTER ON RACE, RELIGION AND POLITICS

97. ROOSEVELT, THEODORE. President and Vice President. Remarkable Typed Letter Signed, while serving on the U.S. Civil Service Commission, on official imprinted stationery. 1 1/2 separate pages, 4to. Washington, February 9, 1893. To Capt. John G. Bourke, Third Cavalry, War Department, Washington.

> "I am glad you saw my allusion to your book. I make a religious point of puffing it on all occasions. I wish you could see the speech too....All of the incidents you wrote of and names you mentioned are familiar to me. In my speech, however, I was, as a matter of fact, considering the thing chiefly from the American standpoint. I hate to bring in any question of race origin into our politics, and I want to see us all act simply and purely as Americans; in other words, my dear sir, act precisely as you have always acted. To me it is equally abhorrent to object to a man because he is of a certain race origin, or to bid for the voters of that race origin by a plank put in specially for them as such, and not as American citizens. I can no more understand, for instance, voting against a man because he is a Catholic by conviction, and Irishman by descent, than I can understand putting in an American political platform an Irish home-rule plank with which we have nothing at all to do. I know you sympathize with me in both these respects...."

Certainly one of the finest declarations of a President pertaining to race, religion and politics we have seen expressed in a letter. Roosevelt has supplied eight words in his own holograph, and cancelled four typed words. An outstanding letter! 1750.00

98. COOLIDGE, CALVIN. President and Vice President. Typed Letter Signed, as Vice President, on imprinted stationery of that office. 1 page, 4to. Washington, March 23, 1921. To S.H. Church of the Carnegie Institute, Pittsburgh, Penn. Writing during his first month in the office of Vice President, Coolidge states that he is "...contemplating with pleasure visiting your institution. My wife will accompany me. We expect to leave here Wednesday night, and leave Pittsburgh late Thursday night, or in good season Friday morning...." Letters of Coolidge during the relatively brief period of his Vice Presidency are scarce. Fine. 250.00

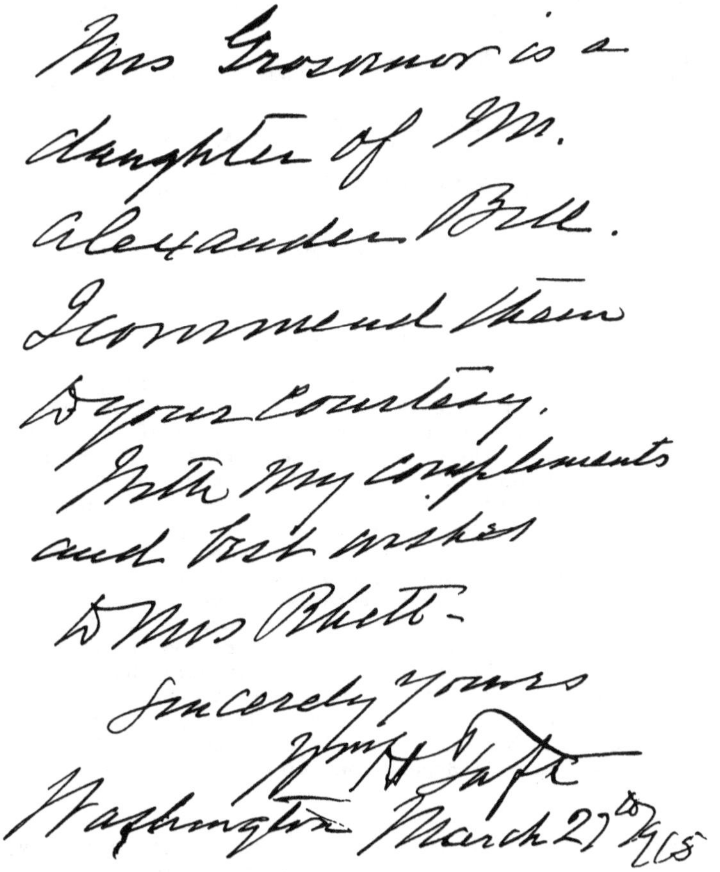
Mrs Grosvenor is a
daughter of Mr.
Alexander Bell.
I commend them
to your courtesy.
With my compliments
and best wishes
to Mrs Rhett -
Sincerely yours
Wm H Taft
Washington March 27th /05

99. TAFT, WILLIAM H. President; Chief Justice, U.S. Supreme Court. Autograph Letter Signed. 2 full separate pages, 8vo. Washington, March 27, 1905. To Mr. Rhett, prominent Charleston, South Carolina citizen, and at one time its mayor. Taft writes: "This will be presented to you by my cousins Mr. & Mrs. Gilbert Grosvenor of Washington. Mr. Grosvenor is the Manager and Editor of the National Geographic Magazine. Mrs. Grosvenor is a daughter of Mr. Alexander Bell. I commend them to your courtesy...." Nice association! Fine. 450.00

Messrs Josiah Foster, William Stetson, Charles C. P. Waterman,
Melatiah Bourne, William Fessenden junr Elisha Pope
and N. B. Gibbs - Sandwich

Quincy 11. October 1842

Fellow Citizens.

I tender you my warm and hearty thanks for the honour of your invitation to a public dinner, which I should take pleasure in accepting, but for engagements which will detain me here and in this vicinity until the necessity of my return to Washington for the Winter

Your approbation of my public service heretofore will be cheering to my last days. and as they can-not be far remote, I hope and trust they will introduce others to your service, who will labour with equal zeal, and with better success. Especially may your future representatives never slum-ber till the full and entire restoration of the right of petition.

With great respect, Gentlemen, I am your
friend and fellow Citizen
John Quincy Adams

"NEVER SLUMBER TILL THE FULL AND ENTIRE RESTORATION OF THE RIGHT OF PETITION"

100. ADAMS, JOHN QUINCY. President. Highly attractive and interesting Autograph Letter Signed, written after his presidency, while representing Massachusetts in Congress. One page, quarto. Quincy, October 11, 1842. To Josiah Foster and a Committee of Gentlemen from Sandwich on Cape Cod. Blank integral leaf. The venerable Adams writes: "I tender you my warm and hearty thanks for the honour of your invitation to a public dinner, which I should take pleasure in accepting, but for engagements which will detain me here and in this vicinity until the necessity of my return to Washington for the Winter. Your approbation of my public service heretofore will be cheering to my last days, and as they cannot be far remote, I hope and trust they will introduce others to your service, who will labour with equal zeal, and with better success. Especially may your future representatives never slumber till the full and entire restoration of the right of petition...." Adams had angered his Southern colleagues in the House of Representatives by introducing a series of petitions which he had received from slaves. He did not insist that they be acted upon, but only that they be accepted by the House and referred to the proper committee. Southerners maintained that since slaves were property they did not have the right of petition. Adams' persistence in this matter forced the House to adopt a rule that suspended the right of petition. Hence the background for the last sentence in the above letter. Superb condition!! 1750.00

CANDIDATE WILSON IS DISTURBED BY FALSE REPORTS IN THE PRESS

101. WILSON, WOODROW. President. Typed Letter Signed, on his imprinted stationery, while campaigning for his first presidential term. Full page, 4to. Sea Girt, N.J., August 16, 1912. To George A. Armes, Washington, D.C. Wilson writes: "I have been very much disturbed by statements in the papers that I was expecting to take part in the planting of a tree on your place at some future time. I appreciated your courtesy in extending the invitation to me but you will remember that I did not accept, and I am very sure that it will not be possible for me to do so. I beg that you will take any proper occasion to correct this misunderstanding...." Highly unusually content, in which Wilson shows his obvious irritation. Fine. 395.00

THE FIRST LADY WRITES A SOLDIER BOY TO BECOME HIS PEN-PAL

102. ROOSEVELT, ELEANOR. First Lady. Typed Letter Signed, as First Lady, on gilt-imprinted White House stationery. Full page, small 4to. Washington, May 28, 1942. To [Thomas] Castorino. Remarkable letter reaching out to an American GI: "Miss Ilma tells me that you like to be called Tom, but as this is my first letter I feel a little bit shy about doing so. Miss Ilma has asked the members of the board if they will write to a few of the boys in the Services, saying that you like to get letters and packages now and then. I am very glad to do so and I hope that I shall get to know you better and if you will write me of your interests and what you like to do and the kind of things you would like to have sent you, I can be more intelligent. I notice you are working in a station hospital, and I wonder if that means that you are in the Medical Corps? Camp Eustis might mean that you would sometime get a chance to be in Washington, and if that happens, I hope you will let me know as I should like to have a chance to meet you as it is easier to write to people once you have met them. I hope you get on well in the army and that you will write me...." As we said, quite remarkable!! 250.00

A FOLLOW-UP LETTER TO HER SOLDIER PEN-PAL

103. ROOSEVELT, ELEANOR. First Lady. Typed Letter Signed, as First Lady, on gilt-imprinted White House stationery. 1 page, small 4to. Washington, June 9, 1942. To Tony [Castorino]. She writes: "I was glad to get your letter and to know you are out of the hospital. What kind of a unit are you attached to? Is it just an infantry group or some other part of the Service? Your wants sound very similar to those of all the other boys I know. If you will let me know what kind of cigarettes you like, I will see that you get some every now and then. I sent you some hard candy because I thought it would keep better but if you would rather have something different, just say so. I will continue to send you some reading material, but you had better tell me what your interests are. Do you like mechanics or sports or mystery stories? The President will like your message and I will be sure to give it to him...." Fine. 250.00

INVITING THE SON OF THE FORMER PRESIDENT TO THE WHITE HOUSE

104. BUCHANAN, JAMES. President. Superb Autograph Letter Signed, as President. Very full page, 8vo. Washington, April 7, 1859. To Robert Tyler, son of President John Tyler, and two years later Register of the Confederate Treasury. Buchanan writes:

> "I have received your favor of yesterday & rejoice that you have accepted the Chairmanship of the Committee. The right man in the right place.
>
> I am happy to infer from your letter that you intend soon to pay us a visit; and I write to say that you must come directly to the White House. This will be but charity as Miss Lane & myself are now its only occupants.
>
> I am sorry to learn that our friends desire to fiddle away both Convention & Platform. This I think must be confined to Philadelphia. So far as I can judge the tone of feeling is healthy throughout the State. Your friend..."

At this time young Tyler was living near Philadelphia. When the Civil War broke out he returned to Virginia and remained loyal to the Confederacy. Buchanan's stand in favor of the Lecompton Constitution in Kansas fragmented the Democratic Party into northern and southern factions, thus paving the way for Lincoln's victory the following year. Once framed, this letter has a light stain at the extremities; otherwise in fine condition. Quite scarce of presidential date, with choice association and content!! 2000.00

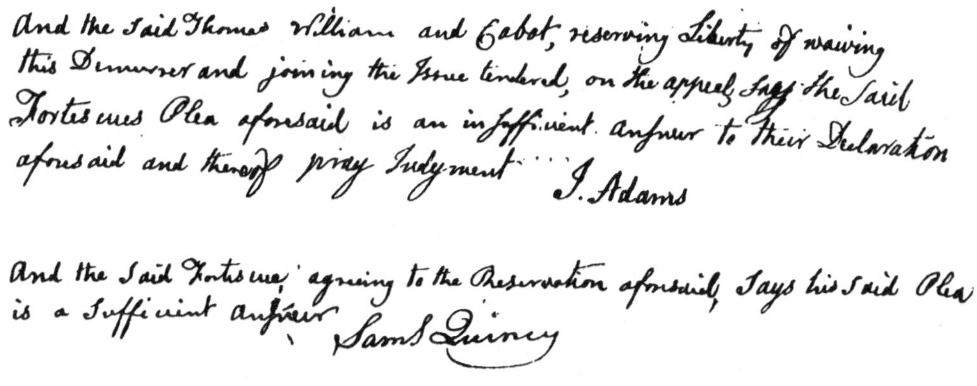
And the Said Thomas William and Cabot, reserving Liberty of waiving this Demurrer and joining the Issue tendered, on the appeal, say the Said Fortescues Plea aforesaid is an insufficient answer to their Declaration aforesaid and thereof pray Judgment... J. Adams

And the Said Fortescue, agreeing to the Reservation aforesaid, Says his Said Plea is a Sufficient answer Saml Quincy

105. ADAMS, JOHN. President and Vice President. Autograph Document Signed. One page, oblong 8vo. No place or date. [Ca. 1769]. Fine early legal document penned as a young attorney before the commencement of his career in public affairs. Attractive specimen. 1250.00

106. TAFT, WILLIAM H. President; Chief Justice, U.S. Supreme Court. Typed Letter Signed, as President, on imprinted White House stationery. 1 page, 4to. Washington, February 10, 1910. To J. C. Shaffer, Chicago Evening Post, Chicago, Illinois. President Taft acknowledges his correspondent's letter "...with respect to the Baltimore judgeship, and thank you for the information which you give...." Nice presidential example. Excellent condition. 375.00

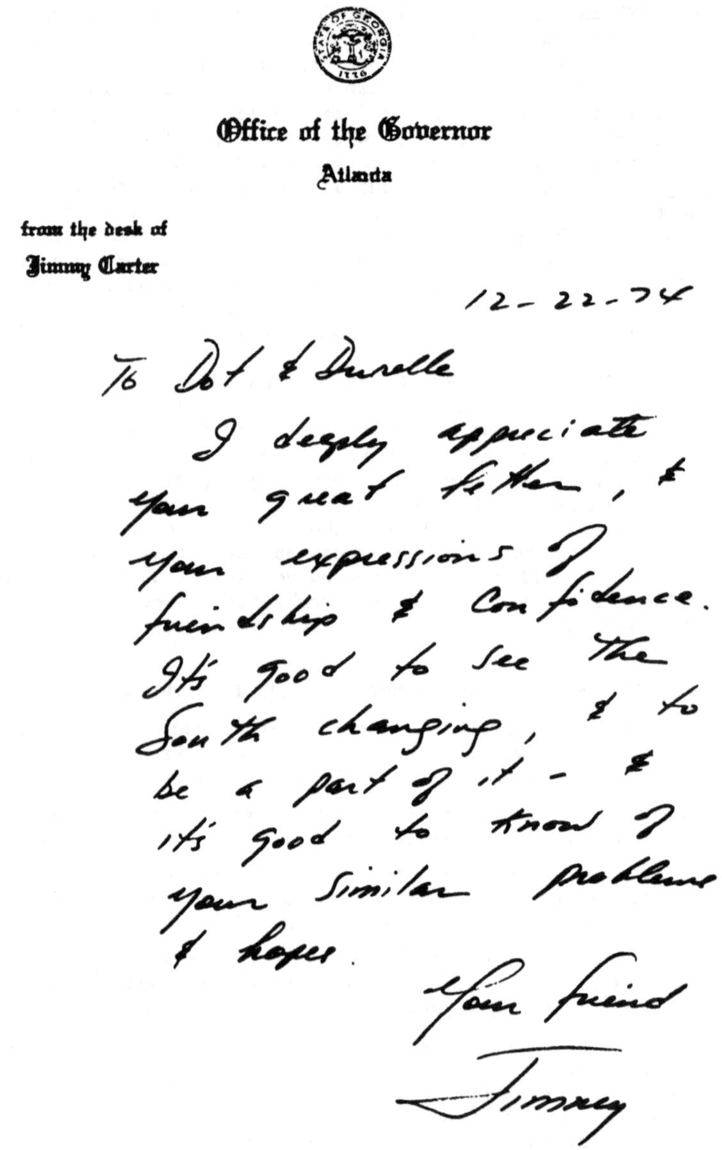
Office of the Governor
Atlanta
from the desk of
Jimmy Carter
12-22-74
To Dot & Durelle
I deeply appreciate your great letter, & your expressions of friendship & confidence. It's good to see the South changing, & to be a part of it - & it's good to know of your similar problems & hopes.
Your friend
Jimmy

"IT'S GOOD TO SEE THE SOUTH CHANGING..."

107. CARTER, JIMMY. President; Governor of Georgia; farmer. Autograph Letter Signed "Jimmy", as Governor of Georgia, on imprinted stationery. 1 page, 4to. Atlanta, December 22, 1974. To "Dot & Durelle ______", some Georgia friends. Original metered envelope with typed address. The future President writes: "I deeply appreciate your great letter, & your expressions of friendship & confidence. It's good to see the South changing, & to be a part of it -- & it's good to know of your similar problems & hopes...." Choice condition. 2,500.00

"I ALWAYS GO ALONG WITH MY BOSS"

108. EISENHOWER, DWIGHT D. President and General; planned the Allied Invasion of Europe. Typed Letter Signed "Ike", as Commander of NATO, on his gilt-initialed five-star stationery. Full page, 4to. Supreme Headquarters, Allied Powers Europe, November 13, 1951. To Robert W. Woodruff, President of Coca Cola, Atlanta, Georgia. In this "Dear Bob" letter, Eisenhower first expresses his concern about the "queer disease that you picked up in France", adding: "Please tell Nell [Woodruff's wife] for me that, if she finds herself unable to make you follow the doctor's orders, a ball bat applied in a suitable spot is quite frequently effective in quieting any tendencies to be up and about...." Turning to other matters, Ike continues: "I am delighted that Jim Farley liked the letter I wrote to him. His two little talks were chock-full of common sense and practical wisdom. Ralph Hayes' comment must have given Jim a real laugh! During my hectic visit to the United States, I had a chance to see, very briefly, Cliff, my brother Milton, Bill Robinson, and Doug Black. They all came to my plane at La Guardia. Wish you could have joined us -- I'd far rather have talked about Ichauway than about political duties. Mamie sends love to you and Nell -- and, of course, I always go along with my boss ...." Eisenhower was nominated by the Republican Party for President the following year, and defeated Adlai Stevenson in the November (1952) Election. Very nice letter! 450.00

A VISITOR TO THE MILITARY ACADEMY AT WEST POINT

109. ADAMS, JOHN QUINCY. President. Choice Autograph Letter Signed, after his presidency, while representing his District in Congress. Full page, 4to. Washington, May 15, 1840. To Samuel A. Turner, Scituate, Mass. Adams encloses a letter from the Secretary of War "inviting you to attend as one of the Visitors next month at the Military Academy at West Point." Turning to local concerns within his District, he continues: "Your Memorial for an appropriation for the improvement of the North River, is with your marked map before the Committee of Commerce; but they have the counter Memorials from Marshfield and Hanover, praying for another survey also before them, and by the law of counterbalancing forces, I fear their action will be neutralized, and no report made this Session...." Fine. With engraved portrait. 975.00

110. VAN BUREN, MARTIN. President and Vice President. Autograph Letter Signed, as Vice President. 1 3/4 pages, 4to. No place, March 28, 1833. To Mr. Flagg. Van Buren writes: "Gov. Cass did me the honor to ask me to look at the recommendation for cadets, and finding amongst them one from you which could not I thought be wrong...on account of the source it came from -- and the breed which the lad appears to be of, I have taken the liberty of asking his appointment. You may send him the Warrant. Remember me kindly to...Gov. & Mrs. Marcy and all my friends -- that is to some of them...." Fine letter, and somewhat scarce as Vice President. 750.00

MELANCHOLY LETTER PENNED AFTER HIS WIFE'S DEATH

111. PIERCE, FRANKLIN. President. Autograph Letter Signed, penned on black-bordered mourning paper. 2 full pages, tall 8vo. Concord, New Hampshire, Sunday Morning, November 20 [1864]. To "My dearest Sister" [actually his sister-in-law, Mrs. Mary Aiken, his deceased wife's sister]. The bereaved former president writes: "When your kind note...was rec'd I was suffering too keenly to read any part of the heavy mail which was accumulating day by day. This is my first attempt to write, one which I shall prosecute no further than to thank you for your kind offer to come to me and to say that I am decidedly better, and expect soon to be firmly on my feet again. I came down from my chamber Friday for the first time -- passed the whole of yesterday in this little parlor which you will remember and am still better this morning. But these days are so full of memories of her [his late wife's] sufferings -- of my own isolation and keen heart-aches that I have sometimes been inclined to look upon acute physical suffering as a messenger of relief...." His beloved wife, Jane, died at her sister's home in Andover, Mass., the previous December 2, 1863. An unusual out-pouring of grief and melancholy by a former president. Excellent condition. 750.00

112. ARTHUR, CHESTER A. President and Vice President. Manuscript Document Signed, as Quarter Master General for the State of New York during the Civil War. Full page, 4to. Albany, September 23, 1862. Above Arthur's bold signature has been penned the text of Special Orders No. 629, which states that "Lieut. Colonel Henry P. Casey, Quarter Master of the 6th Division, is hereby detached from that Division and assigned for duty in the Department of the Quarter-Master General at New York City, as Acting Deputy Quarter-Master General." Arthur, who was then the Quarter-Master General, certified with his signature that the above is a true copy. Arthur is uncommon of Civil War date. Choice condition. 450.00

113. ROOSEVELT, ELEANOR. First Lady. Typed Letter Signed, as First Lady, on gilt-imprinted White House stationery. 1 page, 8vo. Washington, December 29, 1944. To Harry and Louise [Hopkins]. "I was delighted to have a photograph of you with Diana, and I love the cotton print. We had a very quiet family day, with five grandchildren contributing some real Christmas spirit. I hope you had a happy Christmas Day...all good wishes for the New Year..." Fine. 95.00

114. GRANT, ULYSSES S. President and General. Handsome autograph specimen boldly penned on an oblong 8vo leaf: "Yours Truly, / U. S. Grant / Lt. Gen. U.S.A. / Washington, D.C. / March 20th 1866." The writing covers most of the page. With engraved portrait. 150.00

115. ROOSEVELT, ELEANOR. First Lady. Complete envelope, personally franked "Free / Anna Eleanor Roosevelt" in blue ink in upper right corner. Postmarked New York, Jan. 22, 1947. Neatly addressed by typewriter to a lady in Cambridge, Ohio. The cancellation runs across Mrs. Roosevelt's signature. Her address is imprinted on the verso. Scarce in personally franked covers, as she usually employed a rubber stamp. Fine. 125.00

116. FORD, GERALD R. President and Vice President. Typed Letter Signed "Jerry Ford", as Minority Leader of the U.S. House of Representatives, on imprinted letterhead. 1 page, 4to. Washington January 28, 1966. To Howard K. Barker, Belmont, Michigan. Ford agrees to place several names on his mailing list to receive the newsletter, Your Washington Review, and sends a booklet entitled Our American Government, adding "I hope they will find it of value and interest. I am glad to have the opportunity of serving you..." Fine example. 125.00

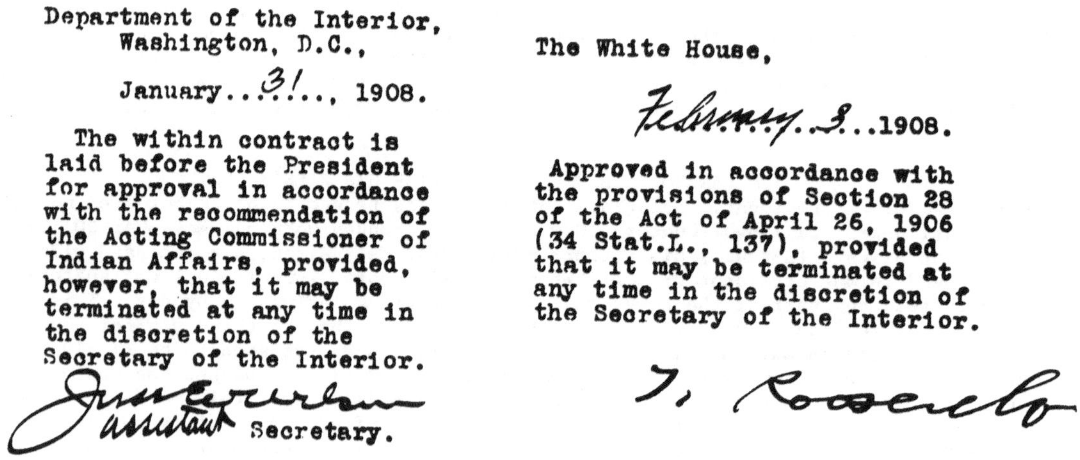
Department of the Interior,
Washington, D.C.,

January..31..., 1908.

The within contract is laid before the President for approval in accordance with the recommendation of the Acting Commissioner of Indian Affairs, provided, however, that it may be terminated at any time in the discretion of the Secretary of the Interior.

Assistant Secretary.

The White House,

February..3..1908.

Approved in accordance with the provisions of Section 28 of the Act of April 26, 1906 (34 Stat.L., 137), provided that it may be terminated at any time in the discretion of the Secretary of the Interior.

T. Roosevelt

THE GREAT WHITE FATHER APPROVES A CHEROKEE NATION CONTRACT FOR EMPLOYING WILLIAM W. HASTINGS AS AN ATTORNEY

117. ROOSEVELT, THEODORE. President and Vice President; Governor of New York; leader of the Rough Riders at Battle of San Juan Hill; Civil-Service Commissioner; author, rancher and big game hunter. Typed Endorsement Signed "T. Roosevelt", as President, on the verso of the second page of a typewritten Agreement between the Cherokee Nation and William W. Hastings, whom they desired to employ as their attorney. The White House [Washington], February 3, 1908. The Agreement is signed by William C. Rogers, Principal Chief of the Cherokee Nation, and by Hastings. There are also two other related documents pertaining to this matter. The whole contained in a file wrapper stamped "Office of Indian Affairs". Unusual, and fine. 850.00

FRONTIER MUSTER ROLL FOR LABORERS AT FORT CRAWFORD

118. TAYLOR, ZACHARY. President; General on American frontier; achieved hero status in Mexican War. Attractive and rare partly printed Document Signed "Z. Taylor, Col. / 1st Regt. U.S. Infty / Comd." One page, large folio [16 3/4 x 20 3/4 inches]. Fort Crawford [Michigan Territory, now in the State of Wisconsin], November 1832. Muster roll of "non-commissioned officers and privates employed on extra duty as mechanics and laborers..." Taylor, as the commanding officer, has certified that the muster roll is correct. Excellent condition. 950.00

119. DAVIS, JEFFERSON. 1808-1889. American statesman and soldier; President of the Confederate States of America; saw frontier army service after graduation from West Point; officer in Mexican War; Congressman and Senator from Mississippi; Secretary of War (Pierce). Autograph Letter Signed. Full page, 4to. No place, November 15, 1851. To an unnamed recipient concerning payment of his mileage account, probably for travelling between Washington and his home in Mississippi, while serving in the U.S. Senate. Davis writes: "...The contingency which you mention in relation to the mileage account will induce me to provide for the payment of the bill drawn in favor of Corcoran & Riggs. I will direct my factor in New Orleans to send you a draft which I hope will reach you before the date at due. And this will enable me to act freely hereafter on the matter of the mileage account..." With engraved portrait. 500.00

120. TAFT, WILLIAM H. President; Chief Justice, U.S. Supreme Court. Typed Letter Signed, on his imprinted stationery. 1 page, 4to. New Haven, Conn., October 8, 1915. To Dr. Edward L. Gulick, Fairlee, Vermont, concerning the title of Taft's address for the Civic Forum. He writes: "...I would like to talk on A League of Nations to Enforce Peace, and would be entirely willing to have questions asked in regard to it. The subject is one that is being considered in various parts of the country, and it seems to me it might interest your audience. I would be glad to hear from you and to know whether this meets Doctor Vernon's approval and yours...." Interesting letter written while the Great War was raging in Europe but a year and a half before the United States entered the conflict. Fine condition. 200.00

"SO MANY...PERSONS...STRANGERS TO MY HUSBAND...HAVE UNDERTAKEN...HISTORIES, ALL CLAIMING SUCH INTIMATE KNOWLEDGE OF THE LAMENTED PRESIDENT THAT I HAVE BEEN FREQUENTLY STARTLED WITH THEIR INACCURATE ACCOUNTS."

121. LINCOLN, MARY TODD. First Lady. Superb Autograph Letter Signed "Mrs. A. Lincoln". 4 full pages, 8vo. Chicago, March 7, 1868. To A. D. Worthington, Hartford, Conn. With original stamped envelope bearing a circular Chicago postmark, and addressed by Mrs. Lincoln. Headed Private.

> "For reasons which are unnecessary to mention, I have concluded it is best for me not to accede to the proposition you have made me. My health is far from being restored and rest and quiet are now absolutely necessary for my life. The temptation to me is sometimes very great that many incidents that occurred in so momentous a time, under my immediate notice connected with my beloved husband & the country, should be truthfully placed before the public. So many pretentious persons, who were quite strangers to my husband & my household have undertaken their histories, all claiming such intimate knowledge of the lamented President, that I have been frequently startled with their varied & inaccurate accounts. It will be impossible for me, under present circumstances, to subject myself to the annoyance of public clamor. You understand the American people quite as well as myself and will appreciate my feelings in preferring silence. I am sure our noble friend, Col. Deming will do so. I have mentioned to no one, the subject of our correspondence & trust in the future you will guard it as well -- as also the contents of this letter, which has been so freely expressed...."

At this time, Mrs. Lincoln was suffering considerably from seemingly endless newspaper stories and a published account in the spring of 1868 of the Lincolns in the White House by Elizabeth Keckley, Mrs. Lincoln's personal friend and maid during the White House years. In the present letter Mary Lincoln expresses her frustration over such revealing and often inaccurate publications, while at the same time delines to write her own memoir. Choice!! 4500.00

APPOINTMENT OF A CONSUL FOR THE HAWAIIAN ISLANDS

122. BUCHANAN, JAMES. President. Attractive partly printed Document Signed, as President. Small oblong folio. Washington, October 3, 1859. Countersigned by LEWIS CASS, Secretary of State. Embossed white wafer seal of the State Department affixed with red wax at lower left. President Buchanan appoints Henry A. Pierce "Consul of the Kingdom of the Hawaiian Islands for Boston and New Bedford, in the State of Massachusetts; Portsmouth, New Hampshire; and Portland, Maine, to reside in Boston..." Actually this is the recognition of a Consul who was appointed by the Hawaiian Government. Fine condition. With engraved portrait. 750.00

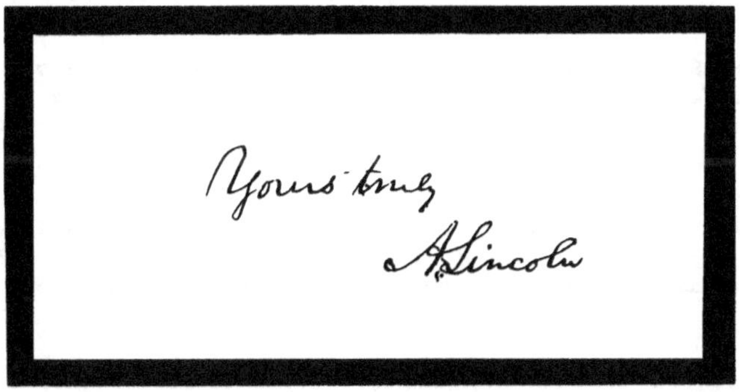

123. LINCOLN, ABRAHAM. President. Choice signature: "Yours truly / A. Lincoln" penned on a pastel green 24mo leaf. Superb specimen, with ample margins on all sides for framing. With handsome steel-engraved portrait. 850.00

"WHILE I AM COMMISSIONER THE LAW IS GOING TO BE OBSERVED; AND THAT'S ALL THERE IS TO IT...."

124. ROOSEVELT, THEODORE. President and Vice President. Strongly expressive Typed Letter Signed, on the imprinted letterhead of the President's Office, Police Department, City of New York. 1 page, 4to. New York, July 3, 1895. To his friend Madison Grant, New York City. Roosevelt begins: "The Knickerbocker Club at eight on Monday evening. I am very glad you can come..." Then turning to the difficulties he was having with the Mayor in the uniform enforcement of the law, Roosevelt continues: "I think you should say halved instead of doubled when you speak that way of myself and the Mayor. I do not care a rap; while I am Commissioner the Law is going to be observed; and that's all there is to it...." Fine condition. Letters dating from Roosevelt's relatively brief tenure as Police Commissioner are scarce. 495.00

MATCHING PAIR OF HAYES PRESIDENTIAL PHOTOGRAPHS

125. HAYES, RUTHERFORD B. and LUCY W. President and First Lady. Two superb matching sepia photographs, in the very scarce tall cabinet size, by Sarony of New York. Taken while President and First Lady in 1878. Each signed on the lower image area against the lighter area of the background. An unusual pair of matching photographs taken by Napoleon Sarony at his gallery in New York City when the Hayes family visited on October 2, 1878, two days prior to the President's 56th birthday. Receiving the finished product a few days later, Hayes recorded in his diary, "...Lucy's are beautiful, mine good." Triple matted in rich brown with tan and cream lips, thus ready to frame. Overall size 16 x 15 inches. Very, very choice!! 1750.00

126. CLEVELAND, FRANCES FOLSOM. First Lady. Handsome engraved vignette of the front approach to the Executive Mansion, showing numerous people and carriages in the wide drive. Signed by Mrs. Cleveland on the lower white margin. 12mo. Attractive and in choice condition. 125.00

127. ROOSEVELT, EDITH KERMIT. First Lady. Petite envelope, addressed and franked "Free / Edith K. Roosevelt" in top, right corner. Clear "Oyster Bay, N.Y. / Aug. 7, 1933" postmark. Addressed in her hand to Mrs. Amos Little, Timestone Farm, Marlboro, Mass. Very fine. 65.00

128. TRUMAN, HARRY S. President and Vice President. Typed Letter Signed, as U. S. Senator from Missouri, on imprinted Senate letterhead. 1 page, 4to. [Washington] April 3, 1936. To Howard McMillan, Dorchester, Mass. Senator Truman encloses "a pass to the Senate Gallery, which is good for this session of Congress..." Accompanying this letter is the original imprinted Senate Pass which Truman has filled out in his holograph for McMillan, but bearing a stamped facsimile signature. It is rather unusual that a Senator from Missouri would be sending such a pass to a resident of Massachusetts. Fine condition. The two pieces: 225.00

129. ROOSEVELT, ELEANOR. First Lady. Typed Letter Signed, as First Lady, on gilt-imprinted White House stationery. 1 page, 4to. Washington, November 14, 1942. To Diana [Hopkins], daughter of presidential advisor Harry L. Hopkins. She writes: "I am sending you these war stamps as a birthday gift with every good wish for your birthday. I hope you have a very pleasant day and that you will enjoy the books. Affectionately..." Nice association. 95.00

130. HARRISON, WILLIAM HENRY. President; General in War of 1812. Manuscript Document Signed "Wm. H. Harrison / A.D.C." One page, narrow 12mo. Greenville, December 2, 1794. Early frontier document ordering ten complete rations for a barge crew for two days. Somewhat irregularly trimmed at top and bottom (as usual), else fine. With engraved portrait. 475.00

THE HANDLING OF CONSCIENTIOUS OBJECTORS

131. ROOSEVELT, FRANKLIN D. President. Choice war-date Typed Letter Signed, as President, on imprinted White House stationery. 2/3 page, large 4to. Washington, March 29, 1944. To Reverend G. Bromley Oxnam, Resident Bishop, The Methodist Church, Boston, Mass. Roosevelt writes: "Your letter...in reference to procedures for handling conscientious objectors has been referred to the Director of Selective Service who is now engaged in studying this entire matter. He will advise you of his recommendations and conclusions on this subject at an early date. I am glad to have the expression of your views on conscientious objectors and appreciate your writing me in this connection...." Choice war-dated letter. Fine condition. 750.00

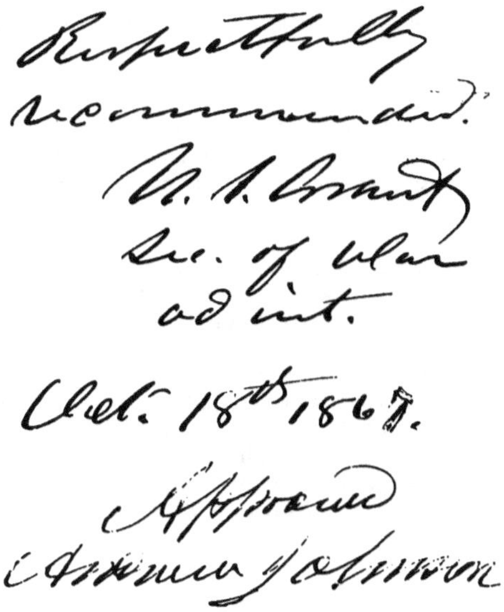

SIGNED ENDORSEMENTS BY GENERAL GRANT AND PRESIDENT JOHNSON

132. JOHNSON, ANDREW. President and Vice President. Autograph Endorsement Signed "Approved / Andrew Johnson" as President, penned directly under an Autograph Endorsement Signed "Respectfully recommended / U. S. Grant / Sec. of War / ad int. / Oct. 18th 1867". These endorsements have been penned on the integral leaf of a Manuscript Letter Signed, on imprinted War Department stationery, by B. W. BRICE, Paymaster General, addressed to General Grant in his capacity as Secretary of War ad interim. Brice recommends that Simeon Francis, Paymaster U.S. Army, be placed on the retired list of officers due to his age (62 years), and that "if the President shall see fit to make the vacancy [filled]...that Isaac S. Stewart...be appointed...." All the writing is on separate leaves, thus rendering the double combination of presidential signatures suitable for framing or display. Excellent condition. Choice!! 950.00

133. HAYES, RUTHERFORD B. President. Handsome partly printed Document Signed, as President. Oblong folio. Washington, April 9, 1877. Countersigned by D. M. KEY, Postmaster General. Embossed gilt wafer seal of the Post Office Department (pony express rider) affixed at bottom left. President Hayes appoints Albert Davis to serve as Postmaster in South Abington, Massachusetts. Hayes' name is boldly imprinted at top, and the magnificent spread-eagle vignette is the same as used on the front cover of this catalogue. Handsomely preserved. 425.00

134. COOLIDGE, CALVIN. President and Vice President. Printed Speech: Address...Accepting the Statue of President Andrew Jackson at Washington, D.C., April 15, 1928. Printed pamphlet with self-covered printed wrappers. Government Printing Office: Washington, 1928. 6 pages, small 4to. Signed by Coolidge on the last page beneath the final line of text. Bound in 3/4 blue morocco; gilt-lettered spine; decorated endpapers. Bookplate of Stuart W. Jackson. We cannot recall having seen this speech signed before. Fine condition. 350.00

135. HARRISON, BENJAMIN. President. Attractive partly printed Document Signed, as President. Oblong folio. Washington, June 18, 1889. Countersigned by JOHN WANAMAKER, Postmaster General. Gilt-embossed seal of the Post Office Department (pony express rider), at lower left, with blue silk ties. President Harrison appoints John T. Stansfield to serve as postmaster at Mount Carmel, Illinois. Harrison's name is imprinted at head, and there is a spread-eagle vignette like the one found on the front cover of this catalogue. Very fine. 425.00

136. CLEVELAND, GROVER. President. Attractive partly printed Document Signed, as President. One page, 4to. Washington, March 2, 1889. Two days before leaving office in his first term, President Cleveland authorizes the Secretary of State to affix the Seal of the United States to "a warrant for the pardon of Charles W. Penrose..." Choice condition. 350.00

137. CLEVELAND, GROVER. President. Autograph Statement, in pencil, and unsigned, written as President. 1 1/3 pages, large 8vo. Executive Mansion, February 8, 1888. Apparently a memorandum prepared for a cabinet member concerning the eligibility of a man named Rimker for a **pardon.** Cleveland writes: "The inference plainly is, it seems to me, that on the 29th of November 1872, the facts passed and the proceedings as developed by the report of the Judge Advocate General was submitted to the President [Grant] and he thereupon signified his approval of the proceedings and sentence, orally and definitely to the Secretary of War. Whereupon the latter officer on the next day personally endorsed upon the assent the finding and conclusion of the President, as they had been communicated to him....The endorsement on the record recites that the proceedings of the Court had been submitted to the President. Without having the Rimker case now before me I am of the opinion that this recital was precisely what was held to be fatally wanting in that case and that the decision turned entirely upon that omission. If that be so the record in this case is complete and valid." An unusual presidential draft showing the attention Cleveland gave to minor details, and his insistence that the record be allowed to speak for itself. Fine. 150.00

138. HOOVER, HERBERT. President. Strikingly handsome studio photograph by Harris & Ewing showing a near full-face bust image of Hoover. On the lower blank margin he has penned: "Kind Regards of / Herbert Hoover". Not inscribed to a named person. Choice item! 250.00

139. GARFIELD, JAMES A. President; assassinated. Manuscript Letter Signed "J. A. Garfield", while serving in Congress from Ohio, on ornately printed Thirty Eighth Congress letterhead, featuring a lovely vignette of the U.S. Capitol Building. Full page, 4to. Washington, March 23, 1867. To Hon. Milton Sutliff, Warren, Ohio. Garfield writes: "...I called on the Secretary of War this morning and presented the claims of Capt. Hadley to a brevet stating the points which you made in your former communication, and the secretary ordered a brevet to be conferred upon him. I hope it will be sent to the Senate before the adjournment of that body. I ...return you Capt. Hadley's letter which shows that the Southern climate has not weakened his faith in the cause of freedom nor made him unworthy to receive the decoration of the government...." Interesting southern reference. Fine condition. 350.00

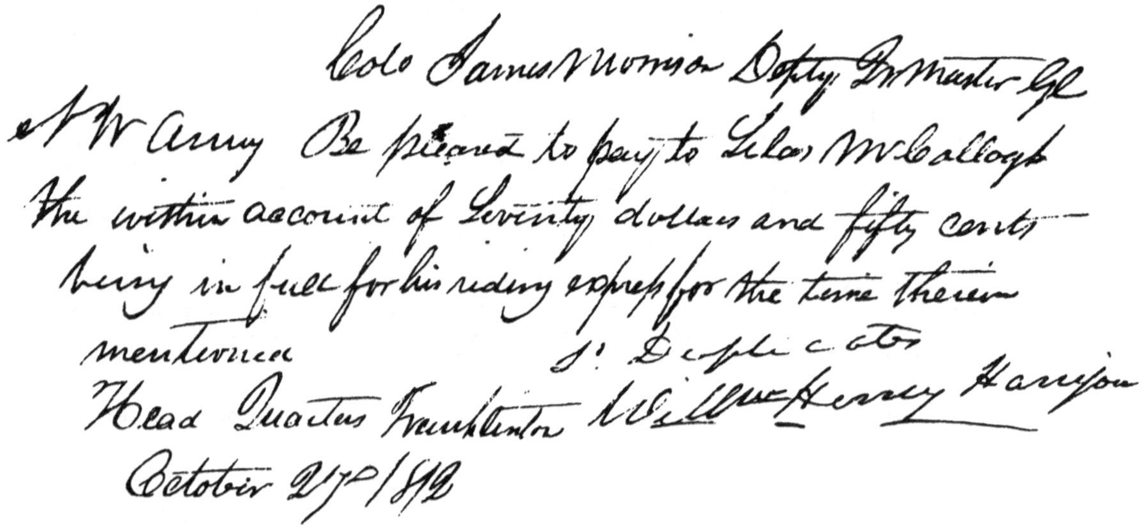
Colo James Morrison Depty Qr Master Gl
N W Army Be pleased to pay to Silas McCullogh
the within account of Seventy dollars and fifty cents
being in full for his riding express for the time therein
mentioned
Duplicate
Head Quarters Franklinton Willm Henry Harrison
October 27th 1812

140. HARRISON, WILLIAM HENRY. President; General in War of 1812; Governor of the Indiana Territory. Manuscript Document Signed. 1 page, oblong 8vo. Head Quarters, Franklinton, October 27, 1812. Pay order directed to Colonel James Morrison, Deputy Quartermaster General of the Northwest Army. Harrison approves payment of $70.50 to Silas McCullogh "being in full for riding express for the time therein mentioned." On the verso appears McCullogh's account for 38 days riding express. With handsome engraved portrait of General Harrison. 500.00

141. ROOSEVELT, FRANKLIN D. President. Lengthy Typed Letter Signed, as Governor of New York, on the blue and gilt crested stationery of his office. Full page, 4to. Albany, August 10, 1929. To C. Allen Dunham, Arcade, New York, acknowledging his letter concerning the needs of the deaf in New York. He writes: "...It is impossible...to forecast what the future relation of the state to the schools for the deaf now under private management will be, for any plan looking toward the taking over of these schools as state institutions will necessarily include consideration not only of the Rome, Rochester and Malone schools...but also the three schools in New York City. It would be unfortunate to present to the Legislature a proposition affecting the future of these schools without first carefully considering the whole situation... I can...assure you that I am personally interested in the schools for the deaf and shall...see to it that their problems and needs are given the consideration which they deserve...." With another fine paragraph on the same subject. Excellent. 295.00

142. GRANT, ULYSSES S. President; Union General; accepted Lee's surrender. Gorgeous albumin carte de visit photograph showing a 3/4 length seated likeness of Grant in military attire. Imprint of Henry Ulke, Photographer, Washington, 1868, on verso. Boldly signed on the lower white mount: "U. S. Grant / General." Pristine condition. 950.00

143. [EISENHOWER, DWIGHT D.] President and General. Leatherette bill (paper money) case, gilt-lettered: "Trip of President Dwight D. Eisenhower / Washington to Panama and Return / July 20 to July 24, 1968 / Pan American World Airways / [Pan Am logo]". Interesting presidential souvenir from trip made by a commercial carrier. 35.00

144. [HOOVER, HERBERT]. Imprinted visiting card. 15.00

145. PIERCE, JANE M. First Lady. On a narrow slip cut from an ALS she has penned her full signature "Jane M. Pierce" followed by "My husband's kind remembrance." Very nice, and seldom offered in simple signature format. 75.00

146. ADAMS, LOUISA C. First Lady (wife of John Quincy Adams). Autograph Letter, in the third person. 1 page, 4to. Quincy [Mass.], September 25, 1835. To [Asher B.] Durand, the engraver and painter. She writes: "Mrs. Adams encloses a small pattern in paper, at the request of her daughter, who is desirous of having the Miniature of the Portrait, as nearly of that size as possible, if he can procure it. If not able to do so, Mrs. Adams wishes it to be as small as convenient, so that she may have it set for wear when it is finished. Mrs. Adams is happy to sieze the present opportunity of returning her thanks to Mr. Durand for the Portrait of her Grand daughter so elegantly presented, and begs Mr. Durand to accept the sentiment of her high respect and esteem...." Some expert restoration work to the folds on verso, else fine. With an attractive steel-engraved portrait. Very scarce. 575.00

147. HARRISON, BENJAMIN. President. Typed Letter Signed, as President, on imprinted Executive Mansion stationery. 2/3 page, 4to. Washington, October 21, 1889. To Hon. H. J. Spooner, Providence, R.I. Original imprinted envelope bearing a Washington postmark in place of a postage stamp. Harrison acknowledges his correspondent's letter, and states "...I notice what you say about the appointment of a collector at Providence. I had a brief conversation with Senator Aldrich upon the subject the other day, when he was here, of which he will advise you, I am sure...." Fine example, and rather scarce as President. 450.00

148. COOLIDGE, CALVIN. President and Vice President; Governor of Mass. His book: Have Faith in Massachusetts / Speeches and Addresses. Gilt-lettered deep blue cloth. Boston, 1919. Second Edition Enlarged, containing material not in the first edition. Inscribed on the front endpaper by Collidge, while serving as Governor: "To Irvin L. Lindabury / With regards / Calvin Coolidge / 1920". Bookplate. With worn dust jacket. Book is very fine. Dust jacket says Coolidge was elected on a "LAW AND ORDER"platform. 150.00

149. [NIXON, RICHARD M.]. President and Vice President. Gold-plated tie bar bearing Nixon's facsimile signature stamped across the bar. On the right end of the bar is the Presidential Seal (gilt, with a blue background). Original plain box. This White House souvenir was given out by the President himself, or by staff members, and was not commercially available. 35.00

150. HOOVER, HERBERT. President. Printed pamphlet containing his speech: This Crisis in American Life. Address [before]...The Republican National Convention, Philadelphia, June 22, 1948. Octavo, printed wrappers. Signed by Hoover in bright blue ink on the front wrapper, which also serves as the title-page. Very fine copy. 150.00

151. MC KINLEY, WILLIAM. President; assassinated (1901). Typed Letter Signed, as President, on imprinted Executive Mansion stationery. 1 page, 4to. Washington, November 19, 1900. To E.P. Briggs, Kansas City, Missouri, acknowledging his "cordial words of congratulation", upon being elected to a second presidential term. Presidential letters by McKinley are relatively scarce, and this is a nice clean specimen. 650.00

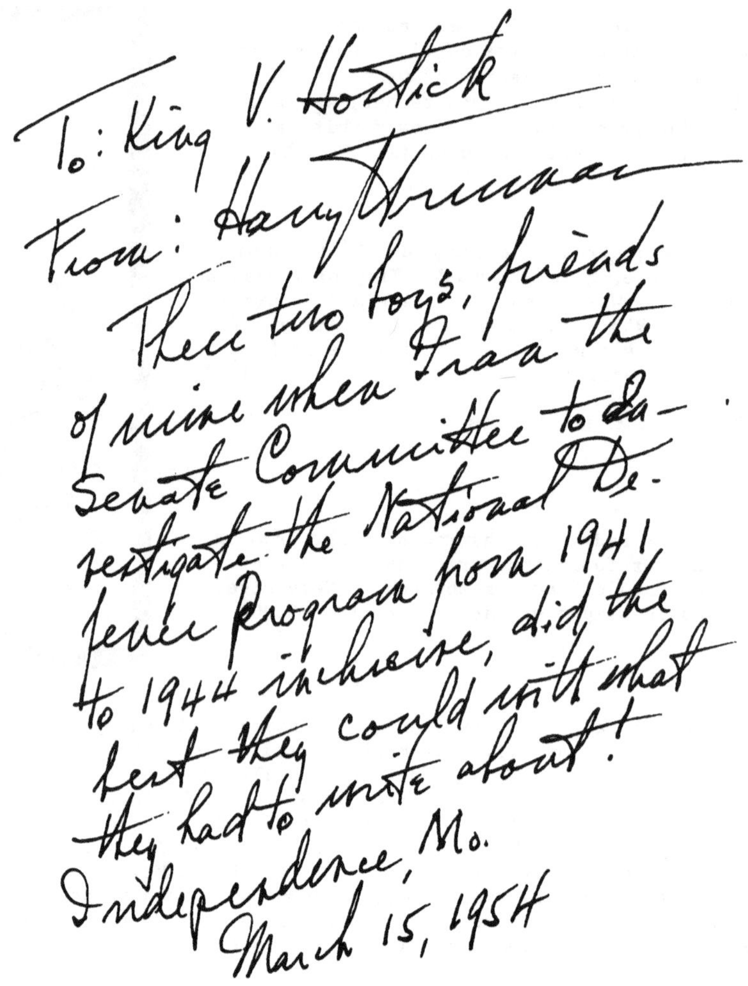
To: King V. Hostick
From: Harry Truman
These two boys, friends
of mine when I ran the
Senate Committee to In-
vestigate the National Defence Program from 1941
to 1944 inclusive, did the
best they could with what
they had to write about!
Independence, Mo.
March 15, 1954

RARE HOLOGRAPH STATEMENT BY THE FORMER PRESIDENT

152. TRUMAN, HARRY S. President and Vice President. Rare Autograph Statement Signed, in the form of an inscription (removed from a book). Full page, 8vo. Independence, Missouri, March 15, 1954. The former president has boldly penned: "To: King V. Hostick / From: Harry S. Truman / These two boys, friends of mine when I ran the Senate Committee to Investigate the National Defence Program from 1941 to 1944 inclusive, did the best they could with what they had to write about!..." Undoubtedly this refers to the picture book about Truman and his presidency entitled MR. PRESIDENT, by Hillman and Wagg. A remarkable inscription penned by the former president for a mid-western retired autograph dealer. 1250.00

153. GRANT, ULYSSES S. President. Partly printed Document Signed, as President. 1 page, quarto. Washington, August 19, 1873. President Grant authorizes the Secretary of State to affix the Seal of the United States to "a Warrant for the pardon of Edmond Ross..." Fine condition, except for light rectangular stain in top left margin (caused by another sheet of paper). Bold signature. With steel-engraved portrait. 350.00

GOVERNOR WILSON'S DEMOCRATIC CLUB SPEECH

154. WILSON, WOODROW. President. Printed pamphlet: Address by GOVERNOR WOODROW WILSON of New Jersey, Delivered at the Dinner of the Democratic Club in Philadelphia, on Tuesday Night, February 21, 1911. Printed stiff wrappers. No place, no date. 15 pages, 8vo. Signed by Wilson on the last page beneath the final line of printed text. Choice condition, and a very rare and desirable signed Wilson speech. 350.00

PRESIDENT JOHNSON'S AMNESTY PROCLAMATION

155. [JOHNSON, ANDREW]. President and Vice President. Historic printed document signed in type headed By the President of the United States of America: A Proclamation. 1 1/2 pages, legal folio. Washington, May 29, 1865. President Johnson sets forth conditions granting amnesty in accordance with the document issued by President Lincoln, March 26, 1864. "I, Andrew Johnson, President of the United States, do proclaim and declare that I hereby grant to all persons who have, directly or indirectly, participated in the existing rebellion,...amnesty and pardon..." Accompanied by a printed Circular Letter from William H. Seward, Secretary of State, transmitting the President's Proclamation. Some very light stains, else fine. Very rare and historic printed items. 450.00

THE FORMER CONFEDERATE PRESIDENT EXPLAINS WHY HE DID NOT SEEK AN AUDIENCE WITH THE LATE POPE PIUS IX

156. DAVIS, JEFFERSON. President of the Confederate States of America. Remarkable Autograph Letter Signed. 2 pages, 4to. Beauvoir, Harrison Co., Mississippi, March 20, 1878. To "My dear Friend". Davis expresses his appreciation and approval at seeing his previous letter printed in The Catholic Universe. He continues: "...It has given satisfaction to my Catholic friends hereabouts and I am happy to have been permitted to add a pebble to the pile of stones which signify and commemorate the good deeds and virtues of his departed Holiness [Pope Pius IX]. I was anxious...to have paid my respects and to have made my personal acknowledgments to The Holy Father and to you. I will explain why I did not do this; when in Paris I received a message from Cardinal Antonelli who had been informed of the obstacles in the way of my making a visit to Rome, that, he would give me permission to enter the city, so as to relieve me of the necessity of getting a passport from the American Minister. But as I foresaw that this might expose The Holy Father to embarrassing inquiries by the U.S. Charge at Rome, I failed to avail myself of the last opportunity to gratify my earnest desire to see him, and to thank him for his benevolent and fair course towards the South during the War, as well as for his personal friendship to myself...." Originally worn at the folds, they have been expertly repaired with mending tissue. Quite a remarkable letter!! 950.00

157. HARDING, WARREN G. President. Typed Letter Signed, as President, on imprinted White House stationery. 1 page, 4to. Washington, September 12, 1922. To Mrs. Charles L. Bird, Overmoor, Peterborough, N.H. Original envelope. In part: "I greatly appreciated your kind and sympathetic expressions and I very much like what you said concerning Mrs. Harding. I really think she deserves the kindly things you said...We did pass three or four exceedingly anxious days and...great comfort...was found in expressions of sympathetic...friends..." Fine! 650.00

158. GARFIELD, JAMES A. President; assassinated. Manuscript Letter Signed. Full page, 4to. Mentor, Ohio, July 3, 1880. To George G. Mullins, Chaplain U.S.A., St. Louis, Missouri, acknowledging his letter of June 9th. "...Could not answer sooner, was so crowded with work -- and even at this late date can only thank you...." Garfield had just received the Republican Presidential nomination. Fine example. 250.00

159. TAYLOR, ZACHARY. President; General in Mexican War, and the hero of Buena Vista; military officer on American frontier. Manuscript Document Signed "Z. Taylor, Col. / Comdg." One page, oblong 8vo. Fort Crawford, Michigan Territory, March 1833. Requisition for One cord of wood to be used as fuel in the Commanding Officer's office at Fort Crawford. Taylor, of course, was the commanding officer. With handsome steel-engraved portrait. Choice! 650.00

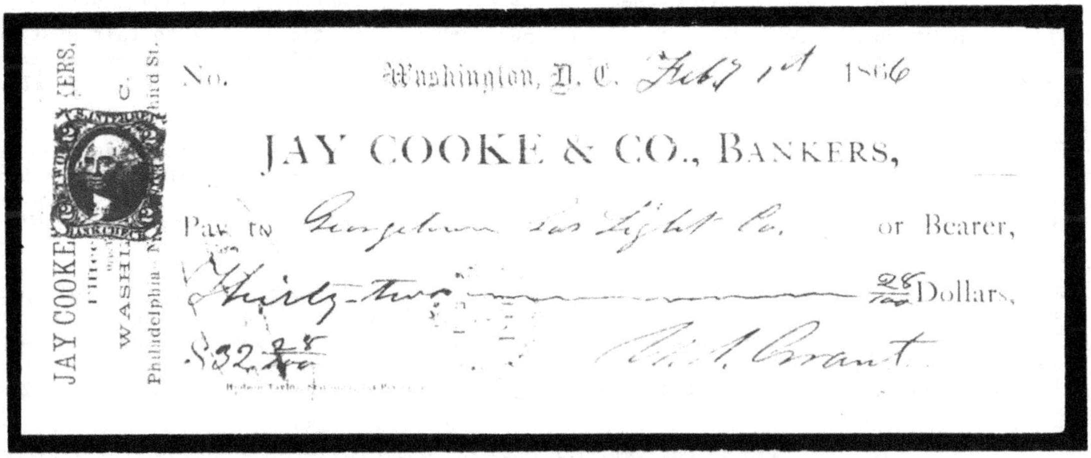

160. GRANT, ULYSSES S. President and Union General. Partly printed Signed Bank Check, accomplished in his hand. Oblong 12mo. Washington, February 1, 1866. Drawn on Jay Cooke & Co., Bankers, and made payable to the Georgetown Gas Light Co. Adhesive revenue stamp at top left. Cut-cancelled (nothing missing), and two stamped bank cancellations. Excellent condition. Grant is very rare in check format. With handsome engraved portrait. 1250.00

161. HOOVER, HERBERT. President. Typed Letter Signed, as President, on imprinted White House stationery. 1 page, 4to. Washington, August 13, 1932. To E. C. Lampson, Editor, The Jefferson Gazette, Jefferson, Ohio. Original stamped envelope. Hoover writes: "I am deeply interested to learn of your praiseworthy efforts to erect suitable memorials at Jefferson, Ohio, to Joshua Reed Giddings and B. F. Wade, who played so large a part in the founding of the Republican Party, and to my dear friend, the late Senator Theodore R. Burton, whose life was a noble pattern of the high-minded public servant...." Choice! 425.00

162. WILSON, WOODROW. President. Scarce Autograph Note Signed, as President of Princeton University. 1 page, 12mo. Princeton, N.J., May 8, 1905. To Miss Sophie Knowlton Smith, taking pleasure in sending his autograph. Although brief, attractive and scarce. 350.00

163. ROOSEVELT, THEODORE. President and Vice President. Typed Letter Signed "T. Roosevelt", as Acting Secretary of the Navy, on imprinted Navy Department stationery. 1 page, 4to. Washington, August 4, 1897. To Passed Assistant Engineer George E. Burd, U.S.N., Boston, Mass. The future President orders his correspondent to "Proceed to New York, N.Y., and report to the Commandant of the Navy Yard at that place, for such duty as he may assign you at that Yard. This employment on shore duty is required by the public interests. The unexpired portion of the leave of absence granted you...is hereby revoked...." Several endorsements, one in lower blank margin, others on verso. Interesting naval content. Fine. 225.00

164. TRUMAN, BESS W. First Lady. Typed Letter Signed, as First Lady, on gilt-imprinted White House stationery. 1 page, small 4to. Washington, May 24, 1945. To baseball executive and owner of the Washington Senators, Clark C. Griffith. She writes: "I am delighted to have that annual pass which you have so courteously sent me on behalf of the American League of professional baseball clubs. I am looking forward to making good use of this during the current season..." Interesting and fine. 100.00

THE CHIEF JUSTICE SEEKS TO AVERT A BAD JUDICIAL APPOINTMENT

165. TAFT, WILLIAM H. President; Chief Justice, U.S. Supreme Court. Highly unusual and candid Typed Letter Signed, as Chief Justice, on imprinted Supreme Court stationery. Very full page, 4to, with the postscript running four lines on to a second leaf. Washington, November 18, 1923. To Warren F. Martin, Special Assistant to the Attorney General, Washington. Headed Confidential. Taft writes:

> "If Thomas F. Graham is the State Judge in San Francisco whom Senator Shortridge recommended for appointment to the last vacancy...I have no hesitation in saying, from the unanimous testimony of many prominent, able and patriotic lawyers from San Francisco and California who have spoken to me...with great concern lest he be appointed, that he is utterly without qualifications for the place. If he is the man whom I think him to be, he acquired his prominence as a Judge in divorce cases by sensational attempts to reconcile the parties, and not by any manifestations of judicial learning or needed judicial qualities in any respect. I don't think it is unjust to him to say that until Senator Shortridge presented him as a candidate, he was regarded as a joke by serious minded members of the Bar, and that it would greatly lower the standard of the Federal Bench in California to have him appointed. I never met Judge Graham and have no possible reason for saying this except the desire to avoid an unworthy appointment. I would much perfer that Senator Shortridge...should succeed in having his recommendation for the Judgeship acted upon favorably by the President, but in this case I must think that the Senator has been blinded by his friendly feelings toward Judge Graham and has not been prompted by unbiased judgement..."

Accompanying this remarkable letter is a typed carbon of Martin's reply to Taft stating that the Senator will not press the nomination, and that considerable other negative letters have been received. Truly, a splendid judicial letter!! 875.00

166. GRANT, ULYSSES S. President; Union General. Partly printed Document Signed, as President. One page, 4to. Washington, May 10, 1871. The President authorizes and directs "the Secretary of State to affix the Seal of the United States to a Warrant for the pardon of James Geary." Excellent condition, with Grant's signature particularly choice. With portrait. 425.00

167. BUCHANAN, JAMES. President. Manuscript Letter Signed, as Secretary of State. Full page, 4to. Department of State, Washington, August 6, 1846. To C. Porter, Consul of the United States at Frontern de Tabasco. Buchanan acknowledges receipt of several despatches and informs his correspondent that his Bond has been received, approved, and sent to the Treasury Department to be placed on file. Fine condition. With engraved portrait. 250.00

SIGNED PRESENTATION COPY OF NIXON'S LATEST BOOK

168. NIXON, RICHARD M. President and Vice President. His book: Leaders / Profiles and Reminiscences of Men Who Have Shaped the Modern World. Paper-covered boards, cloth back. New York, 1982. First edition. Inscribed by the former President on the half-title: "To William Livingston / With best wishes / from / Richard Nixon / 12-8-82". Mint copy, in original decorated publisher's dust-jacket. 125.00

AN EXCEPTIONALLY EARLY LETTER

169. JOHNSON, LYNDON B. President and Vice President. Typed Letter Signed, as National Youth Administration Director for Texas, on primitively imprinted letterhead. Full page, 4to. Austin, Texas, September 25, 1935. To William H. Sealy, Kosse, Texas. Johnson encloses a bulletin (present) which "explains the type of aid available to college students under the National Youth Administration, as well as the requirements and procedure necessary to securing it. Students who have been awarded high school scholarships are eligible to participate....This program is now under way in Texas, and colleges have been accepting applications for some time... Denominational and religious colleges are eligible to participate in the National Youth Administration program...." The bulletin describing the program is attached to Johnson's letter. This is the earliest Johnson letter we can recall being offered for sale. Fine. 450.00

SUPREME HEADQUARTERS
ALLIED EXPEDITIONARY FORCE

Soldiers, Sailors and Airmen of the Allied Expeditionary Force!

You are about to embark upon the Great Crusade, toward which we have striven these many months. The eyes of the world are upon you. The hopes and prayers of liberty-loving people everywhere march with you. In company with our brave Allies and brothers-in-arms on other Fronts, you will bring about the destruction of the German war machine, the elimination of Nazi tyranny over the oppressed peoples of Europe, and security for ourselves in a free world.

Your task will not be an easy one. Your enemy is well trained, well equipped and battle-hardened. He will fight savagely.

But this is the year 1944 ! Much has happened since the Nazi triumphs of 1940-41. The United Nations have inflicted upon the Germans great defeats, in open battle, man-to-man. Our air offensive has seriously reduced their strength in the air and their capacity to wage war on the ground. Our Home Fronts have given us an overwhelming superiority in weapons and munitions of war, and placed at our disposal great reserves of trained fighting men. The tide has turned ! The free men of the world are marching together to Victory !

I have full confidence in your courage, devotion to duty and skill in battle. We will accept nothing less than full Victory !

Good Luck ! And let us all beseech the blessing of Almighty God upon this great and noble undertaking.

170. EISENHOWER, DWIGHT D. President and General. His book telling of his experiences in World War II: Crusade in Europe. Brown cloth. New York, 1948. First edition. Copy No. 71 of 1426 numbered copies containing the facsimile printing of Ike's historic D-Day Order personally signed by Eisenhower in the lower blank margin. Very fine copy. 950.00

ARRANGING A MEETING WITH HIS FUTURE COMMERCE SECRETARY

171. WILSON, WOODROW. President; Governor of New Jersey; President of Princeton University; only president to hold a Ph.D. Typed Letter Signed, as President-elect, on his imprinted stationery 1 page, 4to. Trenton, N.J., December 19, 1912. To Honorable William C. Redfield, Brooklyn, New York. In part: "...I would be very much obliged if you would give me the pleasure of seeing you at 2:30 on Monday afternoon the thirtieth of December here in Trenton. In haste..." Redfield, a prominent industrialist and politician, was offered by Wilson, and accepted the position of Secretary of Commerce. This planned meeting might have been to discuss the make-up of Wilson's cabinet. Fine. 325.00

172. ROOSEVELT, EDITH KERMIT. First Lady. Autograph Letter Signed, as First Lady of New York State, on silver-imprinted Executive Mansion stationery. 3 full pages, 12mo. Albany, no date [Ca. 1899-1900]. To Doctor Morgan. She writes: "Mr. Elisha Roosevelt tells me that you can arrange to come to Albany to see my boy. Any date and hour will be convenient for me except Wednesdays, I am always engaged on that day. I hope you may be able to fix an early date....I feel that my boy has never been successfully fitted with glasses, and you have done such wonders for others that I feel sure you can help him...." Mrs. Roosevelt was probably referring to her son, Archibald. Very scarce of this period. Fine. 150.00

PRESIDENT GERALD R. FORD

SWEARING-IN CEREMONY FOR THE 38TH PRESIDENT OF THE UNITED STATES, IN THE EAST ROOM AT THE WHITE HOUSE ON AUGUST NINTH, ONE THOUSAND NINE HUNDRED AND SEVENTY-FOUR

OATH OF OFFICE

I, Gerald R. Ford, do solemnly swear that I will faithfully execute the Office of President of the United States, and will, to the best of my ability, preserve, protect and defend the Constitution of the United States, so help me God.

REMARKS

Mr. Chief Justice, my dear friends, my fellow Americans:

The oath that I have taken is the same oath that was taken by George Washington and by every President under the Constitution. But I assume the Presidency under extraordinary circumstances, never before experienced by Americans. This is an hour of history that troubles our minds and hurts our hearts.

Therefore, I feel it is my first duty to make an unprecedented compact with my countrymen. Not an inaugural address, not a fireside chat, not a campaign speech—just a little straight talk among friends. And I intend it to be the first of many.

I am acutely aware that you have not elected me as your President by your ballots, and so I ask you to confirm me as your President with your prayers. And I hope that such prayers will also be the first of many.

If you have not chosen me by secret ballot, neither have I gained office by any secret promises. I have not campaigned either for the Presidency or the Vice Presidency. I have not subscribed to any partisan platform. I am indebted to no man, and only to one woman—my dear wife—as I begin this very difficult job.

I have not sought this enormous responsibility, but I will not shirk it. Those who nominated and confirmed me as Vice President were my friends and are my friends. They were of both parties, elected by all the people and acting under the Constitution in their name. It is only fitting then that I should pledge to them and to you that I will be the President of all the people.

Thomas Jefferson said the people are the only sure reliance for the preservation of our liberty. And down the years, Abraham Lincoln renewed this American article of faith asking, "Is there any better way or equal hope in the world?"

I intend, on Monday next, to request of the Speaker of the House of Representatives and the President pro tempore of the Senate the privilege of appearing before the Congress to share with my former colleagues and with you, the American people, my views on the priority business of the Nation and to solicit your views and their views. And may I say to the Speaker and the others, if I could meet with you right after these remarks, I would appreciate it.

Even though this is late in an election year, there is no way we can go forward except together and no way anybody can win except by serving the people's urgent needs. We cannot stand still or slip backwards. We must go forward now together.

To the peoples and the governments of all friendly nations, and I hope that could encompass the whole world, I pledge an uninterrupted and sincere search for peace. America will remain strong and united, but its strength will remain dedicated to the safety and sanity of the entire family of man, as well as to our own precious freedom.

I believe that truth is the glue that holds government together, not only our Government, but civilization itself. That bond, though strained, is unbroken at home and abroad.

In all my public and private acts as your President, I expect to follow my instincts of openness and candor with full confidence that honesty is always the best policy in the end.

My fellow Americans, our long national nightmare is over.

Our Constitution works; our great Republic is a Government of laws and not of men. Here the people rule. But there is a higher power, by whatever name we honor Him, who ordains not only righteousness but love, not only justice but mercy.

As we bind up the internal wounds of Watergate, more painful and more poisonous than those of foreign wars, let us restore the golden rule to our political process, and let brotherly love purge our hearts of suspicion and of hate.

In the beginning, I asked you to pray for me. Before closing, I ask again your prayers, for Richard Nixon and for his family. May our former President, who brought peace to millions, find it for himself. May God bless and comfort his wonderful wife and daughters, whose love and loyalty will forever be a shining legacy to all who bear the lonely burdens of the White House.

I can only guess at those burdens, although I have witnessed at close hand the tragedies that befell three Presidents and the lesser trials of others.

With all the strength and all the good sense I have gained from life, with all the confidence my family, my friends, and my dedicated staff impart to me, and with the good will of countless Americans I have encountered in recent visits to 40 States, I now solemnly reaffirm my promise I made to you last December 6: to uphold the Constitution, to do what is right as God gives me to see the right, and to do the very best I can for America.

God helping me, I will not let you down.

Thank you.

Gerald R. Ford

This is number 93/175

[Item No. 173]

MAGNIFICENT NEWLY-ISSUED PRESIDENTIAL BROADSIDE

173. FORD, GERALD R. President and Vice President. Strikingly handsome multi-colored broadside containing the Oath of Office and the full text of President Ford's Remarks made after being sworn in as President by Chief Justice Warren Burger, following Nixon's resignation. The right third of this remarkable broadside is comprised of a 3/4 length color portrait of Ford. Large oblong folio [22 x 15 inches]. Gilt Presidential Seal at top left. Limited to just 175 copies (only edition) signed by Ford beneath his portrait. Due to the small quantity printed, historic significance of the content, and beauty of the lay-out and printing, we feel that the price will soon be increased to a considerable degree. 225.00

174. REAGAN, NANCY. First Lady. Handsome, and most unusual quarto photograph showing a very young future First Lady dusting the books on the top shelf in a bookcase. Boldly signed in red ink against a light background area. Pristine condition. 75.00

DATED PRESIDENTIAL PRESENTATION

175. JOHNSON, ANDREW. President and Vice President. Superb 3/4 length albumin photograph depicting the embattled Chief Executive seated, his left hand resting on a table. Johnson has signed this carte de visit photograph on the lower white margin. On the otherwise blank verso he has also penned: "Presented / June 4th 1868 / Andrew Johnson", thus dating the piece from his incumbency. Pristine condition. Very rare and desirable photograph. 2000.00

"I AM NOT IN PUBLIC LIFE..."

176. COOLIDGE, CALVIN. President and Vice President. Highly interesting Typed Letter Signed, on his imprinted stationery. 1 page, 4to. Northampton, Mass., May 23, 1930. To S. J. Woolf, New York City. The former President, who had been out of office for just over a year, writes: "For a great many years I have been assisting individuals and newspapers to prepare articles. I am not in public life and should like very much to be relieved of that kind of work. You do not know what a great burden it gets to be when you have to pursue it day after day after you are out of office. Later I expect to have the picture men all together after which the picture business of my residence I hope will be closed...." 375.00

177. MC KINLEY, WILLIAM. President; assassinated. Typed Letter Signed, as Governor of Ohio, on imprinted Executive Chamber stationery. Full page, 8vo. Columbus, Ohio, January 21, 1892. To Hon. Charles Townsend, Athens, Ohio. McKinley writes that he had heard of Mr. Brown's candidacy only the day before his correspondent's letter arrived. "...I do not know whether I shall be able to give him the first vacancy, although I could have done it had I known of it sooner...." Nice political letter. Fine. 225.00

COPYRIGHTS AND RADIO BROADCASTING

178. HOOVER, HERBERT. President. Typed Letter Signed, as Secretary of Commerce, on official imprinted stationery. 1 page, 4to. Washington, November 14, 1925. To Hon. Wallace H. White, House of Representatives, sympathizing with his "difficulty in finding time to serve as committee chairman in the recent radio conference", and adding: "The subject of copyrights...is perhaps the most vexatious one with which the broadcasters now have to deal. I am very hopeful that the action which you took will result in its final solution...." Fine. 150.00

PRESIDENTIAL PARDON FOR A CRIMINAL GONE INSANE

179. JOHNSON, ANDREW. President and Vice President. Manuscript Document Signed, as President. 1½ pages, tall legal folio. Washington, October 25, 1866. Countersigned by WILLIAM H. SEWARD, Secretary of State. Large embossed white wafer seal of the State Department affixed on the second page to the left of Johnson's fine signature. A full and unconditional pardon granted to Robert Warner, who was convicted of Assault and Battery, and sentenced to one year's confinement in the County Jail, because "he has become insane and his pardon has been requested by the Judge who sentenced him and the Warden of the Jail..." Some fold separations neatly reinforced with mending tissue, else in fine condition. 950.00

180. WILSON, WOODROW. President. Handsome, partly engraved Document Signed, as President. Tall folio, vellum. Washington, May 27, 1916. Countersigned by JOSEPHUS DANIELS, Secretary of the Navy. Embossed blue wafer seal of the Navy Department at bottom center. President Wilson commissions Weyman P. Beehler a Lieutenant in the U. S. Navy. Small spread-eagle vignette at top center, this time showing our national bird perched on a rock in the ocean with fully rigged clipper ships in the background. A most attractive vignette of sea-nymphs and flags appears at the bottom. Very ornate and decorative presidential document. Fine! 450.00

LEMONS FOR THE PRESIDENT?

181. FILLMORE, MILLARD. President and Vice President. Autograph Letter Signed, probably written either as Vice President or President, but undated. 2 pages, 8vo. No place, no date. To "My Dear Miss Wilhelmina". Fillmore writes: "I received with great pleasure your kind note accompanied by a very acceptable New Year's Present of some very fine Lemons; for which please accept my grateful acknowledgements. These are evidently the growth of this climate and I intend to preserve them till my wife & daughter arrive that they may see what fine specimens of tropical fruits are grown in the national metropolis...." Interesting!! 350.00

182. MC KINLEY, WILLIAM. President; assassinated. Imprinted (blue) Executive Mansion card, boldly signed by McKinley as President. Washington, no date. Lightly pressure-mounted, else fine. Getting scarce in this format. 250.00

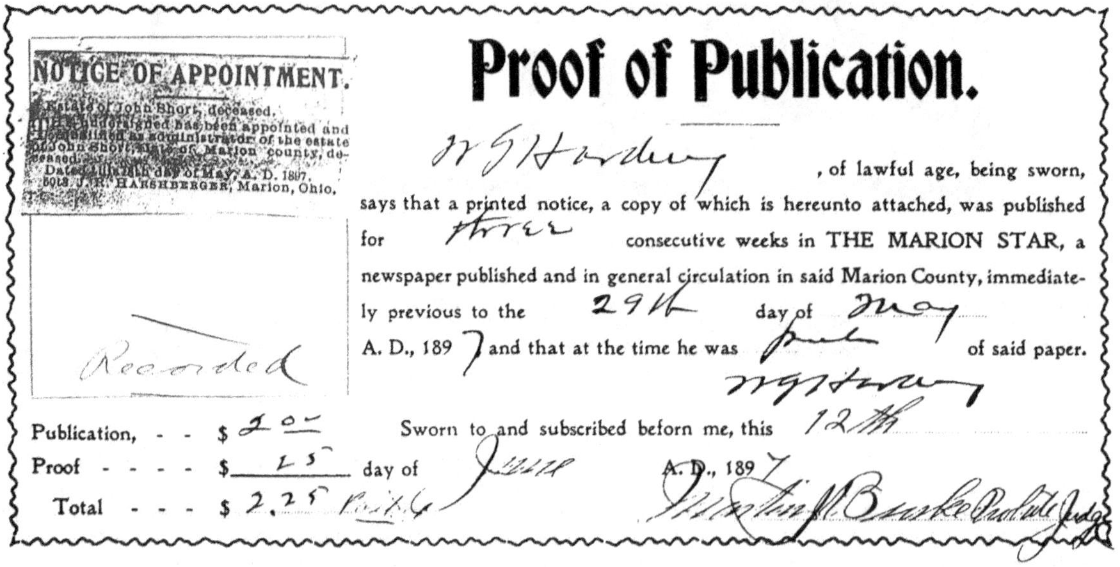
NOTICE OF APPOINTMENT.
Estate of John Short, deceased.
The undersigned has been appointed and qualified as administrator of the estate of John Short, late of Marion county, deceased.
Dated this 11th day of May, A. D. 1897.
J. H. HARSHBERGER, Marion, Ohio.

Proof of Publication.

W G Harding, of lawful age, being sworn, says that a printed notice, a copy of which is hereunto attached, was published for three consecutive weeks in THE MARION STAR, a newspaper published and in general circulation in said Marion County, immediately previous to the 29th day of May A. D., 1897 and that at the time he was [illegible] of said paper.

W G Harding

Recorded

Publication, - - $2.00
Proof - - - - $ .25
Total - - - $2.25 [illegible]

Sworn to and subscribed before me, this 12th day of June A. D., 1897

[illegible] Probate Judge

183. HARDING, WARREN G. President. Partly printed Document Signed as owner and editor of The Marion Star. 1 page, oblong 8vo. [Marion, Ohio] June 12, 1897. "Proof of Publication" form completed by the future President with his signature "W. G. Harding" appearing twice on the document. Also signed by a Probate Judge. The printed "Notice" clipped from Harding's paper is affixed at top left. Fine condition. 225.00

184. HOOVER, HERBERT. President. Printed pamphlet containing his speech: The Constructive Character of the Republican Party. October 18, 1952, New York City. Self-covered printed wrappers. Boldly signed by Hoover in bright blue ink on the front wrapper beneath his printed name. 18 pages. Small 8vo. Excellent condition. 150.00

THE PRESIDENT CONGRATULATES THE GERMAN KAISER

185. CLEVELAND, GROVER. President. Interesting partly printed Document Signed, as President. One page, 4to. Washington, March 15, 1893. President Cleveland authorizes the Secretary of State to affix the Seal of the United States to an "envelope containing my letter addressed to the Emperor of Germany, on the marriage of his sister Princess Feodora of Prussia, to Prince Constantine of Hesse, January 25, 1893..." Pristine condition. 425.00

REMARKABLE LETTER DEALING WITH THE CRITICISM LEVELLED AGAINST KENNEDY FOR HIS ABSENCE FROM THE U. S. SENATE DURING THE VOTE TO CENSURE SENATOR JOSEPH R. MC CARTHY

186. KENNEDY, JOHN F. President. Revealing Autograph Letter Signed "Jack", brightly penned on four separate sheets of plain yellow stationery. No place or date [October, 1954]. To "Dear Langdon" [Langdon P. Marvin, Jr., legislative assistant and consultant to Kennedy; his father was Franklin D. Roosevelt's law partner, and FDR was his Godfather.] Since this testy letter is Kennedy's reaction to a notice that appeared in Drew Pearson's Washington Merry-Go-Round column, we quote in full Pearson's observations:

"MC CARTHY & MASSACHUSETTS
Sen. Jack Kennedy of Massachusetts, will probably go to the hospital during the debate to censure McCarthy. Kennedy has a legitimate excuse -- an old war wound. But he will choose the particular moment of the McCarthy debate to be hospitalized because of his huge McCarthy following in Massachusetts ....Sen. Saltonstall, also from Massachusetts and now up for re-election, would like to go to the hospital if the censure vote comes before November. Saltonstall has stood well with the Boston Irish ever since, as governor, he vetoed the birth control bill. So he's been worried sick about the prospect of voting on McCarthy....Young Kennedy might have a second political purpose for going to the hospital -- skipping any campaigning for Foster Furcolo, the capable state treasurer, who's opposing Saltonstall. John is said to figure a second Democratic senator would diminish his own political stature and perhaps pit popular Salty against him in 1958."

In response to the above article, Kennedy reacted as follows:

"Foster Furcolo had already sent me the Pearson column. It demonstrates my previous point. My guess is that it came either from Furcolo himself who is close to Pearson -- or perhaps from Ed Michaelson.

In any case the facts are wrong. As you know the operation was set in advance of the McCarthy Censure business and 2nd ly it is doubtful if Furcolo could beat Saltonstall in 1954 if I would have to worry about him in '58'.

I will leave it to your judgement -- but it demonstrates that [Jack] Anderson etc. is unfriendly & I am inclined to say to hell with them -- Thanks.

Jack"

Accompanied by the newspaper clipping of Pearson's column. One of the most revealing letters of the future president to appear on the market. Excellent condition. 3500.00

THE DAY WILSON SOUGHT A DECLARATION OF WAR

187. ROOSEVELT, FRANKLIN D. President. Interesting Typed Letter Signed, as Assistant Secretary of the Navy, written on the imprinted letterhead of the Secretary of the Navy. 1 page, 4to. Navy Department, Washington, April 2, 1917. To Alfred B. Williams, Washington, D.C. In response to this older man's volunteering for Reserve Duty, Roosevelt writes: "The age limit for the Reserve is placed at fifty-eight years and up to the present time we have not taken in any volunteers in excess of that age. I have...had your letter placed where it will be within reach if the future should necessitate our taking in men over the present age limit. I want to tell you how much the Department appreciates your offer of services and the fine spirit expressed in your letter. It is the proper spirit and just what the country needs today more than anything else. You may be sure that if the necessity arises you will hear from us...." On the very day this letter was written, President Wilson addressed a Joint Session of Congress, asking for a Declaration of War against Germany. Choice association! 325.00

188. NIXON, PATRICIA. First Lady. Autograph Letter Signed "Pat", penned on stationery imprinted "Mrs. Richard Nixon". 2 full pages, 8vo. [Los Angeles, January 15, 1962]. Original postmarked envelope, addressed by Mrs. Nixon, and bearing her full imprinted name and address on flap verso. To Mrs. Jack Stuart, Washington, D.C. She writes: "It was wonderful to hear Julie's report of her visit with you -- it made me envious! The permanent you gave her is, as always, beautiful. You are still the champion. Our house still is not completed -- the usual excuses which most people encounter in building! At any rate, we do hope you can visit us and inspect it! Louise Johnson wrote about her experience in a strange land. Apparently she is still finding it fascinating....While the rest of the country has been freezing, we have had 80° temperatures and beautiful flowers galore. You better hurry out to this garden spot. (Chamber of Commerce talking!)..." Nice personal letter, and scarce in full holograph. 175.00

189. POLK, JAMES K. President. Attractive partly engraved Document Signed, as President. Tall folio, vellum. Washington, May 26, 1847. Countersigned by WILLIAM L. MARCY, Secretary of War. Embossed white wafer seal of the War Department affixed with red wax. In this striking document dating from the Mexican War, President Polk commissions Josiah P. Chadbourne a Second Lieutenant in the Ninth Regiment of Infantry. Spread-eagle vignette at head, with another choice military vignette of flags and accoutrements at bottom. Excellent condition. Documents signed by Polk as President have become quite scarce. 1250.00

DOCUMENT FRAGMENT SIGNED BY MONROE AND ADAMS

190. MONROE, JAMES. President. Fragment cut from a Four-Language Sea Letter boldly signed as President, above the printed legend "BY THE PRESIDENT". Also signed in full by JOHN QUINCY ADAMS, as Secretary of State. Oblong 8vo. Choice signatures! With matching portraits. 350.00

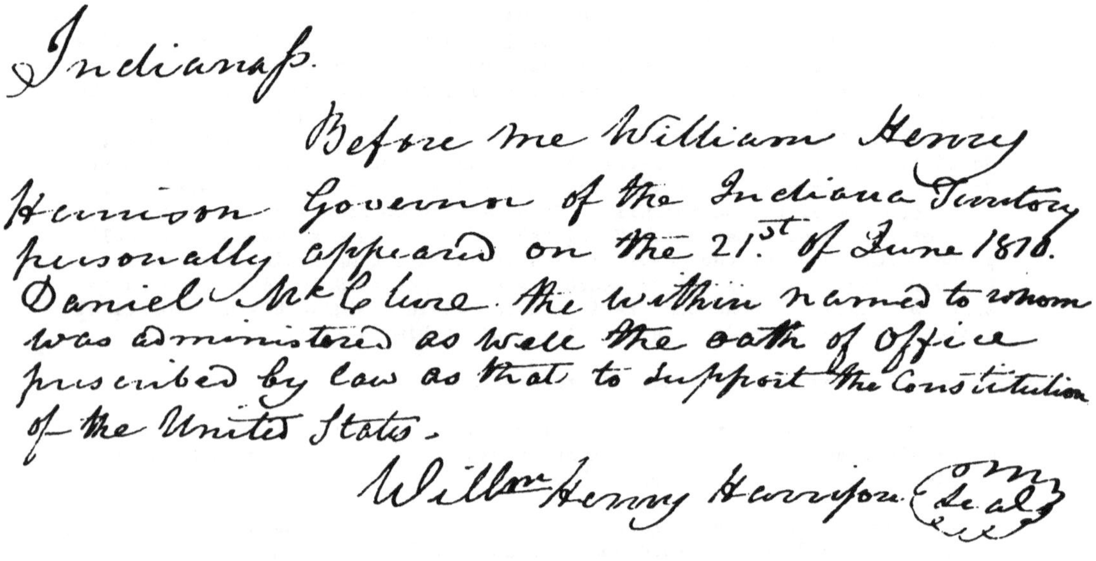
Indianap.
Before me William Henry Harrison Governor of the Indiana Territory personally appeared on the 21st of June 1810. Daniel McClure the within named to whom was administered as well the oath of Office prescribed by law as that to support the Constitution of the United States.
Willm Henry Harrison (Seal)

AS GOVERNOR OF THE INDIANA TERRITORY, HARRISON SIGNS THE APPOINTMENT OF A JUDGE AND THEN PERSONALLY ADMINISTERS HIS OATH ON THE VERSO

191. HARRISON, WILLIAM HENRY. President. Extremely rare partly printed Document Signed, as Governor and Commander in Chief of the Indiana Territory. Small legal folio. Vincennes, June 21, 1810. Countersigned by Jno. Gibson, Secretary. Embossed wafer seal of the Territory affixed with red wax at lower left. Governor Harrison appoints Daniel McClure of Knox County to be a Judge of the Court of Common Pleas. On the verso, in an eight-line Autograph Document Signed (illustrated above), Harrison has personally administered the oath of office to the new Judge. Thus this document is fully signed by Harrison twice, on front and verso. Fine. 1250.00

COLLECTING INFORMATION TO ATTACK THE NEW DEAL

192. HOOVER, HERBERT. President. Important, lengthy Typed Letter Signed, on his imprinted stationery. Very full page, 4to. No place, August 24, 1940. To O. Glenn Saxon, Dept. of Finance and Control, Hartford, Conn. Interesting letter written during the presidential campaign of 1940. Hoover writes: "I have to make some speeches in the campaign and there are certain things that I would like to bring out. One of these is that there has been a steady increase in the tariff since the New Deal came into power due to the imposing of processing and excise taxes on goods of foreign origin -- especially those that have taken place on food imports and which are really tariffs in disguise. In any event, the New Deal has steadily increased the tariffs on many items. I am wondering if there is anybody...who can dig out this sort of stuff. I would want to be able to deliver some statistics on the total intellectual dishonesty of the New Deal and cite these actions as proof. I am in hopes that you are finding this campaign better than the last one. Certainly there is a great deal of response over the country...." Excellent content and condition. 450.00

INSCRIBED COPY OF TRUMAN'S STATE OF THE UNION ADDRESS

193. TRUMAN, HARRY S. President and Vice President. Printed pamphlet, with self-covered printed wrappers, containing Truman's The State of the Union / Address...delivered before a Joint Session of the Two Houses of Congress / January 6, 1947. U.S. Government Printing Office: Washington, 1947. 12 pages, small 4to. Boldly inscribed on the front wrapper: "To Mrs. Winifred D. Biorck / from / Harry S. Truman / 12-10-56". Fine, and very scarce! 350.00

PRESIDENTIAL ARREST WARRANT

194. JOHNSON, ANDREW. President and Vice President. Excellent partly printed Document Signed, as President. 1 page, 4to. Washington, June 20, 1868. President Johnson authorizes the Secretary of State to affix the Seal of the United States to "a Duplicate Warrant for the arrest of Edward C. Mevulton..." Clean, fresh condition. With engraved portrait. 495.00

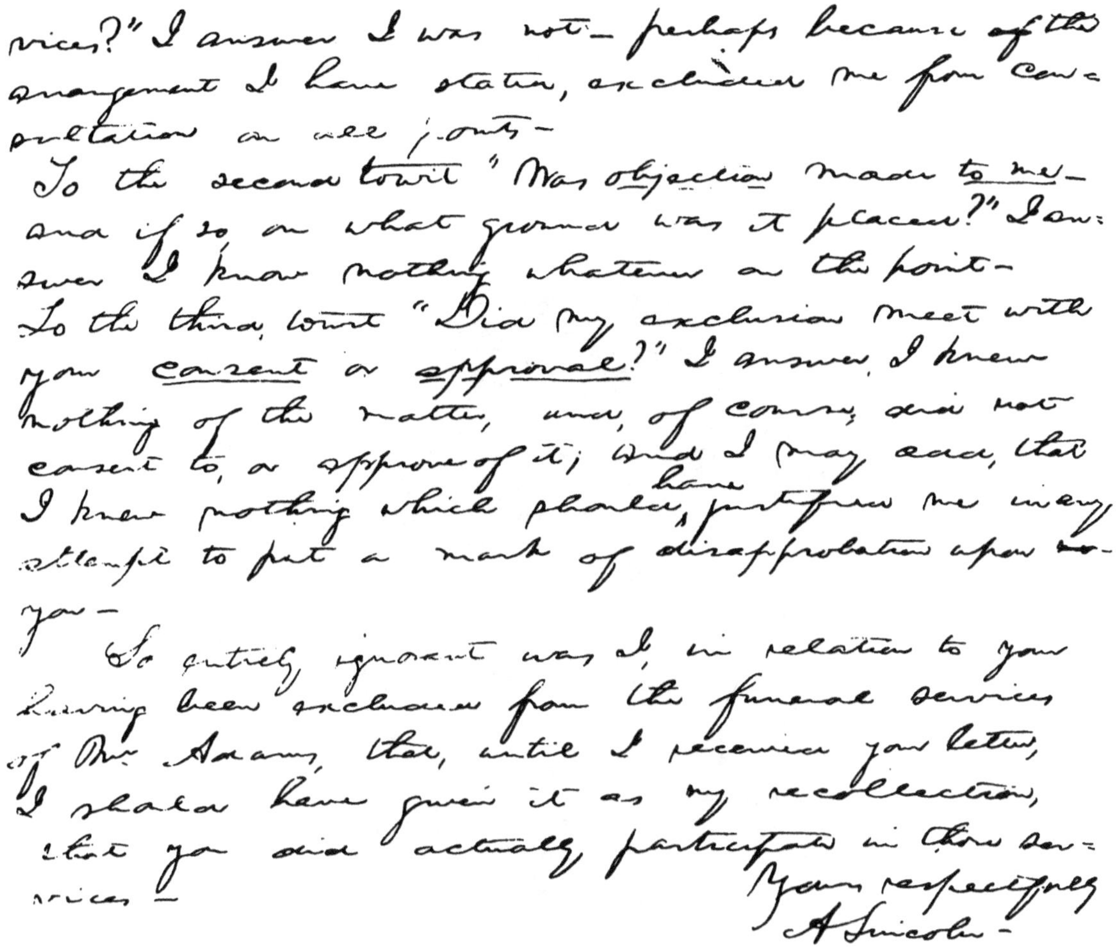
vices?" I answer I was not — perhaps because of the arrangement I have stated, excluded me from consultation on all points —
To the second, to wit "Was objection made to me — and if so on what ground was it placed?" I answer I know nothing whatever on the point —
To the third, to wit "Did my exclusion meet with your consent or approval?" I answer, I knew nothing of the matter, and, of course, did not consent to, or approve of it; and I may add, that I knew nothing which should have justified me in any attempt to put a mark of disapprobation upon you —
So entirely ignorant was I, in relation to your having been excluded from the funeral services of Mr. Adams, that, until I received your letter, I should have given it as my recollection, that you did actually participate in those services —
Your respectfully
A. Lincoln —

CONGRESSMAN LINCOLN DECLARES HIS LACK OF COMPLICITY IN THE EXCLUSION OF THE REVEREND MR. SLICER FROM THE FUNERAL OF JOHN QUINCY ADAMS

195. LINCOLN, ABRAHAM. President. Autograph Letter Signed "A. Lincoln", while serving his only term in the House of Representatives. 2 pages, 4to. Washington, June 1, 1848. To the Rev. Mr. Henry Slicer, Methodist minister and Chaplain of the U.S. Senate. Docketed integral leaf. A long letter from the young Congressman explaining to Slicer that he had no part in the exclusion of the minister from the funeral services of former President John Quincy Adams conducted in the House. Lincoln, a member of the large committee of thirty appointed by the House to oversee the funeral arrangements, writes: "...the committee being much too numerous for convenience, we delegated our authority to a sub-committee, of a smaller number of our own body, of which...I was not a member. Whatever was done...was done by this sub-committee." Lincoln goes on to answer three questions put to him by the minister: "To your first special interrogation, to wit 'Were you consulted in regard to my exclusion from the services?' I answer I was not...To the second, to wit 'Was objection made to me and if so on what ground was it placed?' I answer I know nothing whatever on the point. To the third, to wit 'Did my exclusion meet with your consent or approval?' I answer I knew nothing of the matter, and of course did not consent to it or approve it, and I may add that I knew nothing which should have justified me in any attempt to put a mark of disapprobation on you...." Lincoln concludes by saying: "So entirely ignorant was I, in relation to your having been excluded from the funeral services of Mr. Adams, that until I received your letter I should have given it as my recollection that you did actually participate in those services...." An extremely interesting and early letter, in quite fine condition.

15,000.00

AN OUTSTANDING SIGNED PHOTOGRAPH OF GREAT RARITY!

196. DAVIS, JEFFERSON. President of the Confederate States of America. Magnificent large albumin photograph of the Confederate statesman. Oval image 6 1/2 x 8 1/2 inches, mounted to an overall size of 9 1/2 x 12 inches. A formal half-length image. Signed twice by Davis, once as "Jeffn: Davis" on the lower blank part of the photographic surface, and a second time on the bottom mount: "Very respectfully / and truly yours / Jeffn: Davis". The photograph is a post-war production of a war-time photo by William Davies of the Lee Gallery in Richmond. Davis is known to have directed requests for his likeness to this photographer in the early 1870's. Without question, the finest signed photograph of Davis we have ever seen! Excellent condition. 2500.00

197. JOHNSON, ANDREW. President and Vice President. Scarce partly printed Document Signed, as Governor of Tennessee. 1 page, 4to. Nashville, June 24, 1856. Countersigned by F.N.W. Burton, Secretary of State. Governor Johnson commissions A. R. Reed to serve as Justice of the Peace in Madison County. Printed on light blue paper. With engraved portrait. Fine. 450.00

CHARACTERISTIC APPEAL FOR AN ARMY OFFICER AT DEATH'S DOOR

198. JACKSON, ANDREW. President; General in War of 1812 and Seminole Indian War; hero of the Battle of New Orleans. Superb Autograph Letter Signed. Nearly 2 full pages, 4to. Hermitage, [Tennessee], October 15, 1822. To Colonel George Gibson, Washington. With the integral address-leaf, addressed in Jackson's hand, and bearing a black circular Nashville postmark. A sympathetic and characteristic appeal for an army officer in difficulties.

> "I am just informed, that Capt. Thornton being in arrears with the Government $2000 had made arrangements with the Government to pay the some (sic) by the appropriation of one half of his pay, untill the whole debt was sunk; by the act of Congress of last session he has been deprived of this arrangement, and of course is to support himself on the wind -- The Capt. has been allways (sic) considered a valuable officer, and his misfortunes ought to have been visited with a more lenient hand. He has...by the first arrangement with the Government shown a disposition to be honest & just to his Government. I am aware that the executive government can do nothing for him now, unless he is not receiving the full extent of the limitation of the law for his extra service. If this should be the fact that he does not receive $20 pr month for his extra services, justice to him would require that the executive government should increase it to the limit -- his attention to his extra duty will deserve it -- and humanity under existing circumstances demand it -- and the god of Justice will smile with great complacency upon this act of Justice. I learn he has been at deaths door in Pensacola with the raging fever there. I make this application without any knowledge of his, and trust in God it will be granted -- if his extra pay has not reached the highest limit of the law. If it has, I will only regret, that humanity and justice has been so much triffled with by the last Congress, that the executive government cannot extend relief where in my opinion it is so much merited...
>
> My friend Colonel Gadsden, who is now with me, informs me you were well & doing well when he left the city.
>
> Mrs. J has not forgot you, & begs to be presented to you, and accept assurances of my continued friendship & esteem...."

Handsomely preserved, and a letter of compassion and human interest. 4500.00

CREDENCE AND RECALL OF AMERICAN AMBASSADORS TO PERSIA AND HAWAII

199. CLEVELAND, GROVER. President. Interesting partly printed Document Signed, as President. Full page, 4to. Washington, May 12, 1893. President Cleveland authorizes the Secretary of State to affix the Seal of the United States to "four envelopes as follows: 1. Credence of Alexander McDonald M.R. & C.G. to Persia. 2. Recall of Watson R. Sperry... 3. Credence of James H. Blount E.E. & M.P. to Hawaii. 4. Recall of John L. Stevens [from Hawaii]..." Attractive, clean and fresh. With portrait. The Hawaiian reference is particularly nice. 475.00

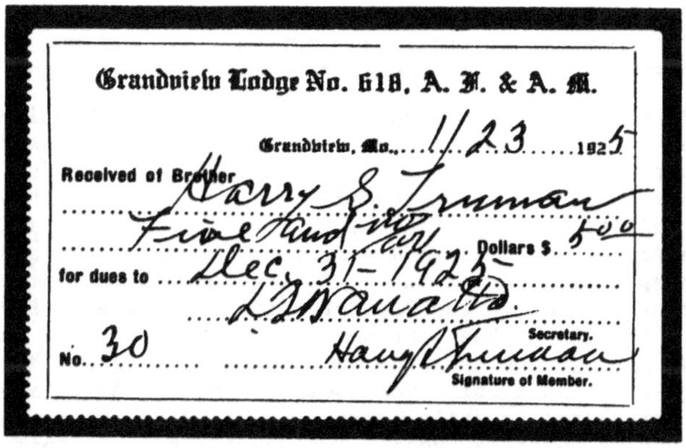

Grandview Lodge No. 618, A. F. & A. M.

Grandview, Mo., 1/23 1925

Received of Brother Harry S. Truman

Five and no/100 Dollars $ 5.00

for dues to Dec. 31-1925

Secretary.

No. 30 Harry S Truman

Signature of Member.

200. TRUMAN, HARRY S. President and Vice President. Unusual, early, partly printed Document Signed. 1 page, 24mo. Grandview, Missouri, January 23, 1925. Receipt for five dollars issued to Truman for his membership dues in the Grandview Lodge No. 618, A.F. & A.M. [Masons]. Accomplished and also signed by the Lodge secretary, and blindstamped with the Lodge's Seal. While a receipt, this document also served as Truman's membership card. Rare item! 325.00

HOOVER'S ADDRESS TO THE 1952 REPUBLICAN NATIONAL CONVENTION

201. HOOVER, HERBERT. President. Printed pamphlet containing his <u>Address...at the Republican National Convention / Chicago / July 8, 1952</u>. Self-covered printed wrappers. 14 pages, tall narrow 8vo. Boldly signed in bright blue ink by Hoover on the front wrapper beneath the title. Pristine condition. 150.00

GENERAL JOHN E. WOOL'S APPOINTMENT TO THE PEACE CONVENTION

202. TYLER, JOHN. President and Vice President of the United States; Virginia statesman and governor. Partly printed (blue ink) Document Signed "John Tyler", as President of the Peace Convention. 1 page, 8vo. Conference Convention, Washington, February 4, 1861. Docketed integral leaf. President Tyler certifies that "Mr. John E. Wool / Delegate from New York / ... [is] a member of the Convention." In a letter published in the Richmond Enquirer, Jan. 17, 1861, Tyler recommended a convention of border states for the purpose of devising some method of adjusting the difficulties brought on by the secession of South Carolina. In acting upon

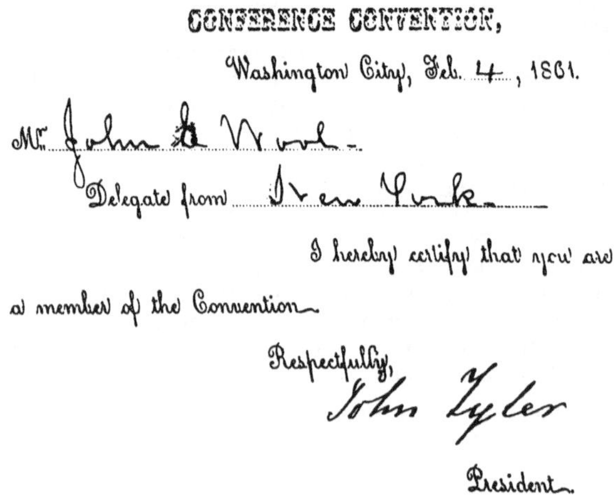
CONFERENCE CONVENTION,
Washington City, Feb. 4, 1861.
Mr. John E. Wool
Delegate from New York
I hereby certify that you are
a member of the Convention
Respectfully,
John Tyler
President

Tyler's suggestion, the Virginia legislature enlarged it into a proposal of a peace convention to be composed of delegates from all the states. The Peace Convention, consisting of delegates from thirteen northern and seven border states, met at Washington on February 4, 1861, and chose Tyler as its president. Several resolutions were adopted and reported to Congress, where they were rejected in the Senate. General Wool, here appointed a delegate from New York, had a distinguished military career and is perhaps best remembered for his service in the Mexican War. Because of his advanced age he saw limited service in the Civil War. Fine condition, and a romantic piece of history, showing the aged ex-President's unsuccessful attempt to avert Civil War. 750.00

WILLIAM PINKNEY'S COMMISSION, SIGNED BY JEFFERSON AND MADISON, TO SERVE AS MINISTER PLENIPOTENTIARY OF THE UNITED STATES TO GREAT BRITAIN

203. JEFFERSON, THOMAS. President. Manuscript Document Signed, as President. 1 page, small square folio. Countersigned by JAMES MADISON, Secretary of State. Embossed (spread-eagle) perforated wafer seal at lower left. Washington, May 12, 1806. Text reads: "Reposing special Trust and Confidence in your Integrity, Prudence and Ability, I do appoint you the said William Pinkney, Minister Plenipotentiary of the United States of America at the Court of His Britanic Majesty, authorizing you hereby to do and perform all such matter and things as to the said place or Office doth appertain, or as may be duly given you in charge hereafter, and the said Office to Hold and exercise during the Pleasure of the President of the United States for the time being, and until the end of the next Session of the Senate of the United States, and no longer...." Pinkney, a prominent Maryland lawyer and legislator, had been appointed by George Washington in 1796 to serve as a Joint Commissioner in England to adjust American claims for maritime losses, as stipulated in Jay's Treaty (1794). He remained in England on that assignment until 1804, returning home that year. Two years later, by this document, Jefferson appointed Pinkney ambassador to Great Britain where he served until 1811 (seeking his own recall just prior to the outbreak of the War of 1812 which he had sought to avoid through diplomacy). He negotiated a treaty with England in 1807, but Jefferson was so dissatisfied with its provisions that he refused to submit it to the U.S. Senate for advice and consent. Much has been written of Pinkney's diplomacy in the history of America's foreign relations. Our commission is in very good condition with several tiny holes along the horizontal fold not affecting any text (blank area), and some mounting traces on the verso. Madison's signature is strong, with Jefferson's very slightly light but completely legible. One of the most important diplomatic appointments ever to pass through our hands. 3,500.00

204. PIERCE, FRANKLIN. President. Attractive full signature. With engraved portrait. 125.00

205. GRANT, ULYSSES S. President; Union General; accepted Lee's surrender. Handsome mounted proof engraving of Grant's likeness. Legal folio. No place or date. Ca. 1867. Legal folio (including paper mount). Boldly signed in ink "U. S. Grant / Lt. Gen." Also signed in pencil by the artist (engraver), William E. Marshall. Marked "1st Proof" in lower margin. Striking portrait of General Grant, in uniform, before his election to the presidency. Choice! 950.00

206. FORD, GERALD R. President and Vice President (not elected to either office). Typed Letter Signed "Gerald R. Ford", on his gilt-embossed engraved stationery. 1 page, 4to. [Rancho Mirage, California] July 17, 1978. To James E. Sherburne. Original envelope bearing the former President's franking signature in facsimile. Gracious letter to a collector, in part: "...Your hobby sounds like an extremely interesting one, and your collection one which should be treasured. It is with great pleasure that I make my personal contribution to your project, and I am honored to be included among so many impressive individuals...." Pristine condition, and a fine post-presidential specimen. 150.00

207. EISENHOWER, DWIGHT D. President and General in World War II; commanded the Allied Invasion of Europe, and afterwards headed NATO. Typed Letter Signed "Ike E", as President of Columbia University, on the blue-imprinted stationery of that office. 1 page, 8vo. New York, September 14, 1948. To Robert Woodruff, president of the Coca-Cola Company. In this friendly "Dear Bob" letter, Eisenhower writes: "Though I realize you may not be in New York next month, I am sending you this invitation in the hope that you might be here. Please disregard the September 15th deadline which is mentioned. An affirmative reply from you will be most welcome at any time...." Scarce with this form of intimate signature. Fine condition. 195.00

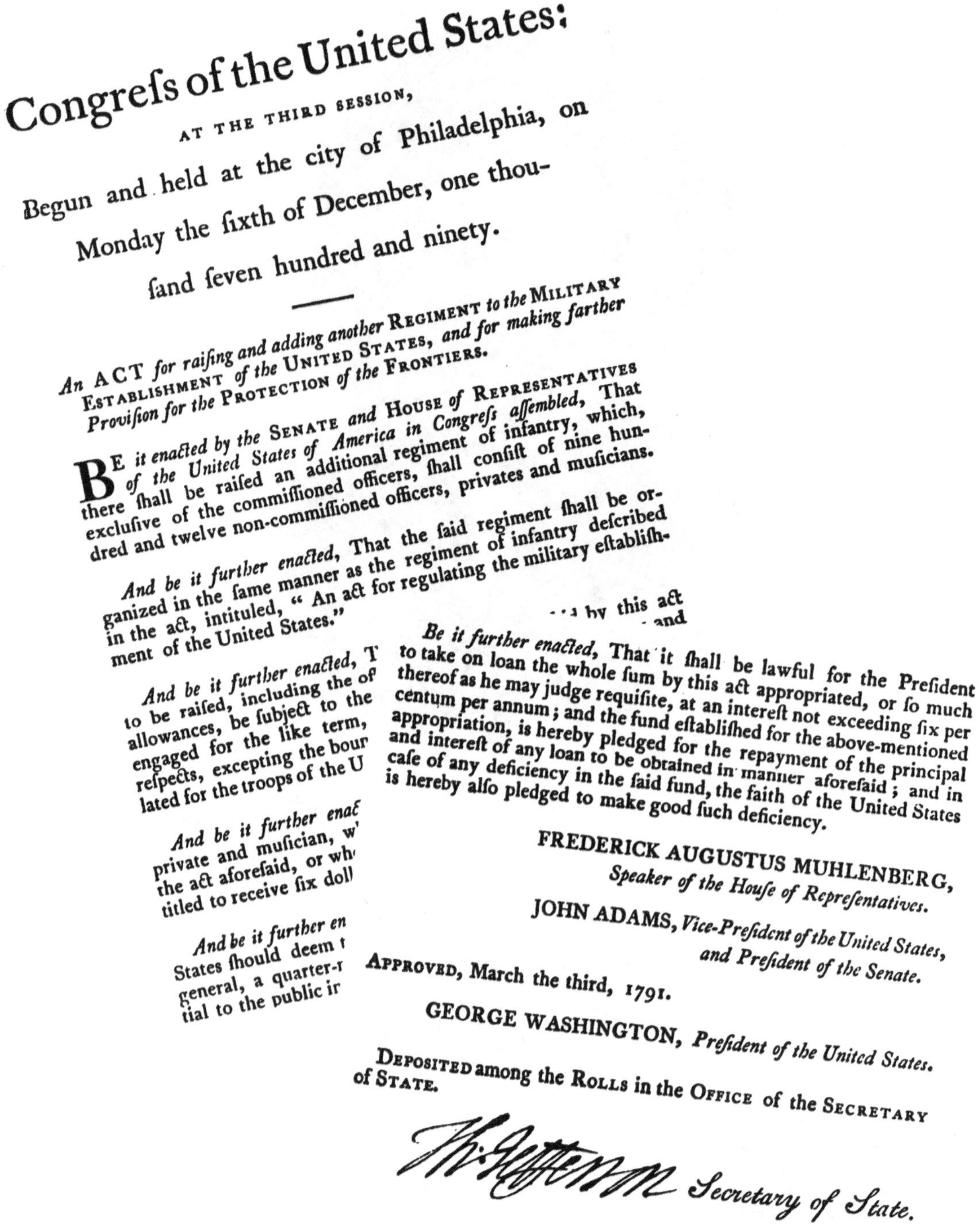
Congrefs of the United States:

AT THE THIRD SESSION,

Begun and held at the city of Philadelphia, on Monday the fixth of December, one thoufand feven hundred and ninety.

An ACT for raifing and adding another REGIMENT to the MILITARY ESTABLISHMENT of the UNITED STATES, and for making farther Provifion for the PROTECTION of the FRONTIERS.

BE it enacted by the SENATE and HOUSE of REPRESENTATIVES of the United States of America in Congrefs affembled, That there fhall be raifed an additional regiment of infantry, which, exclufive of the commiffioned officers, fhall confift of nine hundred and twelve non-commiffioned officers, privates and muficians.

And be it further enacted, That the faid regiment fhall be organized in the fame manner as the regiment of infantry defcribed in the act, intituled, " An act for regulating the military eftablifhment of the United States."

... by this act ... and

And be it further enacted, T
to be raifed, including the of
allowances, be fubject to the
engaged for the like term,
refpects, excepting the boun
lated for the troops of the U

And be it further enac
private and mufician, w
the act aforefaid, or wh
titled to receive fix doll

And be it further en
States fhould deem t
general, a quarter-r
tial to the public ir

Be it further enacted, That it fhall be lawful for the Prefident to take on loan the whole fum by this act appropriated, or fo much thereof as he may judge requifite, at an intereft not exceeding fix per centum per annum; and the fund eftablifhed for the above-mentioned appropriation, is hereby pledged for the repayment of the principal and intereft of any loan to be obtained in manner aforefaid; and in cafe of any deficiency in the faid fund, the faith of the United States is hereby alfo pledged to make good fuch deficiency.

FREDERICK AUGUSTUS MUHLENBERG,
Speaker of the Houfe of Reprefentatives.

JOHN ADAMS, *Vice-Prefident of the United States, and Prefident of the Senate.*

APPROVED, March the third, 1791.

GEORGE WASHINGTON, *Prefident of the United States.*

DEPOSITED among the ROLLS in the OFFICE of the SECRETARY of STATE.

Th: Jefferson Secretary of State.

"THE PROTECTION OF THE FRONTIERS"

208. JEFFERSON, THOMAS. President and Vice President. Remarkable printed Act of the First Congress "for raising and adding another REGIMENT to the MILITARY ESTABLISHMENT of the UNITED STATES, and for making farther Provision for the PROTECTION of the FRONTIERS." Signed in ink by Jefferson, as Secretary of State, at the conclusion of the printed text. Four pages, tall legal folio. Philadelphia, March 3, 1791. Printed by Francis Childs and John Swaine: Philadelphia, 1791. Evans 23855. Signed in type by Frederick A. Muhlenberg, Speaker of the House; John Adams, Vice President and President of the Senate; and George Washington, President. By this act a new regiment is created, with its structure and remuneration fully prescribed, and in case of an emergency the President is allowed to raise an additional regiment of two thousand troops. Payment for these troops was to come from taxes upon imported and domestic distilled spirits. It was this tax on distilled spirits which precipitated the Whiskey Rebellion in 1794. This copy once belonged to SAMUEL HUNTINGTON, the Connecticut Signer and Governor, and bears a four-line docket in his hand on the fourth page. Near mint condition, and a fascinating conversation piece!! 5750.00

"ONCE OUT IN THE STREET, HE [FRANKLIN PIERCE] IS CONSTANTLY BESIEGED"

209. PIERCE, JANE M. First Lady. Autograph Letter Signed "J. M. Pierce". 3 1/2 pages, 4to. Concord, N.H., July 25, 1852. To her sister, Mrs. Mary Aiken. Interesting letter written just one month after her husband had unexpectedly received the Presidential Nomination of the Democratic National Convention meeting in Baltimore. Speaking of her only surviving child, Benjamin, who was tragically killed at the railroad station while accompanying his parents to Washington the following year for Pierce's inauguration, she writes: "...The poor boy is not at his brightest just now, and does not go to school..." And in reference to her husband, now the presidential candidate, she writes: "I am hoping our travellers are [having] a pleasant journey and will have the comfort of less dusty roads of the rain of today. I shall expect them back on Wednesday morning -- for Mr. P. said he could not be absent longer. They went in great haste at last -- for once out in the street, he is constantly besieged -- and there is no end to the variety of demands upon his time and attention...." She hopes to be able to spend some time that summer at Rye Beach with her husband, and then comments: "...but how short our summer is! one does half what they intend to, it is gone -- as for the future, I cannot bear to look forward and have no ability to do more than take care of the present, without making preparation or calculation for any thing more...." After much family talk she tells of painted portraits and photographs being made of her husband. "...The same painter [Harding] has taken a likeness of Mr. Pierce -- pretty good -- by far the best which has ever been taken before, but which might be improved. I hope this will be the last which Mr. P will be troubled with at present.I do not want to see another of the wretched daguerrotypes and engravings which are about in such abundance...." And in closing, she states that her husband plans to be in Brunswick at their great celebration. Pierce was a graduate of Bowdoin College in Brunswick, Maine, and Mrs. Pierce's father had served as president of the college. Highly interesting content, showing the mood of the candidate's wife during the early stages of the presidential campaign. Also, letters of Mrs. Pierce signed with her full signature are very scarce. Excellent condition. 1250.00

210. ROOSEVELT, THEODORE. President and Vice President. Printed Program for the "Ceremony of the Unveiling of the Lincoln Monument, Van Horn Bequest, Newark, New Jersey, May 30th 1911." 8vo. Boldly signed in bright blue ink by Roosevelt on the front cover. Contains a sepia portrait of the seated image of Lincoln by Gutzon Borglum. Roosevelt delivered the Speech accepting the statue, and presenting it to the City of Newark. Text pages include the Order of Ceremony and a brief history of the statue. Tied with white silk ribbon. Excellent! 250.00

211. EISENHOWER, DWIGHT D. President and General. Typed Letter Signed, with initials "D. E.", on his gilt-imprinted stationery. Very full page, 4to. Gettysburg, Pa., May 11, 1962. To Hon. Robert Dechert, Philadelphia. Original mailing envelope bearing Eisenhower's metered frank. In part: "...As to your suggestion about a luncheon of the World Affairs Council of Philadelphia, I really think you must count me out -- certainly as of this year. I am not sure when Mrs. Eisenhower and I shall leave for California, but it will not be too long after the end of October, and I know you cannot and do not want to schedule another luncheon, even if I could find the time, so soon after the one at which Allen Dulles is to appear. We hope to spend five or six months in Southern California...." Excellent condition. 250.00

212. HARRISON, BENJAMIN. President. Typed Letter Signed, on his imprinted stationery. ½ page, 4to. Indianapolis, Indiana, December 26, 1900. To David A. Munro, New York City. Writing to the magazine editor, the former president states: "...I beg to say that I can probably get something ready for your February number, if it will not be needed too soon. About what time must you have the manuscript?..." Fine example. 225.00

213. TAFT, WILLIAM H. President; Chief Justice, U.S. Supreme Court. Typed Letter Signed, on his imprinted stationery. 1 page, 4to. New Haven, Conn., November 22, 1913. To Professor F. W. Hooper, The Brooklyn Institute of Arts and Sciences, Brooklyn, N.Y. Taft has received his correspondent's letter "...advising me that at a meeting of the Board of Trustees...I was, on the recommendation of the council unanimously elected an honorary member of the Institute. I beg to express to you, and to the Board, through you, my very sincere thanks for this honor ...." Fine condition, written the year Taft left the presidency. 150.00

214. HARDING, WARREN G. President. Typewritten Statement Signed "W. G. Harding", on imprinted U.S. Senate letterhead. 2/3 page, 4to. [Washington], September 4, 1917. Headed "To Whom it May Concern". Senator Harding states that he has "...known Dr. D. F. Spicer for a number of years and...have only known favorable things concerning him. He is a man of thorough education, manifest ability and unquestionable honesty and integrity, and possesses a most agreeable personal character. I cannot speak from personal knowledge of his professional attainments, but I do know him to be very highly regarded and I think he deserves the full confidence of those who have occasion to turn to him in a professional capacity...." Mounting traces from verso show through slightly at top corners, else fine. 250.00

SIGNATURES OF VICE PRESIDENT NIXON AND THE EISENHOWER CABINET

215. [EISENHOWER, DWIGHT D.] Handsome quarto photograph depicting a crystal glass globe of the world, mounted on a wooden base, with a plaque inscribed "With the Affectionate Regards of His Cabinet", and dated on the etched globe "December 1959". This was apparently a Xmas gift from the Cabinet to President Eisenhower. Signed on the lower otherwise blank foreground by RICHARD NIXON, Vice President, and by the ten members of Ike's Cabinet: JAMES P. MITCHELL, FREDERICK A. MUELLER, CHRISTIAN A. HERTER, THOMAS SLATER, ARTHUR C. FLEMMING, FRED A. SEATON, WILLIAM P. ROGERS, ROBERT B. ANDERSON, ARTHUR E. SUMMERFIELD and EZRA TAFT BENSON. From the celebrated Greenway Collection. Highly unusual photograph, probably unique with this assemblage of signatures, and in very fine condition. 450.00

216. TAFT, WILLIAM H. President; Chief Justice, U.S. Supreme Court. Fine signature boldly penned on a plain visiting card. Note on verso indicates that Taft probably signed this card while serving as Secretary of War in 1907. Nice specimen! 75.00

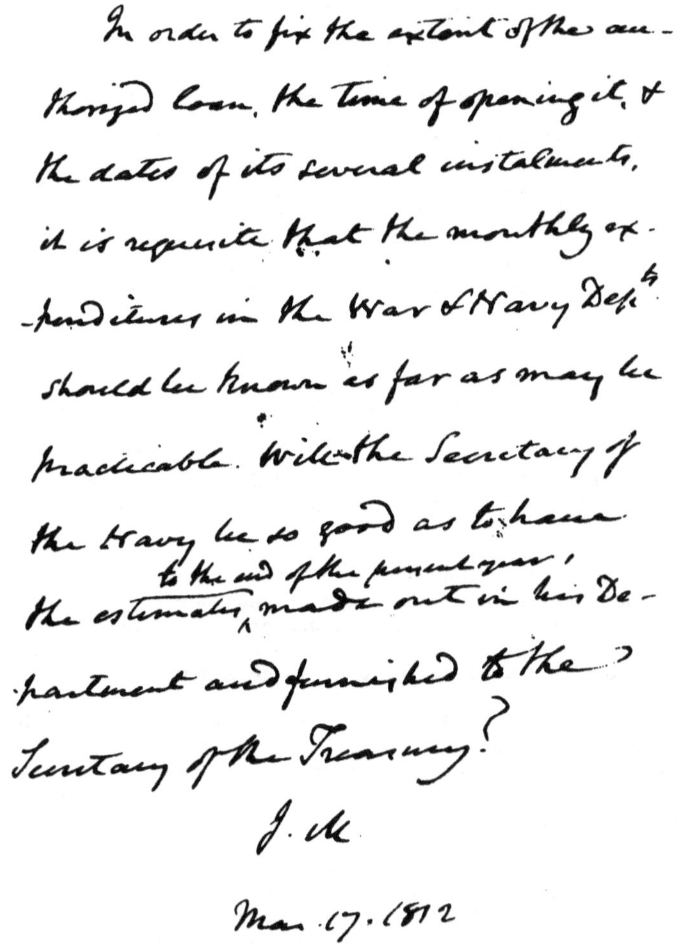
In order to fix the extent of the au-
thorized loan, the time of opening it, &
the dates of its several instalments,
it is requisite that the monthly ex-
-penditures in the War & Navy Depts
should be known as far as may be
practicable. Will the Secretary of
the Navy be so good as to have
the estimates, to the end of the present year, made out in his De-
-partment and furnished to the
Secretary of the Treasury?
J. M.

Mar. 17. 1812

217. MADISON, JAMES. President; Secretary of State; Signer of U.S. Constitution. Autograph Message Signed, with initials "J. M.", as President. Full page, 8vo. [Washington] March 17, 1812. To the Secretary of the Navy [Paul Hamilton]. Integral address-leaf in Madison's hand. He writes "In order to fix the extent of the authorized loan, the time of opening it, & the dates of its several instalments, it is requisite that the monthly expenditures in the War & Navy Depts. should be known as far as may be practicable. Will the Secretary of the Navy be so good as to have the estimates to the end of the present year, made out in his Department and furnished to the Secretary of the Treasury?..." Docketed on overleaf. Excellent condition. 750.00

AN APPEAL ON BEHALF OF THE IMPOVERISHED CHILDREN OF PORTO RICO

218. ROOSEVELT, FRANKLIN D. President. Typed Letter Signed, as Governor of New York, on his personally imprinted letterhead. Very full page, 4to. Albany, November 6, 1930. To Mrs. Benjamin Arnold, Albany, N.Y. Roosevelt states that he has accepted the State Chairmanship in New York of the Committee "which is making an appeal on behalf of the impoverished children of Porto Rico", and hopes that his correspondent will accept a place on the Committee. "Governor Theodore Roosevelt of Porto Rico is the Honorary Chairman." He continues: "As a result of the survey made...at the request of President Hoover, it was revealed that over 150,000 American school children are seriously undernourished -- some slowly starving....The Porto Rico hurricane which destroyed crops, roads and homes, left all but destitute more children in peril of death from malnutrition and the scourge of tuberculosis than anywhere under the American flag. The fact that black coffee without sugar or milk is the only breakfast for tens of thousands of children in Porto Rico today tells its own story....I am sure that we all want to help in this good work...." An interesting letter with a scarce reference to President Hoover, whom FDR resoundly defeated at the polls two years later. Fine. 450.00

219. EISENHOWER, DWIGHT D. President; General in World War II; planned the Allied invasion of Europe. Typed Letter Signed, with initials "D.E.", on his gilt-imprinted "DDE" stationery. One page, 4to. Palm Desert, California, February 3, 1965. To Hon. Robert Cutler, Boston, Mass., who had served in the Eisenhower Administration as a Security Council aide. Eisenhower writes: "Mamie and I were happy to receive your recent note and I know that you must feel great relief now that your book is completed. I will...be most interested in seeing it once it is in print. We both hope that you will have a restful vacation and that your blood pressure will get back to a normal level. Take good care of yourself...." Fine. 150.00

THE FUTURE PRESIDENT SUPERVISES DOLLY MADISON'S FINANCIAL AFFAIRS

220. BUCHANAN, JAMES. President. Magnificent Autograph Letter Signed. 2 very full pages, quarto. Wheatland, near Lancaster, June 27, 1849. To the Hon. John Y. Mason, of Virginia, who had served in President Polk's cabinet with Buchanan. Docketed integral leaf. Buchanan writes:

> "I returned from Washington last night, having done the best I could for Mrs. Madison. I found it difficult to persuade her that she ought not to have the whole premium placed in her hands at once, in which event it would have been of little or no service to her. According to the present arrangement her income will be increased from $1200 to 1800 per annum for a longer period than she may probably survive. I hope you will approve what we have done. The old lady has greatly changed since I saw her last. She is now very feeble.
>
> It is my purpose, God willing, to pass the next winter at New Orleans: and I may in going there avail myself of your kind invitation to visit Richmond. I hope, however, before that time to enjoy the pleasure of seeing you here. As President of the James River Company, you will probably have occasion to visit the North....
>
> It would do your heart good to see [Robert J.] Walker. He is as plump as a partridge & as lively as a lark. He has already got 21 cases in the Supreme Court.
>
> Should a judicious selection be made of a Candidate for Canal Commissioner at Pittsburg...we shall redeem this State in handsome style in October; but the day has passed in Pennsylvania when a Democratic nomination is equivalent to an election. The popular will must now be consulted in the selection of Candidates: and this being done, we have as large a Democratic majority as ever.
>
> I could invest about $25,000 of my own within a fortnight or three weeks and should have been glad to do it permanently in Virginia Bonds....Mr. Corcoran told me that I could procure Chesapeake & Ohio Bonds guaranteed by the State of Virginia at 97 or 98; but I would rather give par for the Bonds of the State, though I have no doubt both are equally secure...."

The venerable former First Lady, Dolly Madison, died later the same year. Living in near poverty, several years earlier she sold to the United States Government all her late husband's papers, and was able to live comfortably from the annuity this sale produced. This choice letter of Buchanan is in excellent condition, and besides the Dolly Madison business, has other political and financial news of interest. 2500.00

SUPERB SIGNED PRESIDENTIAL PHOTOGRAPH

221. ROOSEVELT, THEODORE. President and Vice President. Handsome small studio photograph by Clinedinst, of Washington, showing a 3/4-length image of Roosevelt seated at his desk in the White House, his left hand resting on some papers. Signed as President on the dark-colored bottom mount: "with regards of / Theodore Roosevelt / Feb. 1st 1904". While the mount color is a dark gray, Roosevelt has used even darker ink, and the contrast is satisfactory. The copyright date on the photograph is 1902. Size is quarto. Handsome display piece! 575.00

SETTING UP A COMMISSION TO HELP IN EUROPE

222. TAFT, WILLIAM H. President; Chief Justice, U.S. Supreme Court. Important Typed Letter Signed, on his imprinted letterhead. 1 page, 4to. New Haven, February 8, 1917. To Eli Whitney, New Haven,Conn., inviting him to attend "an important conference-luncheon...at the Hotel Taft to consider a large constructive program arising out of the present war." Taft continues: "Mr. John R. Mott, together with Mr. Brockman and Mr. Eddy, who have been engaged in conducting the great work in the prison camps of Europe and with the armies of the countries now at war, will meet with us to consider a large and far-reaching program to help the nations suffering from the war and to devise, if possible, some adequate means through the Y.M.C.A. ... of fulfilling our Christian obligation to the nations which are in such need at this critical time...." Interesting letter written just prior to the United States active involvement as a combatant. John R. Mott, herein mentioned, was the recipient of the Nobel Peace Prize. Very nice letter! 500.00

223. MC KINLEY, WILLIAM. President; assassinated. Partly printed Signed Counter Check, drawn on the Sergeant-at-Arms of the U.S. House of Representatives. Oblong 12mo. Washington, March 13, 1882. Accomplished by Mc Kinley and made payable to himself. Minor wear, else fine. Very clear, early signature. Scarce in this format. 275.00

224. TAYLOR, ZACHARY. President; General on the American frontier and in the Mexican War. Manuscript Letter Signed "Z. Taylor, Col. / 1st Regt. U.S. Infy. / Comdg." Full page, 4to. Head Quarters, Fort Crawford, April 16, 1835. To General R. Jones, Adjutant General U.S. Army, Washington. As commanding officer of this important frontier post in the Michigan Territory (now in the state of Wisconsin), Taylor transmits various returns and reports, and explains that since no men were recruited or enlisted in October and November 1834, no reports were made out. Fine specimen. With portrait. 850.00

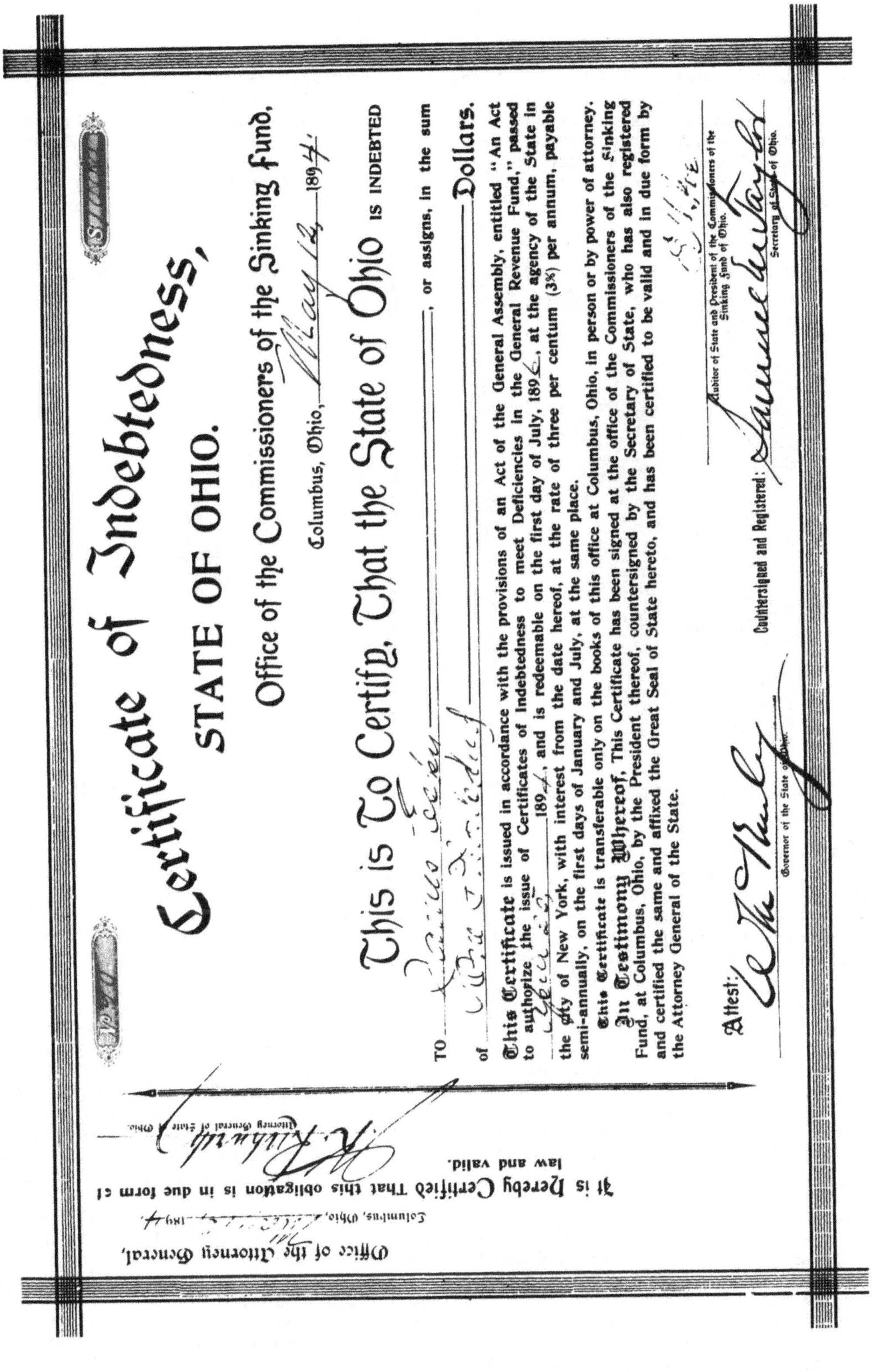

Certificate of Indebtedness,

STATE OF OHIO.

Office of the Commissioners of the Sinking Fund,

Columbus, Ohio, May 12 1894.

This is To Certify, That the State of Ohio IS INDEBTED

TO ______, or assigns, in the sum

of ______ Dollars.

This Certificate is issued in accordance with the provisions of an Act of the General Assembly, entitled "An Act to authorize the issue of Certificates of Indebtedness to meet Deficiencies in the General Revenue Fund," passed ______ 1894, and is redeemable on the first day of July, 1896, at the agency of the State in the city of New York, with interest from the date hereof, at the rate of three per centum (3%) per annum, payable semi-annually, on the first days of January and July, at the same place.

This Certificate is transferable only on the books of this office at Columbus, Ohio, in person or by power of attorney.

In Testimony Whereof, This Certificate has been signed at the office of the Commissioners of the Sinking Fund, at Columbus, Ohio, by the President thereof, countersigned by the Secretary of State, who has also registered and certified the same and affixed the Great Seal of State hereto, and has been certified to be valid and in due form by the Attorney General of the State.

Attest: ______ Governor of the State of Ohio.

Countersigned and Registered: ______ Secretary of State of Ohio.

______ Auditor of State and President of the Commissioners of the Sinking Fund of Ohio.

Office of the Attorney General,

Columbus, Ohio, ______ 1894.

It is Hereby Certified That this obligation is in due form of law and valid.

______ Attorney General of State of Ohio.

SCARCE OHIO CERTIFICATE OF INDEBTEDNESS

225. MC KINLEY, WILLIAM. President (assassinated); Governor of Ohio; Congressman. Partly printed (red and blue) Document Signed, as Governor of Ohio. 1 page, oblong legal folio. Columbus, May 12, 1894. Also signed by E. H. Poe, State Auditor; Samuel M. Taylor, Secretary of State; and J. K. Richards, Attorney General. Interest-bearing "Certificate of Indebtedness" [bond] issued to James Espy for One Thousand Dollars. Payable in 1896 at 3% interest. Cut cancelled (nothing missing, and not affecting Mc Kinley's fine signature). Unusually attractive specimen in much above average condition. Desirable financial item. 1250.00

ENGROSSED RESOLUTION OF THE U. S. SENATE

226. TRUMAN, HARRY S President and Vice President. Exceedingly rare partly printed Document Signed, as Vice President of the United States. Legal folio. [Washington] February 1, 1945. Also signed by LESLIE L. BIFFLE, Acting Secretary of the U. S. Senate. Engrossed "Resolution of the Republican Conference in the United States Senate expressing deep appreciation of the Distinguished Service and the great sense of loss at the passing of Edwin A. Halsey, Secretary of the Senate." Heavy gilt-ruled borders. Gilt-embossed wafer seal of the U.S. Senate with green silk ribbon. Truman's autograph as Vice President is very scarce as he served for only three months in that capacity. A strikingly handsome and colorful document. 575.00

227. FILLMORE, MILLARD. President and Vice President. Magnificent albumin carte de visit photograph by J. T. Upson & Co., Buffalo, N.Y., depicting the full-length image of the former President. Boldly signed "M. Fillmore" on the lower white mount. On the verso Fillmore has penned: "For Mrs. Lampson / [revenue stamp] / Millard Fillmore / Jany. 25, 1866." Pristine condition, and without question the finest signed photograph of Fillmore we have seen. Extremely rare, and very, very choice!! 3750.00

228. VAN BUREN, MARTIN. President and Vice President. Autograph Letter Signed, as Vice President. 3 full pages, 4to, with a lengthy postscript filling the fourth page. New York, November 7, 1833. To William L. Marcy, Governor of New York. Headed Private. In part: "I regret from the bottom of my heart the incident to which you refer. It comes upon me by surprise & excites in me the same feelings that it has in you. I have not had an opportunity to ascertain... that the idea that it has rec'd countenance in the quarter to which you allude is principally, if not wholly, founded in mistake. I shall however know. If the association is made however wrong I do not now see how it can be remedied. A charge would render the circumstances not be expected and would cost more than the thing is worth. If it be so you and Mr. K____ must make a strong appeal to the Doctor's sense of what is due to his standing and high character and prevent him from falling into the common error of disappointed men. I entertain the sincerest respect and warmest regard for him and his family and nothing would mortify me more than to hear of his making a noise upon the subject. He is too valuable a man to sink to that. The injustice he has rec'd followed up by a forbearing and dignified course...would do him a great deal more good than the place, especially in his independent circumstances....How little is the art of making advantage out of our disappointments understood. Really, these continued vexations would, one would suppose, make us all sick of politics, and yet when the Theatre upon which we act is considered we ought to expect these almost constant annoyances....This time I trust Mr. K____ is satisfied with the Message without the aid of his ingenious constructions. It hits his nail upon the head. You see what violence is preparing for us at W[ashington]. So be it...." With another interesting political paragraph about a temperance advocate whom Van Buren hopes will not bolt the party. Very fine. 950.00

229. MADISON, JAMES. President. Choice full franking signature boldly penned in jet-black ink on the address-panel of a Department of State address-leaf. Addressed in a secretarial hand to Charles Simms, Alexandria, Virginia. Clear circular "WASH·CITY / FREE" postmark. Docketed as 1801. Accompanied by a handsome steel-engraved portrait. Clean and fresh! 325.00

230. GRANT, ULYSSES S. President; Union General; accepted Lee's surrender. Choice Autograph Letter Signed, as Lieutenant General, on imprinted U.S. Army stationery. 2 full pages, 4to. City Point, Virginia, November 10, 1864. To Hon. E. M. Stanton, Secretary of War. Grant writes: "I would respectfully recommend the promotion of Brig. Gen. R. Ingalls, now Brigadier General of Volunteers, to the same grade, by brevet, in the regular army, to take rank as such from the 16th day of June 1864, the date of his assuming the duties of Chief Quartermaster of the Combined Armies operating against Richmond. This is also the date of the crossing of the James River after the Campaign from the Rapidaun, by the Army of the Potomac.... For the skillful manner in which Gen. Ingalls has conducted the affairs of his Department he deserves this recognition of his services. He was the first officer of his Dept., I believe, who proved capable of organizing and running all the machinery in it for the Army of the Potomac. There has been no other Army in the United States where the duties of Quartermaster have been nearly as well performed. The services of General Ingalls are too well understood at Washington for me to add more than my testimony that since I have been directly with the Armies where he has acted as Chief Quartermaster his services have been all that could be asked, and such as but few could perform...." Excellent war-dated letter! 2000.00

231. BUCHANAN, JAMES. President. Fine signature, as Sec. of State. With portrait. 125.00

232. JOHNSON, ANDREW. President and Vice President. Partly printed Document Signed, as President. 1 page, 4to. Washington, December 28, 1866. Authorizes the Secretary of State to affix the Seal of the United States to "a Warrant for the unconditional pardon of Stephen Smith." Very light offset paper stain in upper left marginal corner, else quite fine. With a handsome engraved portrait. 400.00

233. TYLER, JOHN. President and Vice President. Huge signature "J. Tyler", as President, cut from an official document. Also signed by A.P. Upshur, Secretary of State. With portrait. 150.00

234. COOLIDGE, CALVIN. President and Vice President. Printed Proclamation Signed, as Governor of Massachusetts. Broadside, Executive Chamber, Boston, November 13, 1919. Coolidge sets aside Thursday, November 27, 1919, as A DAY OF THANKSGIVING AND PRAISE. Also signed by Alben F. Langtry, Secretary of the Commonwealth. Margins slightly reduced, otherwise fine. 250.00

235. ROOSEVELT, ELEANOR. First Lady. Unusual Autograph Letter Signed, in the third person, penned on "Executive Mansion, Albany" stationery. Full page, August 10, 1932. She writes: "The Governor & Mrs. Franklin D. Roosevelt accept with pleasure Mr. & Mrs. Arthur Bellinger's kind invitation to the marriage of their daughter and Mr. Earl Ralph Miller on Thursday, the eighth of September." Also, an ALS in the third person of FDR's mother, Mrs. James Roosevelt, penned on imprinted Campobello Island stationery, accepting the same invitation. Miller had served as Roosevelt's bodyguard, and the bride was on Mrs. Roosevelt's staff. Fine. 125.00

236. HOOVER, HERBERT. President. Autograph Message Signed, penned on a 16mo leaf bearing the imprint "Stanford University, California". February 14, 1945. Entire message reads "This is to express both my hopes and good wishes for your recovery. Herbert Hoover" Dated on Valentines Day, this message probably accompanied a gift. Holograph messages of Hoover are very scarce. Choice example. 250.00

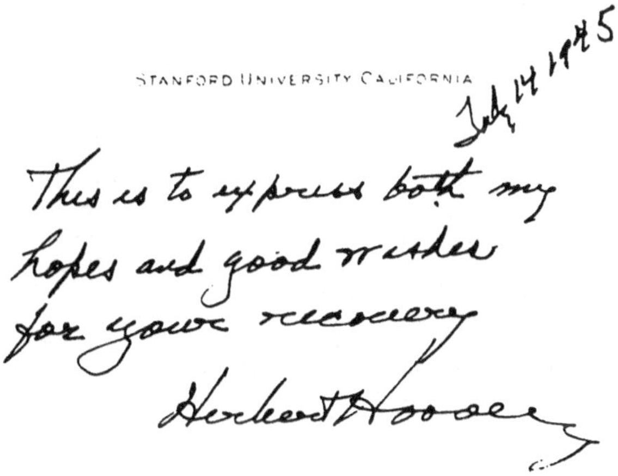
STANFORD UNIVERSITY CALIFORNIA

Feb 14 1945

This is to express both my hopes and good wishes for your recovery

Herbert Hoover

237. PIERCE, FRANKLIN. President; General in Mexican War. Attractive Autograph Letter Signed, penned on lightly lined blue stationery. Full page, 4to. Concord [New Hampshire], February 18, 1851. To Perley Dodge, Amherst, N.H. Docketed integral leaf. Having retired from Congress and Washington life some ten years earlier, Pierce devoted his time to his family and law practice, serving briefly in the Mexican War. In 1852 he unexpectedly received the nomination of his party to stand as their presidential candidate. In this letter, written one year prior to the nomination and consequent election, Pierce is concerned with some missing legal papers. He writes: "Since my return I do not find my docket and having sent to Manchester, learn that it was not left in my room at Shepherds. And think I must have left it in the Court Room or at your room. Please to write me and if you find the docket send it over to Manchester....I hope you will get this in season to send tomorrow as I cannot make my charges and credits without the docket...." Nice letter for a lawyer's set of presidential autographs. Fine condition. With handsome steel-engraved portrait. 550.00

IN A MOVING LETTER OF TRIBUTE ROOSEVELT OFFERS CONDOLENCES TO
THE WIDOW OF HIS FORMER COMMERCE SECRETARY

238. ROOSEVELT, FRANKLIN D. President. Interesting Typed Letter Signed, as President, on imprinted White House stationery. Full page, 4to. Washington, April 12, 1943. To Mrs. Daniel C. Roper, Washington. Original envelope present. The President extends his sympathy to Mrs. Roper on the death of her husband, a South Carolina Democrat whom Roosevelt had known and worked with since the Wilson Administration, and who had served in his cabinet as Secretary of Commerce from 1933-38. Roosevelt continues:

> "...In a long and versatile public career Daniel Roper served his day well and faithfully. In the great office of Secretary of Commerce, whose burdens he assumed in a time of national depression and disaster, he worked indefatigably in the national interest, ignoring every consideration but the public welfare. He never lost faith in the guiding principle that a partnership between government and business would win the fight and he saw this principle vindicated in the restoration of prosperity and with prosperity, hope and happiness to a sorely tried people. The Nation which he served so faithfully and the grand old home State, of whose traditions he was so proud, will long revere his memory.
>
> To me his passing brings a deep sense of personal sorrow in the loss of a staunch and loyal friend of many, many years...."

A moving letter of considerable association and historic value. Pristine condition. 1500.00

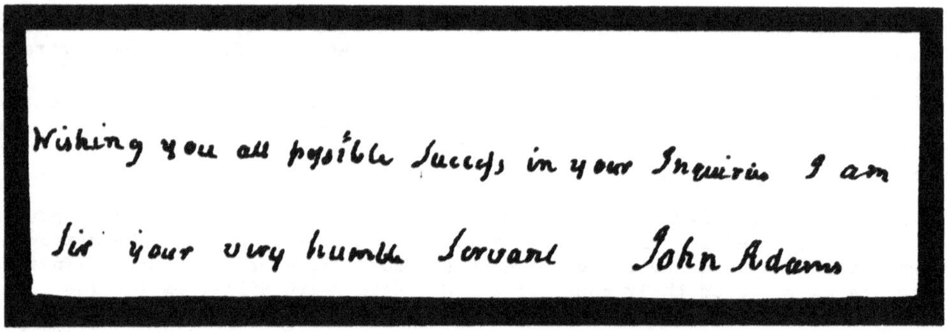
Wishing you all possible Success in your Inquiries I am
Sir your very humble Servant John Adams

239. ADAMS, JOHN. President and Vice President. Autograph Sentiment Signed "John Adams" (actually the concluding two lines from an ALS). One page, oblong 16mo. On the verso appears the date "Quincy, June 2, 1816" in Adams' hand. The sentiment reads: "Wishing you all possible success in your Inquiries I am Sir your very humble Servant..." With engraved portrait. 750.00

PRESIDENTIAL ALS TO A CABINET MEMBER

240. TYLER, JOHN. President and Vice President. Autograph Letter Signed, as President. 1 1/3 pgs. 4to. Washington, July 15, 1845. To Hon. Mr. [John C.] Spencer, Secretary of War. Tyler writes: "I redeem a promise made sometime ago in bringing to your notice Mr. La Fayette M. Ringgold who has been recommended to you for office by Mr. Monroe of the City of New York. His family connexions (sic) are highly respectable and he stands allied to President Monroe. A clerkship would be well bestowed upon him, but I have said to his mother that the appointment must proceed from yourself as I was not only ignorant of the wants of your office but was also unaware of vacancies when they occured...." Interesting presidential content with fine association. Fine condition. 1250.00

PANORAMA VIEW OF TRUMAN'S 1949 INAUGURATION

241. TRUMAN, HARRY S. President and Vice President. Striking 10 x 8 photograph showing Chief Justice Fred Vinson administering the Presidential Oath of Office to Harry S. Truman, with Vice President Barkley, Sam Rayburn, Dean Acheson, George Marshall and other dignitaries looking on. Boldly inscribed against the white area of the platform: "To Rev. Bill Warford, kind regards from / Harry S. Truman / 2-5-64". The photograph is from a negative in the Department of the Army files and bears their imprint on verso. Very scarce in this format! 495.00

"THE TRUE AMERICAN SPIRIT"

242. WILSON, WOODROW. President. Early Typed Letter Signed, while serving on the faculty at Prince ton University. 1 page, small 4to. Princeton, N.J., July 13, 1892. To Rev. H. A. Bridgman, Boston, Mass. Wilson writes: "I take pleasure in sending you the article I promised. I have called it The True American Spirit. It contains...about fifteen hundred words. Having said my thought in that space, I did not care to take advantage of you and stretch it to your full limit of eighteen hundred...." Wilson was the author of numerous books and articles. 395.00

243. POLK, JAMES K. 1795-1849. President; Congressman from Tennessee (1825-39); Speaker of the U.S House of Representatives; Governor of Tennessee. Autograph Letter Signed. Full page, 4to. Washington City, July 4th 1832. To Hon. Levi Woodbury [Secretary of the Navy], Washington. Integral address-leaf addressed by Polk. Congressman Polk writes: "My countryman Mr. Goodrich is now employed in an inferior clerkship in the Post Office, with a salary of only $800 -- His talents and business habits entitle him as I think to a better situation. His salary is not

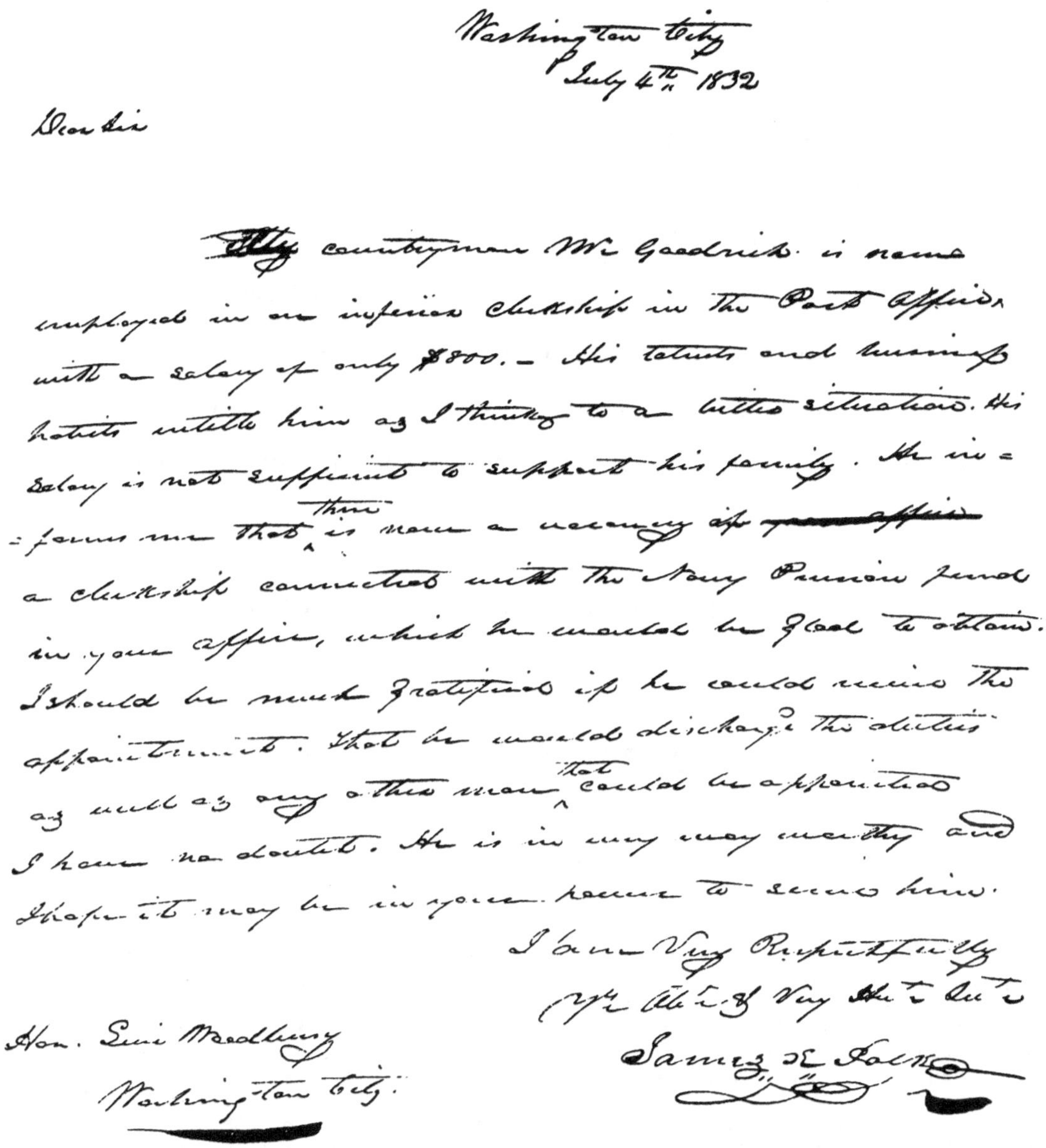

Washington City
July 4th 1832

Dear Sir

My countryman Mr Goodrich is now employed in an inferior clerkship in the Post Office, with a salary of only $800. — His talents and business habits entitle him as I think to a better situation. His salary is not sufficient to support his family. He informs me that there is now a vacancy of ~~post office~~ a clerkship connected with the Navy Pension fund in your office, which he would be glad to obtain. I should be much gratified if he could receive the appointment. That he would discharge the duties as well as any other man that could be appointed I have no doubt. He is in every way worthy and I hope it may be in your power to serve him.

I am Very Respectfully
Yr Obt. & Very Hble Servt
James K. Polk

Hon. Levi Woodbury
Washington City.

sufficient to support his family. He informs me that there is now a vacancy of a clerkship connected with the Navy Pension fund in your office, which he would be glad to obtain. I should be much gratified if he could receive the appointment. That he would discharge the duties as well as any other man that could be appointed I have no doubt. He is in every way worthy and I hope it may be in your power to serve him...." Boldly penned in jet-black ink, the letter is in pristine condition. With a handsome engraved portrait. 1500.00

244. BUCHANAN, JAMES. President; Secretary of State; Minister to England; Senator from Penn. Autograph Letter Signed. 2/3 page, 4to. Wheatland [his home near Lancaster], June 14, 1852. To C. L. Ward, Towanda, Penn. Addressed by Buchanan on verso. Buchanan sends the Pennsylvania Democratic leader a copy of an address: "...I would thank you to let me know what you think of it, & to take care that it is accurately printed. I have often suffered horribly from misprinting. I am just on the wing for Franklin County..." Buchanan had been a leading candidate for the Democratic Presidential nomination of 1852, which went by compromise to Franklin Pierce. Some wear and mounting evidence on verso, otherwise fine. With a fine steel-engraved portrait. Ideal for framing. 450.00

No. 511. five hundred eleven

Additional instruction to the public and private armed vessels of the United States.

THE public and private armed vessels of the United States are not to interrupt any vessels belonging to citizens of the United States coming from British ports to the United States laden with British merchandize, in consequence of the alledged repeal of the British Orders in Council, but are on the contrary to give aid and assistance to the same; in order that such vessels and their cargoes may be dealt with on their arrival as may be decided by the competent authorities.

By command of the President of the United States of America,

Secretary of State.

"ADDITIONAL INSTRUCTIONS TO THE PUBLIC AND PRIVATE ARMED VESSELS OF THE UNITED STATES"

245. MONROE, JAMES. President. Small printed broadside, signed in ink as Secretary of State. One page, small quarto. No place or date. [Washington, ca. 1814-1815]. Numbered in ink at the top "No. 511. five hundred eleven". Full text, after the heading which captions this description, reads: "THE public and private armed vessels of the United States are not to interrupt any vessels belonging to citizens of the United States coming from British ports to the United States laden with British merchandize, in consequence of the alleged repeal of the British Orders in Council, but are on the contrary to give aid and assistance to the same; in order that such vessels and their cargoes may be dealt with on their arrival as may be decided by the competent authorities. By command of the President of the United States of America, [signed] Jas Monroe / Secretary of State." Dramatic broadside calling for the end of privateering against British shipping during the War of 1812, when it was perceived that an end to the war was near. Fine. With a handsome steel-engraved portrait of Monroe. 750.00

TEN DAYS ON THE STUMP IN CONNECTICUT

246. GARFIELD, JAMES A. President; assassinated. Manuscript Letter Signed, as a Member of Congress from Ohio. Full page, 4to. Washington, April 10, 1875. To G. A. Hine, Freedom Station, Portage Co., Ohio. Garfield acknowledges receipt of his correspondent's letter which he found "awaiting me here on my return from Connecticut where I had been absent ten days on the stump. I staid (sic) at home about one week and then came back to go to Connecticut. I received a letter...from Halsey Hall in reference to the vacancy on the A.G.W. R.R. That vacancy is in Mr. Sessions District and the Department has concluded they must fill it by appointing a N.Y. man. So it does not come to me. I am surprised that Deveraux does not find a place for you on his road...." Minor wear to the folds, else fine. 375.00

THE MESS IN CALIFORNIA!!

247. HOOVER, HERBERT. President. Typed Letter Signed, on his imprinted stationery. 1 page, 4to. No place, April 10, 1936. To Dr. John Wesley Hill, Washington, D.C. "...If you noticed it at all, you will see that I adopted much of your condensation at Fort Wayne. We are in a great deal of a mess out here in California due to entirely inconsiderate actions. However, we will have to wait and see how it comes out...." Excellent condition. 150.00

248. TYLER, JOHN. President and Vice President. Autograph Endorsement Signed, as President, on the integral leaf of an Autograph Letter Signed addressed to "His Excellency The President" by JAMES M. PORTER, Secretary of War. [Washington] November 20, 1843. Porter transmits a letter (not present) from General [Zachary] Taylor and a report from Adjutant General Jones which have led them to recommend that Captain Gustavus Dorr of the 6th Infantry "be dropped from the rolls of the Army..." President Tyler responds: "Let Capt. Dorr be dropped from the rolls of the Army - and these opinions of the Secretary of War, M. General Scott and Adjt. Gen'l Jones be filed..." There is also an Autograph Endorsement Signed by General Jones stating that the orders of the Executive have been executed, and Captain Dorr has been duly notified. Choice presidential item, penned on separate leaves, and thus displayable. 650.00

COLLEGE MEN AND SERVICE IN THE WAR

249. TAFT, WILLIAM H. President; Chief Justice, U.S. Supreme Court. Highly important Typed Letter Signed, on his imprinted stationery. Full page, 4to. New Haven, Conn., June 2, 1917. To Frank Prentiss Rand, Editor, The Signet of Phi Sigma Kappa, North Amherst, Mass. Taft writes:

> "It has been gratifying to me to note the real patriotic spirit shown by the young men of the universities and colleges of this country. There is among them no jingo spirit, no rejoicing that we have war, only a determination to their duty and to vindicate the environment of academic education as stimulant of patriotic ideals. Young college men of this country are going to fill the most important part of the younger officers in the Army of the Republic, and we can count on their making a great record as representatives of the educated men of the country. Every college man worth his salt is looking about to find a place in which he can be most useful. If he is deprived of the opportunity of going to the front, there are other places in which he can serve. They also serve who only stand and wait -- that is, those who are so young as not to be eligible for commissions may well keep themselves in preparation for graduation when they will be eligible. Those who are engaged in technical profession indispensable to our proper military preparation, like the medical profession and the profession of engineering, should continue that preparation at all hazards."

Outstanding content letter written by Taft just one month after the United States entered the Great War. Taft has supplied three words in his own holograph. Excellent! 750.00

EARLY CHECK ON CARTER'S [PEANUT] WAREHOUSE ACCOUNT

250. CARTER, ROSALYNN S. First Lady. Partly printed Signed Bank Check, accomplished in her hand. Oblong 8vo. Plains, Georgia, December 6, 1960. Drawn on the Plains Mercantile Co., c/o Bank of Commerce, Americus, Georgia. Payable to Roosevelt Middlebrooks. Stamped Carters Warehouse / Plains, Georgia in magenta ink above Mrs. Carter's signature. Fine. 75.00

251. ROOSEVELT, THEODORE. President and Vice President. Typed Letter Signed "T. Roosevelt", on imprinted letterhead of The Outlook. 1 page, 8vo. New York, July 24, 1912. To E. Wentworth Prescott, State House, Boston, Mass. Writing shortly after being nominated for President by the newly-formed Progressive Party, Roosevelt writes that he has forwarded his correspondent's letter to Senator Dixon in New York, "...in the hope that he may suggest some way for you to be of further help in this campaign...." Uniformly tanned, else fine. 195.00

ACKNOWLEDGING CONGRATULATIONS ON BEING ELECTED VICE PRESIDENT

252. ARTHUR, CHESTER A. President and Vice President. Manuscript Letter Signed, as Vice President-elect. 1 page, 8vo. New York, November 8, 1880. To John L. Parker, Moravia, acknowledging his "...letter of the 4th inst. and [I] beg to thank you for your congratulations and kind expressions regarding myself..." Touching on another matter, possibly campaign expenses, Arthur adds: "I think the remittance you refer to has been made to you -- if not please let me know." Fine specimen. 450.00

253. TAFT, WILLIAM H. President. Imprinted White House card on which President Taft has boldly penned: "For F. W. Chamberlain / with best wishes / Wm. H. Taft / Dec. 5th 1912." 275.00

VERY EARLY LETTER AS A YOUNG ATTORNEY

254. MC KINLEY, WILLIAM. President; assassinated. Autograph Letter Signed, on his imprinted Law Office stationery. 1/2 page, 4to. Canton, Ohio, October 19, 1868. To A. H. Smith, Lancaster, Penn, a client, notifying him that he has been successful in obtaining a judgement on some notes. Probably the earliest McKinley letter we have encountered. Fine. 350.00

255. ROOSEVELT, FRANKLIN D. President. Typed Letter Signed, as Assistant Secretary of the Navy. 1 page, 4to. Washington, March 30, 1918. To Hon. Clayton L. Wheeler, U. S. Marshal, Utica, N.Y. Writing on official imprinted stationery, the future President says he will look into the matter of John Evans, and informs his upstate New York friend: "We have moved from N Street to 2131 R. Street, and the next time you are here you must come and see our new house ...." Fine example. 275.00

256. HAYES, RUTHERFORD B. President. Plain visiting card on which the former President has penned: "Rutherford B. Hayes / Spiegel Grove / 29 Sept. 1891". Very fine. 125.00

Sincerely yours,

Theodore Roosevelt

Let me repeat, that of course I want the fullest and most open expression of preference at the primaries; that I will stand heartily for whatever you, yourself ~~and~~ and the rest of the leaders really finally do, and have no intention of "forcing the nomination", or of trying to; but that, unless you object, I should like, as a good Republican and party man and a staunch believer in you to tell you my judgement, for whatever it is worth.

Hon. Herbert Parsons, M.C.,
52 William Street,
New York, N.Y.

257. ROOSEVELT, THEODORE. President. Remarkable and highly important Typed Letter Signed, as President, on imprinted White House stationery, with a holograph postscript covering most of the last page. 3 full pages, large 4to. Oyster Bay, N.Y., August 27, 1908. To Congressman Herbert Parsons of New York City, concerning the effort to deny Charles Evans Hughes the Republican re-nomination to the governorship of New York. In part: "I have far too many necessary encounters with men I do not like, to permit myself to feel even a passing irritation at sharp words from men whom I not only like but thoroly respect, as I do you....I am not in the least opposed...to having the Republicans of any county express their wishes on primary day.... I earnestly hoped we could get just such a free expression of the voters wishes. You are entirely right in saying that you understood that I was unwilling, in view of Hughes' conduct toward you...to ask any of you to support him....You were very strong in your statements of what the men under you said as to Hughes' unpopularity....When Bennet tells me...that the sentiment is very strong for the renomination of Hughes I have got to take notice of it. I entirely agree with all you say as to your just reasons for complaint against Governor Hughes, and furthermore with all you say as to the fact that many of those who desire his renomination desire it chiefly for the purpose of hurting the Republican party. Moreover, my dear Parsons, you can hardly seriously suppose that, to quote your own words, I am trying to 'treat you as a puppet' -- that is , if you mean <u>me</u> when you say 'those in charge of the national campaign', which of course I am not. On the contrary I have written again and again to Taft and to Hitchcock not to make any open statement, and I haven't the slightest intention of 'telling you what to do' and never will 'tell the newspapers that you will be told what to do'....You wrote me requesting to see me, and asking that I say nothing until I had seen you. I saw you. We went over the situation. I afterwards saw Bennet and various others, including Sherman, and the situation as they related it was so totally different that I felt I ought to tell you that this, with other knowledge brought to me, has made me alter my mind as to what was the wise thing to do. But surely my letter most explicitly disclaims any intention to dictate to you...." The remainder of this remarkable letter is illustrated above. In addition to the lengthy holograph postscript, Roosevelt has made several corrections in the typed text, adding fifteen holograph words. One of the most important political Roosevelt letters to come on the market. Fine condition. 4500.00

258. [HARRISON, BENJAMIN]. Printed ticket, complete with stub, for the Inaugural Stand, State, War, and Navy Departments, March 4, 1889. Allows admission "to the corridors of the building." Under printed vignette of American eagle. Nice souvenir of Harrison's inauguration. 25.00

EYE-WITNESS ACCOUNT OF THE FIRST ATTEMPTED PRESIDENTIAL
ASSASSINATION BY A FUTURE FIRST LADY

259. PIERCE, JANE APPLETON. First Lady (wife of President Franklin Pierce). Magnificent Autograph Letter Signed "Your aff. Jeanie". 4 pages, 4to. Washington, February 1, 1835. To her mother, Mrs. [Elizabeth] Appleton, Amherst, New Hampshire. With the postmarked integral address-leaf franked "Free / Fr. Pierce / M.C." by her husband. Mrs. Pierce devotes the first part of this lengthy letter to the attempted assassination of President Andrew Jackson, the first such attempt made on the life of an incumbent President. She writes: "...I attended the funeral of Mr. Davis on Friday -- and witnessed for the first time the imposing ceremonies attending the death of a member of Congress. The day was exceedingly unpleasant and I did not ride to the burying ground. And the circumstance which occurred just as the procession was starting prevented many others. You will have heard before this reaches you of the attempt to take the President's life -- which was most happily frustrated. The man was siezed in the Rotunda while I was in it. From all accounts, it seems to me that he must be deranged altho' it is not thought so by others. I saw the President this morning at Mr. Posts church, where he appears very attentive and devout...." Mrs. Pierce then details the events of that evening, when the Pierces and another couple were riding across town in a carriage to attend a party, and the carriage overturned. She describes how her husband crawled out to get help for the others trapped in the carriage, and mentions the minor injuries they all sustained. An exceptionally fine content letter from the Pierce-Aiken family archives, and never before offered for sale. Choice condition. 2,000.00

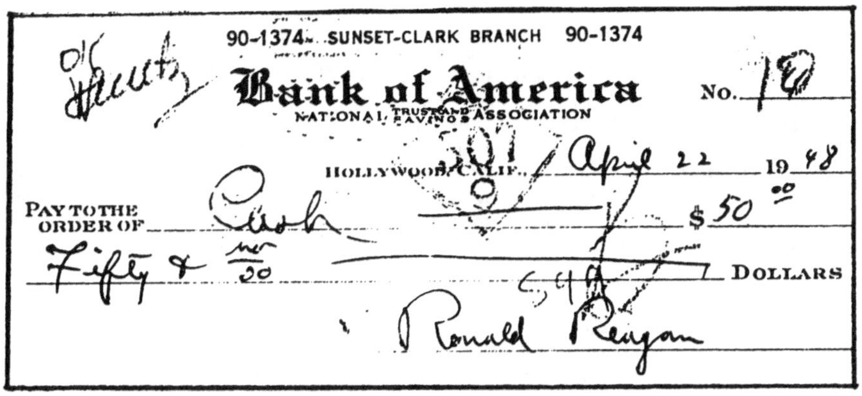

260. REAGAN, RONALD. President; movie actor and President of the Screen Actors' Guild. Rare partly printed Signed Bank Check, accomplished in his hand. Oblong 12mo. Hollywood, California, April 22, 1948. Drawn on the Bank of America, and made payable to "Cash" for fifty dollars. Stamped endorsement of "The Players" on verso. Tiny punch-hole cancellation does not affect Reagan's fine signature. Rare in this format. 1250.00

TO PRESIDENT ANDREW JACKSON WITH HIS INITIALED ENDORSEMENT

261. POINSETT, JOEL R. 1779-1851. South Carolina statesman and diplomat; first U.S. Minister to Mexico (1825-29); Secretary of War (1837-41); introduced the poinsetta, named in his honor, to the United States. Choice Autograph Letter Signed. Full page, 4to. The Homestead, Greenville, South Carolina, no date. To Gen'l Andrew Jackson, President of the United States, Washington. With integral address-leaf bearing Jackson's four-line initialed endorsement. Fine letter in favor of Mr. Rolando of Charleston who "visits Washington in hopes of obtaining a warrant to enter the Navy...[His] father is well known to me, and has been always distinguished for his firm attachment to the government. His conduct and principles entitle him to the favorable consideration of the administration, and your friends in Charleston will ...be much gratified by the success of his application. Mr. Legare will...accompany young Mr. Rolando to Washington, and will inform you of the singular state of parties in our city, and of the revolution this State seems destined shortly to undergo...." Jackson writes: "Referred to the Secretary of the Navy for his consideration. A. J." Small blank corner missing from the address-leaf, else in very fine condition. Great content & association! 325.00

262. HOOVER, HERBERT. President. His book: An American Epic / Introduction / The Relief of Belgium and Northern France 1914 - 1930. Volume One of a projected series which the former President was unable to complete due to his death. Silver-lettered blue cloth. Chicago, 1959. First edition. Boldly inscribed in jet-black ink on the front endpaper: "To the Capitol Hill Club / With the Good Wishes / of / Herbert Hoover." Original dust-jacket. Fine. 150.00

263. TAFT, WILLIAM H. President; Chief Justice, U.S. Supreme Court. Magnificent studio photograph by Harris & Ewing, bearing a copyright date of 1908. Full-face bust pose. Inscribed on the lower area of the photographer's mount: "For Mary L. D. Ferris / with best wishes of / Wm. H. Taft". Ideal for framing or display. Excellent condition. 295.00

"THE TROUBLOUS TIMES THROUGH WHICH WE WERE OBLIGED TO GO"

264. WILSON, WOODROW. President of the United States during the Great War; President of Princeton University; Governor of New Jersey; professor, historian and lecturer. Typed Letter Signed, on his imprinted "S Street" stationery. Full page, 4to. Washington, January 23, 1922. To Mrs. Sidney Sherwood, Cornwall, New York. In part: "...I wish with you that Sidney might have been at my side in the troublous times through which we were obliged to go. I remember him with admiration and affection. I warmly congratulate you on the record your children are making. I have not had the pleasure of seeing any of them but Sidney since that time so long ago when I took a meal with you at Roland Park. With warmest regard and the hope that the children will all attain the distinction they now seem bound for...." Nice letter! 325.00

265. LINCOLN, ABRAHAM. President. Autograph Endorsement Signed "A. Lincoln", as President, penned on the verso of an Autograph Letter Signed by FRANCIS H. PIERPONT, Governor of loyal Virginia, later the state of West Virginia. 1 1/4 pages, 4to. Wheeling, September 20, 1862. To Hon. Secretary of War [E.M. Stanton]. Pierpont recommends for a Brigadier's commission "Col. George R. Latham of the 2 Va. Vol. Inft. now stationed in the defences of Washington ...[He] has distinguished himself for Ability and bravery. I would refer you to Gen'l Millroy for definite information. Latham has been under his command ever since the Gen. went into the field -- and been in all the battles from Rich Mountain to the last fight at Bull Run...." Lincoln has boldly penned: "Respectfully submitted to Gen. Halleck. A. Lincoln / Sep. 30, 1862". Latham, later breveted Brigadier General, did not get the commission recommended by Governor Pierpont. Penned on scarce imprinted stationery "The Commonwealth of Virginia / Executive Department / Wheeling, Va." The loyal government attempting to operate from Wheeling agreed to formation of West Virginia as a state (admitted to the Union 20 June 1863) when the Civil War did not end quickly as had been hoped. In fine condition throughout, and not published in Basler. 2500.00

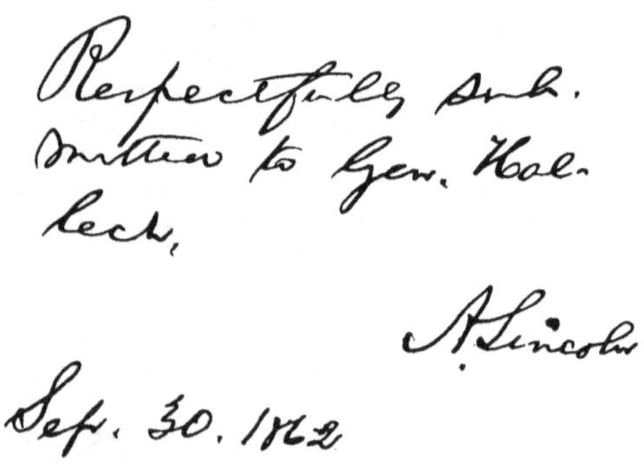

266. ARTHUR, CHESTER A. President and Vice President. Manuscript Document Signed, as Collector of the Port of New York, on imprinted Custom House stationery. 1/2 page, 4to. New York, February 11, 1873. To the Deputy Collectors. Arthur writes: "In order that the quantities and weights of Essential Oils 'may be accurately ascertained by the Examiner of Drugs' ... as suggested in [a] letter of Hon. Secretary of the Treasury...you will please order to the U.S. Public Store 'all such dutiable Oils'." Initialed dockets by the various Deputy Collectors appear at the top of this document. Fine presidential item. 395.00

267. TRUMAN, BESS W. First Lady. Autograph Letter Signed, as First Lady, penned on gilt-imprinted White House stationery. 2 separate pages, 8vo. Washington, no date. To [Paul] Wooten, the noted journalist. She writes: "Thank you so much for the clippings. We had not seen them and are delighted to have them. Margaret and I had a wonderful time in your city [New Orleans] -- it could not have been nicer...." Scarce in holograph as First Lady. Fine. 150.00

SOUVENIR DINNER PROGRAMME SIGNED AS PRESIDENT

268. FORD, GERALD R. President and Vice President. Handsome colored printed Programme for the Annual Dinner of the Nashua, New Hampshire, Chamber of Commerce, celebrating its 50th anniversary in 1976. Signed "Gerald R. Ford", as president, beneath the handsome printed colored portrait of his likeness on the front cover. Ford was the guest speaker. Mint. 150.00

269. MONROE, JAMES. President; Secretary of War and State; Minister to England; Governor of Virginia. Handsome partly engraved Document Signed, as President. Large folio, vellum. Washington, December 29, 1817. Countersigned by Benjamin W. Crowninshield, Secretary of the Navy. Ornate blind-stamped wafer seal affixed with red wax. The President commissions James E. McDonald to serve as a Lieutenant in the U. S. Navy. Handsome vignettes of a spread eagle at head, and several implements of war at the bottom. Very slightly yellowed with Monroe's signature a trifle light. Otherwise fine. 650.00

270. COOLIDGE, CALVIN. President and Vice President. Strikingly handsome sepia studio photograph by Allison Spence, Northampton [Mass.], showing a formal bust image of Coolidge. Boldly inscribed in bright dark blue ink on the wide lower margin: "To Frank S. Cummings / With regards, / Calvin Coolidge". Pristine condition, in photographer's presentation folder. We have not encountered Coolidge photographs by his home-town photographer. 250.00

271. ROOSEVELT, EDITH KERMIT. First Lady. Complete envelope, franked "Free / Edith K. Roosevelt", and addressed in her hand. Postmarked: "Oyster Bay, N.Y., March 28, 1942". Fine. 65.00

LATE LETTER OF GRANT REFERRING TO HIS ARTICLE ON THE BATTLE OF SHILOH, THE WRITING OF HIS MEMOIRS AND HIS PAINFUL CANCER

272. GRANT, ULYSSES S. President; Union General. Magnificent Autograph Letter Signed, in the last year of his life. Full page, tall 8vo. New York City, February 4, 1885. To Birwell Smith, Publisher, Century Co. Grant writes: "I am much obliged to you for the ten copies of the Century containing my article on Shiloh, which you were kind enough to send me Saturday last. I am also pleased at the success of the Magazine. For three or four weeks prior to about last Saturday I suffered so much pain that I did but little work on my book. I am now however able to devote from four to six hours each day upon it, and, if this continues, I shall hope in the course of two or three weeks to have progressed far enough to justify me in making arrangements for its publication...." The entry in DAB concerning Grant's activities at this time is most relevant: "The life was short. A dangerous cancer of the throat was wearing Grant away, though he was fighting the disease in order to carry to completion the only civil task that he had learned how to do well. In 1884 he wrote for the publishers of the Century Magazine an article (Feb. 1885) on the battle of Shiloh. This paid him handsomely and was an immediate success....He set to work upon his Personal Memoirs, writing in his sickroom and in the quiet of the house at Mount McGregor where he was taken to die. Mark Twain, then in business as a publisher of subscription books, waited for the copy, to put on the market one of the most suc cessful of American books." Grant barely finished the last chapter when he died on July 23, 1885. Truly a fascinating and highly important Grant letter. Fine condition. 1500.00

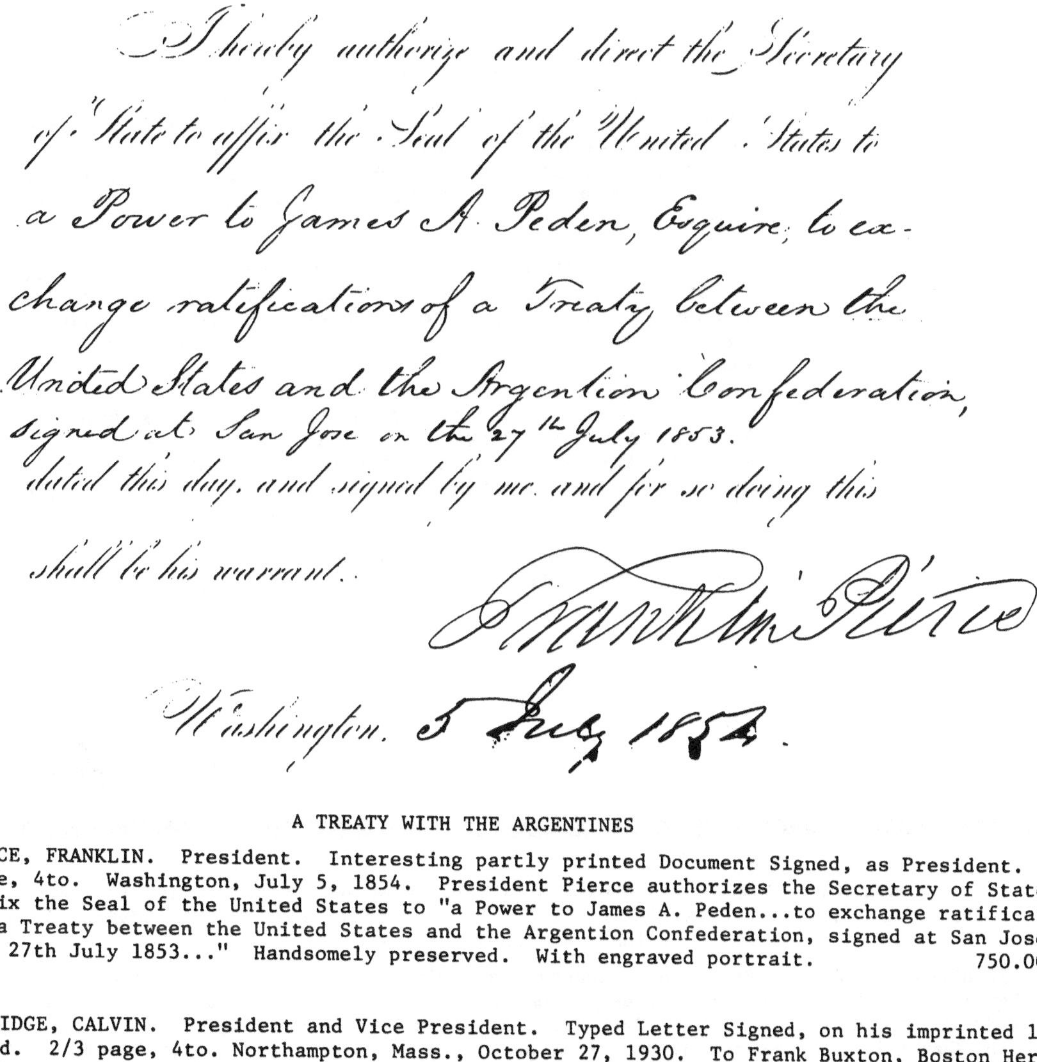
I hereby authorize and direct the Secretary of State to affix the Seal of the United States to a Power to James A. Peden, Esquire, to exchange ratifications of a Treaty between the United States and the Argention Confederation, signed at San Jose on the 27th July 1853. dated this day, and signed by me, and for so doing this shall be his warrant.

Franklin Pierce

Washington, 5 July 1854.

A TREATY WITH THE ARGENTINES

273. PIERCE, FRANKLIN. President. Interesting partly printed Document Signed, as President. One page, 4to. Washington, July 5, 1854. President Pierce authorizes the Secretary of State to affix the Seal of the United States to "a Power to James A. Peden...to exchange ratifications of a Treaty between the United States and the Argention Confederation, signed at San Jose on the 27th July 1853..." Handsomely preserved. With engraved portrait. 750.00

274. COOLIDGE, CALVIN. President and Vice President. Typed Letter Signed, on his imprinted letterhead. 2/3 page, 4to. Northampton, Mass., October 27, 1930. To Frank Buxton, Boston Herald, Boston, Mass. The former president writes: "Enclosed is a copy of a radio speech which I suppose is to be made at the time and place indicated...To be perfectly sure about this you should check it up (sic. out) with Mr. Taylor at the State Committee Headquarters...." Nice clean specimen, showing Coolidge's continuing interest in state politics. 225.00

275. BUCHANAN, JAMES. President. Ornate, partly-printed Document Signed, as Secretary of State. One page, large legal folio. Washington, April 17, 1848. United States passport issued to Casper J. Beleke, who has also signed this document beneath his physical description. Printed seal of the State Department. Highly ornate printed heading, including a spread-eagle (head to the right) not found on any other type document. Handsome display piece. 325.00

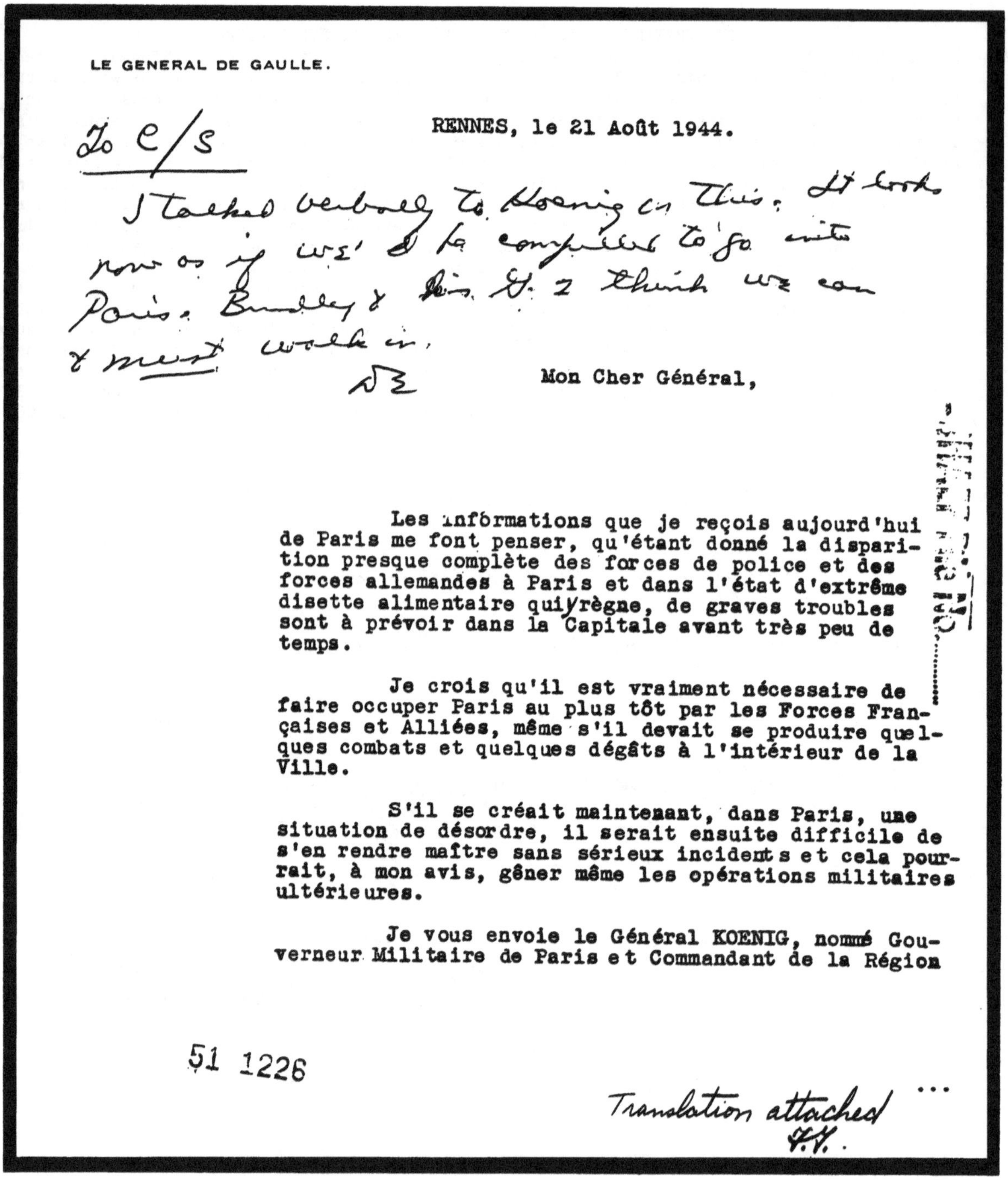

LE GENERAL DE GAULLE.

RENNES, le 21 Août 1944.

To C/S

I talked verbally to Koenig on this. It looks now as if we'd be compelled to go into Paris. Bradley & his G-2 think we can & must walk in.

DE

Mon Cher Général,

Les informations que je reçois aujourd'hui de Paris me font penser, qu'étant donné la disparition presque complète des forces de police et des forces allemandes à Paris et dans l'état d'extrême disette alimentaire qui règne, de graves troubles sont à prévoir dans la Capitale avant très peu de temps.

Je crois qu'il est vraiment nécessaire de faire occuper Paris au plus tôt par les Forces Françaises et Alliées, même s'il devait se produire quelques combats et quelques dégâts à l'intérieur de la Ville.

S'il se créait maintenant, dans Paris, une situation de désordre, il serait ensuite difficile de s'en rendre maître sans sérieux incidents et cela pourrait, à mon avis, gêner même les opérations militaires ultérieures.

Je vous envoie le Général KOENIG, nommé Gouverneur Militaire de Paris et Commandant de la Région

51 1226

...

Translation attached
F.H.

DE GAULLE'S LETTER TO EISENHOWER GIVING HIS CONSENT FOR THE ALLIES TO MARCH INTO PARIS, WITH IKE'S INITIALED HOLOGRAPH ENDORSEMENT STATING THAT GENERAL BRADLEY THINKS "WE CAN & MUST WALK IN."

276. EISENHOWER, DWIGHT D. President; General in World War II; planned and executed the D-Day landings on the French beaches; as Supreme Allied Commander in Europe planned the strategy that led to the defeat of Nazi Germany. Autograph Endorsement Signed "D.E.", as Supreme Allied Commander, at the top of the first page of a two-page Typed Letter Signed by GENERAL CHARLES DE GAULLE addressed to Eisenhower. Writing from Rennes, in Brittany, on August 21, 1944, De Gaulle states: "The information which I've received today from Paris makes me think that, given the virtually complete absence of German forces and police in the city, and the extreme food shortages which exist there, there will be serious trouble in the Capital before long. I think that it is quite necessary to have the French and Allied Forces occupy Paris as soon as possible, even if that means some minor combat and destruction has to occur within the city limits. If Paris were to fall into disorder now, later on it would be difficult to master the situation without serious incidents, which would, in my opinion, endanger ulterior military operations. I am sending you General Koenig, the Military Governor of Paris, and Commandant of the Parisian Region, to study with you the matter of the occupation in case you decide to go ahead with it without delay...." Eisenhower has penned: "To C/S / I talked

de Paris, pour étudier, avec vous, la question de l'occupation au cas où vous décideriez d'y procéder sans délai.

Bien cordialement à vous

C. de Gaulle

RECEIVED
9623
AUG 20 15 57 1944
SHAEF.SECY.GEN.STAFF

Monsieur le Général EISENHOWER,

Commandant Suprême des Forces Expédionnaires

Alliées.

51 1227

RECEIVED
23 AUG Entd
SUPREME HQ ALLIED E.F
SECRETARY GENERAL
STAFF

verbally to Koenig on this. It looks now as if we'd be compelled to go into Paris. Bradley & G-2 think we can & must walk in. / D.E."

Both Eisenhower and Bradley had hoped that Paris could be temporarily by-passed as the Allies rushed toward the Seine, but they had not reckoned on the French resistance organization. In his Crusade in Europe, Eisenhower writes concerning this matter: "...A special problem that became acute toward the end of August was that of determining what to do about Paris. During all preliminary operations we had been at great pains to avoid direct bombing of the French capital....At the moment we were anxious to save every ounce of fuel and ammunition for combat operations...and I was hopeful of deferring actual capture of the city, unless I received evidence of starvation or distress among its citizens....Information indicated that no great battle would take place and it was believed that the entry of one or two Allied divisions would accomplish the liberation of the city...." The plan was set in motion, and on the morning of August 25, 1944, General Dietrich von Choltitz, the Reich's Commandant in Paris surrendered to General LeClerc, Commander of the French 2nd Armoured Division (the first to march into Paris).

Probably the greatest letter from World War II ever to appear on the market. Several stamped dockets and two punch-file holes in top blank margin. A super letter!! 45,000.00

277. MADISON, JAMES. President; Signer of U.S. Constitution; co-author of The Federalist Papers. Superb Printed Letter Signed, as Secretary of State in Jefferson's cabinet. 3 full pages, legal folio. Department of State, Washington, August 1, 1801. Headed Circular, and addressed "To the Consuls and Commercial Agents of the United States." Docketed integral leaf. This lengthy message deals with a multitude of problems resultant from our trading with foreign nations. He first takes up the question of American citizens purchasing vessels in foreign ports, in some cases prize vessels, and how the paper work for these transactions is to be handled. Madison suggests that Health Certificates be issued to guard against contagion; the spending of public monies is forbidden "without the special direction of a Minister of the United States, except for the relief of seamen". He discusses the evil of seamen being discharged from the crews of American vessels in foreign ports because new crews could be hired at less wages. Madison then turns to the problem of forged Sea-Letters: "We have to lament that our Sea-letters have been forged and assumed by foreign vessels...Whilst no law exists to oblige the masters of American vessels to present their papers to the Consuls, it is difficult to suggest that means of detecting and counteracting the abuse...Enclosed [not present] you will find a copy of the Sea-letter as now issued. The types in the future will remain the same; the paper will be sometimes varied. Besides the means of comparison afforded by the signatures, seal and typography, we have caused a stamp to be impressed upon them....It is evident that the admission of the existence of forged papers should be delicately made, so as not to excite a magnified opinion of their extent...." In a one-sentence holograph postscript beneath Madison's bold signature, a secretary has penned: "The affixing the stamp is for the present omitted and therefore no sea letter is inclosed". Excellent condition. 1250.00

278. ROOSEVELT, ELEANOR. First Lady. Typed Letter Signed, with initials "E. R.", as First Lady, on gilt-imprinted White House stationery. 1 page, 4to. Los Angeles, Calif., March 23, 1939. To Harry [Hopkins], Secretary of Commerce, Department of Commerce, Washington. Original envelope bearing Air Mail postage, and marked Personal. She writes: "I am very much distressed to hear that you have been ill again. If you have to be away for any length of time, don't you want Diana to come over to the White House with her nurse and settle down? We will be enchanted to have her and even if I am away, you may be sure that every one will look after her as everybody is always very happy to have her around. I do hope things will go better before long with you. My love to Diana, Affectionately..." Choice, highly personal content, and very scarce as such. 150.00

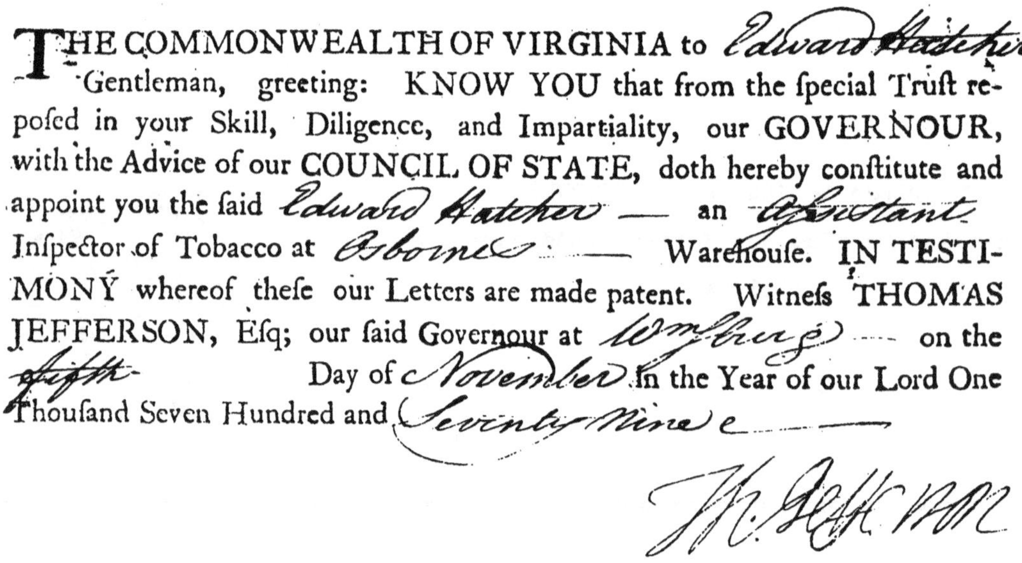
THE COMMONWEALTH OF VIRGINIA to Edward Hatcher Gentleman, greeting: KNOW YOU that from the ſpecial Truſt repoſed in your Skill, Diligence, and Impartiality, our GOVERNOUR, with the Advice of our COUNCIL OF STATE, doth hereby conſtitute and appoint you the ſaid Edward Hatcher — an Assistant Inſpector of Tobacco at Osborne — Warehouſe. IN TESTIMONY whereof theſe our Letters are made patent. Witneſs THOMAS JEFFERSON, Eſq; our ſaid Governour at Wmsburg — on the fifth Day of November in the Year of our Lord One Thouſand Seven Hundred and Seventy Nine —

Th: Jefferson

APPOINTMENT OF A TOBACCO INSPECTOR

279. JEFFERSON, THOMAS. 1743-1826. President of the United States; Vice President and Secretary of State; Governor of Virginia; Signer, and principal author of the Declaration of Independence. Choice and highly unusual partly printed Document Signed, as Governor of Virginia. Oblong 8vo. Williamsburg, November 5, 1779. Jefferson appoints Edward Hatcher "with the Advice of our Council of State...an Assistant Inspector of Tobacco at Osborne Warehouse..." Docketed on verso. Handsome document of revolutionary war date. Choice steel-engraved portrait accompanies this fine document. 2250.00

280. ROOSEVELT, FRANKLIN D. 1882-1945. President. Typed Letter Signed, as Acting Secretary of the Navy, on imprinted Navy Department stationery. 1 page, 4to. Washington, June 7, 1917. To the Honorable, The Secretary of the Treasury [William G. McAdoo]. Roosevelt acknowledges receipt of a letter from McAdoo enclosing a letter from Mr. Wrightsman "in regard to alleged inefficiency of aircraft...." He continues: "I wish to assure you that the situation is not quite in accordance with Mr. Wrightsman's letter, and that every care is being taken in the construction and operation of Naval aircraft...." Interesting war content. Fine. 225.00

281. MONROE, JAMES. President; Secretary of War and State; Minister to England; Governor of Virginia. Autograph Letter Signed, as Secretary of War. Full page, 4to. Richmond, May 28, 1815. To George Graham, on official business. In part: "You will have rec'd the brevet comm. with my signature before this reaches you. Maj. Taliaferro of King George County, the son of James, has not rec'd his warrant for the military academy, which I thought had [been] issued in July, & was given to Col. Goodwyn. Will you be so good as [to] send it to him, or a duplicate, as I presume the place stands open for him? I have written to Col. Bankhead...& hinted that it was possible that as satisfactory evidence of his meritorious service, he might be breveted to higher rank. I heard from many that his conduct was highly meritorious...." In a brief postscript, Monroe adds: "My health continues to improve." When Monroe became President two years later, he appointed Graham, the recipient of this letter, Commissioner of the General Land Office. Some minor wear and paper repairs to folds on verso. Basically in fine condition. With engraved portrait. 1,200.00

282. PIERCE, FRANKLIN. President. Interesting Autograph Letter Signed. 1 1/3 pages, 4to. Concord, August 10, 1840. To "My dear Sister" [his sister-in-law, Mrs. Mary Aiken, sister of his wife] In part: "...I write now merely to tell you how well we have all been and how satisfactorily we are settled again. Jane is perfectly satisfied with everything at our new quarters, finds the rooms more commodious and pleasant than she anticipated and will be able in a day or two to fill up the details of a very pleasant account of ourselves. Our ride up was delightful and Frank Robert [his eldest son] proved as good a little traveller as need be. The Mother and the boy both seem to me to be better than at any time since my return. Frank is as gay as a little bird -- perfectly delighted with the variety of new objects around him especially with the dog and the variety of flowers in the garden & yard...." Pierce did not seek re-election to Congress as he wanted to return to Concord to be near his wife and children. His son Frank, died two years later. Both his children, and his wife were continuously in bad health. Interesting family letter. Fine condition. 750.00

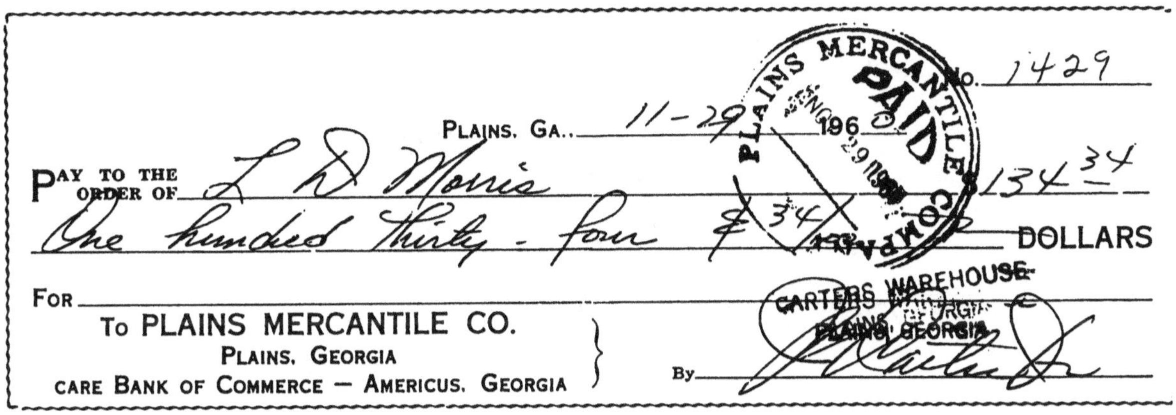
No. 1429
PLAINS, GA. 11-29 196
PAY TO THE ORDER OF L D Morris $134 34/
One hundred Thirty-four $34/ DOLLARS
FOR
To PLAINS MERCANTILE CO.
PLAINS, GEORGIA
CARE BANK OF COMMERCE — AMERICUS, GEORGIA
By
PLAINS MERCANTILE COMPANY PAID
CARTERS WAREHOUSE PLAINS, GEORGIA

EARLY CHECK ON CARTER'S [PEANUT] WAREHOUSE ACCOUNT

283. CARTER, JIMMY. President. Partly printed Signed Bank Check, accomplished in his hand. Oblong 8vo. Plains, Georgia, November 29, 1960. Drawn on the Plains Mercantile Co., c/o Bank of Commerce, Americus, Georgia. Payable to L. D. Morris. Stamped "Carters Warehouse / Plains, Georgia" in magenta ink above Carter's signature. Signed "J. E. Carter, Jr.", the scarce early form of his signature. Very rare! Excellent condition. 1250.00

284. POLK, JAMES K. President; Speaker of the U.S. House; Governor of Tennessee. Autograph Letter Signed, as Speaker. 1 page, 4to. Washington City, February 16, 1839. To James E. Root, Saratoga Springs, New York. With the integral address-leaf in Polk's hand. Polk writes: "In compliance with the request contained in your letter of the 9th instant, I herewith send you my autograph; and am Very Respectfully Your obt. Sevt..." Attractive specimen, in fresh condition. With handsome steel-engraved portrait. Well suited for display. 850.00

285. NIXON, RICHARD M. President and Vice President. Attractive, and most unusual cacheted postal cover marking the Cease-fire agreement in Vietnam, and postmarked "Washington, January 27, 1973", the date the agreement became effective. Printed in red on the envelope is the newspaper announcement of the agreement from Paris, and also President Nixon's statement concerning same. Nixon's picture is also printed on the envelope. Signed "Richard Nixon" in a blank area above his statement. The first cover of this type we have encountered. 150.00

286. ROOSEVELT, ELEANOR. First Lady. Handsome engraved proof vignette of the back side of the White House. Oblong 8vo. Signed on the lower white margin. The vignette is by the Bureau of Engraving and Printing, and differs from the view usually encountered. Undated, but probably signed as First Lady. Fine. 100.00

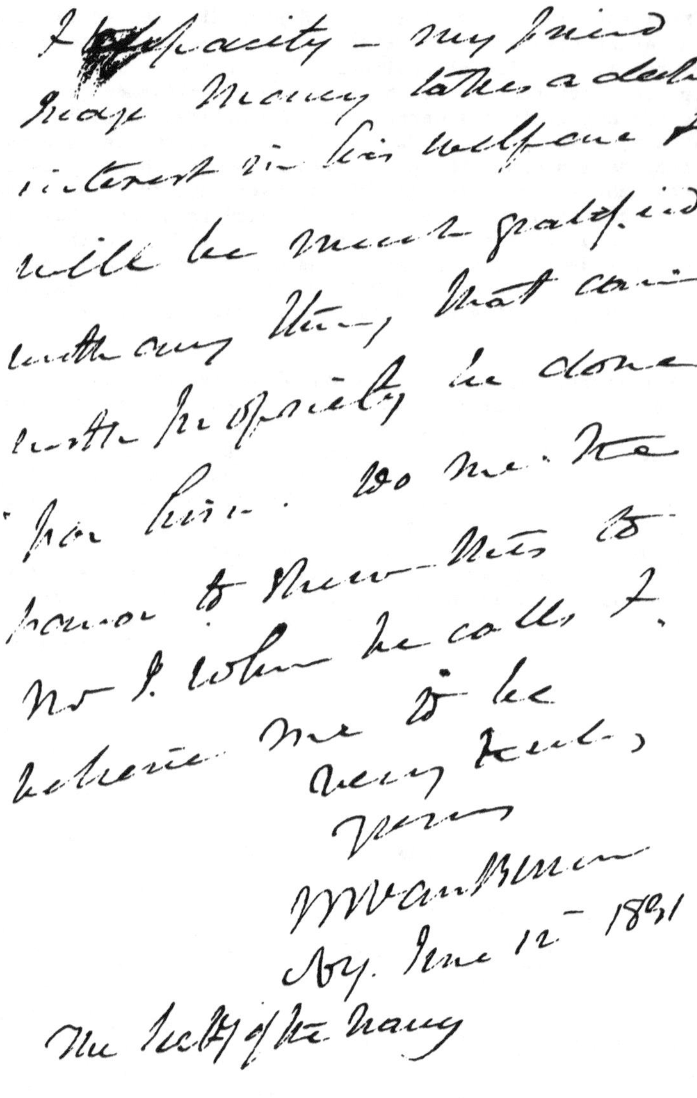
& capacity – my friend
Judge Marcy takes a deep
interest in his welfare &
will be much gratified
with any thing that can
with propriety be done
for him. Do me the
favor to remember me to
Mrs. W. when he calls &
believe me to be
very truly
yours
M Van Buren
N.Y. June 12 – 1831
The Secty of the Navy

287. VAN BUREN, MARTIN. President; Vice President; Secretary of State; Minister to England (not confirmed by U.S. Senate). Autograph Letter Signed, at about the time of his resignation as Secretary of State. 2 full pages, 8vo. New York, June 12, 1831. To [Levi] Woodbury, Secretary of the Navy. With the docketed integral address-leaf. Van buren informs his correspondent that "Mr. L. Jones will apply to you for an appointment in the Marine Corps. He has been a Cadet at West Point & will doubtless explain to the satisfaction of [the] Government the cause of his leaving that Institution. I believe him to be a young gentleman of worth and capacity -- my friend Judge Marcy takes a deep interest in his welfare and will be much gratified with any thing that can with propriety be done for him...." Fine condition. 395.00

288. FORD, GERALD R. President and Vice President. His book: A Vision for America, being the text of his Address to the Republican National Convention, Joe Louis Arena, Detroit, Michigan, July 14, 1980. Silver-lettered blue cloth. Lord John Press: Northridge, California, 1980. First edition. Limited to 500 numbered copies [400 in this binding] signed by Ford on the colophon leaf. Mint, as issued. 95.00

289. FORD, GERALD R. Same book as above, only one of 100 numbered copies bound in full blue morocco, and laid in a presentation box. Signed by Ford on the colophon page. This leather edition will become quite rare, as we were able to obtain only three copies, and the limitation is very small. Mint. 195.00

290. CLEVELAND, GROVER. President. Lower half of a partly printed Document Signed, as President. 1 page, oblong folio. Countersigned by T. F. BAYARD, Secretary of State. Washington, April 16, 1886. Blind-stamped Seal of the Department of State at lower left. Although a fragment, complete in itself. Pristine condition, with an unusually bold signature of Cleveland. Ideal for framing or display. 125.00

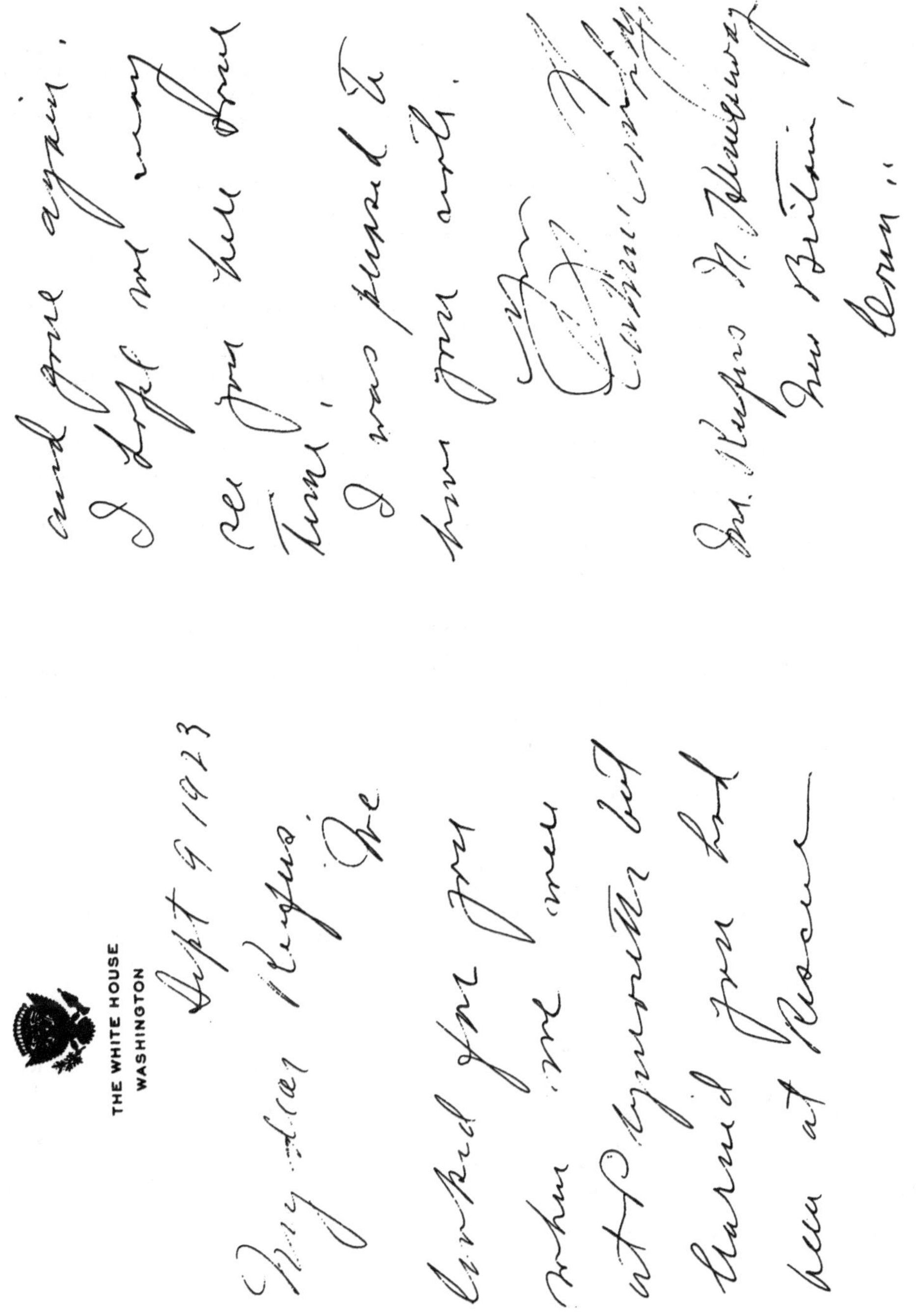

THE WHITE HOUSE
WASHINGTON

Sept 9 1923

My dear Rufus: We looked for you when we were at Plymouth but learned you had been at Rescue and gone again. I hope we may see you here some time. I was pleased to have your note.

Yours
Calvin Coolidge

Mr. Rufus N. Hemenway,
New Britain,
Conn.

RARE HOLOGRAPH LETTER AS PRESIDENT

291. COOLIDGE, CALVIN. President and Vice President. Extremely rare Autograph Letter Signed, as President, penned on green-crested White House stationery. 2 full separate pages, 8vo. Washington, September 9, 1923. To Rufus N. Hemenway, New Britain, Connecticut. Original postmarked White House envelope, addressed by Coolidge, and marked "Personal" by him in the top left corner. Coolidge writes: "We looked for you when we were at Plymouth but learned you had been at Rescue and gone again. I hope we may see you here some time. I was pleased to have your note...." Written just one month after Coolidge became President following the death of Harding. Fine condition, and rarely offered in full holograph as president. 2500.00

"AN HONEST MAN IS THE NOBLEST WORK OF GOD"

292. JACKSON, ANDREW. President; General in War of 1812, and hero of the Battle of New Orleans. Extremely choice Autograph Letter Signed, as United States Senator from Tennessee, penned two months after being defeated for the presidency by John Quincy Adams. Nearly a full page, legal folio. Washington City, January 31, 1825. To E. K. Ingersol, who apparently had named his son after "Old Hickory".

> "Your letter of the 21st instant is just rec'd. From your kind feelings expressed, as well as the evidence of respect in calling your son for me, receive my thanks. I send my blessing to the child; may he live, grow & prosper, and be to his parents a comfort in old age -- be serviceable to himself & country, and an ornament to the society in which he may live. You say you are poor -- your own industry with proper occonomy (sic) will soon remove poverty from your door; It is not material what occupation a man follows; all are equally honourable when pursued with honesty & industry -- always keepin (sic) in view that an honest man is the noblest work of God...."

Truly, a moving letter by the future president! A United States Senator from 1823, Jackson was put forth as the Democratic Presidential candidate in the following year. The highest office of the land went to John Q. Adams in the 1824 election and Jackson returned to his Senate seat until October 14, 1825, when he resigned. He was elected President over Adams in 1828. Several paper repairs to the folds on verso, not affecting the fine appearance of this choice letter. With handsome steel-engraved portrait. 5750.00

293. COOLIDGE, CALVIN. President and Vice President. Typed Letter Signed, as Lieutenant Governor of Massachusetts, on imprinted stationery bearing the seal of the Commonwealth. Full page, 4to. State House, Boston, August 18, 1917. To Arthur H. Tuttle, Chairman, Republican Committee, Sheffield, Mass., concerning Coolidge's candidacy for the Governorship. He writes: "The nomination paper you were so kind as to circulate for me has been returned....I appreciate your services and support....The faithful, efficient, and unselfish work of our Committeemen, and those who aid them, is the strength of our party and is worthy of every honorable recognition...." Interesting political content. Fine condition. 175.00

294. HARDING, WARREN G. President. Typewritten Statement Signed, as President, on a plain oblong 12mo white card. No place or date, but dated in pencil in an unidentified hand Nov. 3, 1921. Harding writes: "We hear much of the traditions of famous universities, but if we look into them we commonly find that they concern men, men who have stamped their personalities, who have given of their generous natures, who have colored the intellectual atmosphere about them ...." An unusual presidential expression! Fine condition, with a bold signature. 450.00

GRANT ATTENDS GENERAL SCOTT'S FUNERAL

295. GRANT, ULYSSES S. President and Union General. Autograph Letter Signed, on stationery imprinted "Head-Quarters Armies of the United States". 1 1/2 pages, 8vo. No place [Washington] May 31, 1866. To "Dear Jones". Grant writes: "I start this evening for West Point to attend the funeral of Gen. [Winfield] Scott. From there I shall start for St. Louis via Chicago, reaching there on Sunday morning. Mrs. Grant will be with me and we propose becoming regular boarders at your house during our stay. If we should remain over Monday evening I would have no objection to meeting about four of your friends socially until say 2 in the morning. I presume Mrs. J. let you down light upon that subject I wrote to her about...." Heavy vertical fold crease, else fine. 575.00

WRITTEN ON BOARD THE STEAMER POWHATAN

296. PIERCE, FRANKLIN. President. Autograph Letter Signed. 2 full pages, 4to. Steamer Powhatan, December 9, 1857. To his nephew, John Aiken, Andover, Mass. Pierce writes: "We have been laying here at anchor near Norfolk waiting for some slight repairs to a valve of the engine since yesterday morning. We shall probably be under way again tomorrow....Our accomodations are so ample and complete on board this noble ship that the detention is not irksome. Your aunt has been quite bright today, and passed an hour or two on the poop deck. Every thing seems to promise a pleasant voyage and several Officers on board, who have visited Madiera confirm the agreeable impression we have received from the first of its climate and attractions. Rev. Mr. Wood formerly of Concord is Chaplain of the Powhatan will prove an agreeable and instructive companion, full of minute information with regard to the Holy Land and the East generally. Your aunt is writing a letter which she will send back by the Pilot when he parts with us off Cape Henry. With much love to all..." Pierce wrote this letter some nine months after leaving the presidency. Excellent condition. 950.00

297. TAFT, WILLIAM H. President; Chief Justice, U. S. Supreme Court. His book: Ethics in Service. Lilac cloth. Yale University Press: New Haven, 1915. First edition (one of 1000 copies). Inscribed by the former president on the front endpaper: "For J. B. McGhee / with best wishes / Wm. H. Taft / Jany. 30 1921". Uncommon title. Fine. 250.00

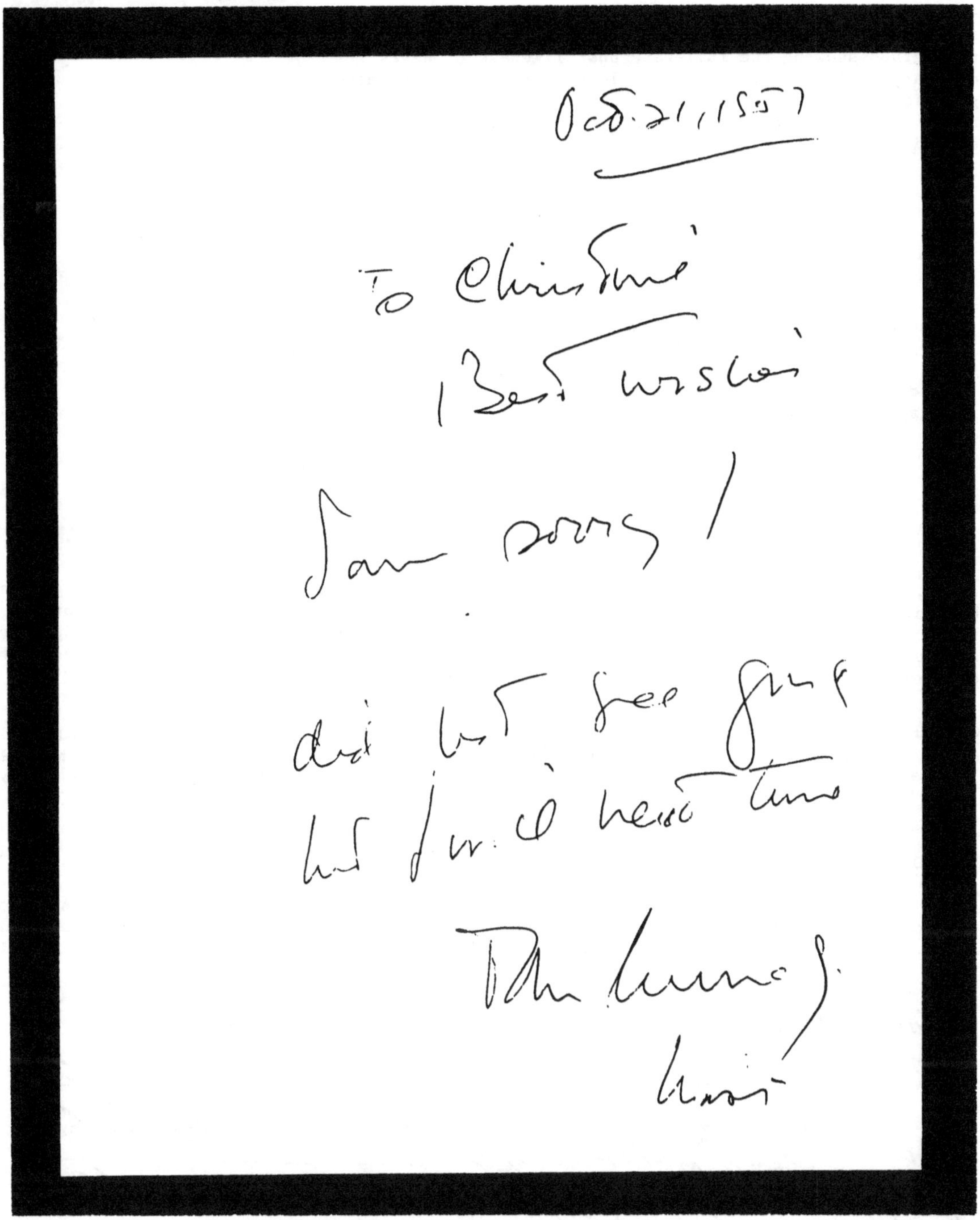
Oct. 21, 1957

To Christine

Best wishes

I am sorry

I did not see you

but I will next time

John Kennedy

Mass.

298. KENNEDY, JOHN F. 1917 - 1963. President; assassinated. Autograph Note Signed "John Kennedy / Mass.", written in blue ball-point ink, while serving in the United States Senate. Full page, small 4to. No place, October 21, 1957. Entire message reads: "To Christine / Best wishes / I am sorry I did not see you but I will next time / John Kennedy / Mass." Attractive, boldly penned example. Fine condition. 1250.00

HONORABLE DISCHARGE FROM THE TANK CORPS

299. EISENHOWER, DWIGHT D. President; General in World War II; planned the Allied Invasion of Europe. Choice, early Partly Printed Document Signed, as "Major, Tank Corps, U.S.A., Commanding". Full page, 4to. Camp Colt, Gettysburg, Penn., September 14, 1918. Certifies that James C. Beene "a Private of 334th Battalion of the Tank Corps...is hereby HONORABLY DISCHARGED from the UNITED STATES ARMY...to accept a commission as 2nd Lieutenant Tank Corps..." Signed "D. D. Eisenhower". Private Beene's "Enlistment Record" is on the verso. 350.00

300. FILLMORE, MILLARD. President and Vice President. Complete address-leaf bearing an oval Buffalo postmark, addressed and franked "Free / M. Fillmore / M.C." in the upper right corner. Addressed by then Congressman Fillmore to David E. Evans, Batavia, New York. Recipient's docket indicates the year to be 1837. Fine example. 250.00

301. HAYES, RUTHERFORD B. President; Governor of Ohio; Union officer in Civil War. Extremely rare albumin carte de visit photograph showing the full-face bust likeness of Hayes in military uniform. Signed on the lower portion of the photographic surface: "R. B. Hayes / Col. 23d Ohio". Identity of photographer not shown. Probably the earliest known signed photograph of the future President. 1500.00

302. GRANT, ULYSSES S. President and General. Handsome proof engraving of President Grant, in formal civilian dress, bust profile likeness, by the Bureau of Engraving & Printing. Small 8vo. Boldly signed by Grant, probably while President, in bright violet ink, beneath his image. Very fine specimen, and rather scarce in this format. 750.00

303. WILSON, WOODROW. President. Typed Letter Signed, as Governor of New Jersey, on the gilt-embossed, crested stationery of his office. 1/2 page, 4to. Executive Department [Trenton], February 20, 1911. To Conrad Reno, Boston, Mass. Original envelope. Wilson acknowledges receipt of "the Tri Partnership bill now before the Massachusetts Legislature", and assures his correspondent: "It will have my careful perusal and consideration...." Fine. 250.00

304. ROOSEVELT, FRANKLIN D. President. Autograph Note Signed. 1 page, oblong 8vo. No place or date. Ca. 1932. To Mr. Philipp. Complete message reads: "Please come up to Dem. Nat. Headquarters 57 St & B'way next Tues or Wed p.m. about 3 o'clock. Sincerely / Franklin D. Roosevelt." Fine holograph specimen with obviously political overtones! 575.00

305. EISENHOWER, DWIGHT D. President and General. Handsome full-face bust photograph, as President Boldly inscribed on the wide lower white margin: "with best wishes from / Dwight D. Eisenhower". Above this inscription a secretary has neatly penned "For: Chester Wiggin". A pencil note on verso indicates that the photograph was delivered to Senator Bridges, probably for a staff member or constituent. Pristine and choice! 200.00

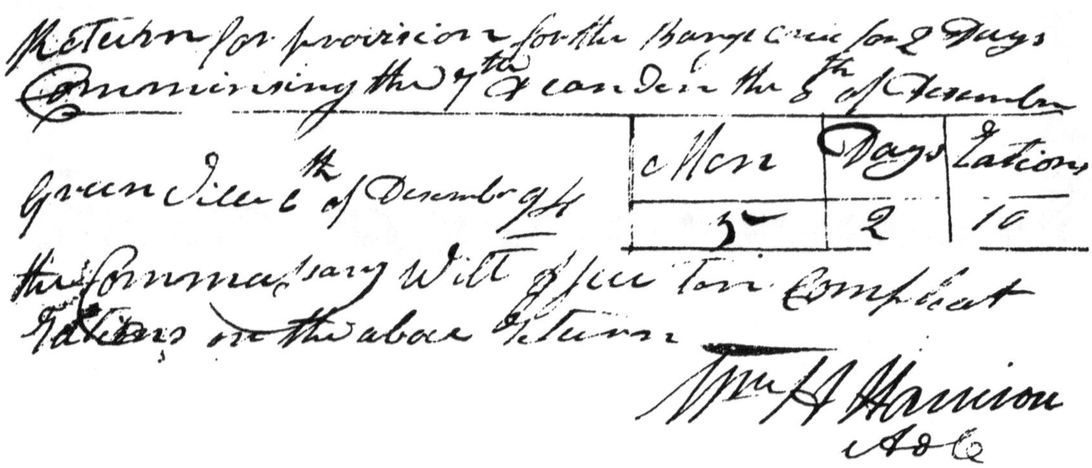
Return for provision for the Barge Crew for 2 Days
Commencing the 7th & ending the 8th of December

Men	Days	Rations
5	2	10

Green Ville 6th of December 94

the Commassary Will issue Ten Compleat
Rations on the above Return

Wm H Harrison
ADC

PROVISION RETURN FOR A BARGE CREW IN THE NORTHWEST TERRITORY

306. HARRISON, WILLIAM HENRY. 1773-1841. President; Secretary of the Northwest Territory; Governor of Indiana Territory; General, commanding the Army of the Northwest in War of 1812; Congressmen and Senator from Ohio. Early Manuscript Document Signed "Wm. H. Harrison / A D C". 1 page, oblong 8vo. Greenville, December 6, 1794. Provision Return for a five-man Barge Crew for two days service. "The Commassary(sic) will issue ten compleat(sic) Rations on the above return." Boldly signed, and in fine condition. With engraved portrait. 495.00

307. TAFT, WILLIAM H. President; Chief Justice, U.S. Supreme Court. Lengthy Autograph Letter Signed, on his imprinted stationery. 7 1/2 pages, 8vo. Hotel Belvidere, Baltimore, 11.30 PM, no date [ca. 1915]. To Mrs. Rhett, wife of the mayor of Charleston, South Carolina, who was recuperating from an illness at Johns Hopkins Hospital. Taft begins by saying that he is pleased that she chose Johns Hopkins for it is "the place where you can be put right more certainly and more expeditiously than any where else in the country....I am very sorry I didn't know you were here for I would have made an effort to go to the Hospital and demand admission to see that you were properly treated. I know a lot of those Johns Hopkins medical men. They are good many of them Yale Men -- Dr. Welsh, Dr. Halstead, Dr. Janeway and Dr. Howland...Then Dr. Llewellyn Barker was consulting physician in Mrs. Taft's case...." Turning to politics, Taft continues: "How is that dear old Democratic husband of yours? Why doesn't the Party put your good men to the front? I believe you have by some mistake a good Governor in South Carolina now. Why not give us all a shock of heart disease and send a gentleman and one with the making of a statesman in time to the Senate. Think it over. Your husband ought to come. They must have forgotten that you and he entertained me by this time ..." And then the Taft children: "Mrs. Taft and I have just been to Bryn Mawr to see Helen gratuate. I am very proud that after having been out of Bryn Mawr for three years in ... gayety at the White [House] Helen had the courage to go back and finish her remaining two years and graduate third in a class of 84 and to win the literary prize of the College. I am hoping she will take three years in graduate work at Yale and receive a Ph.D. degree at Yale. Then with Charley, Bob & Helen we'll have three Yale degrees and one Bryn Mawr. I made the Commencement address at Bryn Mawr and came down here and made another one at Bryn Mawr preparatory school today. I have entered myself for the long distance talking prizes. Bryan and I are the only entries. This war business has given me an advantage. He has to spend at least one day a week in Washington and that is a handicap in our race. Mrs. Taft is better than she has been since she was first stricken in Washington. She likes New Haven. The Society is very pleasant there. We are comfortably situated and New York is near enough to delight the shopper's and the matinee seeker's heart. We had your boy at the house once but I find the boys so busy that visiting a professor's house is something of a burden...." With much more not quoted. A fine rambling, lengthy, yet interesting letter. 1250.00

308. GRANT, ULYSSES S. President; Union General; accepted Lee's surrender. Manuscript Letter Signed "U. S. Grant / Lt. Gen." 1 page, 4to. No place or date. Ca. 1865. Headed "Gentlemen". Grant writes: "I regret that I shall be unable to be present at the meeting of Officers of the Army & Navy, called for the purpose of considering the best means of procuring employment for disabled Soldiers & Sailors &c. I need hardly say that I heartily approve of its object and trust that you will succeed in devising some plan by which work may be provided for all the brave and unfortunate defenders of our Country...." With engraved portrait. Fine. 575.00

LIMITED TO 100 COPIES

309. ROOSEVELT, FRANKLIN D. President. His book: Records of the Town of Hyde Park / Dutchess County. Edited by Franklin D. Roosevelt for the Dutchess County Historical Society. Lettered brown cloth. Hyde Park, N.Y., 1928. On the verso of the front endpaper, opposite the title-page, the future president has penned the limitation notice in his own hand: "No. 44 of 100 Copies / Franklin D. Roosevelt / Hyde Park, 1928". Minor soiling to cloth covers, and front inner hinge neatly repaired. Very scarce. We cannot recall having had this FDR title before. 475.00

310. EISENHOWER, DWIGHT D. President and General. Typed Letter Signed, as President, on imprinted White House stationery. 1 page, 4to. Washington, December 22, 1954. Typed "PERSONAL" twice. To Mrs. George W. Sutton, Jr., New York City. Ike writes: "How very nice of you to send me the Jungle Rugs and Slippers for each of the grandchildren. I am sure they will capture the youngsters' imaginations and that they will present great possibilities for creative play. I am interested to know of your new venture and wish you every success. With best wishes of the season..." Choice condition, with an exceptionally dark bold signature. 450.00

RARE ENVELOPE FRANKED AS PRESIDENT

311. TAYLOR, ZACHARY. President; General on the American Frontier and in Mexican War; died after serving as President for only two years. Complete envelope franked "Z. Taylor" at top right, as President. Addressed in a secretarial hand to Mr. Elias C. Page, Canton, St. Lawrence Co., N.Y. Indistinct "Washington / FREE" postmark. There are some minor tears at the sides, and the envelope is open on three sides. Red wax seal fragment on the verso. An extremely rare presidential frank in satisfactory display condition. Taylor's signature is particularly choice. 1250.00

312. ROOSEVELT, ELEANOR. First Lady. Autograph Letter Signed "Cousin Eleanor", as First Lady, on the vignette-imprinted letterhead of Detroit's Hotel Statler. Full page, small 4to. Detroit [November 17, 1936]. To Mrs. H. C. Milholland, Jr., New York City. Postmarked White House envelope. She writes: "Nancy dear / I just heard from your Mother the sad news & I am so sorry dear for you and Milt. It is a cruel disappointment. I hope when you are better you will come & lunch with me in my New York apartment. May your birthday be a happy day in spite of this sorrow. With love / Cousin Eleanor" Nice family letter! 125.00

313. GARFIELD, JAMES A. President. Manuscript Letter Signed, on imprinted "Mentor, Ohio" stationery. Full page, 8vo. September 11, 1880. To Mr. C. B. Waite, New York, acknowledging receipt of "the portfolio which you so kindly sent me from Paris..." Fine example, signed while a candidate for the Presidency. Garfield was elected in November. 250.00

314. HAYES, LUCY WEBB. First Lady. Attractive sepia cabinet photograph by McKecknie & Oswald, Toledo, Ohio, showing her profile bust image. Signed "Lucy W. Hayes / 1877" on the lower mount area, with the year actually penned on the lower portion of the photograph. Her husband was inaugurated President on March 4, 1877, so this photograph could have been signed as First Lady. Ornate imprint of the photographers on verso. Fine and scarce! 450.00

SCARCE PRESIDENTIAL PARDON

315. JOHNSON, ANDREW. President and Vice President. Manuscript Document Signed, as President. 2 pages, tall folio. Washington, November 11, 1868. Countersigned by F. W. Seward, Acting Secretary of State. The President grants William Connell, alias William Carroll, who was convicted at the age of fourteen for larceny, and was sentenced to three years' imprisonment, pardon after serving nineteen months in prison. Large embossed eagle-vignette wafer seal affixed near the signatures on the second page. Fine condition. 950.00

316. TAFT, WILLIAM H. President; Chief Justice, U.S. Supreme Court. Bound souvenir booklet of the Fourth Annual Banquet of the Ohio Society of Philadelphia held at the Bellevue-Stratford, January 14, 1908. Contains a handsome printed portrait of Taft as Secretary of War, who was the main speaker. In the top blank margin of the portrait Taft has penned: "For Wm. V. Alexander Esq., / With the best wishes of / Wm. H. Taft". The booklet also includes the menu (featuring an eagle vignette), the Program, portraits of the Society's officers, and the names of the participants. Gilt-decorated leather binding. Octavo. Choice! 150.00

MAGNIFICENT STUDIO-SIZE ENGRAVED PORTRAIT

317. GRANT, ULYSSES S. President and General; accepted Lee's surrender. Handsome engraved bust portrait of Grant in civilian dress, probably as President. [Likeness resembles that found on the fifty-dollar bill]. Boldly signed (huge signature) by Grant on the wide margin beneath his image. Attractively mounted and matted, and thus ready for framing. Most impressive. Overall size, including the matt 15 x 20 inches. Some very light foxing which is really not objectionable. Striking exhibition piece. 750.00

318. PIERCE, FRANKLIN. President. Autograph Letter Signed. 3 full pages, 8vo. Rome, March 28, 1859 To Hon. Carroll Spence, Florence, Tuscany. Interesting social letter written by the ex-president while on his tour of the Continent. He writes: "I was very glad to receive your kind note by Mr. Bulen, and intended to send an answer by Mrs. Marcy who left for Florence with her daughter this morning. Circumstances prevented me from seeing her last night, but this may perhaps reach F. as soon as she will and I am sure you will be glad to call on her at once. Mr. French, Brother in law of Mrs. M now Consul at Aix la Chapelle, is detained here by illness and hence any attentions you may find it convenient to extend to Mrs. M...will be doubly acceptable ...We talked of you while they were here as she knows the high esteem which you had for Gov. Marcy. I hope to join them at F. about the 20th of April, and then we may proceed to Venice together....Mrs. Pierce, I regret to say, has been quite indisposed for several days, but I hope she may soon so far recover as to enjoy at least a few days in Rome...." Fine. 750.00

KEEPING FAITH: Memoirs of a President
Jimmy Carter

319. **PRESENTATION EDITION**
This edition is signed, numbered, and limited to 2,500 copies. The book cover is finished in one-piece top-grain cowhide and the spine is hubbed and capped. The binding is Smythe-sewn and the text edges are gilded. 325.00

320. **DELUXE EDITION**
This edition is signed and slipcased. The book cover and slipcase are finished in Centennial blue Buckram cloth. The binding is Smythe-sewn with blue and gold head and foot bands. 95.00

MAGNIFICENT SIGNED IMPERIAL ALBUMIN PHOTOGRAPH

321. GRANT, ULYSSES S. President and Union General. Superb imperial albumin photograph of General Grant, in uniform, by F. Gutekunst, Philadelphia. Boldly signed on the lower mount between his image and the identifying imprint: "U. S. Grant / Lt. Gen. U.S.A.". In fine print under Grant's printed name, it reads: "Entered according to Act of Congress, in the year 1863, in the Clerk's Office of the District Court of the United States for the Eastern District of Pennsylvania, by F. Gutekunst, 712 Arch Street, Philadelphia." On the verso there is an adhesive 5¢ U.S. Internal Revenue stamp, and Gutekunst's imprinted label. Overall size: 11 x 14 1/2 inches. Without question the finest signed photograph of Grant we have handled, and very rarely encountered in this large a size. Excellent condition. 2500.00

ADAMS TO ELBRIDGE GERRY DISCUSSING JEFFERSON'S APPOINTMENT
AS MINISTER TO FRANCE AND MENTIONING DOCTOR
FRANKLIN

322. ADAMS, JOHN. Second President of the United States; Signer of Declaration of Independence; Minister to France, Holland and England. Absolutely superb Autograph Letter Signed, while serving as Minister to France. 4 full pages, 4to. Auteuil near Paris, September 9, 1784. To [Elbridge] Gerry, fellow revolutionary patriot and Signer from Massachusetts. We are able to quote extensively, but not fully, from this magnificent letter.

"The Appointment of Mr. Jefferson is a very happy one. He is as active in Business as he is able, and has nothing so much at Heart as the real Service of his Country. I have known him of old. We have acted together formerly upon trying occasions, and have always been Friends. Neither He nor I, are altered, and I am under no Apprehensions but We shall preserve the Confidence and Friendship of each other. Dr. Franklin has the Stone, which confines him to his House and now and then a Walk of a mile round it. He never goes to Versailles or to Paris, as he can not ride in a Carriage; for this Reason, and to accomodate him, Mr. Jefferson and I have agreed to meet him always at Passy, and do our Business there. Your late Arrangement has done him much good. It has obliged him to Subdue or conceal those Passions, which have tormented him and others for many years. I never saw him in such apparent good Humour, and I shall certainly do nothing to disturb it.

[David] Humphreys is an accomplished Secretary, and a well bred Man. Mr. [W.T.] Franklin has no more Cause of Grief, upon this occasion than Mr. Thaxter, whose education, family, profession and character are as much superior as his Services have been more laborious, hazardous, successful and important, and his rewards have been less....Schemes will be laid to reward the one, while the other will modestly and silently retire. I must pursue the same Course with my Son [John Q. Adams], whom I must send to the Bar, although I know not how to do without him. I don't mean however to oppose or wish to prevent any Notice which any Member of Congress may think proper to propose to be taken of Mr. Franklin.

We have begun to give Notice of our Appointment, and shall probably go on well enough with Several Powers. Spain and England will be difficult. Whether France and Holland & Sweden will agree to the Allerations or any of them I know not. With the Barbary Powers, We cannot treat for Want of Oath....

Our Countrymen, by flying to London with all their Trade and Ships have flattered the Vanity of the English So much that We shall have a thousand Prejudices to contend with in treating with them. They think and Say, that their Trade is so essential to America...the Americans will force their Way to their Ports and Marketts. Treaty or no Treaty, they shall have all our Trade, and therefore they had better keep them selves unbound and free. We will do the best we can but your Limitation of two years will soon be out, and not half the work done.

There is another Limitation too which will shackle Us, very much. You have reduced our Salaries so low, that it is absolutely impossible for Us to live in Character, and see the Company which it is your interest We should see. It is peculiarly hard upon me as I am obliged to furnish my House here with many Articles after having furnished one before in Holland. You will remember you never allowed Us any Thing as all other Nations do to furnish Houses and Tables. Is it your Interest, to give yourselves and your Representatives in Europe an Air of Despicable Meanness, beyond even the Ministers of every petit, two penny Sovereignty, nay even below common Merchants, and ordinary House Keepers, nay I might add below the Style of Living of the Common Girls of the Town, many of whom live in Houses and in Furniture of Twenty Thousand Pounds Stirling Value and at a Rate of Three Thousand Pounds a Year.

However it is your Character not mine that is at State. If you allow me but one hundred Pounds, I wont Spend above 99 of it. When the Cause required it, I Starved my Family. Now it does not and you have Fish & Fur & Leather enough to pay, I will not Starve them any longer...."

Handsomely preserved, this historic letter associates the names of four Signers of the Declaration of Independence, Adams, Jefferson, Franklin and Gerry. It is interesting to note that a few years after this letter was written there developed a serious break in the good relationship between Adams and Jefferson, a deep-seated difference over Federalism as practiced by Adams, and the Democratic Republicanism espoused by Jefferson. 9,500.00

323. MONROE, JAMES. President; Secretary of State; Minister to England. Partly printed Document Signed, as Governor of Virginia. 1 page, small folio, vellum. [Richmond] November 28, 1801. Grant of 19 acres, in exchange for a Land Office Treasury Warrant, in the County of Berkeley. The land is described in terms of poles and stakes. Small wafer seal affixed with red wax. Excellent condition. With engraved portrait. 325.00

TRANSMITTING LETTERS OF MARQUE COMMISSIONS

324. MONROE, JAMES. President. Superb Manuscript Letter Signed, as Secretary of State. Full page, legal folio. Department of State [Washington], June 26, 1812. To the Collector of the Customs, Portsmouth, New Hampshire. Docketed integral leaf. Interesting letter written at the start of the War of 1812 concerning Letters of Marque. In part: "I send...five blank Commissions from No. 171 to 175 inclusive, for such private armed vessels as may be fitted out in your District with a corresponding number of blank bonds, printed instructions, and copies of an act passed this day concerning Letters of Marque, Prizes and Prize goods. These you will deliver to such Citizens of the United States as may apply....In filling up the bonds, you will particularly observe that if the compliment of men belonging to the vessel is no more than one hundred and fifty, the bond is to be for five thousand dollars, if more than that number, then the bond is to be for ten thousand dollars....You will observe that the Commissions are numbered, and for the sake of regularity, it will be proper that you should place corresponding numbers on the instructions and on the bond[s]..." Fine letter showing what was necessary to operate a privateering vessel during the War of 1812. Excellent condition, with Monroe's signature particularly dark and bold. With engraved portrait. 1250.00

325. JOHNSON, ANDREW. President and Vice President. Ornate, partly engraved Document Signed, as President. Tall folio, vellum. Washington, June 1, 1865. Countersigned by EDWIN M. STANTON (stamped signature), Secretary of War. Embossed blue wafer seal of the War Department. Appointment of Samuel M. Mansfield to serve as Captain in the Corps of Engineers. Spread-eagle vignette at head, with another interesting military vignette of flags, rifles, swords, etc., at lower center. Highly decorative document for the den or office. Very clean. 650.00

DEDICATION OF THE MC KINLEY MEMORIAL ORGAN

326. ROOSEVELT, THEODORE. President and Vice President. Typed Letter Signed, as President, on imprinted White House stationery. 1 page, 4to. Washington, December 11, 1908. To Rev. John Wesley Hill, New York City. Roosevelt writes: "I regret that I can not be present with you on the occasion of the dedication of the McKinley Memorial Organ. With all good wishes for the success of the occasion..." President McKinley was assassinated some seven years earlier, and Roosevelt then became President. Fine example. 595.00

327. CLEVELAND, GROVER. President. Partly printed Document Signed, as President. Oblong folio. Washington, March 5, 1894. Countersigned by RICHARD OLNEY, Attorney General. Embossed red wafer seal of the Justice Department at lower left. President Cleveland appoints Anson S. Taylor a Justice of the Peace for the City of Washington. Pressure-mounted to another sheet of paper, and with one closed tear. Excellent appearance. 350.00

328. COOLIDGE, CALVIN. President and Vice President. Impressive partly printed Document Signed, as President. Oblong folio. Washington, June 23, 1924. Countersigned by HARRY S. NEW, Postmaster General. Embossed seal of the Post Office Department (pony express rider) at lower left. Appointment of Howard S. Kiess to serve as Postmaster at Blossburg, Pennsylvania. Attractive condition, with Coolidge's name boldly imprinted at top, and a superb spread-eagle vignette. Ideal for framing or display. 325.00

329. GRANT, ULYSSES S. President; Union General. Brief Autograph Letter Signed, on the embossed monogrammed stationery of his wife. 1 page, 8vo. No place, January 4, 1882. To Mrs. [Hamilton] Fish, wife of his former Secretary of State. The former president writes: "Mrs. Grant asks me to say that it will give her & me pleasure to dine with you on the 17th inst. at 1/2 past seven o'clock...." A polite, clean social note, but still nice association. 350.00

ACKNOWLEDGING A SHIP'S MODEL FOR HIS COLLECTION

330. ROOSEVELT, FRANKLIN D. President. Typed Letter Signed, as President, on imprinted White House stationery. 1 page, 4to. Washington, February 26, 1937. To Andrew T. Durbin, Kenton, Ohio. In part: "...I have been deeply interested in what you say about your father and, of course, I am most appreciative of your kind thought in regard to his desire to present the ship model to me. It has been delivered to me here, and I am delighted to have it...." Fine condition, and a good letter showing FDR at one of his favorite hobbies. 495.00

RECOGNITION OF THE ARGENTINE CONSUL AT PHILADELPHIA

331. BUCHANAN, JAMES. President. Attractive partly printed Document Signed, as President. Small oblong folio. Washington, June 11, 1860. Countersigned by LEWIS CASS, Secretary of State. Embossed white wafer seal of the State Department affixed with red wax at lower left. President Buchanan recognizes Jose Costas y Pujol as "Consul of the Argentine Confederation at Philadelphia..." Excellent condition, and well-suited for display. Portrait. 650.00

332. TAFT, WILLIAM H. President; Chief Justice, U.S. Supreme Court. Typed Letter Signed, as President, on imprinted White House stationery. 1 page, 4to. Beverly, Mass., July 4, 1912. To Hon. John W. Griggs, St. John's Salmon Club, Gaspe, P.Q., Canada. Writing from the Summer White House on the North Shore in Massachusetts, Taft thanks President's McKinley's Attorney General "...for the salmon which you were good enough to send us, and which has arrived in good condition. We will enjoy it immensely...." Nice association! Fine. 425.00

333. TAFT, WILLIAM H. President; Chief Justice, U.S. Supreme Court. Typed Letter Signed, on his imprinted stationery. 1 page, 4to. New Haven, Conn., October 8, 1914. To Hon. Charles G. Washburn, Worcester, Mass. Says that it would be hard for him to come on June 10th, but he would be delighted to do so, and explains: "...I have agreed to go to a classmate's school in Connecticut on the 8th of June, to deliver a commencement address at Wellesley on the 15th and another one at Swarthmore College on the 16th. I submit to you whether that is not all that I ought to undertake, considering the fact that the first part of June I shall be occupied in correcting examination papers of my class and with the details of the end of the college year. I have such a warm friendship for you and for Worcester, that I really hate to decline...." Fine condition, and an interesting post-presidential letter. 195.00

334. HOOVER, HERBERT. President. His book: "The Ordeal of Woodrow Wilson". Blue cloth. New York, 1958. First edition. Lenthy signed presentation inscription to a nurse penned on the front endpaper: "To Mrs. Gladys T. Bolanz / With the Good Wishes / of / Herbert Hoover / May 1, 1958 10.20 A.M. / Presbeterian Hospital / New York." Fine. 150.00

335. GARFIELD, JAMES A. President. Autograph Letter Signed, on imprinted House of Representatives letterhead, while serving in Congress from Ohio. 1 page, 4to. Washington, December 27, 1876. To Hon. Edwards Pierrepont, U. S. Minister, London, England. Congressman Garfield introduces Mr. Thomas J. Wise, "...a worthy Citizen of Youngstown, Ohio, who goes to England for the purpose of transacting some business with the department of Patents. Any attention you may be able to show him will be gratefully received, and will oblige his friends at home...." Handsome letter, boldly penned, and in choice condition. 575.00

336. HOOVER, HERBERT. President. Handsome 8 x 6 engraved vignette of the United States Capitol Building, executed by the Bureau of Engraving & Printing. Boldly signed in bright blue ink by Hoover on the lower white margin. Pristine condition! 195.00

ADVICE FOR A HANDICAPPED PERSON SEEKING A DRIVER'S LICENSE

337. ROOSEVELT, FRANKLIN D. President. Typed Letter Signed, as Governor of New York, on the blue and gold imprinted stationery of that office. 1 page, 4to. Executive Chamber, Albany, December 18, 1929. To Albert Rivington Stone, Hoboken, New Jersey. The future president, himself confined to a wheelchair, offers his handicapped correspondent information on obtaining a driver's license. "...The requirements for a driver in New York are that one has to pass a driver's test. In other words, the New York law says nothing about one having to have the full and free use of both legs and both arms. However, I do not know what the New Jersey law is but some states do have a clause which bars parals. I hope that you will be successful in getting your driver's license. Perhaps I shall see you soon in Warm Springs...." 350.00

POSTMARKED FRANKED ADDRESS-LEAF

338. BUCHANAN, JAMES. President; Secretary of State (Polk); Minister to England; Pennsylvania Senator. Complete address-leaf bearing a light circular Washington postmark, and FREE. Franked (signed) "Free / James Buchanan" in the upper right corner. Addressed by Buchanan to "Col. Reah Frazer / Lancaster / Pennsylvania." Docket by the recipient on verso indicates the year as 1841. With a fine steel-engraved portrait. Nice for framing or display. 225.00

339. EISENHOWER, DWIGHT D. President and General. Typed Letter Signed, as President, on imprinted White House stationery. 1 page, 4to. Washington, October 16, 1959. To Mr. and Mrs. Harry A. Lee, San Francisco. In this "Dear Collie and Harry" letter Ike expresses thanks for their message, adding: "I am truly grateful for your good wishes for my anniversary..." Signed with initials "D. E." Original stamped envelope. Excellent. 295.00

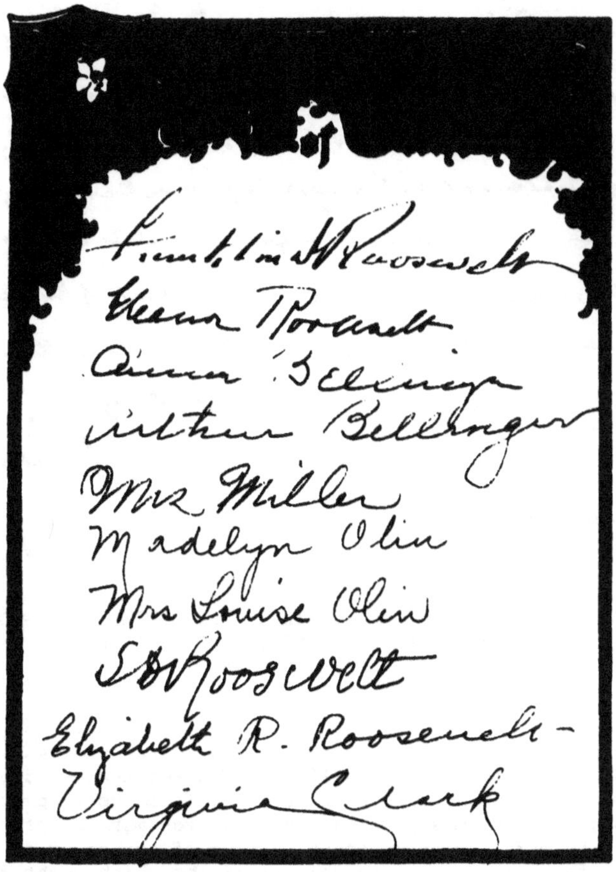

TWO MEMBERS OF ROOSEVELT'S "FAMILY" GET MARRIED AT HYDE PARK, N.Y.

340. ROOSEVELT, FRANKLIN D. President; Governor of New York. His signature, as Governor of New York and Presidential Candidate at the head of the first (of five) pages headed "Congratulations of Guests". Bound in a 12mo white cloth booklet with the gilt imprint Our Wedding on the front cover. Published by The Methodist Book Concern, no date. Souvenir book containing the "Form for the Solemnization of Matrimony with [Marriage] Certificate". The groom was Earl R. Miller, a member of the N.Y. State Police and FDR's personal bodyguard; his bride was Ruth T. Bellinger, a secretary and aid to Mrs. Roosevelt. The marriage was held at Val Kill Cottage, in Hyde Park, September 8, 1932. The Marriage Certificate is signed by Ralph S. Thorn, Pastor of the Methodist Episcopal Church, and witnessed with the signatures of two of the Roosevelt's children, Anna Roosevelt Wall and Elliott Roosevelt. Beneath FDR's signature is that of his wife, Eleanor, and his mother Sara Delano Roosevelt. In addition to family members of the bride and groom, other signing of note include: Grace G. Tully, Marguerite A. [Missy] LeHand, Ernest K. Lindley, Judge Samuel Rosenman and his wife, Malvina Thompson Scheider, Franklin D. Roosevelt, Jr., John Roosevelt, Marion Dickerman and Molly Goodwin. Truly a remarkable assemblege of signatures gathered in a single small volume! Choice condition. 750.00

341. HARRISON, BENJAMIN. President. Bottom half of a partly printed Document Signed, as President. Oblong folio. Washington, June 20, 1889. Countersigned by JAMES G. BLAINE, Secretary of State. Large embossed (eagle vignette) white wafer seal of the Department of State. Although a fragment, complete in itself, and suitable for framing or display. Choice condition, bearing handsome, darkly penned signatures. 150.00

342. TRUMAN, HARRY S. President and Vice President. Typed Letter Signed, on his imprinted stationery. 1 page, 4to. Independence, Missouri, February 14, 1964. To Norman Hostler, Princeton, New Jersey. Gracious letter to an autograph seeker: "It has come to my attention that you would like to have my autographed picture. It is enclosed, herewith. Your wanting it is quite a compliment...." Fine example. 100.00

343. WILSON, WOODROW. President. Typed Letter Signed, as President, on imprinted White House letterhead. Full page, 4to. Washington, May 5, 1914. "To the Diplomatic and Consular Officers of the United States". With original addressed envelope. Wilson writes: "At the instance of Senator Overman, I have pleasure in introducing to you Mr. Phillip S. Henry, an influential citizen of the State of North Carolina, who is about to proceed abroad as a Special Commissioner appointed by the Governor of his State, to investigate Municipal Governments, Conditions and Public Utilities in England and Europe. Mr. Henry will report the result of his investigations to the Governor of North Carolina. I cordially commend Mr. Henry to you for such courtesies and assistance as you may be able to render..." Fine example. 450.00

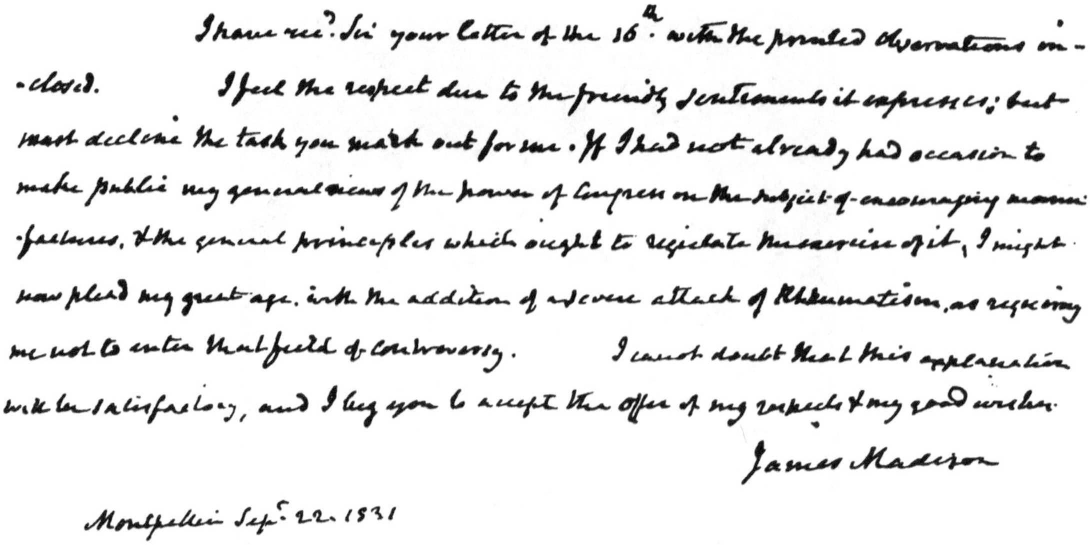
I have rec.d Sir your letter of the 16th with the printed observations in-
-closed. I feel the respect due to the friendly sentiments it expresses; but
must decline the task you mark out for me. If I had not already had occasion to
make public my general views of the power of Congress on the subject of encouraging manu-
-factures, & the general principles which ought to regulate the exercise of it, I might
now plead my great age, with the addition of a severe attack of Rheumatism, as requiring
me not to enter that field of controversy. I cannot doubt that this explanation
will be satisfactory, and I beg you to accept the offer of my respects & my good wishes.
James Madison
Montpellier Sepr 22. 1831

MADISON DECLINES TO ELABORATE ON "MY GENERAL VIEWS OF THE POWER OF CONGRESS ON THE SUBJECT OF ENCOURAGING MANUFACTURES..."

344. MADISON, JAMES. President. Autograph Letter Signed. 1/2 page, 4to. Montpellier [Virginia], September 22, 1831. Recipient not identified. Madison acknowledges his correspondent's letter and printed observations. He continues: "I feel the respect due to the friendly sentiments it expresses; but must decline the task you mark out for me. If I had not already had occasion to make public my general views of the power of Congress on the subject of encouraging manufactures, & the general principles which ought to legislate the exercise of it, I might now plead my great age, with the addition of a severe attack of Rheumatism, as requiring me not to enter that field of controversy...." Fine example. With a superb engraved portrait of Madison suitable for display with his letter. 1,750.00

345. COOLIDGE, CALVIN. President and Vice President; Governor of Massachusetts. Typed Letter Signed, on his imprinted stationery. 1 page, 4to. Northampton, Mass., May 26, 1930. To Rufus N. Hemenway, New Britain, Conn., acknowledging his note and invitation. He writes: "...I am obliged to be in Springfield on Decoration Day so I cannot go to Vermont. I trust you may have a very pleasant day and wish you would give my remembrance to Mrs. Hemenway in which Mrs. Coolidge joins...." Attractive, clean letter! 150.00

346. ROOSEVELT, FRANKLIN D. President. Detailed Typed Letter Signed, as President, on imprinted White House stationery. 1 1/3 separate pages, large 4to. Washington, October 11, 1939. To Hon. James A. Farley, Chairman, Democratic National Committee, Washington, concerning the procedure in filling positions in the Department of Agriculture. FDR explains in detail the meaning of Bureau of the Budget Circular No. 349, issued on July 26, 1939, stating that he does not see how it interferes with the personnel procedures of the Department of Agriculture. He goes on to mention several times the Works Projects Administration as a source for workers. The typist original wrote "My dear Mr. Farley" as the salutation, and Roosevelt crossed out "Mr. Farley", and wrote in "Jim". Splendid association of names! Choice. 950.00

FISHING AND THE BUSINESS CLIMATE

347. CLEVELAND, GROVER. President. Autograph Letter Signed. 3 full closely written pages, 8vo., on stationery embossed with Cleveland's summer address. Gray Gables, Buzzards Bay, Mass., August 24, 1902. To his friend and financial adviser, Commodore E. C. Bennedict, Greenwich, Conn. Original stamped and addressed envelope. In part: "...I have had no particular fishing news to impart that would be interesting to you. I have not been after squeteagues but once since you left, and then with Mr. [Joseph] Jefferson. We caught plenty on that trip, but I had grown sort of tired of that kind of fishing, and have since then turned my attention to bottom and pond fishing and unsuccessful trips after birds. So far as I can hear Brad and I are the only persons who have lately caught any tautog worth talking about. We have had some fine catches by dint of bait other people don't seem to get....I think we can give you some good fishing..." Then turning to the business climate, Cleveland observes: "I have been thinking a great deal lately about the business and financial outlook. If the coal strike and some other matters don't change soon, I believe there will be serious trouble before we are six months older. I don't like to see so many things depending on one man's nod...." This last remark probably refers to President Theodore Roosevelt. Choice condition and content. 450.00

348. CLEVELAND, GROVER. President. Handsome sepia cabinet photograph by Gutekunst, Philadelphia. Shows a dignified formal bust profile of the former President. Signed and dated "1906" by Cleveland on the photographer's mount beneath his image. Choice condition. 495.00

349. TAFT, WILLIAM H. President; Chief Justice, U.S. Supreme Court. Typed Letter Signed, on his imprinted stationery. 1 page, 4to. New Haven, Conn., February 8, 1916. To H. A. Truby, New Kensington, Penn. Original stamped envelope. Taft writes: "...I am sure I don't know where you can secure a set of Mr. Moore's Digest of International Law. I had some difficulty in getting a set myself, but what you ought to do is to write to W. H. Laudermilk and Company, Booksellers...My impression is that I purchased my set through that firm. At any rate, they are the collectors of government publications...." Fine example. 150.00

"WE MUST CARRY THE BATTLE TO EVERY QUARTER"

350. HOOVER, HERBERT. President. Typed Letter Signed, on his imprinted stationery. 1 page, 4to. New York, November 10, 1939. To Hon. David H. Blair, Washington, D.C. Hoover promises to keep in touch with Mr. Morehead, adding: "In the meantime...we will have to see how the situation develops. Certainly we must carry the battle into every quarter...." The "battle" was undoubtedly his fight against most of Franklin Roosevelt's New Deal policies. 125.00

351. COOLIDGE, GRACE. First Lady. Autograph Letter Signed, as the wife of the Vice-President-elect 2 full separate pages, 8vo. Adams House, Boston, November 13, 1920. To Wallace W. Anderson, Manager of the Football Association, Amherst, Mass. Original stamped & addressed envelope. "Thank you very much for your invitation to attend the Amherst - Williams football game in Amherst on Saturday afternoon, November 20th. Nothing would please me better than to take my place on the stand and shout for good old Amherst, but it looks now as though I should have to be in Boston...Here's to Amherst and may she win!..." Fine condition. 95.00

352. ROOSEVELT, FRANKLIN D. President. Typed Letter Signed "F.D.R.", as Governor of New York, on the gilt-embossed stationery of that office. 1 page, 4to. Albany, April 5, 1929. To Jouett Shouse, Kansas City, Missouri. "...I am looking forward with real pleasure to seeing you in Washington at the dinner..." Nice example. 125.00

RONALD REAGAN
WARNER BROS. STUDIOS . BURBANK, CALIFORNIA

Oct. 2

Dear Mrs. Bert

Just a line to tell you how happy I was to see you in Eureka and how much I wish I could have sat and talked to you about old times.

All of us who attended Eureka in those days have some very happy memories — thanks to you; and you can be very proud of the place you have in so many hearts.

College is over for each of us in four years but the memories go on year after year and I think that is the nicest part. I dont have to tell you how many of us will always remember the campus as including a little store up the hill where coffee was waiting right after those 8 oclock classes.

I must close now but again let me say I was happy you could get back — it wouldn't have been Eureka without you.

Love

Dutch

[Item No. 353]

RECALLING HIS UNDERGRADUATE YEARS AT EUREKA COLLEGE

353. REAGAN, RONALD. President of the United States. Remarkable Autograph Letter Signed "Dutch", on his imprinted "Warner Bros. Studios" stationery. 2 separate pages, 8vo. Burbank, California, October 2 [1947]. To Mrs. Bert Hogbin, Danville, Illinois. Original postmarked envelope, addressed by Reagan, and bearing his return-address in his hand (upper left): "Reagan / Warner Bros. / Burbank, Calif." Nostalgic letter to the former proprietor of a little store young Reagan, known as "Dutch" to his friends, used to frequent while a student at Eureka College. He writes: "Just a line to tell you how happy I was to see you in Eureka and how much I wish I could have sat and talked to you about old times. All of us who attended Eureka in those days have some very happy memories -- thanks to you; and you can be very proud of the place you have in so many hearts. College is over for each of us in four years but the memories go on year after year and I think that is the nicest part. I dont have to tell you how many of us will always remember the campus as including a little store up the hill where coffee was waiting right after those 8 o'clock classes....I was happy you could get back -- it wouldn't have been Eureka without you. Love / Dutch" Reagan went back to his alma mater once again in May, 1982, where he delivered the Commencement Address and received an honorary degree. Fine condition, and very scarce with the familiar form of his signature. 1,500.00

354. WILSON, WOODROW. President. Typed Letter Signed, as President, on imprinted White House letterhead. 1 page, 4to. Washington, January 30, 1914. To Mr. E.R.L. Gould. Original stamped envelope. Wilson expresses his appreciation for Gould's letter "...outlining a project for the extension of industrial credits to persons of small means. I have been very greatly interested in reading what you say of the movement, and am gratified to note that it is so well under way...." A fine letter in pristine condition. 400.00

355. HOOVER, HERBERT. President. His fascinating book criticizing the New Deal: The Challenge to Liberty. Gilt-letterd blue cloth. New York, 1934. First edition. Inscribed in bright blue ink on the front endpaper: "To Herbert Clark / With the Kind Regards of / Herbert Hoover." This book may possibly have been inscribed to a relative of Hoover's, as his middle name was Clark. Mint. 125.00

356. CLEVELAND, GROVER. President. Engraved oval proof portrait by the Bureau of Engraving and Printing showing the bust profile image of Cleveland (as depicted on the $1,000 bill). Mounted to octavo size and boldly signed by Cleveland on the mount beneath his likeness. Probably signed while President, but undated. Quite uncommon in this format. Fine. 450.00

357. TRUMAN, HARRY S. President. Typed Letter Signed, on his imprinted stationery. 1 page, 4to. Kansas City, Mo., December 30, 1953. To Hon. Carl H. Claudy, Masonic Service Association, Washington, acknowledging his Christmas note. "I enjoyed our association very much, and I think we made a contribution to the welfare of a great many people...." Fine. 125.00

358. COOLIDGE, CALVIN. President and Vice President. Handsome half-length formal quarto photograph by Bachrach. Probably taken in 1925 while Coolidge was President. Inscribed by Coolidge on the darker area of the photograph, again probably as president: "To Marguerite W. Stoddard / With best wishes, / Calvin Coolidge." Part of Coolidge's large signature is on a lighter part and there are ample white margins on all sides. Stunning pose! Fine. 225.00

359. VAN BUREN, MARTIN. President and Vice President; Secretary of State; Governor of New York. Complete address-leaf franked "Free / M. Van Buren" at upper right. Addressed by the former President to Henry C. Wiley, Saxtons River, Vermont. Faint postmark which does not show in the illustration. Choice condition. With handsome steel-engraved portrait. 225.00

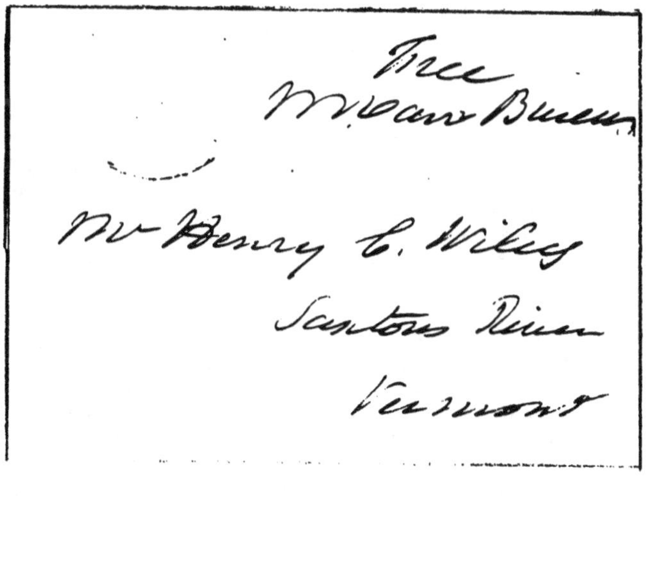
Free
M. Van Buren
Mr Henry C. Wiley
Saxtons River
Vermont

360. [HARRISON, WILLIAM HENRY]. President. Two-page social ALS written by a man from Boston to a friend in Hartford on imprinted political campaign letterhead in support of Harrison's candidacy for the presidency. June 27, 1840. Postmarked integral address-leaf. Only one political remark is made in this letter: "Whigs are wide awake here in B[oston]." Fine. 75.00

PICTORIAL WHITE HOUSE CHRISTMAS CARD

361. ROOSEVELT, ELEANOR. First Lady. Single-panel, postcard-size Christmas Greeting Card from President and Mrs. Roosevelt, dated 1935. Mounted on the left half of the card is an original photograph depicting the Roosevelts seated at a table located on a porch adjacent to the White House garden. She is knitting; he has just looked at the morning paper. In addition to the printed greeting, Mrs. Roosevelt has penned "With love / Cousin Eleanor". Choice! 75.00

BOTH VOLUMES INSCRIBED BY TRUMAN

362. TRUMAN, HARRY S. President and Vice President. His Memoirs: Year of Decision (Volume 1), and Years of Trial and Hope 1946-1952 (Volume 2). New York, 1955-56. Black cloth. First edition. On the half-title page of each volume the former President has penned the following inscription: "To Harry N. Burgess / kindest regards / from / Harry S. Truman / 5-5-59" A fine set of these important Memoirs, with the original imprinted dust-jackets, featuring Truman's portrait on the back portion of the jacket. 325.00

363. WILSON, WOODROW. President. Handsome studio photograph by Harris & Ewing depicting the bust image of the president. Boldly signed "Woodrow Wilson" on the wide lower white margin. Not inscribed to a named person, just signed. Ideal for framing or display. Fine. 450.00

"AS THE LEADER OF THE PARTY..."

364. WILSON, WOODROW. President. Choice Typed Letter Signed, as Governor of New Jersey and President-elect, on the black and gilt-imprinted letterhead of the governorship. 1 page, quarto. Executive Department, State of New Jersey, November 15, 1912. To Mr. M.J. Verdery, New York City. Interesting letter written about ten days after Wilson won the historic three-way contest for the presidency. He writes: "I want to give myself the pleasure not only of acknowledging your kind telegram of congratulation but of expressing in turn my appreciation of the active and intelligent work you have done. As the leader of the party, I feel that I owe you a direct personal expression of sincere thanks...." Fine condition. 350.00

WHO'S WHO IN AMERICA QUESTIONAIRE FORM COMPLETED BY ROOSEVELT

365. ROOSEVELT, FRANKLIN D. President. Printed form sent by the editors of Who's Who in America, containing the entry as it appeared in the previous edition, seeking an update for Volume 14. 1926-1927. Full page, 4to. Ca. 1925. Roosevelt has deleted the lawfirm name of Emmet, Marvin & Roosevelt, and substituted in his own hand "Roosevelt & O'Connor, 1924 - " He adds the fact that he served as Overseer at Harvard University from 1918-24; and that he serves as a Trustee of Vassar College, and the Woodrow Wilson Foundation. He has also penned in the names of his five children which had not previously appeared. An important and interesting piece of FDR memorabilia for the Roosevelt enthusiast!! Fine condition. 450.00

366. CLEVELAND, GROVER. President. Partly printed Document Signed, as President. Oblong folio. Washington, March 10, 1887. Countersigned by WILLIAM F. VILAS, Postmaster General. Gilt-embossed seal of the Post Office Department with red silk ties at lower left. President Cleveland appoints Andrew W. Bingham to serve as postmaster at Littleton, New Hampshire. Cleveland's name is imprinted at top, and there is a spread-eagle vignette like the one illustrated on the front cover of this catalogue. Attractive presidential document. 350.00

SIGNED AS SECRETARY OF WAR, AD INTERIM

367. GRANT, ULYSSES S. President; Union General. Partly printed Document Signed, as Secretary of War, ad interim. Full page, 4to. War Department, Adjutant General's Office, Washington, October 19, 1867. Embossed blue wafer seal of the War Department affixed with blue silk ties. Beneath a signed document by E. D. TOWNSEND, Assistant Adjutant General, stating that an appended document is a true copy from the files, Grant has placed his signature attesting to the fact that Townsend is indeed the Assistant Adjutant General. Documents signed by Grant in this capacity are quite scarce. Fine condition. With portrait. 395.00

THE LIMITATION OF ARMAMENTS CONFERENCE ** 1921

368. HARDING, WARREN G. President. Interesting Typed Letter Signed, as President, on imprinted White House stationery. Full page, 4to. Washington, December 23, 1921. To Mrs. Charles Sumner Bird, Washington, D.C. Harding writes: "I want to tell you how greatly I was pleased when Senator Lodge brought me the other day the remarkable volume of endorsements from Massachusetts Republicans, of the effort which is represented in the Convention for the Limitation of Armament....Such a wonderful testimonial, from the entire Republican organization of the great State of Massachusetts, always a pioneer in every good and human cause, is greatly calculated to encourage and enhearten those who are endeavoring to accomplish this work for the advance of all mankind. I do not need to tell you that we now feel a firm confidence that the Conference is destined to an eminent success. In an impressive measure, that success will be due to the splendid support of the people of the United States, attested in just such testimonials as you have sent to me. Be assured that I shall always preserve this testimonal volume as a particularly prized memento of a notable historic event...." Mrs. Bird, the recipient of this letter, was a member of the Advisory Council to the U.S. Delegation at this historic conference. The letter is very slightly browned in a uniform manner, otherwise fine. 950.00

369. TAYLOR, ZACHARY. President; army officer on the American frontier. Manuscript Letter Signed "Z. Taylor, Maj. Gen'l / U.S.A. Comdg." 1 page, 4to. Head Quarters, Army of Occupation, Camp near Monterey, June 8, 1847. To the Adjutant General of the Army, Washington, concerning his communication "relative to the re-organization of Company G, 2nd Dragoons..." Taylor suggests that "Point Isabel or Matamrovos as a suitable position for the purpose, that is, if it be intended to assign the Company to this line of operations. Capt. Howe has doubtless reported to you under my instructions...." Fine. The following year Taylor was drafted to run for the presidency, and although he did not actively seek it, was easily elected. With engraved portrait. Excellent condition. 850.00

PRESIDENT BUCHANAN PURCHASES CAMDEN & AMBOY RAILROAD BONDS

370. BUCHANAN, JAMES. President; Secretary of State; Minister to England; Pennsylvania Congressman. Autograph Letter Signed, as President. Full page, 4to. Soldiers Home, near Washington, September 26, 1858. To C. H. Fisher. Buchanan writes: "Being in the Country I did not receive your favor...until yesterday at too late an hour to go to Town & obtain a draft on Philadelphia or New York. Tomorrow (Monday) morning, I shall send you a draft for $3320 the price of four Camden & Amboy Bonds of $1000 each, No's 128, 131, 143 & 419 payable in 1889, with Coupons payable on the 1st December and June...." With engraved portrait. Interesting financial letter, and very choice in full holograph as president. 1500.00

371. MC KINLEY, WILLIAM. President; Governor of Ohio; Congressman. Handsome small engraved vignette of the White House [Bureau of Engraving & Printing]. 12mo. Boldly signed by McKinley, as President, on the lower white margin. View shows the back side of the Executive Mansion with children at play on the lawn. Pristine condition. 450.00

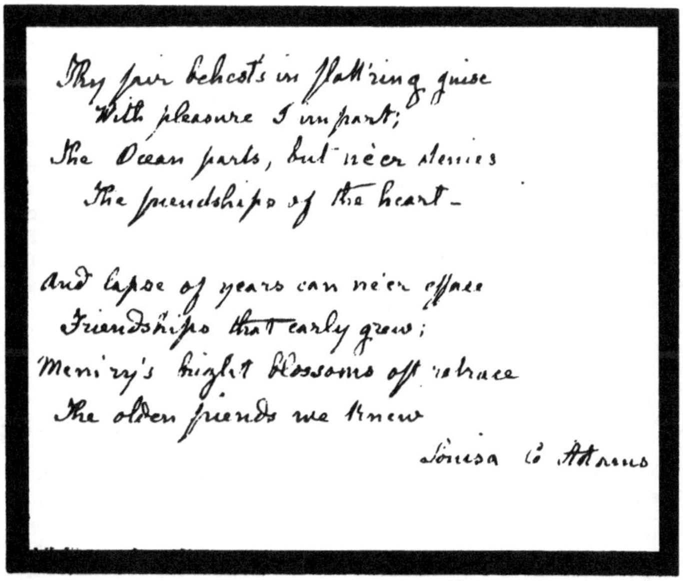

Thy fair behests in flatt'ring guise
With pleasure I impart;
The Ocean parts, but ne'er denies
The friendships of the heart -

And lapse of years can ne'er efface
Friendships that early grow;
Mem'ry's bright blossoms oft retrace
The olden friends we knew
Louisa C Adams

372. ADAMS, LOUISA CATHERINE. First Lady; wife of John Quincy Adams. Autograph Manuscript Poem Signed. 1 page, 12mo. No place or date. Two four-line stanzas about old friends and friendships. John Quincy Adams remains the only President who has been published as a poet, and one occasionally encounters manuscripts of his poetry. However, original poetry of his wife is seldom seen. With handsome steel-engraved portrait. 950.00

UNABLE TO GET HIS PRESIDENTIAL PAPERS IN ORDER

373. CLEVELAND, GROVER. President. Autograph Letter Signed. 2 full pages, 8vo. Princeton, N.J., March 23, 1900. To H. Lockelson. Cleveland writes: "I am ashamed to say that any papers I may possibly have that would be useful to you are in such a state of confusion that I don't think, even if I have them in possession they can be made available. Ever since I left Washington I have been intending to arrange them -- a very little at least -- but nothing of the kind has been done; and it is not likely to be entered upon at present...." Cleveland agrees to meet with his correspondent at a later date. The subject of a former president's papers is always of much interest to autograph collectors. Fine condition. 325.00

SUPERB COLOR PHOTOGRAPH OF THE WHITE HOUSE SIGNED BY 7 FORMER RESIDENTS

374. [PRESIDENTS AND FIRST LADIES ** A CHOICE GROUPING]. Striking, brilliantly colored 10 x 8 colored photograph of the White House in summer, showing the rising fountain and lots of yellow flowers. Signed against the light background of the blue sky by former Presidents GERALD R. FORD and JIMMY CARTER; and by First Ladies BESS TRUMAN, MAMIE D. EISENHOWER, JACQUELINE KENNEDY, BETTY FORD and ROSALYNN CARTER. Remarkable assemblege of autographs!! 650.00

375. JOHNSON, ANDREW. President and Vice President. Attractive partly printed Document Signed, as President. Oblong folio. Washington, February 20, 1866. Countersigned by HUGH MC CULLOCH, Secretary of the Treasury. Embossed seal of the Treasury Department at lower left. Appointment of Jeremiah S. Putnam to be Collector of Customs for the District of York in the State of Maine. Johnson's name is imprinted at top, and there is a different type eagle vignette, this time showing the bird perched on a rock in the ocean. Folds repaired with tissue on verso, else fine. Nice appearing document, and somewhat scarce in this format. 575.00

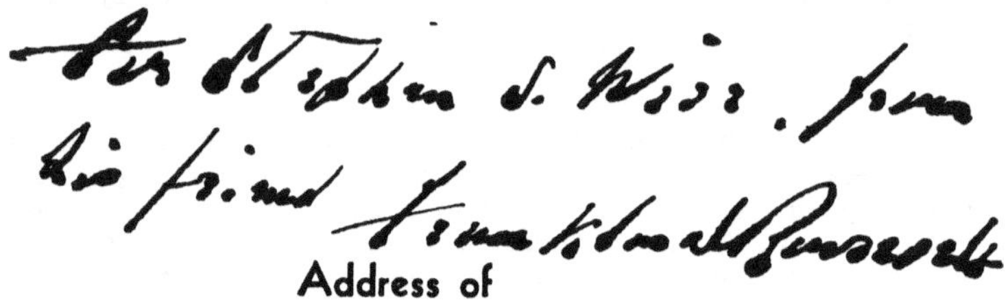
Address of

President Franklin D. Roosevelt

to the

Joint Session of Congress

January 4, 1939

STATE OF THE UNION ADDRESS -- 1939

376. ROOSEVELT, FRANKLIN D. President. Printed self-covered pamphlet containing the text of Roosevelt's Address...to the Joint Session of Congress / January 4, 1939. 8vo. 10 pages. Boldly inscribed in bright blue ink at the top of the front wrapper above the title and his name: "For Stephen S. Wise, from / his friend / Franklin D. Roosevelt". The recipient of this inscribed state of the union message which deals with the impending crisis in Europe and the rebounding domestic economy, was the founding rabbi of the Free Synagogue in New York City; Wise was also founder of the first section of Federation of American Zionists, and of the Zionist Organization of America; he was president of the delegation of American Jewish Congress at the Peace Conference in Paris (1919); president of the American Jewish Congress; founder and president of the Jewish Institute of Religion. Wonderful association! Fine condition, save for two horizontal folds for mailing. 750.00

377. MADISON, JAMES. President. Complete address-leaf franked with Madison's full signature as Secretary of State. Quarto. [Washington, April 1808]. Circular Washington postmark. Addressed in a secretary's hand to the Governor of Pennsylvania, Lancaster. Stamped FREE. At this time THOMAS MC KEAN, the Signer, was Governor of Pennsylvania. Docketed. Very bold franking signature!! With engraved portrait. 350.00

378. FILLMORE, MILLARD. President and Vice President. Autograph Letter Signed. Very full page, tall 8vo. Buffalo, October 17, 1861. To John O. Sergeant, sending "...a letter of introduction to Mr. George Peabody who is the only person that I feel at liberty to address that will be likely to be of service to you. I regret exceedingly the necessity which compels you to leave the country at this time, but sincerely hope that your European tour may prove beneficial to Mrs. S. and that you may both return in safety to your native land...." Attractive, and somewhat intriguing letter, in view of the fact that it was written early in the Civil War. One wonders why Sergeant had to leave the country at that moment!! 325.00

CHOICE HOLOGRAPH LETTER AS PRESIDENT, TO JOHN TYLER'S SON

379. BUCHANAN, JAMES. President. Autograph Letter Signed, as President. 1 1/2 pages, tall 8vo. Washington, October 3, 1859. To Robert Tyler, son of the former president, and shortly to be Register of the Confederate Treasury. Buchanan writes: "...You have indeed performed your entire duty as chairman of the State Convention. Whatever may be the result of the election, you may feel proudly conscience that none of your predecessors have written addresses equal to your own. Indeed they have been marked by signal ability and excellent good sense. I am sorry you have been so badly sustained. Mr. Westcott has been treated very leniently: and this according to my wishes. He has never seemed to recognise in its true character the nature of the offense for which he was removed...." Intriguing political content. Holograph letters of presidential date by Buchanan are quite scarce. 1250.00

DISARMAMENT AND THE NUCLEAR TEST BAN TREATY

380. FORD, GERALD R. President and Vice President. Typed Letter Signed, while representing Michigan's Fifth District in Congress, on imprinted House of Representatives stationery. 1 1/2 separate pages, 4to. Washington, April 26, 1963. To Howard K. Barker, Belmont, Michigan. Ford writes: "...The Burleson-Curtis Resolution...is presently with the House Committee on Foreign Affairs. The Committee has scheduled no action on the resolution but I certainly agree with you that the purpose and intent of the resolution is desirable. It is imperative that any disarmament or nuclear test ban treaty should include fool-proof safeguards to protect the interests of the United States. It seems to me that the proposals...are modest and justifiable and ought to be adopted as the policy of our country as far as disarmament proposals are concerned. I understand that President Kennedy in a speech in Massachusetts did comment on Pope John's encyclical and stated in effect that he applauded it both as a Catholic and as an American...." The remainder of this lengthy letter deals with suggestions for motel accomodations in the Washington area, as his correspondent was planning to visit Washington. 250.00

381. WILSON, WOODROW. President of the United States. Autograph Note Signed "W. W.", as President, on imprinted White House stationery. 1/2 page, 8vo. Washington, December 11, 1917. To [Newton D.] Baker, his Secretary of War. Writing shortly after America's entry into World War I, President Wilson expresses his gratitude for "Summaries" supplied to him by Baker. These were probably war summaries. Wilson is very rare in full holograph, particularly as President. Pristine condition. 350.00

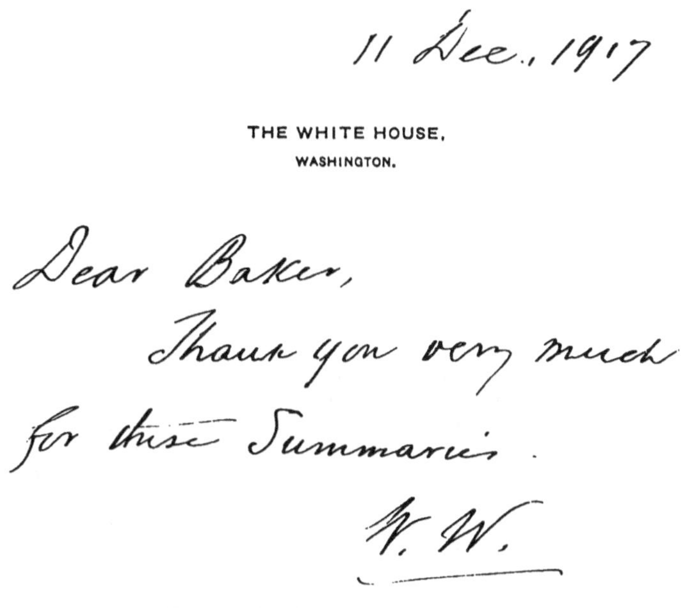
11 Dec., 1917

THE WHITE HOUSE,
WASHINGTON.

Dear Baker,
Thank you very much
for these Summaries.
W. W.

RARE HOLOGRAPH LETTER AS FIRST LADY

382. PIERCE, JANE M. First Lady (wife of President Franklin Pierce). Autograph Letter Signed "J. M. Pierce", undated but as First Lady. 4 pages, 8vo. [Washington] Thursday P.M., no date. To her sister, Mary Aiken, in Andover, Mass. In part: "I think about the dear ones at Andover so constantly that I cannot refrain from writing....I imagine all, and my heart overflows with sympathy and sorrow, and tender & agonising remembrances. We cannot mingle our sighs and tears with yours, beloved friends -- but oh! how deeply do we feel for & with you. My dear brother, who has not dared to admit hope to mingle with his fears from the first, how truly did you see the end of your hopes in regard to the dear boy...." After more on the death of [Alfred], her nephew, and an allusion to the tragic death of her own son, Mrs. Pierce continues: "I am alone. I do not know whether or when we shall go away -- & have even less inclination to now than before. The mail closes soon. My husband is much engaged in his office with urgent affairs -- he intends writing, but feels that he can express so later...." Letters of Mrs. Pierce are very scarce, especially with her full signature. Fine condition. 750.00

383. VAN BUREN, MARTIN. President and Vice President. Manuscript Letter Signed, as Secretary of State in Jackson's cabinet. 1 page, 4to. Department of State, Washington, December 28, 1830. To Anthony Butler, in Mexico, introducing "Mr. George Champley, a citizen of New York who is about to embark for Mexico, on a tour through the Southern Republics. His views are partly commercial & partly scientific; and any friendly attention you may have in your power to show him will be esteemed a favor...." With a fine steel-engraved portrait. 325.00

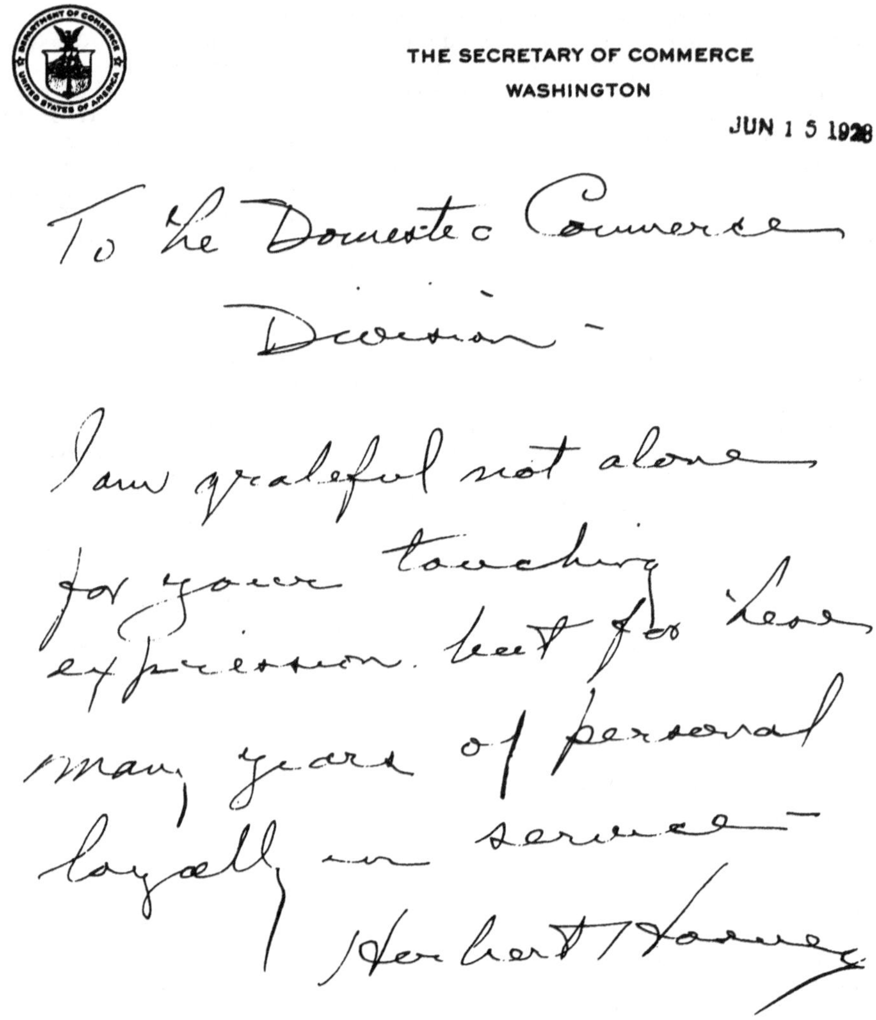

THE SECRETARY OF COMMERCE
WASHINGTON

JUN 1 5 1928

To the Domestic Commerce Division –

I am grateful not alone for your touching expression but for these many years of personal loyalty in service –

Herbert Hoover

384. HOOVER, HERBERT. President; Secretary of Commerce (1921-28). Excessively rare Autograph Letter Signed, as Secretary of Commerce, on imprinted stationery of that office. Full page, 4to. Washington, June 15, 1928. To the Domestic Commerce Division. Hoover resigned his position as head of the Commerce Department when it became obvious that he would be the choice of the Republican Party to run for the Presidency. In this note of appreciation to his colleagues, Hoover writes: "I am grateful not alone for your touching expression, but for these many years of personal loyalty in service. Herbert Hoover" Fine condition, and very rare in full holograph. 2750.00

COMMUTATION OF LIFE SENTENCE FOR A CONVICTED MURDERER

385. MC KINLEY, WILLIAM. President; Governor of Ohio; Congressman and Union officer in Civil War. Ornate partly engraved Document Signed "Wm. Mc Kinley", as Governor of Ohio. Large folio. Columbus, July 23, 1895. Countersigned by Samuel M. Taylor, Secretary of State. Large embossed gilt wafer seal affixed at lower left. Commutation of Walker Henry's life sentence for second degree murder to Sixteen Years, Three Months and Twelve Days (time served) "provided he abstain from the use of intoxicating liquors, and the sale of the same..." Ornate engraved heading with the Ohio State Seal and the Governor's name as "WILLIAM MC KINLEY, JR." A secretary has drawn a red "X" through "JR.", as the Governor's father had died, and he dropped the "JR." from his name and signature at this time. Excellent condition. Choice! 250.00

386. HARDING, WARREN G. President. His Signature " W. G. Harding", as an endorsement, on the integral tab of a partly printed check of The Harding Publishing Company. Oblong 4to. Marion, Ohio, October 25, 1913. Drawn on The Marion County Bank Co., and signed by the treasurer of Harding's company. Payable to Harding for $260 The signed endorsement, instead of being on the verso of the check itself, is conveniently on an integral leaf, so that when opened, one may view both the check and Harding endorsement at the same time. Excellent! 225.00

387. ARTHUR, CHESTER A. President and Vice President. Brief Autograph Document Signed, as Collector of the Port of New York. 1 page, oblong 12mo. No date. Complete text reads: "Referred to Deputy Collector James, Chn. Examing Board. C. A. Arthur / Collector". Fine. 175.00

388. JOHNSON, ANDREW. President and Vice President. Magnificent, ornate, partly engraved Document Signed, as President. Tall folio, vellum. Washington, March 5, 1867. Countersigned by EDWIN M. STANTON (stamped signature), Secretary of War. Lightly embossed seal of the War Department. President Johnson commissions ROBERT D. CLARKE a Paymaster in the U.S. Army. Huge spread-eagle vignette at top center, with another splendid military vignette at bottom. This is a most unusual document in that Johnson very rarely personally signed military commissions after the first several months of his presidency, and it is very rare, indeed, to encounter one as late as 1867. Perhaps the explanation may be that this appointment is for a Paymaster rather than an officer, and because money was involved, the personal signature of Johnson was required. The stamped signature of Secretary Stanton is usually found on Johnson documents of this type. Splendid, fresh condition, and exceptionally clean. Very choice!! 750.00

A COMFORTING EDITORIAL FOR THE BELEAGURED PRESIDENT

389. HARDING, WARREN G. President. Interesting Typed Letter Signed, as President, on imprinted White House stationery. 1 page, 4to. Washington, April 28, 1923. To John C. Shaffer, Chicago Evening Post, Chicago, Illinois. Intriguing letter written at the time of the Teapot Dome scandals when Harding was much under fire: "I appreciate more than I can tell you through this medium, your letter of commendation and approval...and the copy of the Evening Post editorial ...Every day, indeed I may fairly say, is now bringing an increased volume of assurances along the line of your own good letter. To be quite frank with you, I do not believe there will be a very serious burden of opposition to this proposal when it is definitely understood by the country...." Rather astonishing content!! Harding died mysteriously later the same year, his administration rocked with scandal. Excellent condition. 750.00

UNUSUAL PARDON FOR A FARO BANK OPERATOR

390. BUCHANAN, JAMES. President. Highly unusual Manuscript Document Signed, as President. Three pages, tall folio. Washington, January 3, 1861. Countersigned by J. S. BLACK, Secretary of State. Ornately embossed white wafer seal of the State Department affixed with red wax on the third page. President Buchanan commutes the three year sentence imposed on William H. Marquis to one year, citing the following background and reason for executive clemency. Marquis was convicted in the Criminal Court of the District of Columbia for "keeping a faro bank in the City of Washington." The text continues: "And whereas, the conviction...is the first conviction under a statue which has been in force nearly thirty years, but had remained unexecuted on account of the severity of its penalities...I, James Buchanan...[for] good and sufficient reasons...have commuted...the sentence..." This is the first presidential document we can recall having to do with gambling. Strengthened at the folds with tissue, else fine. Truly, a fascinating document for the gaming enthusiast!! 1250.00

A CHRISTMAS REMEMBRANCE FOR LILLIAN [PARKS]

391. EISENHOWER, MAMIE D. First Lady. Imprinted Christmas money envelope bearing the following inscription in Mrs. Eisenhower's hand: "For Lillian from President and Mrs. Eisenhower". The recipient of this gift, a long-time member of the domestic staff at the Executive Mansion, was the subject of the TV docu-drama Back Stairs at the White House. Choice!! 150.00

"REPORT UPON WEIGHTS AND MEASURES"

392. ADAMS, JOHN QUINCY. President. Printed book: Report upon Weights and Measures by...Secretary of State of the United States. Paper-covered boards. Gales & Seaton: Washington, 1821. Probably a First Edition. Inscribed on the inside front cover: "Jonathan Russell Esqr. / From / J. Q. Adams". Bookplate of former owner beneath Adams' inscription. We note that in the Appendix there is the lengthy printed text of a letter from Russell to Adams. Some wear to the paper-covered spine, else very good. Adams is very scarce in signed books, and this one done as Secretary of State, is most desirable. 950.00

PRESIDENT GRANT WRITES THE BELGIAN KING

393. GRANT, ULYSSES S. President. Highly interesting partly printed Document Signed, as President. Full page, 4to. Washington, August 20, 1875. President Grant authorizes the Secretary of State to affix the Seal of the United States to "the envelope of my letter to His Royal Majesty Leopold II, King of the Belgians (Adam Badeau's credentials)..." Badeau served as Military Secretary to Grant from 1864-69, during which time he worked on his three-volume Military History of Ulysses S. Grant. As noted in this document Grant appointed him U.S. Minister to Belgium in 1875. In 1887 Badeau published Grant in Peace. Wonderful association! 500.00

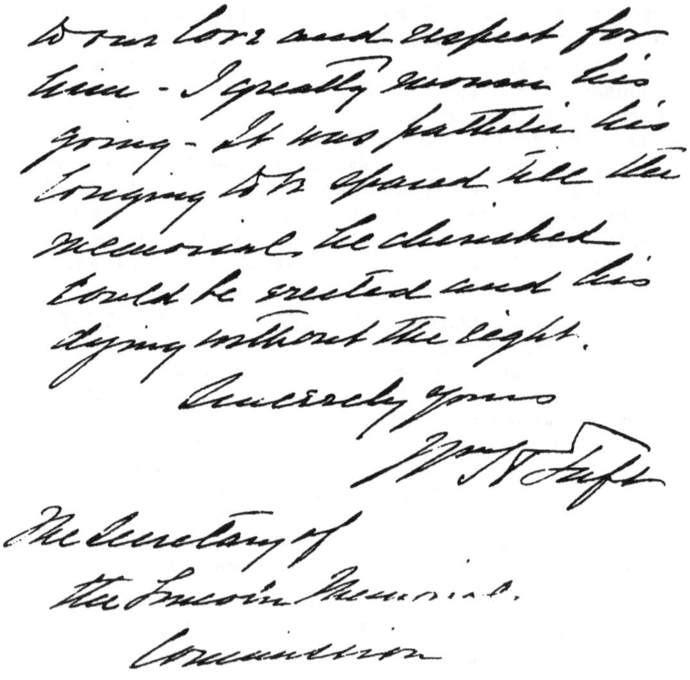
to our love and respect for
him - I greatly mourn his
going - It was pathetic his
longing to be spared till the
memorial, he cherished
could be erected and his
dying without the sight.
Sincerely yours
Wm H Taft
The Secretary of
the Lincoln Memorial
Commission

394. TAFT, WILLIAM HOWARD. President; Chief Justice. Autograph Letter Signed, on the imprinted stationery of Government House. 2 separate pages, 8vo. Ottawa, Canada, January 30, 1914. To the Secretary of the Lincoln Memorial Commission. Taft asks that a meeting be postponed until a time more convenient for him, and taking note of the passing of Senator Shelby M. Cullom of Illinois, who had been Chairman of the Lincoln Memorial Commission. "...The death of Senator Cullom is very sad. I hope he heard of the decision of the Secretary...We must spread some resolutions on our minutes to testify to our love and respect for him. I greatly mourn his going. It was pathetic his longing to be spared till the memorial he cherished could be erected and his dying without the sight...." Scarce in full holograph letters, and an attractive specimen. 750.00

395. EISENHOWER, MAMIE DOUD. First Lady. Autograph Letter Signed, very boldly penned on her gilt-imprinted stationery. 3 full pages, 8vo. [Gettysburg, Pa.] August 31, 1966. To Mrs. Arthur Purvis, Washington, D.C. Original stamped and addressed envelope. She writes: "How very sweet of you to send me the very welcome yellow coat that I borrowed from you twenty-two years ago at West Point. Just a short time ago I sent the picture taken of John and me the day before his graduation to Abilene Museum (Eisenhower) - me, wearing your coat. Now I will send the garment there to be displayed along with the picture. How ever did you keep it so long? Major Dolan called me yesterday from Washington -- she was a nurse at the hospital at West Point and am sure you remember her. She was so good to me when I caught a horrible cold on a Thanksgiving trip up there...." Unusual content! Fine. 150.00

BOOK FROM FILLMORE'S LIBRARY ** SIGNED TWICE AND DATED

396. FILLMORE, MILLARD. President and Vice President. Volume XII of Jared Sparks' Library of American Biography. Second Series. Original pebbled brown cloth. Boston, 1864. Boldly signed by the former President on an early flyleaf, and once again at the top of the title-page: "Millard Fillmore / Jany. 26, 1867". The book contains the biographies of Edward Preble and William Penn. Inner hinges weak, else fine. 350.00

397. TRUMAN, HARRY S. President and Vice President. Typed Letter Signed, as President, on imprinted White House stationery. 1 page, 4to. Washington, February 7, 1946. To Paul Wooton, President, National Press Club, Washington. He writes: "...Mrs. Truman and I enjoyed being present at your inauguration -- our only regret was we couldn't stay through the whole ceremony, but we had made an engagement with Mr. Justice Stone to visit the Art Gallery at nine o'clock. I know you will have a most successful administration because you have the common sense to make it go...." With a newspaper clipping showing a picture of the Trumans and the Wootons together on the occasion referred to above. Very fine. 425.00

398. PIERCE, FRANKLIN. President. Complete address-leaf franked "Free Frank. Pierce" in the upper right corner, and addressed by him to his sister-in-law Mrs. John Aiken in Lowell, Mass. Circular Concord, N.H. postmark. July 12, 1842. Illegal use of the franking privilege to send a three-page ALS of his wife's mother, Elizabeth Appleton, which is also present. Fine example. 275.00

ELEAZER D. WOOD'S COMMISSION AS MAJOR IN THE CORPS OF ENGINEERS
WITH SEVERAL OTHER RELATED WAR OF 1812 LETTERS, ETC. ETC.

399. MADISON, JAMES. President. Important partly printed Document Signed, as President. 1 page, oblong folio. Washington, August 2, 1813. Countersigned by JOHN ARMSTRONG, Secretary of War. With embossed wafer seal of the War Department affixed at top left. President Madison commissions ELEAZER D. WOOD "Major, in the Corps of Engineers, by Brevet". For a biographical account of this important officer in the War of 1812, see Appleton's. Volume VI, page 592. The following important letters are included with this commission.

1. JOHN ARMSTRONG. Manuscript Letter Signed, as Secretary of War. 1 page, 4to. War Department, August 19, 1814. To Lieutenant Colonel Eleazer D. Wood. Armstrong transmits Wood's "Brevet Commission as Lieutenant Colonel...which the President has been pleased to confer upon you as a particular evidence of his approbation of your conduct in the battle of the 25th of July last near the falls of the river Niagara...."

2. ELEAZER D. WOOD. Autograph Letter Signed. 3 full pages, 4to. New York, November 30, 1812. To his sister, Miss Mary Wood, Burlington, Vermont. In part: "...I rec'd...an order to repair with all possible dispatch to the Head Quarters of Gen'l Harrison, who is at or near Detroit, and I am actually thus far on my way to his Army. During the last summer I have been quite actively employed in erecting works and placing New London, and Sag Harbor, on Long Island, in better situation for Defense. I expected to have found Gen'l Dearborn's Army this winter...However as my services are required with the Northern Army, I have no disposition to be elsewhere. I shall spend the winter at Detroit....I have spent 8 years in the Army, for the purpose of imparting myself to render my country a service, and at the same time to promote my own welfare. The period has now arrived when I am to be tested as a soldier -- if I prove to be one, and fortunate; it will no doubt be extremely pleasing & gratifying to you all. If I should fall in the present conflict, you must not grieve nor mourn -- but rejoice that you had a brother to lose for the maintainance and continuation of those sacred rights for which our Revolutionary Patriots bled and fell...."

3. ELEAZER D. WOOD. Autograph Letter Signed. 3 full pages, 4to. West Point, January 24, 1814. To his sister, Miss Mary Wood, Plattsburgh, New York. In part: "...When I was to the Westward, I was surrounded with Indians, and peril of almost losing description; and frequently thought it was doubtful whether I should ever have the pleasure of seeing any of you in this world....When I come home next Spring I'll satisfy you for my long absence. I was out all last winter -- this I hope to spend in the house...."

4. [BATTLE OF FORT ERIE -- AUGUST 15, 1814]. Unsigned manuscript letter, in an unidentified hand, dated Erie, August 16, 1814. 1 1/2 pages, 4to. An important report of the Battle of Fort Erie fought the previous day under the command of Lt. Col. Wood. This letter was probably dictated by Wood right after the battle, but due to his death a few days later, it was left unsigned. The content is highly important as it is a detailed account of this historic battle.

An exceptional small archive of papers from this gallant officer's career. 2500.00

ORATION ON THE LIFE AND CHARACTER OF LAFAYETTE

400. ADAMS, JOHN QUINCY. President. Printed book: Oration on the Life and Character of Gilbert Motier de Lafayette delivered at the Request of Both Houses of the Congress of the United States, before them, in the House of Representatives at Washington, 31st December 1834... First edition in this format. Contemporary gilt-lettered deep blue morocco (slightly worn). Washington, 1835. Bound into this volume after the front endpaper is a special leaf which has been inscribed by the former president: "Joseph B. Anthony / from / John Quincy Adams." Adams sent several of these presentation slips to the publisher for insertion in copies that were bound in full morocco for presentation. Very fine copy. 1250.00

RARE ORDER SIGNED AS BRIGADIER GENERAL

401. GARFIELD, JAMES A. President; Union General in Civil War. Autograph Document Signed " J. A. Garfield / B[rigadier] G[eneral], Chief of Staff". 1 page, oblong 8vo. No place or date. [Early 1863]. Garfield writes: "Cap. J. B. D. / Issue above as Special Order..." What ever was once "above" is now gone. Material signed by Garfield in his capacity as Chief of Staff to General Rosecrans, then commanding the Army of the Cumberland, is scarce. Attractive specimen, in fine condition. With engraved portrait. 275.00

VERY RARE LETTER IN FULL HOLOGRAPH

402. WILSON, WOODROW. President. Autograph Letter Signed, as President of Princeton University. Full page, 8vo. Princeton, New Jersey, October 6, 1902. To Mr. Rich. H. Goebel. The newly elected president of Princeton University writes to an admirer: "I very cheerfully comply with your request for a few lines of my handwriting. A greeting of good cheer go with them!..." Attractive example, and very rare in full holograph. 950.00

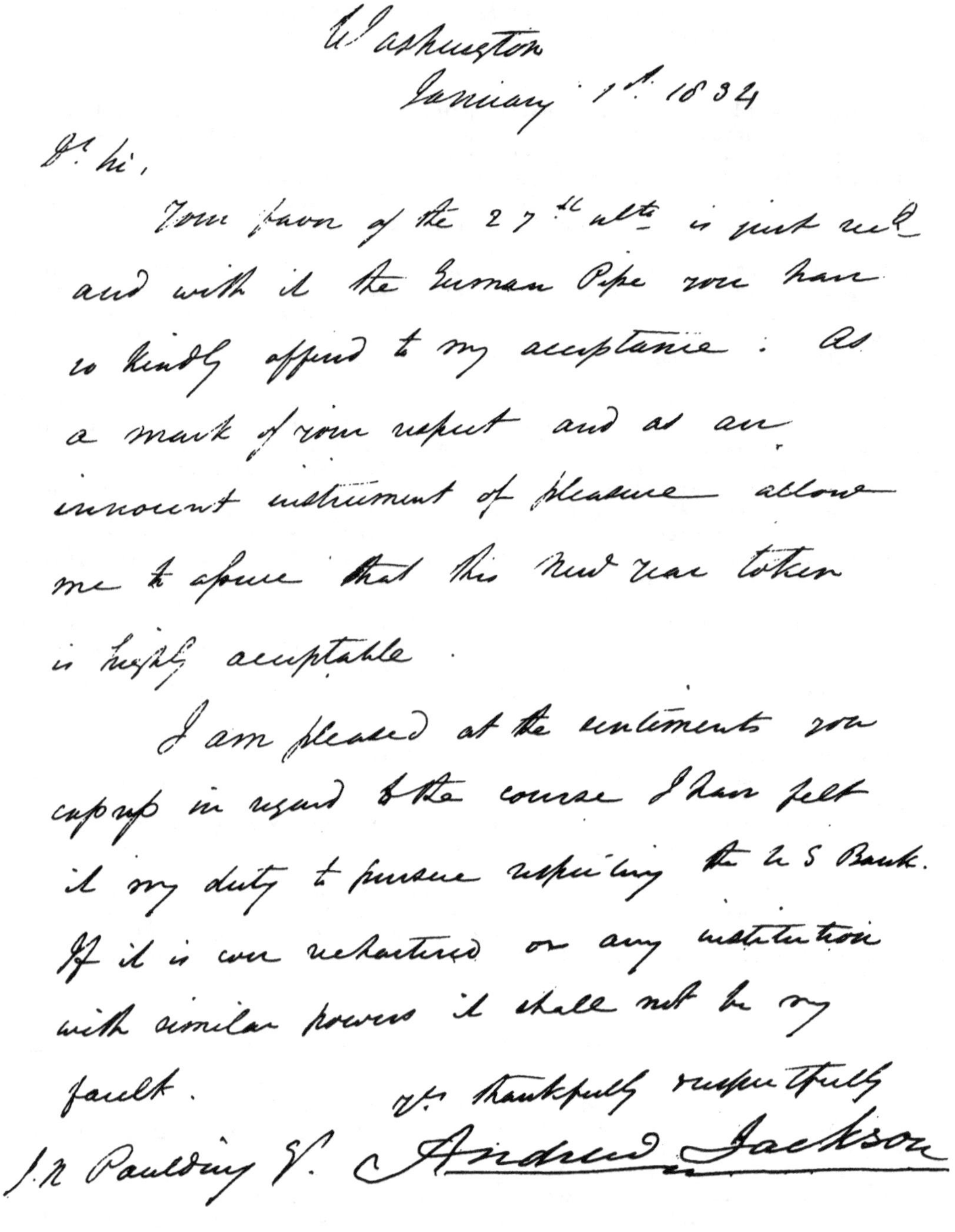
Washington
January 1st. 1834
Dr. Sir,
Your favor of the 27th ulto. is just recd. and with it the German Pipe you have so kindly offered to my acceptance: As a mark of your respect and as an innocent instrument of pleasure allow me to assure that this New Year token is highly acceptable.
I am pleased at the sentiments you express in regard to the course I have felt it my duty to pursue respecting the U S Bank. If it is ever rechartered or any institution with similar powers it shall not be my fault.
Yrs thankfully respectfully
J. K Paulding Esq. Andrew Jackson

PRESIDENT JACKSON SPEAKS OUT ON THE BANKING ISSUE

403. JACKSON, ANDREW. President of the United States; General in War of 1812, where he was the hero of the Battle of New Orleans. Outstanding Manuscript Letter Signed, as President. Full page, quarto. Washington, January 1, 1834. To J[ames] K. Paulding, the writer, then serving as Navy Agent in New York City. President Jackson acknowledges the gift of a German Pipe: "...As a mark of your respect and as an innocent instrument of pleasure allow me to assure you that this new year token is highly acceptable...." In the concluding paragraph he comments on the most important domestic issue of his presidency, the renewal of the Charter of the Bank of the United States: "...I am pleased at the sentiments you express in regard to the course I have felt it my duty to pursue respecting the U.S. Bank. If it is ever rechartered or any institution with similar powers it shall not be my fault...." Excellent condition, and historically important. With handsome steel-engraved portrait. 3500.00

IKE'S FIRST TERM PRESIDENTIAL MEMOIRS

404. EISENHOWER, DWIGHT D. President and General. His presidential memoirs: The White House Years / Mandate for Change / 1953-1956. Olive cloth. New York, 1963. First edition. Copy #199 of a special edition of 1500 numbered copies signed by Eisenhower on an otherwise blank leaf opposite the colophon page. Mint, in publisher's decorated box. 250.00

SCARCE HOLOGRAPH LETTER TO HIS BROTHER-IN-LAW

405. ARTHUR, CHESTER A. President and Vice President. Autograph Letter Signed. 3 very full pages, large 8vo. New York, May 2 [1878]. To John E. Mc Elroy, his brother-in-law, then in Albany. Arthur, then Collector of Customs for the Port of New York, writes: "I received your note... enclosing one from Dr. Herndon. I have had some correspondence with him about his sailing & there has been some confusion in the matter growing out of his supposition that the Devonia (Capt. Craig) sailed on the 18th May. The Anchonia sails on the 18th May & the California on the 25th. I have engaged a state room on the Anchonia & have written to him that if he desired to change & go on the 25th (Capt Craig not being in command of the Anchonia) I could make such arrangement....I do not know yet what the charge will be for passage &c & return - but I have no doubt there will be some reduction at my request. If not there will be time to arrange it through you....I am awfully lonesome & not at all well. Love to Molly...." On the verso of the third page there is a holograph note in pencil by C. A. Arthur III concerning the background of this family letter. Fine condition, and very scarce in holograph. 1250.00

406. ROOSEVELT, FRANKLIN D. President. Attractive sepia quarto photograph, close-up bust pose of FDR as Governor of New York, by the photographer, Ortho. Inscribed on the lower white margin: "For Harold Payson / with my sincere regards / Franklin D. Roosevelt". Mounted. Ideal for framing or display. 225.00

407. PIERCE, FRANKLIN. President. Autograph Letter Signed. 4 full pages, 8vo. Island of Capri, January 22, 1859. To Hon. Carroll Spence, Florida. Long, rambling letter written by the former President while touring Europe. "I intended to write you from Naples, but we remained there only a week and our time was constantly occupied in visiting the various rooms of the Museo Borbonico, Pompeii and other places...At Leghorn I made arrangements without trouble, for sending the box of pictures by a vessel...bound for Boston....We found very satisfactory accomodations at the Hotel Victoria & Washington and had an excellent Steamer (the Vatican) and fine weather for our trip to Naples. On our arrival Mr. Consul Hammet came to the Steamer and was very kind in his attentions. I availed myself of the opportunity to hand him the fourteen Napoleons...At the Custom House we were met by Mr. Chandler who was unremitting in his efforts to contribute to our enjoyment...It was very pleasant to Mrs. Pierce to meet Mrs. C. with whom she was acquainted at Washington....We came here some weeks ago and as we have not been upon the main land since you may well infer that we are pleased with the Island, the climate, and Hotel Tibrio. Mrs. P. has been somewhat indisposed...I think in consequence of too much exposure in her walks and an excursion by boat to the green grotto, but she took a ride on horseback this morning....I infer from letters which I have received from Mr. Hawthorne that we have been better off here than we should have been in the Eternal City so far as climate is concerned. He speaks of the weather as cold and damp and says that his wife and two of his children have been quite ill...." Series of tiny holes in left margin where the letter was originally sewn into a volume, otherwise quite fine. 875.00

SHIP'S PASSPORT IN BLANK, WITH THE VIGNETTE UNCUT AT TOP

408. GRANT, ULYSSES S. President; Union General. Handsome, partly engraved Document Signed, as President. 1 page, tall folio. [Washington], no date. Countersigned by HAMILTON FISH, Secretary of State. Large white wafer seal affixed at lower left. A Mediterranean Ship's Passport, in blank (not filled out), similar in design to Item No. 58 in this catalogue. However, since the document is unissued, the splendid nautical vignette of a fully-rigged clipper ship is in tact. We were told that this is the only known example of an unissued ship's passport signed by Grant, and indeed, we cannot recall having seen one of this type either issued or unissued. Choice, clean condition, and a striking display piece! 1250.00

409. FORD, GERALD R. President and Vice President. Typed Letter Signed, on imprinted House of Representatives stationery. 1 page, 4to. Washington, February 4, 1966. To Anita M. Gilleo, c/o U.S. Embassy, Beirut. Original envelope. In response to Ms. Gilleo's letter concerning "criticisms made of our government by certain persons in Lebanon", Ford replies "The type of charges and claims...appear to be going on from time to time. They may be inspired on certain occasions by efforts of other governments or they may be simply based on rumor or personal feelings of the individuals involved...." Interesting content! 175.00

"I HOPE...THAT I AM THE SORT OF MAN YOU WOULD LIKE TO SUPPORT AND KEEP AS YOUR FRIEND..."

410. WILSON, WOODROW. President. Remarkable Typed Letter Signed, as the Democratic candidate for president, just days before his election to that office, on his imprinted stationery. 1 page, 4to. Trenton, New Jersey, November 1, 1912. To Miss Kittie Petersen, Farnam, Nebraska. With original postmarked envelope. The future president takes time from his busy campaign schedule to write "My dear little Friend" that he "...cannot tell you what gratification it gives me that you should think of me. Your letter has given me a great deal of genuine pleasure, and I hope that as the years go on you will continue to feel that I am the sort of man you would like to support and keep as your friend...." Fine condition, and quite unusual! 450.00

411. GRANT, ULYSSES S. President and Union General. Handsome large cabinet photograph. Boldly inscribed on the lower portion of the photographic surface: "With the compliments / of / U. S. Grant / May 15th 1882." Superb, sharp image. Excellent condition. 950.00

412. VAN BUREN, MARTIN. President and Vice President. Autograph Letter Signed. 4 full pages, 8vo Lindenwald, Kinderhook [New York], September 4, 1861. To J. T. Randolph. Penned on Van Buren's blind-stamped stationery. The aged ex-president writes: "Many thanks...for your very acceptable present & still more for the kind regards of my excellent friend Mrs. R which you have been pleased to communicate. I can say with perfect sincerity that I have seldom met with persons who made such favourable impressions upon me as was the case with both of you during our agreeable sojourn at Shaws. If I ever come to N. York again, which will I hope be the case before long, I shall not fail to find you. The wines are both very superior and I will thank you to inform me...which wines can be ordered here from Spain, & at what prices by the quarter cask...." Fine condition. 495.00

413. POLK, JAMES K. President. Attractive partly printed Document Signed, as President. 1 page, 4to. Washington, November 3, 1845. Authorizes the Secretary of State to affix the Seal of the United States to "the envelope of a congratulatory letter addressed to the Emperor of Austria, on the birth of a Princess..." Mint, fresh condition, with all the writing darkly penned. Accompanied by a handsome steel-engraved portrait. 1000.00

414. DAVIS, JEFFERSON. President of the Confederate States of America; Secretary of War (Pierce); U.S. Senator from Mississippi; Zachary Taylor's son-in-law. Autograph Letter Signed. 3 pages, tall 8vo. New York, July 7, 1873. To Mrs. A. M. Upshur, regarding her father's will. In part: "...You have not told me what was the amount of your claim, nor what provision was made in regard to you in your Father's will. As Executor no doubt Mr. Briscoe could be made responsible for your Father's estate, but the letter of your attorneys implies doubt as to whether a judgement against him would have any money value. The small amount he offers and the delay which he finds it necessary to ask for in the payment of that small amount does not accord with your idea of his wealth. I knew his Father well, not so much of the son, but cannot suppose him capable of fraud or deception..." Davis goes on to discuss the lady's land claims in Louisiana, and finally advises her to rely on some attorney who is on the spot. Davis concludes: "Accept my thanks for your kind wishes for me and mine, but I have to acknowledge that the material prosperity you wish for me has not yet been attained..." Fine. 750.00

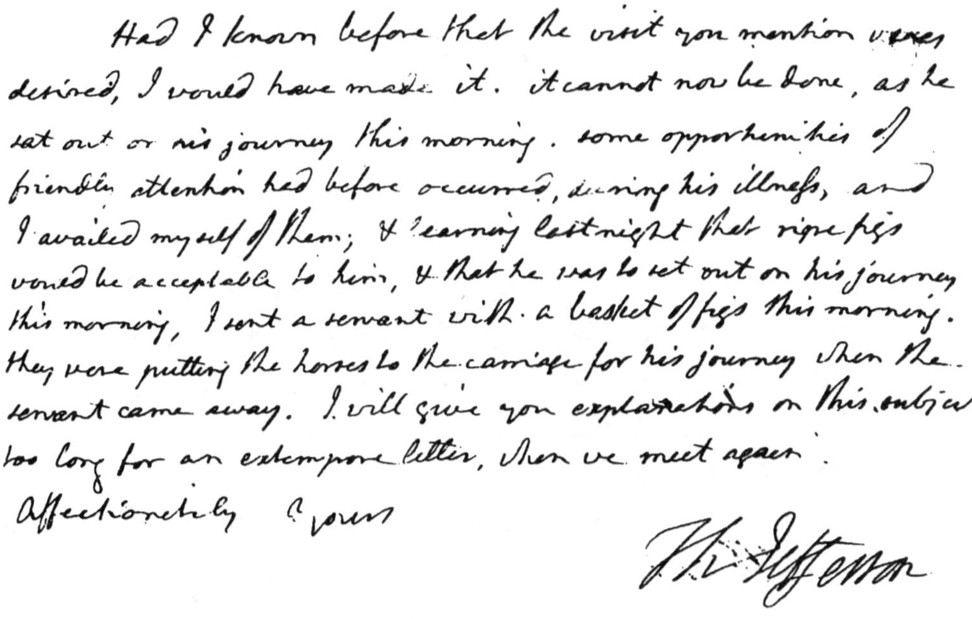
Had I known before that the visit you mention was
desired, I would have made it. it cannot now be done, as he
sat out on his journey this morning. some opportunities of
friendly attention had before occurred, during his illness, and
I availed myself of them; & learning last night that ripe figs
would be acceptable to him, & that he was to set out on his journey
this morning, I sent a servant with a basket of figs this morning.
they were putting the horses to the carriage for his journey when the
servant came away. I will give you explanations on this subject
too long for an extempore letter, when we meet again.
Affectionately yours
Th: Jefferson

TO HIS VIRGINIA NEIGHBOUR, COLONEL JAMES MONROE

415. JEFFERSON, THOMAS. President and Vice President; Signer; Governor of Virginia. Autograph Letter Signed. 1/2 page, 4to. No place, no date. To Colonel [James] Monroe, whose two-line docket appears on the integral address-leaf. Docketed in another hand as being "1809", so possibly written as President, as Jefferson held that office until March 4, 1809. Jefferson writes: "Had I known before that the visit you mention was desired, I would have made it. It cannot now be done, he [Mr. Walker] sat out on his journey this morning. Some opportunities of friendly attention had before occurred, during his illness, and I availed myself of them; & learning last night that ripe figs would be acceptable to him, & that he was to set out on his journey this morning, I sent a servant with a basket of figs this morning. They were putting the horses to the carriage for his journey when the servant came away. I will give you explanations on this subject too long for an extempore letter, when we meet again. Affectionately yours..." Probably written from Monticello, as Monroe's residence was situated less than two miles from Jefferson's. Small seal tear in extreme left blank margin, far from the text, otherwise in extremely fresh condition. Letters exchanged between Presidents are highly desirable, and seldom appear on the market. With engraved portraits of Jefferson and Monroe. 4950.00

416. MC KINLEY, WILLIAM. President. Typed Letter Signed, as Governor of Ohio, on imprinted letterhead of that office. 1 page, 4to. Columbus, June 6, 1894. To Frederick A. Ross, Mayor, Terre Haute, Indiana, regretting his inability "...to join in the reception to be tendered Col. Thompson...on the anniversary of his 85th birthday." McKinley states that "public duties prevent my leaving the state at that time", and concludes: "I beg that you will convey to Col. Thompson my most cordial personal congratulations, and heartfelt wish that he will live many more years to enjoy...the respect and love of all who know him...." Fine. 250.00

417. NIXON, RICHARD M. President and Vice President. His ornately imprinted blue and gold bookplate designed for insertion in his Memoirs. Inscribed: "Etta Capraro / With best wishes for / Christmas - 1978 / from / Richard Nixon". Attractive specimen! 75.00

418. COOLIDGE, CALVIN. President and Vice President. Handsome sepia studio photograph by Harris & Ewing [Washington], showing a bust profile image of "Silent Cal". Boldly inscribed on the lower wide margin: "To Leo C. May, / With Regards, / Calvin Coolidge". Choice! 250.00

419. FILLMORE, MILLARD. President and Vice President. Manuscript Letter Signed, as President, with a two-line initialed holograph postscript in his hand. Full page, 4to. Washington, June 4, 1851. To Alvan Kellogg, East Scott, stating that he forwarded his letter to the Post Master General and "wrote a few words in favor of the appointment of your son-in-law as Post Master at Bath..." Fillmore continues: "But I regret to learn today that another was appointed to fill that place, a few days before your letter was received..." In the holograph postscript, he adds: "Make my kindest regards to Mrs. Kellogg, whom as well as yourself, I recollect with unfeigned satisfaction and esteem. M.F." Fillmore's letters of presidential date are rather scarce, as he held that office for only three years. With engraved portrait. 950.00

Philadelphia Oct. 20th 1792.

Sir,

I have been honored with your polite letter of the 23d of May, together with the works of your late Right Reverend father, Lord Bishop of St. Asaph, which accompanied it.

For the character & sentiments of that venerable & amiable Divine, while living, I entertained the most perfect esteem; and have a sincere respect for his memory, now he is no more. —

My best thanks are due to you for his works, and the mark of your attention in sending them to me, — and especially for the flattering expressions respecting myself, which are contained in your letter. —

I am — Sir
Yr most Obed Hble Ser

G. Washington

The Revd. Doctr. Shipley.

SUPERB HOLOGRAPH LETTER AS PRESIDENT

420. WASHINGTON, GEORGE. First President of the United States; Commander-in-Chief of the American Army during the Revolution. Magnificent Autograph Letter Signed, as President. Full page, 4to. Philadelphia, October 20, 1792. To the Rev. Doctor [William D.] Shipley (1745-1826), the liberal English Unitarian minister who had published the works of his father, Jonathan, the Anglican Bishop of St. Asaph. Washington writes:

> "I have been honored with your polite letter of the 23d of May, together with the works of your late Right Reverend father, Lord Bishop of St. Asaph, which accompanied it.
>
> For the character & sentiments of that venerable & admiable Divine, while living, I entertained the most perfect esteem; and have a sincere respect for his memory, now he is no more.
>
> My best thanks are due to you for his works, and the mark of your attention in sending them to me, -- and especially for the flattering expressions respecting myself, which are contained in your letter...."

Attractive letter in bright, fresh condition; there are very light mounting stains at each blank corner, but these are quite small and inconsequential. Handsome display piece, and an ideal single-page Washington letter of presidential date. 7500.00

421. FORD, GERALD R. President and Vice President (not popularly elected to either office). Typed Letter Signed "Gerald R. Ford", on his gilt-embossed crested stationery. 1 page, 4to. No place, January 5, 1981. To Bill Walker, Middletown, New York. Original addressed envelope bearing Ford's facsimile franking signature. He writes: "I sincerely appreciate the spirit of friendship which prompted you to send your book, THE CLEVELAND INDIANS....Although I do not get to as many games as I would like, I am a baseball fan and the Cleveland Indians do have a great history. Best of success and happiness to you in 1981...." Fine. 225.00

422. CLEVELAND, GROVER. President. Autograph Letter Signed. 2 full pages, 8vo. Tamworth, N. H., July 27, 1905. To Frank D. Marshall, Portland, Maine. Original stamped envelope addressed by the former president. Cleveland responds to an invitation to become a director of the Thomas Brackett Reed Memorial Association. Reed, a Congressman from Maine, had served as Speaker of the House during parts of both of Cleveland's administrations. He writes: "...I had great admiration for Mr. Reed and great respect for his ability. I think it is eminently proper that his high character and public service should be fittingly memorialized. It seems to me, however, that this should be undertaken by those in every way known to him in every way than I can claim to have. Another reason stronger than this for hesitation is found in my reluctance to be identified with a project to which I cannot give the least attention. I am not at all satisfied to be nominally a director in such a movement without performing any useful duty.... I do not want to be suspected of ungraciousness or lack of interest; but if I may be allowed to modestly contribute instead of appearing as a director I shall feel much more comfortable ...." Fine association and content. 350.00

423. POLK, JAMES K. President; Speaker of U.S. House. Partly printed Document Signed "James K. Polk", as Governor of Tennessee. 1 page, tall folio. July 5, 1841. Grant of land in the Ocoee District of Tennessee to Wyatt Stubblefield. Countersigned by the Secretary and Register. Fine condition. All material signed by Polk has become scarce. 650.00

424. TRUMAN, HARRY S President and Vice President. Handsome printed bust portrait from a photograph by Chase-Statler, neatly mounted on heavy paper. Boldly signed, probably as President, on the lower mount: "Best wishes / Harry S Truman". Not inscribed to a named individual. Quarto. Striking portrait study of Truman; full-face bust likeness. Excellent! 125.00

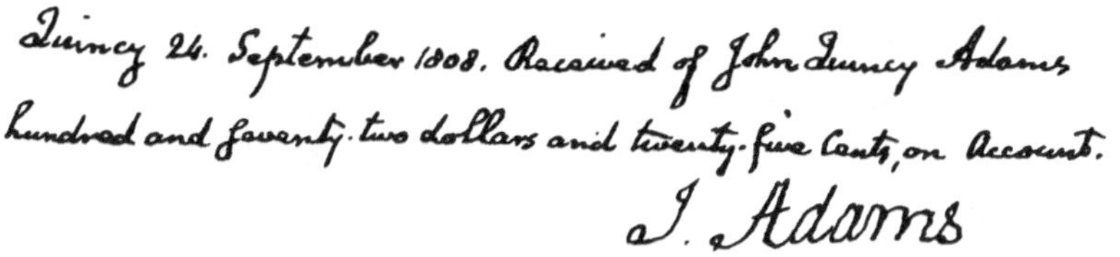
Quincy 24. September 1808. Received of John Quincy Adams
two hundred and seventy-two dollars and twenty-five Cents, on Account.
J. Adams

FATHER AND SON, TWO PRESIDENTS ON THE SAME DOCUMENT

425. ADAMS, JOHN. President and Vice President of the United States; Signer of Declaration of Independence; U.S. Minister to Holland and England. Manuscript Document Signed "J. Adams", the text being fully in the hand of his son, and later President, John Quincy Adams. Oblong 12mo. Quincy [Mass.], September 24, 1808. Receipt given by the elder Adams to his son, reading: "...Received of John Quincy Adams / two hundred and seventy-two dollars and twenty five cents, on Account. / J. Adams". Docketed in the son's hand on the verso "My Father -- 24 Sept'r 1808 / $272.25." Unusual document, bearing the signatures of father and son, the only such combination to both serve as President of the United States. Fine condition. With matching portraits of the two Adams's. Nice ensemble for framing. 2,250.00

EXTRAORDINARILY RARE PRESIDENTIAL FRANK

426. NIXON, RICHARD M. President; Vice President; U.S. Senator from California. Excessively rare free franked envelope, bearing his signature (frank) "Richard Nixon" in the upper right corner. Postmarked "Washington, D.C., Feb. 6, 1951". Stamped address of Russell E. Silvius, a noted collector. Franked while a member of the Senate. This is the first franked envelope of Nixon we have encountered. A modern rarity!! Fine. 1500.00

427. HAYES, RUTHERFORD B. President. Autograph Sentiment Signed "Rutherford B. Hayes", penned on a 12mo leaf. "Truth and Honesty -- Always -- / Rutherford B. Hayes". Neatly matted and newly framed under glass in a 1/2 inch antique-gilt frame, with a handsome engraved portrait. Very scarce in this format, and a striking ensemble. 475.00

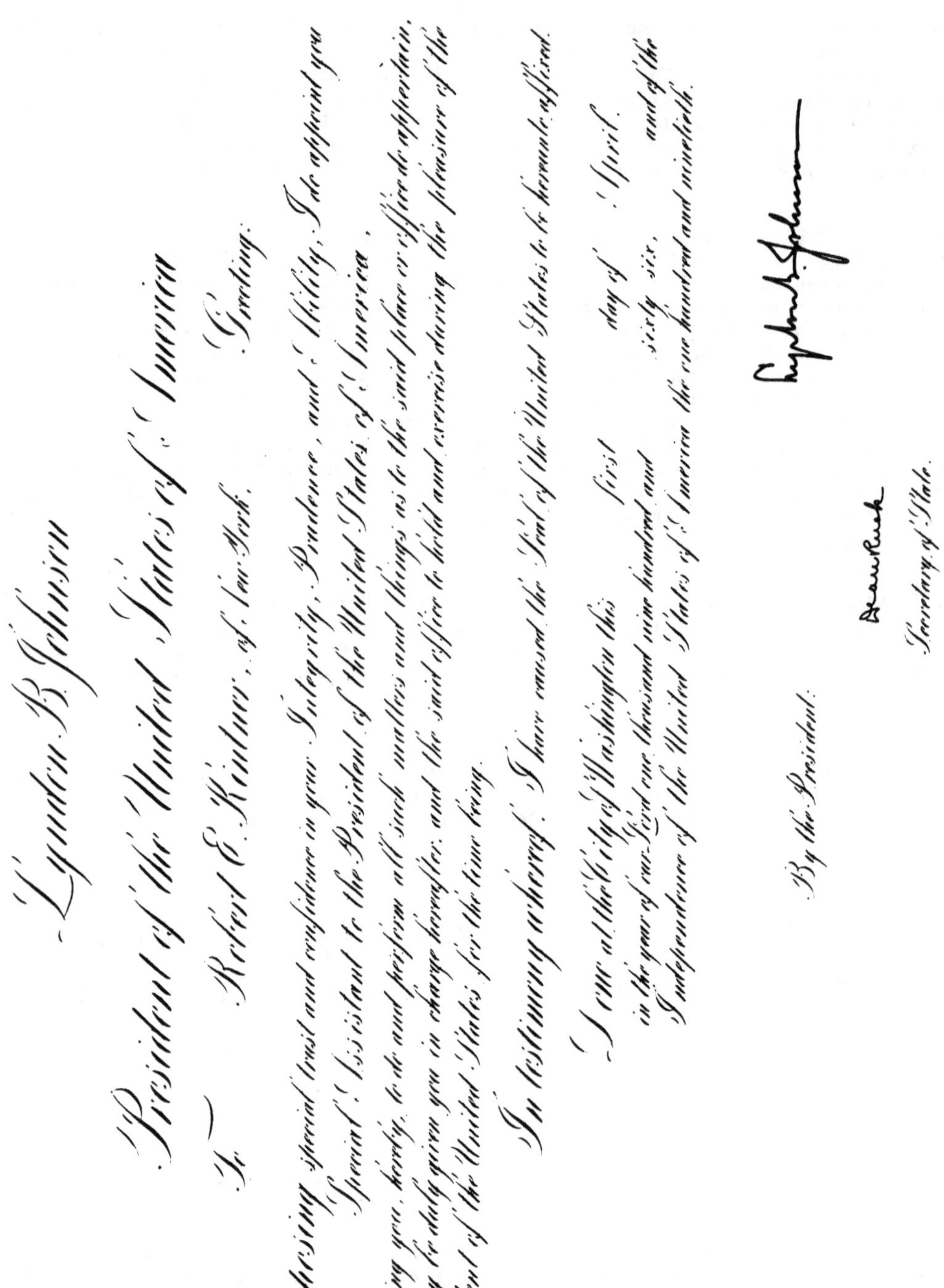
Lyndon B. Johnson
President of the United States of America
To Robert E. Kintner, of New York, Greeting:
Reposing special trust and confidence in your Integrity, Prudence, and Ability, I do appoint you Special Assistant to the President of the United States of America, authorizing you, hereby, to do and perform all such matters and things as to the said place or office do appertain, or as may be duly given you in charge hereafter, and the said office to hold and exercise during the pleasure of the President of the United States for the time being.
In testimony whereof, I have caused the Seal of the United States to be hereunto affixed.
Done at the City of Washington this first day of April, in the year of our Lord one thousand nine hundred and sixty six, and of the Independence of the United States of America the one hundred and ninetieth.
Lyndon B. Johnson
By the President:
Dean Rusk
Secretary of State.

RARE APPOINTMENT OF A SPECIAL ASSISTANT TO THE PRESIDENT

428. JOHNSON, LYNDON B. President and Vice President. Excessively rare partly printed Document Signed, as President. Large oblong folio. Countersigned by DEAN RUSK, Secretary of State. Large ornate embossed seal of the State Department. Johnson appoints Robert E. Kintner of New York to be Special Assistant to the President of the United States. This is the first document of this nature signed by Johnson that we have seen on the market. Choice condition. 1500.00

429. POLK, JAMES K. President; Speaker of U.S. House of Representatives; Governor of Tennessee. Partly printed Document Signed, as President. 1 page, 4to. Washington, July 13, 1847. Polk authorizes the Secretary of State [Buchanan] to affix the Seal of the United States to "the remission of the fine and costs, granted to Lewis Huskey, alias Edward Cairns." Fine, strong signature of Polk. The supplied text, in a secretarial hand, is very slightly light, but is still quite legible. With handsome steel-engraved portrait. Fine. 750.00

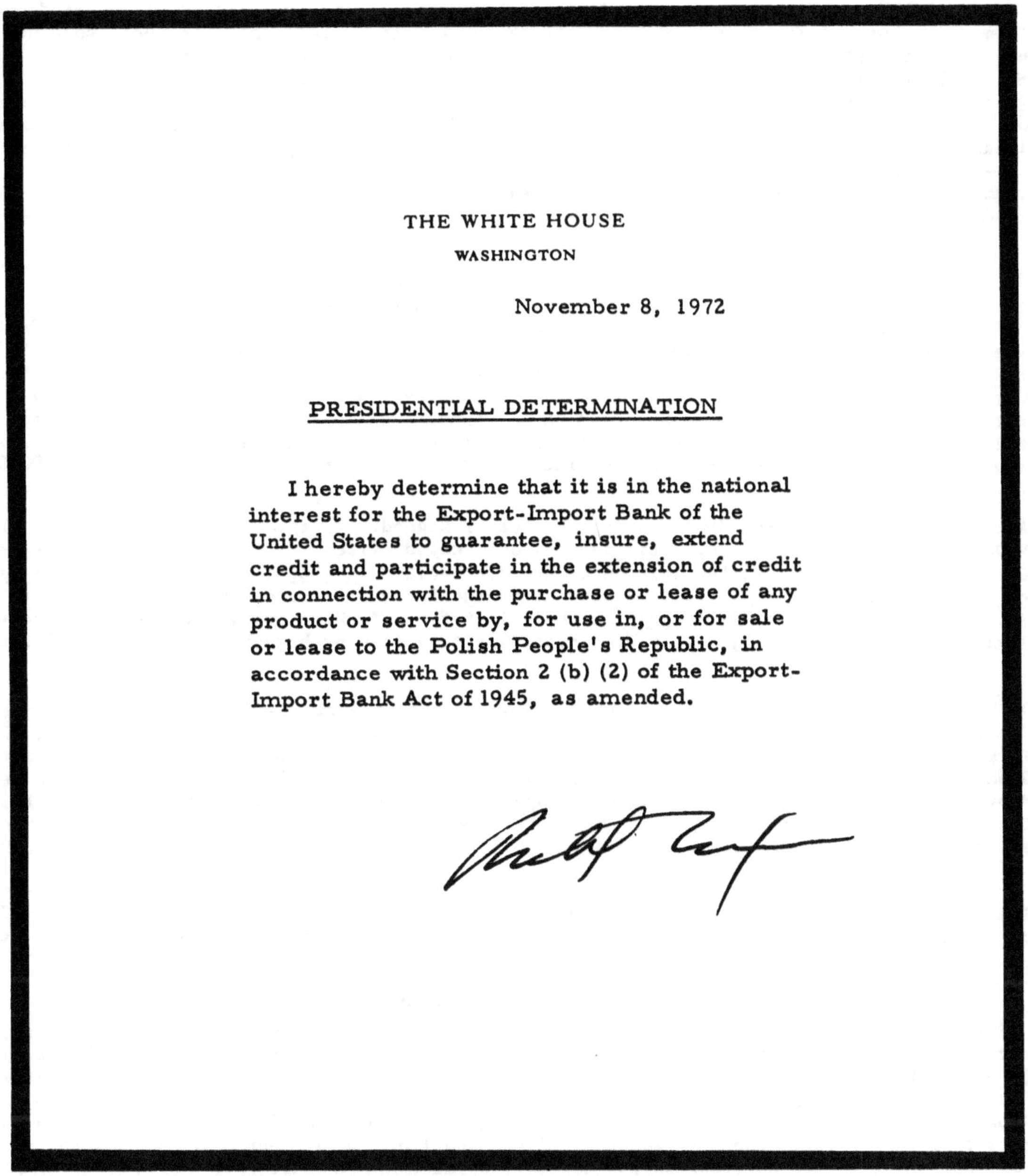

THE WHITE HOUSE
WASHINGTON

November 8, 1972

PRESIDENTIAL DETERMINATION

I hereby determine that it is in the national interest for the Export-Import Bank of the United States to guarantee, insure, extend credit and participate in the extension of credit in connection with the purchase or lease of any product or service by, for use in, or for sale or lease to the Polish People's Republic, in accordance with Section 2 (b) (2) of the Export-Import Bank Act of 1945, as amended.

PRESIDENT NIXON AUTHORIZES FINANCIAL AID FOR POLAND

430. NIXON, RICHARD M. President and Vice President. Excessively rare Typed Document Signed, as President, on the embossed and imprinted stationery of The White House. One page, 4to. Washington, November 8, 1972. Headed PRESIDENTIAL DETERMINATION. Within one week of his resounding re-election victory Nixon orders that it is "in the national interest for the Export-Import Bank of the United States to guarantee, insure, extend credit and participate in the extension of credit in connection with the purchase or lease of any product or service...to the Polish People's Republic..." Pristine condition. We have never seen another document of this nature before. It is probably a souvenir copy signed by Nixon for one of his Polish friends. Remarkable presidential item!! 2500.00

RATIFICATION OF A TREATY WITH NICARAGUA

431. JOHNSON, ANDREW. President and Vice President. Choice partly printed Document Signed, as President. Full page, 4to. Washington, March 12, 1868. President Johnson authorizes the Secretary of State to affix the Seal of the United States to "my Full Power to Andrew B. Dickinson, Minister Resident &c to Nicaragua to exchange with that Government the ratifications of the Treaty concluded between the two Countries on the 21st June 1867..." Very fine condition. With handsome steel-engraved portrait. 650.00

432. HOOVER, HERBERT. President. His book: American Individualism / A Timely Message to the American People. Gilt-lettered blue cloth. New York, 1923. Boldly signed by the future President on the front endpaper. Original printed publishers' dust-jacket. Near mint! 150.00

433. MADISON, DOLLY P. First Lady; rescued Washington portrait and Declaration of Independence from White House just prior to British attack and burning; celebrated hostess; sold her husband's papers to the Library of Congress. Superb Manuscript Letter Signed. 1 page, 4to. Montpellier [Virginia], January 12, 1837. To James H. Causten, Washington. With the integral address-leaf. She writes: "I have received the little volume forwarded at the request of the author, Mr. Lance, with your favor of the 9th and pray you to return him my acknowledgments for this proof of his kind consideration. Were I competent to judge of its merit to which I do not pretend, a painful inflamation of my eyes would not allow their use in reading it as they scarcely permit even my signature...." With engraved portrait. Choice condition, and a very nice social letter. 850.00

CERTIFICATE OF MERIT FOR A PRIVATE WHO FOUGHT AT THE
BATTLE OF CERRO GORDO IN THE MEXICAN WAR

434. POLK, JAMES K. President. Extremely scarce partly engraved Document Signed, as President. One page, small oblong folio, vellum. Washington, November 25, 1848. Countersigned by WILLIAM L. MARCY, Secretary of War. Presidential Certificate of Merit awarded to Private Robert Cowden, Company K of the 2nd Regiment of Dragoons, for distinguished service on April 18, 1847, in the Battle of Cerro Gordo. Handsome spread-eagle vignette at top center. Documents of this type, which exist only for the Mexican War, and were given only to enlisted men for acts of bravery, are very rare and seldom appear on the market. Highly attractive. Choice!! 1500.00

435. HAYES, RUTHERFORD B. President. Autograph Letter Signed. 1 page, large 8vo. Fremont, Ohio, November 29, 1886. To an unidentified Senator. Hayes writes: "President C. H. Payne [of Ohio Wesleyan University] has written an article entitled How to increase the population(?) of liberally educated men. It is published by the Bureau of Education. I would like to have it. Can they not put my name again on their list for all their publications?..." Interesting letter showing how quickly former presidents are forgotten by bureaucrats! Fine. 395.00

436. HOOVER, HERBERT. President. His book: A Remedy for Disappearing Game Fishes. Foreword by French Strother; woodcuts by Harry Cimino. Decorated boards. Huntington Press: N.Y., 1930. First and only edition. Limited to 990 numbered copies. Inscribed on the front endpaper: "To General Milton J. Foreman / With good wishes of / Herbert Hoover". A neat penned note beneath Hoover's inscription indicates that this copy was purchased from Foreman's library in 1935. The inscription was probably penned while President, as Hoover distributed copies of this privately printed volume as presents during his incumbency, Fine. 225.00

437. ADAMS, JOHN QUINCY. President. Darkly penned franking signature "J. Q. Adams" on a small slip of paper. With engraved portrait. Rather small, but still a fine example. 125.00

"VOTING FOR ALL SORTS OF PROGRESSIVE MEASURES"

438. ROOSEVELT, FRANKLIN D. President. Typed Letter Signed, on his name-imprinted stationery, as a candidate for the governorship of New York. 1 page, 4to. [New York City], October 8, 1928. To Hon. John M. Hackett, Poughkeepsie, New York, acknowledging his telegram received at Warm Springs. FDR continues: "...If the betting odds are now correct you and I will both be in Albany this winter, and the Roosevelts will be glad to get more of a chance to see the Hacketts than in the past. Dont forget that if you and I are both elected you become the personal representative of the Governor in the Assembly Chamber and I shall have you voting for all sorts of progressive measures!..." Nice display of the Roosevelt wit!! Fine. 350.00

439. LINCOLN, ABRAHAM. 1809-1865. President; assassinated. Manuscript Document Signed "A. Lincoln" as a young lawyer. Narrow oblong 8vo. Springfield, Illinois, April 6, 1846. The future President acknowledges receipt of $5.00 from William H. Herndon, then an established lawyer who used young Lincoln for small jobs on realty transactions. Later Herndon became Lincoln's sponsor and law partner. Accompanied by a full-page quarto ALS of Sangamon County Judge, James H. Matheny, dated Springfield, April 26, 1884, presenting this Lincoln document to Eleanor Elder, and

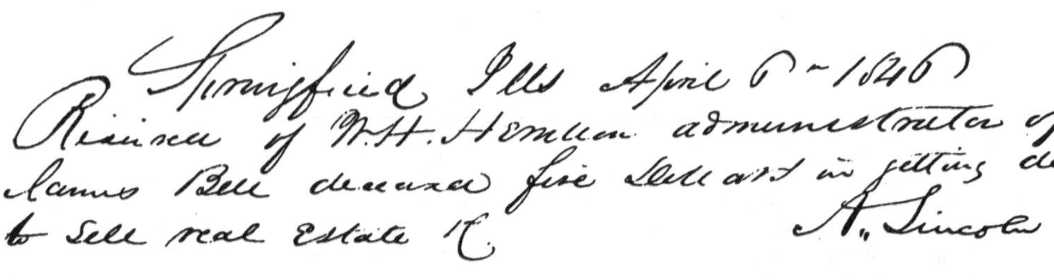
Springfield Ills April 6 - 1846
Received of W. H. Herndon administrator of
James Bell deceased five dollars in getting decree
to sell real Estate &c
A. Lincoln

stating that it was given to him by Herndon. Two years later, in 1848, Lincoln ran successfully for a seat in Congress. This is a very early and desirable Lincoln document dating from his early years in law as a circuit riding attorney. File docket penned on verso. Excellent condition. With a fine engraved portrait. 1950.00

EXCESSIVELY RARE SIGNED ENGRAVED PORTRAIT

440. ADAMS, JOHN QUINCY. President. Handsome engraved portrait of the former President by N. Dearborn, Boston. 12mo. Beneath the image appears the following printed legend: "JOHN QUINCY ADAMS, / 6TH PRESIDENT OF THE U. S. OF AMERICA / [facsimile signature] J. Q. ADAMS". In the upper white margin Adams has boldly penned his signature in full. On the verso the following contemporary inscription appears: "John Quincy Adams born July 11th 1767, at Quincy, Massachusetts, wrote his name hereon July 11th 1842 being on that day 75 years old. Presented to Miss Sarah Ellett with his respects by T. Jones Yorke." Thomas Jones Yorke (1801-1882), was elected to the 27th Congress from New Jersey, serving from 1841 to 1843. Extremely fine condition. The earliest President in a signed portrait to appear on the market. 3000.00

441. TRUMAN, HARRY S President and Vice President. Typed Letter Signed, as President, on imprinted White House stationery. 1 page, 4to. Washington, May 26, 1950. To Hon. Overton Brooks, House of Representatives, Washington. Original addressed envelope. Truman writes: "Thanks very much for the picture which you sent me for my birthday. I am sorry I've been so covered up that we couldn't make the appointment which you asked for but I don't think I've had such a busy time since I have been here. That picture [probably taken on a campaign trip in 1948] brought back some memories of quite a trip and a successful one, I think...." Fine, clean example. 395.00

FORD'S THOUGHTS ON THE LIBERTY LOBBY

442. FORD, GERALD R. President and Vice President. Typed Letter Signed "Jerry Ford", while representing Michigan's 5th District in Congress, on imprinted House of Representatives stationery. 1 page, 4to. Washington, September 14, 1964. To Howard K. Barker, Belmont, Michigan. In part: "...You also asked about the Liberty Lobby. While I am not thoroughly familiar with all the aspects of this organization, I do receive their pamphlets... They are strongly anti-Communistic and present a conservative viewpoint; they effectively present their side of the argument on many issues yet answer some of the more liberal-minded publications. I think therefore, that they serve a need in our country where individual citizens are expected to draw their own conclusions on controvsial issues after hearing all sides of the matter...." In conclusion, Ford, a member of the Warren Commission that looked into the assassination of President Kennedy, comments: "The Warren Commission was originally supposed to make its report to the President today, but this has now been postponed one week. I believe that the report will be available to the public by the end of the month...." Interesting contents. Choice! 250.00

443. BUCHANAN, JAMES. President. Autograph Letter Signed, as Secretary of State in Polk's cabinet. Full page, 8vo. No place, March 30, 1847. To General R. Jones, enclosing letters that show "a mistake has been made in commissioning Lieutenant Gregg by a wrong Christian name. It ought to have been John I. or J. Irvin Gregg instead of James J. Gregg. I would thank you to have the mistake corrected by issuing a new commission...." With engraved portrait. 350.00

444. JOHNSON, ANDREW. President and Vice President. Lower portion of a partly engraved Document Signed, as President. Countersigned by WILLIAM H. SEWARD, Secretary of State. Washington, September 25, 1867. With white embossed wafer seal of the Department of State. The lower third of a presidential appointment, complete in itself. Choice condition. 225.00

445. HAYES, RUTHERFORD B. President. Magnificent partly engraved Document Signed, as Governor of Ohio. 1 page, folio. Columbus, September 28, 1871. Appointment of James B. Bell to serve as a Commissioner of Deeds for the State of Ohio, in Massachusetts. Wonderful engraved heading by the American Bank Note Company, encompassing Hayes' name and title and the Ohio State Seal. Clean and fresh. An outstanding decorative presidential document! 225.00

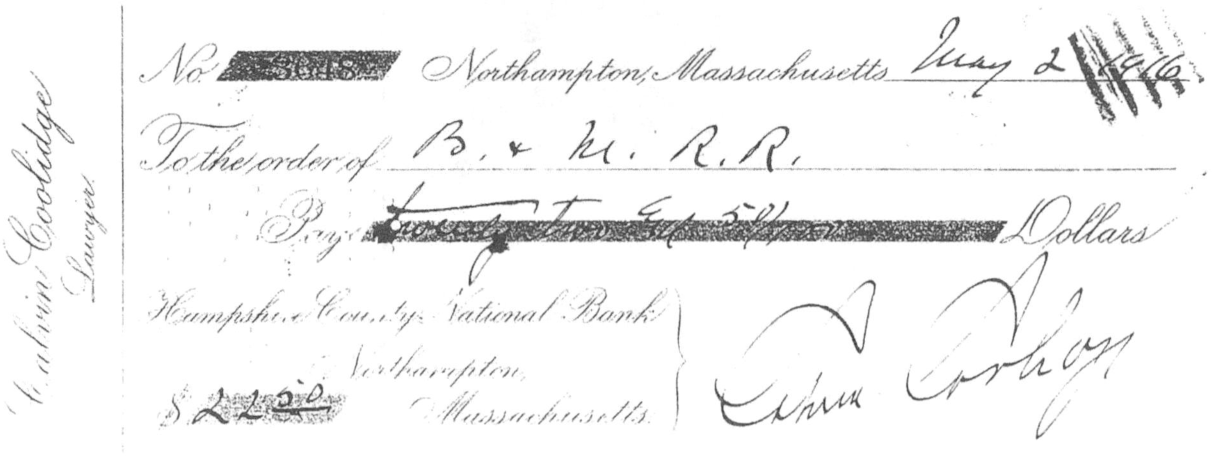

446. COOLIDGE, CALVIN. President and Vice President. Partly printed Signed Bank Check, accomplished in Coolidge's hand. Oblong 8vo. Northampton, Mass., May 2, 1916. Drawn on the Hampshire County National Bank of Northampton. Payable to "B. & M. R.R. [Boston & Maine Railroad]". An early check on Coolidge's law office account. Punch-cancellation holes do not affect Cool' idge's bold signature. Very attractive. 275.00

447. ROOSEVELT, ELEANOR. First Lady. Typed Letter Signed, as First Lady, on gilt-imprinted White House stationery. 1 page, 4to. Washington, February 13, 1941. To Diana [Hopkins], young daughter of presidential advisor and cabinet member, Harry L. Hopkins. She writes: "I am so glad that you got such good marks, and I am delighted with the valentine which you made for me. Daddy will be home soon and I hope you can come here for your Easter holiday. Do you know what time that will be? Tommy sends her love and I do too. Affectionately..." Diana's father, at the time of this letter, was on a special diplomatic mission to Moscow and London. An interesting letter. 125.00

448. TAFT, WILLIAM H. President; Chief Justice, U.S. Supreme Court. Typed Letter Signed, as Secretary of War, on imprinted stationery. 1/2 page, 4to. Manila, November 3, 1907. To Rev. Mercer G. Johnston, Manila, acknowledging a copy of his book Plain American Talk in the Philippines, which "I shall read with much interest..." Nice example. 125.00

449. NIXON, PATRICIA. First Lady. Typed Letter Signed, as First Lady, on imprinted White House stationery. 1 page, small 4to. Washington, November 11, 1971. To Mrs. H. E. Green, Baltimore, Maryland. Original stamped envelope. She writes: "Your thoughtful letter was indeed an encouraging and inspiring message of friendship. Both of us were sincerely touched by the warmth of your words of support and by your kind expression of confidence...." Fine. 95.00

450. REAGAN, RONALD. President. Attractive printed ticket for the Hoosier GOPower $100-a-Plate Statewide Republican Dinner, featuring The Honorable Ronald Reagan, Indiana Convention-Exposition Center, June 19, 1975. Printed in blue ink. 12mo. Signed by Reagan, probably while attending this GOP fund-raising event, above his imprinted portrait. Fine. 125.00

451. EISENHOWER, DWIGHT D. President and General. Striking full-face bust photograph, showing Ike at about the time of his presidency. Quarto. Inscribed in sepia ink on the wide lower white margin: "For Judge John Warren Hill / With best wishes from / Dwight D. Eisenhower". 150.00

452. HOOVER, HERBERT. President. Typed Letter Signed, as Secretary of Commerce, on imprinted stationery of that cabinet post. 1 page, 4to. Washington, June 21, 1928. To Hon. Wallace H. White, Auburn, Maine, acknowledging his letter of congratulation, and saying he appreciates "the fine support you have given me these past months." Written at the time Hoover was nominated for President by the Republican National Convention. Fine. 150.00

453. HARDING, WARREN G. President. Typed Letter Signed, as President-elect, on his imprinted letterhead. 1 page, 4to. St. Augustine, Florida, February 20, 1921. To John C. Shaffer, Evening Post, Chicago, Illinois. Interesting letter written two weeks before his inauguration, in which Harding discusses his selection of Will H. Hays to serve as Postmaster General in his Cabinet. Harding writes: "I was very interested to note what you had to say concerning our mutual friend, Mr. Hays, though I learn from him at the same time that the sense of duty to serve was impelling him to go into the official family. I think he will make a very excellent Postmaster General, though I have a pretty strong conviction that he would do much better for himself in private pursuit. I like him for his consecration to service...." Hays was one of Harding's better choices for his "official family". Fine condition. 450.00

PLANNING FOR THE PEACE FOLLOWING THE GREAT WAR

454. TAFT, WILLIAM H. President; Chief Justice, U.S. Supreme Court. Important Typed Letter Signed as President of the League to Enforce Peace, on their imprinted letterhead listing the numerous members of the Executive Committee. Full page, 4to. New York, September 9, 1916. To Congressman Henry J. Steele, House of Representatives, Washington. Taft solicits a statement of support for the League to Enforce Peace which can later be printed, saying that they have already received statements of support from President Wilson, Justice Hughes, Senators Root and Lodge, and other men in public life. Taft continues: "Our Committee is assured by those who are in close touch with the European situation that while leaders of thought there are so absorbed by events of the war that they have little leisure in which to plan for the future, they will welcome evidence that American public men are giving thought to the erection of safeguards against the recurrence of the calamity which is now devouring their lives and property, and will be disposed to follow leadership which may be furnished from this country ...." The following year, dispite President Wilson's pledge that he would keep American boys out of the European War, the United States declared war against Germany. Fine. 450.00

455. ADAMS, JOHN QUINCY. President; Minister to Russia and England. Autograph Letter Signed, in full, with initialed postscript, while serving as U.S. Minister to England. Full page, 4to. Ealing [England], March 11, 1817. To Thomas Aspinwall, U. S. Consul at London. Adams writes in part: "...I propose to remove very shortly to town, and shall have a number of boxes of Books and other Articles, packed up to be shipp'd for Boston....Mrs. Adams and I go to town this day, to pass the remainder of the week there; at N. 28 Craven Street..." The postscript of this letter is by far the most interesting part, and we quote it fully: "I should have noticed your Letter of 20 Feb[y] enclosing Sibert's Examination. The numbers of Seamen who have applied to you for relief are so great, that I should be glad to have a statement, of the whole number, marking the respective numbers of white men, and men of colour, and a Summary of the principal causes which have brought them in such multitudes to your Office as Applicants for relief. J.Q.A." Handsome letter, in choice condition, and complete with the docketed integral leaf. With a fine engraved portrait. 1500.00

456. ROOSEVELT, EDITH KERMIT. First Lady. Autograph Letter Signed, on her imprinted "Sagamore Hill" stationery. 4 pages, 8vo. Oyster Bay, N.Y., August 7, no year. To Mrs. Little. She writes: "Ever so many thanks for the amusing, & instructive book, and I humbly try to add to your collection one which does not really belong in mine, tho' it has been there for some years. I asked Alice Longworth about the Storer book, and she vaguely remembers a little pamphlet, privately printed, which answers your description, so she is of no assistance. She cannot even recall the title. I have sent your message to Porto Rico...so you may hear soon. I should think it a great opportunity for Porto Rico. They make beautiful embroideries and also many kinds of baskets on that little Island. We must have another day together next July and I shall write the date of one of the country auctions. Each year I shall pull the old house more into shape. I have some bits of lustre for the corner cupboard which are now tucked away in a closet full of reserve china...." Interesting content. 175.00

457. JACKSON, ANDREW. President; General in War of 1812 and Florida Indian Wars; hero of the Battle of New Orleans. Autograph Letter Signed, while representing Tennessee in the United States Senate. Full page, 4to. Washington, March 26, 1824. To Honble. J. C. Calhoun, Secretary of War. Jackson writes: "Major John Peters has made known to me that the office of paymaster at the arsenal at Harpers Ferry has become vacant by the death of the late incumbent; and that from misfortune it would be a convenience for him to obtain that appointment. I am sure he is well qualified to discharge the duties of that appointment: I have barely to add that I have the greatest respect for his character, and that it will afford me pleasure to hear that he has succeeded in his application...." Jackson was defeated for the presidency later this same year by John Quincy Adams. Calhoun was later to serve as Secretary of State and Vice President under Jackson. Expertly backed on the verso only with Japan tissue. Very fine appearance. With engraved portraits of Calhoun and Jackson. 1250.00

INSCRIBED ON THE DAY CONGRESS DECLARED WAR ON GERMANY

458. WILSON, WOODROW. President. Attractive studio photograph of President Wilson by Harris and Ewing, Washington. Inscribed on the lower mount, as president: "To my fellow Jerseyman, John P. Wall, April 6, 1917 / Woodrow Wilson". This was the day that Congress, acting at the request of Wilson, declared war on Germany. Small offset stain, probably from a newspaper clipping, on the lower mount. This stain is very light. Otherwise, quite fine. 450.00

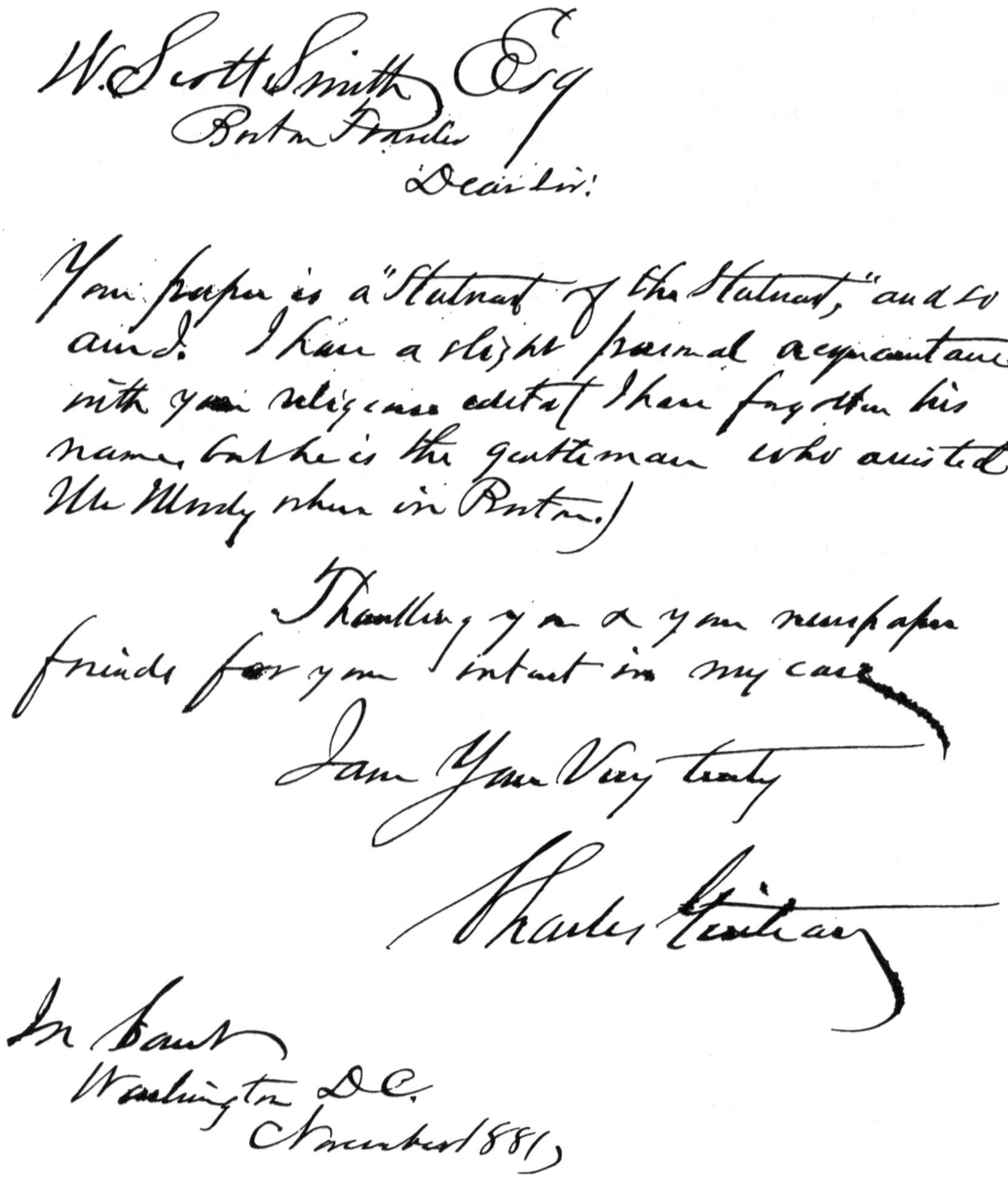
W. Scott Smith Esq
Boston Traveler
Dear Sir:

Your paper is a "Stalwart of the Stalwarts," and so am I. I have a slight personal acquaintance with your religious editor (I have forgotten his name, but he is the gentleman who assisted Mr Moody when in Boston.)

Thanking you & your newspaper friends for your interest in my case

I am Yours Very truly

Charles Guiteau

In Cant
Washington D.C.
November 1881

SCARCE LETTER OF GARFIELD'S ASSASSIN WRITTEN FROM JAIL

459. [GARFIELD, JAMES A.] President; assassinated, July 2, 1881. GUITEAU, CHARLES G. American lawyer and disappointed office seeker who shot President Garfield at the Railroad Station in Washington, D.C., July 2, 1881; tried, convicted and hanged for his crime. Choice Autograph Letter Signed, written from his jail cell. Full page, 4to. In Cant, Washington, D.C., November, 1881. To W. Scott Smith, Boston Traveler, [Boston, Mass.]. Guiteau writes: "Your paper is a Stalwart of the Stalwarts, and so am I. I have a slight personal acquaintance with your religious editor (I have forgotten his name, but he is the gentleman who assisted Mr. Moody when in Boston.) Thanking you & your newspaper friends for your interest in my case, I am Yours Very truly...." Guiteau's letters written from jail are very scarce, and this is a fine specimen in excellent condition. 1250.00

AUTHORIZATION TO NEGOTIATE A TREATY WITH MEXICO

460. BUCHANAN, JAMES. President. Partly printed Document Signed, as President. Full page, 4to. Washington, no date. President Buchanan authorizes the Secretary of State to affix the Seal of the United States to "a Full Power to Robert M. Mc Lane, Esqr., to negotiate a Treaty with the Republic of Mexico..." Excellent condition. With engraved portrait. 675.00

461. TRUMAN, HARRY S. President and Vice President. His book: Truman Speaks. Blue cloth, lettered spine. Columbia University Press: New York, 1960. First edition. Inscribed on the half-title page: "To / Miss Margaret Baker / with kind regards / Harry S. Truman / 6-22-60". Original dust-jacket featuring Truman's profile bust portrait. This book contains the text of lectures delivered by the former President at Columbia University. Very fine. 175.00

QUEEN VICTORIA AND THE RECEPTION OF EX-PRESIDENTS VAN BUREN & FILLMORE

462. BUCHANAN, JAMES. President; Secretary of State; Minister to England. Magnificent Autograph Letter Signed, while representing the United States as Ambassador to the Court of St. James' 4 closely written pages, 8vo. U.S. Legation, London, June 15, 1855. To William Hunter, an official in the State Department. In part:

> "I enclose...a packet of letters with Post Office Stamps upon them written by Miss Lane & myself to our friends in the United States. These are of such a character as to bear the delay incident to sending them to Washington in the Despatch Bag. They are entirely private and do not in the language of the Despatch relate to official business....I shall continue to send some of my private letters by Despatch Bag to Washington, until I can learn the decision of the Department that this would be improper, & that the same foreign postage will be charged upon them as though they were sent direct by the Foreign Mail.
>
> I approve entirely of the pre-payment law. It ought to be extended to all cases. The Queen of Great Britain cannot frank a letter. I did not, however, anticipate that it would deprive me of the use of the Despatch Bag, provided I placed the proper American Stamp upon my letters.
>
> Messrs. Van Buren & Fillmore are both in London and have received much attention, -- indeed, more than I had anticipated. Still, the position has not been assigned to them at Court, to which an Ex President is surely entitled. Her Majesty, however, is an excellent lady as well as excellent Sovereign; and the direct descendant of William the Conqueror may be excused for not appreciating the ex Representatives of the Sovereignty of the American people at their just value.
>
> Please remember me kindly to Judge Dunlap and my old co-laborers in the State Department. Approaching the end of my political career I look back with much pleasure to those friends with whom I have been associated in public life..."

The following year Buchanan was elected President of the United States, thus his political career was not quite at an end when he penned this letter. Fine condition. 2500.00

463. FILLMORE, MILLARD. President and Vice President. Autograph Letter Signed. Full page, small 4to. Buffalo, New York, January 6, 1854. To Haven, his law partner, acknowledging receipt of the third volume of the 5th Series of the Documentary History. He requests that other volumes in the series be sent to replace those lost in the fire at Spaulding's Exchange. He concludes: "We have had a great thaw since Tuesday and lost most of our snow, but the wind changed last night & we have cold weather again this morning...." Fine example, penned on narrow black-bordered stationery. With engraved portrait. 450.00

PANE OF EIGHTY POSTAGE STAMPS SIGNED BY FDR AND ICKES

464. ROOSEVELT, FRANKLIN D. President. Pane of 80 United States Postage Stamps (Scott #808) issued in 1938, four-cent denomination featuring the bust of President Madison. Boldly signed in bright blue ink, as President, by Roosevelt on the left gutter margin. Also signed by HAROLD L. ICKES, Secretary of the Interior. The stamps are mint. Attractive souvenir philatelic item from the administration of the noted stamp collector. 250.00

465. HOOVER, HERBERT. President. His book: On Growing Up / His Letters from and to American Children. Gilt-stamped blue cloth. New York, 1962. Inscribed on the half-title: "To Harry E. ____ / not for instruction but / for entertainment / from / Herbert Hoover." Unusual inscription. Very fine copy in pictorial dust-jacket. One of Hoover's last books. Scarce! 175.00

466. ARTHUR, CHESTER A. President and Vice President. Partly printed Document Signed, as President. Large oblong folio. Washington, July 5, 1884. Countersigned by Frederick Frelinghuysen, Secretary of State. Large white wafer seal of the State Department. Arthur appoints Le Baron B. Colt, of Rhode Island, United States Judge of the First Judicial Circuit. Very light browning at vertical center, otherwise fine. Bold signature of Arthur. 350.00

467. EISENHOWER, DWIGHT D. President and General. Typed Letter Signed "Ike", as President of Columbia University, on blue-imprinted stationery. 1 page, 8vo. New York, June 19, 1950. To Robert W. Woodruff, President of the Coca Cola Company, Atlanta, Georgia. Eisenhower writes: "At lunch the other day Bill Burnham suggested that you might like to have a copy of a letter I wrote him sometime ago concerning the project which we discussed at the University Club. While I am afraid it is needlessly verbose, I think it will serve to give you a few of the highlights....It was indeed a pleasure to see you again...." Fine example. 195.00

468. ROOSEVELT, FRANKLIN D. President. Typed Letter Signed, as Governor of New York, on the blue and gilt imprinted stationery of the governorship. 1 page, 4to. Albany, October 17, 1930. To Dr. John J. Hogan, Aldine Club, New York City. Campaigning for his second gubernatorial term, Roosevelt writes that he had hoped to be able to accept his correspondent's invitation. "However, I regret now to advise you that I have definitely determined upon the itinerery prepared for me by the campaign committee and so it will be impossible for me to be with you..." Fine condition. 250.00

THE FINNISH RELIEF FUND

469. HOOVER, HERBERT. President. Ornate partly printed Document Signed, as National Chairman of the Finnish Relief Fund, 1939-1940. Certificate presented to Henry W. Phelps "in appreciation of sympathetic service during the appeal for funds to aid the stricken civilian population of Finland." Large vignette of American and Finnish Flags. Engraved by the American Bank Note Co. Hoover's signature is in bright blue ink. Pressure-mounted. Fine. 150.00

470. ROOSEVELT, THEODORE. President and Vice President. Attractive unmounted cabinet photograph showing a formal half-length pose of Roosevelt, probably dating from the first year of his presidency. Boldly signed in jet black ink. Impaired only slightly by some uniformly light speckling, the photograph is in fine condition, and makes a striking display item. 375.00

471. MONROE, JAMES. President. Attractive partly printed Document Signed, as President. Small oblong folio, vellum. Washington, February 19, 1818. Countersigned by JOSIAH MEIGS, Commissioner of the General Land Office. Embossed wafer seal affixed at lower left. Grant of 160 acres of land in the Illinois Territory, as authorized by Acts of Congress granting land to the late Army of the United States for Military Bounties. Superb vignette at top left depicting a soldier, his wife and child, receiving a grant of land from the Government (symbolized by Columbia). His rifle may be seen in the foreground. Choice signature of Monroe, and a highly attractive document for framing or display. With portrait. 475.00

472. MC KINLEY, WILLIAM. President. Manuscript Letter Signed, while representing Ohio in the U.S. Congress, on imprinted Congressional letterhead. Full page, narrow 4to. Washington, December 18, 1889. To A. R. Turner, Boston, Mass., sending thanks for his congratulations, and adding "I suppose you have noted that hearings will be had on the several schedules within the next ten days. The subjects and dates were published a day or two ago. I expect to have the pleasure of seeing you during the winter...." The "congratulations" were for Mc Kinley's selection as Chairman of the Committee of Ways and Means, in which role he had a major part in framing and passing the protective tariff act (McKinley Tariff) of 1890. Fine. 250.00

473. JOHNSON, ANDREW. President and Vice President. Handsome signature, boldly written and dated April 8th 1869 (one month after leaving the presidency). Boldly penned in the center of a quarto leaf of blue-lined stationery. Handsome example. With portrait. 225.00

474. ROOSEVELT, THEODORE. President and Vice President. Typed Letter Signed, as President, on imprinted White House stationery. 1 page, 4to. Washington, November 17, 1908. To Claudius B. Spencer, Editor, Central Christian Advocate, Kansas City, Missouri. Roosevelt acknowledges his correspondent's letter, adding: "...I mourn the death of Mr. Thompson; I prized his friendship, and I feel that he was a great moral force and a great force for righteousness in this nation -- as indeed, my dear sir, I have grown more and more to feel of the religious press, the longer I have been in public life...." Fine. 575.00

475. CLEVELAND, GROVER. President. Brief Autograph Letter Signed. Full page, 8vo. [Princeton, N.J.], January 14, 1903. To Holman Conrad, Jr., at the Princeton Inn. The ex-president writes: "I am so situated that I have only time to write a word saying it is impossible for me to see you...." Fine example. With portrait. 225.00

476. HARRISON, CAROLINE SCOTT. First Lady; first wife of Benjamin Harrison; died in the White House. Her scarce full signature on a plain visiting card. Pristine! 125.00

477. PIERCE, FRANKLIN. President. Complete small envelope, boldly franked Free Frank: Pierce, as President, at top right. Clear black circular Washington postmark. Addressed in the hand of Abigail Kent Means, who substituted for the often ill First Lady as White House hostess, to Rev. Daniel P. Noyes, Brooklyn, New York. Remnant of red wax seal on verso. Fine. 275.00

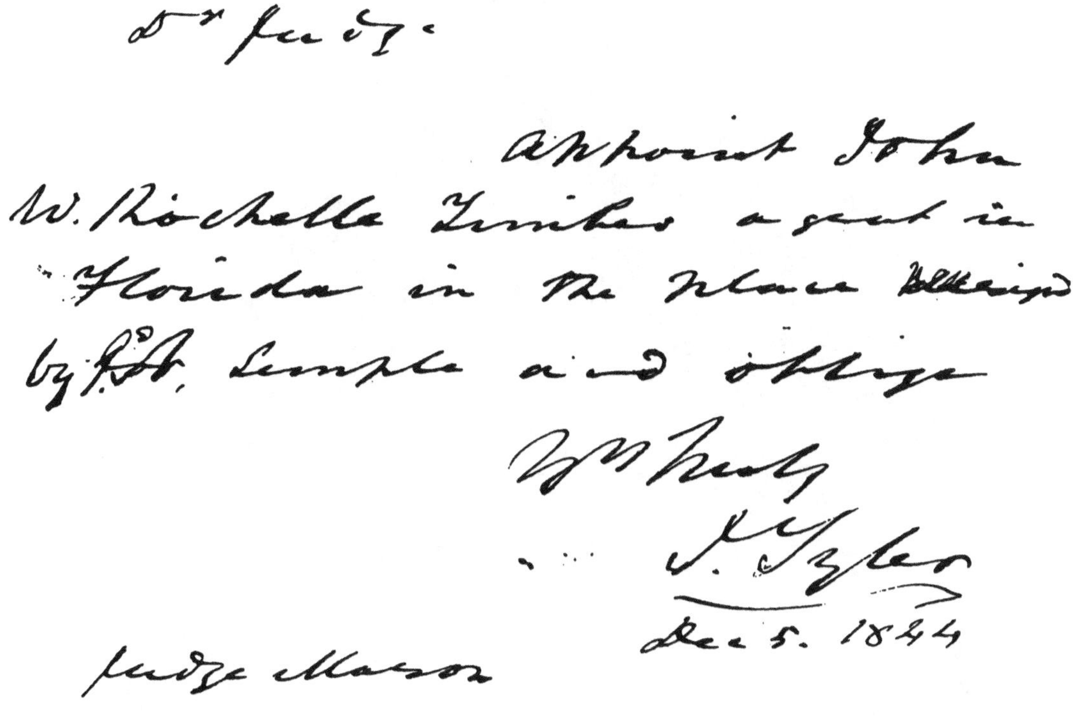
D[ea]r Judge:
Appoint John W. Rochelle Timber agent in Florida in the place resigned by Rob. Semple and oblige
Yrs truly
J. Tyler
Dec 5. 1844
Judge Mason

SCARCE HOLOGRAPH LETTER AS PRESIDENT

478. TYLER, JOHN. President and Vice President. Autograph Letter Signed, as President. 2/3 page, 4to. No place [Washington], December 5, 1844. To Judge [John Y.] Mason, Secretary of the Navy. President Tyler writes: "D[ea]r Judge: Appoint John W. Rochelle Timber agent in Florida in the place resigned by Rob. Semple and oblige / Yrs truly..." Attractive presidential letter, in choice condition. With engraved portrait. 950.00

479. ROOSEVELT, FRANKLIN D. President. Typed Letter Signed, as Assistant Secretary of the Navy, on the imprinted stationery of that office. 1 page, 4to. Washington, July 19, 1917. To Major Willard Straight, U.S.R.F., Governors Island, New York. In this "Dear Willard" letter, the future President writes: "Just a line to tell you of my interest in two young men John Lyons and Leonard Lyons, of Gardiner, Ulster County, New York. They are now at the Norwich University Military Camp and are candidates for the August Officers' Training Camp. I hope they will be allowed to go...." Fine letter, fully signed. 175.00

480. TAFT, WILLIAM H. President; Chief Justice, U.S. Supreme Court. Autograph Letter Signed, on the vignette imprinted stationery of the Blackstone Hotel. Full page, small 4to. Chicago, June 26, 1919. To Charles N. Dietz, Omaha, Nebraska. Taft writes: "I was in Omaha for an hour or less yesterday. I tried through the Governor to get in touch with you but failed. I really was not afraid to sign the letter. I return it herewith. I wish I could write you more at length but I must catch a train...." Fine single-page holograph example. 250.00

481. CLEVELAND, GROVER. President; Governor of New York. Autograph Letter Signed, on the imprinted stationery of the law firm Bissell, Sicard & Goodyear. Full page, 8vo. Buffalo, July 3, 1884. To "My dear General". Writing at the time he received the Democratic Presidential nomination, Cleveland informs his correspondent: "I obtained the photographs more easily than I expected and enclose them for the ladies...." Scarce in one-page letters. Fine. 195.00

482. GRANT, ULYSSES S. President; Union General; recieved Lee's surrender. Lower half (fragment) of a partly printed Document Signed, as President. 1 page, oblong folio. Washington, March 15, 1871. Countersigned by Hamilton Fish, Secretary of State. Embossed (eagle vignette) white wafer seal of the Department of State. An attractive, fresh document, complete in itself, and well suited for framing or display. With engraved portrait. 175.00

483. ARTHUR, CHESTER A. President and Vice President. Manuscript Letter Signed, as Vice President-elect. Full page, 8vo. New York, December 17, 1880. To Hon. Alex. R. Sheperd, Batopilas, acknowledging his letter of June last. "...I thank you cordially for your congratulations and kind expressions regarding myself. With my best wishes for success in your new venture..." Fine. 450.00

MULTI-VIGNETTE ENGRAVED MEMBERSHIP CERTIFICATE FOR THE SOLDIERS MONUMENT ASSOCIATION

484. GRANT, ULYSSES S. President; Union General; accepted Lee's surrender. Magnificent Engraved Document Signed, as President of the Soldiers Monument Association. One page, tall folio. Galena, Illinois, August 28, 1865. Countersigned by J. C. Smith, Secretary. Certificate of Membership, in blank (not filled in), featuring four handsome vignettes at the sides, and an oval portrait of Abraham Lincoln surrounded by draped flags and topped with a spread-eagle at the top center. Truly, a handsome product of the Continental Bank Note Co., New York. Crisp, unfolded, on high quality banknote paper. Wonderful display piece!! 575.00

485. [JACKSON, ANDREW]. President. Holograph invitation penned in an unidentified hand on an octavo leaf: "Gen'l & Mrs. Jackson's compliments to Gen'l Wall and request the pleasure of his company to dinner on Friday at 3 o'clock (the 31st inst). 30th Decr. 1824". Docketed integral address-leaf. Jackson lost the Presidential Election of 1824 to John Quincy Adams. 35.00

"IF YOU LOOK INTO THE JOURNAL OF CONGRESS FOR 1774, YOU WILL FIND A DECLARATION OF RIGHTS OF THE COLONIES AND ANOTHER OF THE VIOLATIONS OF THOSE RIGHTS. THESE DECLARATIONS...WERE DRAWN UP BY TWO COMMITTEES. I WAS ONE OF THE FIRST COMMITTEE AND DREW UP THE REPORT. IN THIS YOU WILL SEE...THE ROUGH MATERIALS OF THE DECLARATION OF INDEPENDENCE..."

486. ADAMS, JOHN. President and Vice President; Signer of Declaration of Independence, and a member of the committee that drafted that document; colonial lawyer. Magnificent Autograph Letter Signed. 3 full pages, 4to. Quincy [Mass.], March 12, 1802. To his son, Thomas B. Adams, suggesting areas of study in pursuit of a legal career. In part: "...It was far from my thoughts to assign you a task. I meant only to turn your mind to a subject, which must necessarily engage much of your contemplations, as long as you live. The Pole Right, the Peoples Right, the common law, is the natural Inheritance of us all. It is our Birth Right. But precious as it is, and dear as it ought to be to all our hearts, it is likely to be a subject of controversy in this country, untill an examination of it...shall be undertaken...by you or some other, whose Industry may be equal to the subject. The assistance to be expected from me, must be very small. I have scarcely a Law Book of any kind left in my office. It is almost 30 years since I abandoned my office and Law Library, and now I have none. My Recollections of the contents of Law Books, you may suppose to be very faint confused and incorrect. A Lawyer should have in his Desk, or Bureau, more pidgeon holes, than a Coiner of constitutions. In these he should deposit, in neat, numerical or alphebetical order, all the effects of his Researches into moot Points..." Adams goes on to discuss Judge Addison's thoughts, as well as those of Lord Chief Justice Hale on the Common Law, and also Blackstone. He then turns to his own experience during the formative years of the United States. "If you look into the Journal of Congress for 1774 you will find a Declaration of the Rights of the Colonies and another of the Violations of those Rights. These declarations of Lists were drawn up by two Committees. I was one of the first Committee and drew up the Report. In this you will see, not only the rough materials of the Declaration of Independence made two years after, but you will see in what light the common Law was seen by that Congress and by all America at that time. Extracts from those Journals, should go into your common Law Pidgeon hole. There is a public printed declaration of the Town of Boston some time anteiour to the meeting of the first congress which will deserve your attention..." In the final paragraph Adams confesses that he is not keeping any copies of his letter to his son, and admonishes him "to keep them Safely or to burn them, that they may not fall into the hands of the Enemy of all good...." Truly, a remarkable letter, and in fine condition. 9500.00

WITH IMPRINTED PRESIDENTIAL ENVELOPE FRANKED BY A SECRETARY

487. JOHNSON, ANDREW. President and Vice President. Attractive full signature penned as president on a small white card. Undated on the card, but with the original postmarked envelope, bearing the imprint "From the President of the United States", and franked by W. A. Browning, Private Secretary. Addressed to Master Geo. H. Woodward, West Troy, N.Y. Circular Washington postmark,bearing the date June 13, 1865. With engraved portrait. 225.00

488. DAVIS, JEFFERSON. President of the Confederate States of America. Manuscript Letter Signed, as Secretary of War in Pierce's cabinet. Full page, 4to. War Department, Washington, May 15, 1856. To Hon. Charles Sumner, Senator from Massachusetts. Davis writes to acknowledge Sumner's letter seeking "to obtain the discharge of Wm. Burke Jr. (enlisted by name of William Bent) from the Army on the ground of his minority." Davis responds: "...I transmit you a copy of a printed circular which states the evidence required by the Department before action can be taken on the case...." Attractive example. With engraved portrait. 350.00

489. HOOVER, HERBERT. President. Strikingly handsome Harris & Ewing studio photograph showing the president seated. Legal folio. Boldly inscribed on the lower blank margin to the American journalist: "To Paul Wooton / With Kind Regards of / Herbert Hoover". Undated, but probably inscribed while president. Pristine condition! 225.00

SCARCE HOLOGRAPH LETTER AS PRESIDENT

490. PIERCE, FRANKLIN. President; General in Mexican War. Autograph Letter Signed, as President. 2 pages, 8vo. Washington, January 1, 1855. To the American Minister in Italy, recommending the sons of a Congressman who were travelling to that country. "I believe you are personally acquainted with Hon. William Appleton now a member of Congress from Boston. His two sons... are now in Europe and expect to visit Naples in the course of a few weeks. I desire to bespeak for them your kind consideration. They are gentlemen in the best sense of the word and I shall acknowledge as a favor to myself anything you may do to enhance the interest and pleasure of their visit...." Written to Robert Dale Owen, former Congressman, and a noted author. William Appleton, a successful Boston merchant, served one term in Congress. He was related to Pierce's wife. Fine. 1500.00

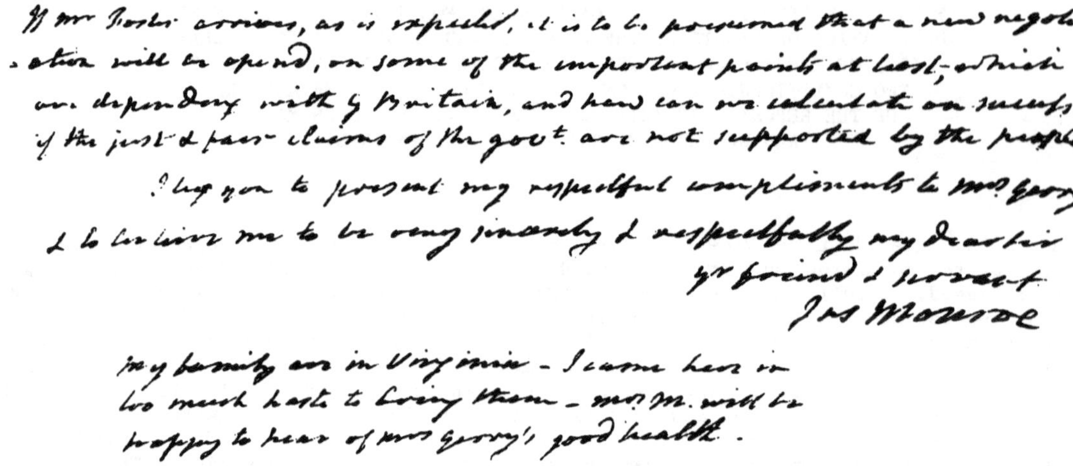
If Mr Foster arrives, as is expected, it is to be presumed that a new negoti-
-ation will be open'd, on some of the important points at least, which
are depending with G Britain, and how can we calculate on success
if the just & fair claims of the govt. are not supported by the people?
I beg you to present my respectful compliments to Mrs Gerry
& to believe me to be very sincerely & respectfully my dear Sir
yr friend & servant
Jas Monroe

My family are in Virginia - I came here in
too much haste to bring them - Mrs M. will be
happy to hear of Mrs Gerry's good health.

"THE UNION AND LAWS MUST BE SUPPORTED, OR WE SINK INTO CONTEMPT"

491. MONROE, JAMES. President. Fascinating and highly important Autograph Letter Signed, as Secretary of State in President Madison's cabinet. 1 1/2 closely-penned pages, 4to. Washington, June 14, 1811. To [Elbridge Gerry, Governor of Mass., and a Signer of the Declaration of Independence]. The next President writes the next Vice President:

> "Two young neighbours and friends of mine, the Mr. Coles, one secretary to the President, intending to visit Boston, permit me to introduce them to your acquaintance. They are very sensible & deserving young men, with whom I am satisfied you will be pleased. They are I recollect nearly connected (the nephews) of Mr. Coles who married a sister of your Lady.
>
> Many years have elapsed since we had the pleasure to meet; but I have always recollected our service together in Congress in 1784, 5, 6, and the confidence which prevailed between us, & the friendship which we then contracted, with great interest and satisfaction. My best wishes for your welfare & for that of your family, have always accompanied you in your publick & private life.
>
> I avail myself of this opportunity to assure you that I was much gratified by a perusal of your speech, lately delivered, to the Legislature of your State. The situation of affairs requir'd decision & firmness -- The union & laws must be supported, or we sink into contempt, inviting aggression from abroad, by proving that, owing to our divisions, we have not energy enough to repress it. You appear to me to have met the crises as you ought to have done, and I have no doubt that the effect will be satisfactory.
>
> If Mr. Foster arrives, as is expected, it is to be presumed that a new negotiation will be open'd, on some of the important points at least, which are depending with G. Britain, and how can we calculate on success if the just & fair claims of the Gov't are not supported by the people?...
>
> My family are in Virginia. I came here in too much haste to bring them. Mrs. M. will be happy to hear of Mrs. Gerry's good health...."

At the time this letter was written problems with Great Britain were mounting. Britain was blockading our ships and capturing our sailors, reducing our commercial trade with Europe, while trade between the U.S. and Britain was at a standstill. People in New England, mostly Federalists, were against having war with Britain for any reason. Monroe soon entered into brisk discussions with Augustus John Foster, who, as British Minister to America, was a very influential figure in pre-war talks. Most important was the fact that New Englanders were on the verge of breaking away from the Union or even trying to overthrow it. The speech to which Monroe refers was made by Governor Gerry to convince the people of New England that America might have to go to war against Great Britain in order to show her that it was a power and would not remain at the merciless hands of the British. He also realized that without the support of the people of New England it would be next to impossible to achieve a successful war -- especially if they sided with the British. In this historic letter Monroe encourages Gerry to continue his support for the survival of the Union. As is evidenced by this letter, the policies of the United States differed from those held by a large group of citizens. Excellent condition, and a marvellous addition to a set of presidents. 2950.00

"WE HAVE BEEN INVADED BY JAPAN AND OUR PURPOSE NOW MUST BE
TO RESIST WITH EVERY POWER WE CAN BRING TO BEAR..."

492. HOOVER, HERBERT. President. Typed Letter Signed on his personally imprinted stationery. One page, 4to. New York, December 10, 1941. To Custis E. Gillis, San Diego, California. Interesting letter written by the former President just three days after the Japanese attack at Pearl Harbor. He writes: "...We have been invaded by Japan and our purpose now must be to resist with every power we can bring to bear. In the meantime, we must need consider the principles upon which a lasting peace can be brought to the world...." Very choice!! 450.00

FDR'S AIRLINE SCHEME

493. ROOSEVELT, FRANKLIN D. President. Important Typed Letter Signed, on the imprinted letterhead of his law firm Emmet, Marvin & Roosevelt. 1 page, 4to. New York, April 4, 1922. To Edward Schildhauer, Washington, D.C. In regard to the proposed dirigible airline in which Roosevelt was interested, he states that he has little time for a conference. "...Unfortunately, the hours in which I am at liberty to take up business matters are so limited by necessary treatment as to make it extremely difficult for me to get through half of my many important personal things I have to do, and this week is too crowded to make it possible for me to give up the time, much as I should like to do so..." FDR indicates that he agrees with the program outlined by Snowden A. Fahnestock, another interested party in the dirigible scheme, and that "Having once decided on a program I think it is extremely inadvisable to change, as it is better to go ahead along a definite line than to be continually shifting our scheme of operations..." Accompanying this letter is Fahnestock's two-page typewritten memorandum, a five-page memorandum by a Mr. Bradley concerning the organizational structure of the proposed airline, which was to be called GENERAL AIR SERVICE, with FDR as Chairman of the Executive Committee, and a photograph of a terrestrial globe on which are indicated some of the intended air routes. Edward Schildhauer, the addressee, was an engineer who had participated in the construction of the Panama Canal and was also interested in the field of aeronautical design. Needless to say the airline scheme was an abortive promotion. It was one of FDR's very few business speculations and is mentioned in most biographies of the President. Fine and interesting. 750.00

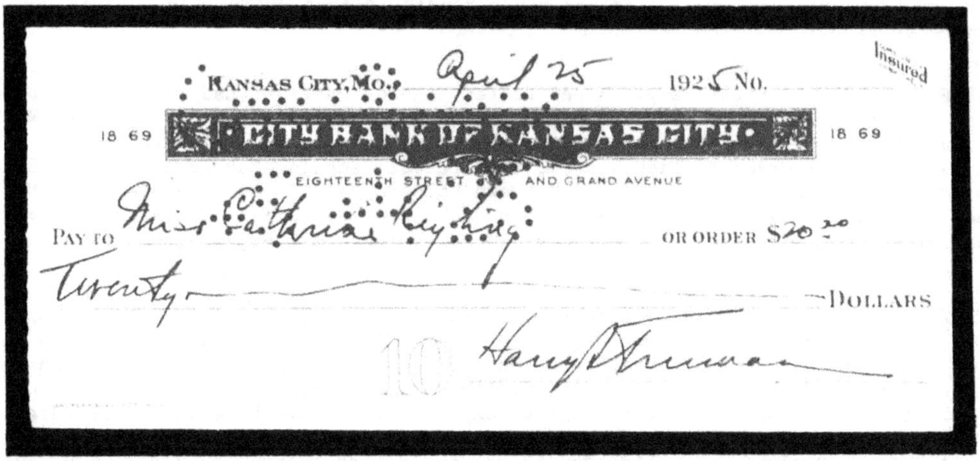

494. TRUMAN, HARRY S. President and Vice President. Partly printed Signed Bank Check, accomplished in his hand. Oblong 12mo. Kansas City, Missouri, April 25, 1925. Drawn on the City Bank of Kansas City, and made payable to Miss Cathrine Reyling. Punch-cancellation holes do not affect Truman's fine signature. Very scarce in this format. Choice specimen. 425.00

495. CLEVELAND, FRANCES F. First Lady. Imprinted Executive Mansion card, Signed. Fine. 75.00

LETTER OF APPRECIATION AND PRAISE FOR A DEPARTING MILITARY AIDE

496. HAYES, RUTHERFORD B. President. Splendid Autograph Letter Signed, as President, on imprinted Executive Mansion stationery. Full page, narrow quarto. Washington, October 10, 1877. To Major C. C. Sniffen. Hayes writes: "In complying with your request...to be relieved from further duty at the Executive Mansion, and assigned to a position in the office of the Paymaster General -- appreciating as I do the honorable motives which actuate you in making the request; I desire to express my acknowledgment of your valuable services during so long a time in the Executive office where your successive promotions show the estimation in which you have been held. In the new duties to which your Commission in the Military service calls you, you will take with you my regard, and I shall always be gratified to hear of your continued prosperity and success...." Handsome presidential letter, neatly inlaid, and in very fine condition. A welcome addition to a set of presidential letters. 1200.00

SEA LETTER FOR A NEW BEDFORD WHALER

497. FILLMORE, MILLARD. President and Vice President. Partly printed Document Signed, as President Large oblong folio. [Washington] 1853. Countersigned by EDWARD EVERETT, Secretary of State. Embossed (Spread eagle) wafer seal of the State Department affixed at center to the left of Fillmore's exceptionally bold signature. Four-language (French, Spanish, English and Dutch) sea-letter, dated New Bedford, May 17, 1853 (two months after Franklin Pierce had been inaugurated as President), for the Barque Superior, Charles L. Norton, Master, "bound for Pacific Ocean and laden with provisions, stores, and utensils for a whaling voyage." This ship returned to New Bedford on March 16, 1857, after a cruise of nearly four years. Unusually fine condition, with no fold breaks, stains or other defects. Fillmore is relatively uncommon in this format. 850.00

498. BUCHANAN, JAMES. President. Autograph Letter Signed. Full page, 4to. Lancaster, March 24, 1841. To John Reynolds. Buchanan writes: "Majors Montgomery & Steinman called on me this morning. The latter informed me that he would not want any portion of our first payment until the 1st of May -- except $1500 & expressed his willingness to let it remain in our hands on interest till that time. I told him that the arrangement would suit me very well and I presumed it would be agreeable to you. I told him he might rely on the $1500 on the 1 April. If you should not be in Town before that day you may send me your check for $750 payable to the order of Steinman. The deeds &c are to be executed as soon after the 1st April as Israel can prepare them....James has returned; but whether he will accept my offer, or his uncle's proposition, I do not know. I think he & Samuel would make a very good pair...." Excellent condition. With a fine steel-engraved portrait. 575.00

499. GARFIELD, JAMES A. President; assassinated. Manuscript Letter Signed "J. A. Garfield", while serving as Congressman from Ohio. 1 1/2 pages, 4to. Washington, December 18, 1872. To S. P. Wollcott, Kent, Portage Co., Ohio. Garfield informs his constituent of his efforts to obtain a position in the Post Office Department. "...I recently called on the P.M. General in regard to vacancies in the Postal Service in our District and found that there are none existing and no immediate prospect of any. It was intended by the Department to put a line of Postal Cars on the Erie Route and that may yet be done. But the dismissal of Sweetzer and other officers from the road has disarranged the business so that the matter is now left in uncertainty. I should be glad to assist your friend, Mr. Reese, but I know of no place that can be had for him, at least at present...." Minor paper repair to fold extremities hardly noticeable, otherwise fine. 350.00

500. ROOSEVELT, ELEANOR. First Lady. Typed Letter Signed, as First Lady, on gilt-imprinted White House stationery. 1 1/3 pages, large 8vo. Washington, April 30, 1935. To Jean Walker Simpson, New York City. Original postmarked envelope. Expresses thanks for "the lovely Easter gift" and asks that her order of last year be duplicated, "sending the same quantities to each person as I have always ordered..." In her own holograph, she has requested that Maple Syrup and candy be sent to Mrs. James Roosevelt, Mrs. John Badtiger and Mrs. Elliot Roosevelt, supplying their addresses. Together, eleven lines in her holograph. Nice association! 125.00

501. CLEVELAND, GROVER. President. Autograph Letter Signed. 2 pages, 8vo. Princeton, March 2, 1907. To Henry S. Watson. The former president writes: "I have written in the copies of Fishing and Hunting Sketches which you sent me for that purpose and have packed them ready to return to you. But I have mislaid your letter and am uncertain how and where you desired me to send them....I suggest that they go by express....I leave home in two or three days for an absence of ten days or two weeks; and perhaps you had better address your letter of instructions to Mrs. Cleveland...." Fine condition, and a nice letter to insert in a copy of Cleveland's delightful sporting book. 250.00

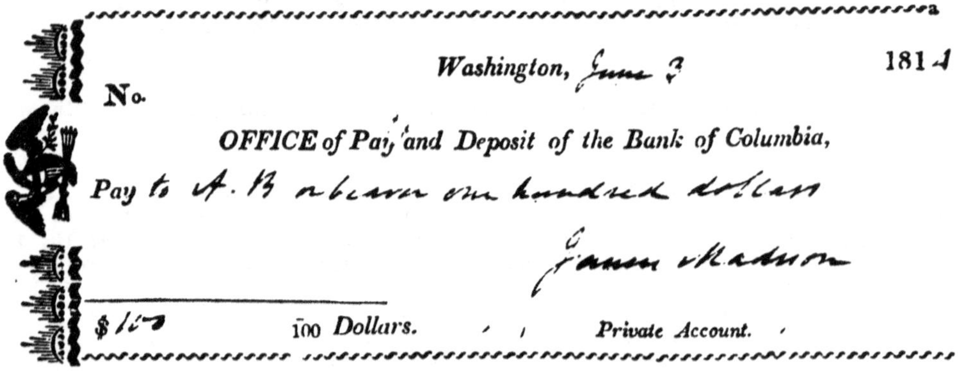

Washington, June 3 1814
No.
OFFICE of Pay and Deposit of the Bank of Columbia,
Pay to A. B. or bearer one hundred dollars
James Madison
$100
100 Dollars.
Private Account.

502. MADISON, JAMES. President. Partly printed Signed Bank Check, accomplished in his hand, as President. Oblong 12mo. Washington, June 3, 1814. Drawn on his "Private Account" of the Office of Pay and Deposit of the Bank of Columbia. Madison directs that One Hundred Dollars be paid "to A. B. or bearer". "A.B." is another way of writing "self". Eagle vignette at left. Closed cancellation slashes and spindle hole (very small). Fine condition for a check of this period. With handsome steel-engraved portrait. 850.00

503. WILSON, WOODROW. President. Partly printed Document Signed, as President. 1 page, small, tall folio. Washington, February 6, 1918. Countersigned by NEWTON D. BAKER, Secretary of War. President Wilson commissions Edgar Jadwin to the rank of Brigadier General in the National Army. Jadwin (1865-1931), was an assistant to General Goethals in building the Panama Canal (1907-1911); he served overseas in the World War (1917-1919), and later as Major General and Chief of Engineers. Eagle vignette at top center. Tiny spattering of ink on the "W" of Wilson in the signature. Unusual form of document apparently reserved for high-ranking officers. Embossed War Department seal at top left. Fine. 225.00

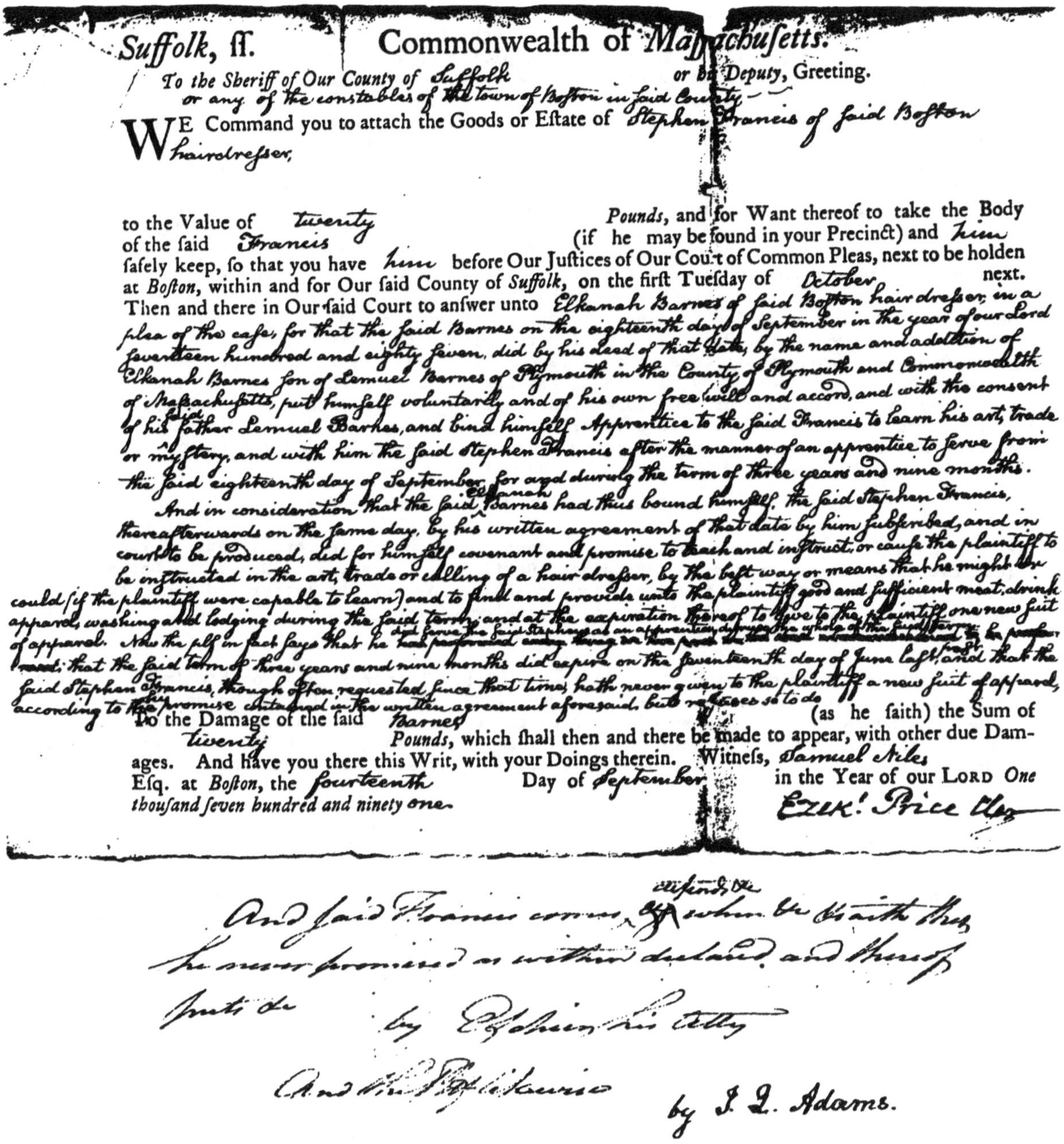
Suffolk, ss. Commonwealth of Massachusetts.

To the Sheriff of Our County of Suffolk or his Deputy, Greeting.
or any of the constables of the town of Boston in said County

WE Command you to attach the Goods or Estate of Stephen Francis of said Boston hairdresser,

to the Value of twenty Pounds, and for Want thereof to take the Body of the said Francis (if he may be found in your Precinct) and him safely keep, so that you have him before Our Justices of Our Court of Common Pleas, next to be holden at Boston, within and for Our said County of Suffolk, on the first Tuesday of October next. Then and there in Our said Court to answer unto Elkanah Barnes of said Boston hair dresser, in a plea of the case, for that the said Barnes on the eighteenth day of September in the year of our Lord seventeen hundred and eighty seven, did by his deed of that date, by the name and addition of Elkanah Barnes son of Lemuel Barnes of Plymouth in the County of Plymouth and Commonwealth of Massachusetts, put himself voluntarily and of his own free will and accord, and with the consent of his said father Lemuel Barnes, and bind himself Apprentice to the said Francis to learn his art, trade or mystery, and with him the said Stephen Francis after the manner of an apprentice to serve from the said eighteenth day of September, for and during the term of three years and nine months.

And in consideration that the said Elkanah Barnes had thus bound himself, the said Stephen Francis, thereafterwards on the same day, by his written agreement of that date by him subscribed, and in court to be produced, did for himself covenant and promise to teach and instruct, or cause the plaintiff to be instructed in the art, trade or calling of a hair dresser, by the best way or means that he might or could (if the plaintiff were capable to learn) and to find and provide unto the plaintiff good and sufficient meat, drink apparel, washing and lodging during the said term, and at the expiration thereof to give to the plaintiff one new suit of apparel. Now the plff in fact says that he [illegible] that the said term of three years and nine months did expire on the seventeenth day of June last, and that the said Stephen Francis, though often requested since that time, hath never given to the plaintiff a new suit of apparel, according to the promise contained in the written agreement aforesaid, but refuses so to do

To the Damage of the said Barnes (as he saith) the Sum of twenty Pounds, which shall then and there be made to appear, with other due Damages. And have you there this Writ, with your Doings therein. Witness, Samuel Niles Esq. at Boston, the fourteenth Day of September in the Year of our LORD One thousand seven hundred and ninety one

Ezek! Price Cler

And said Francis comes & defends &c when &c & saith that he never promised as within declared, and thereof puts &c

by Edw. [illegible] his atty

And the Plff likewise

by J. Q. Adams.

504. ADAMS, JOHN QUINCY. President. Document Signed, penned on the verso of a partly-printed writ-of-attachment accomplished in Adams's hand (hundreds of words). Small oblong 4to. Boston, September 6, 1791. This Suffolk County document authorizes the Sheriff to "Attach the Goods or Estate of Stephen Francis" to satisfy a judgment of 20 Pounds against him. The reason for this action is given in detail and is in Adams' hand. On the verso Edward Wentworth, Constable, and Adams have signed endorsements concerning the subject. Lightly stained in one vertical fold, else fine. Unusual and scarce legal document from the future President's early legal career. 350.00

505. FORD, BETTY. First Lady. Striking full-color quarto photograph showing a close-up facial image of the attractive First Lady. Inscribed against the white background of her blouse: "To Bob Nolder / with best wishes / Betty Ford". Highly attractive!! 75.00

506. ROOSEVELT, THEODORE. President and Vice President. Choice signature measuring five inches in length. Very ample margins. A knock-out! 125.00

507. MONROE, JAMES. President. Partly printed Document Signed, as President. Oblong legal folio, vellum. Washington, June 14, 1824. Countersigned by GEO. GRAHAM, Commissioner of the General Land Office. Embossed wafer seal of the Land Office at lower left. President Monroe grants 80 acres of land at Shawneetown, Illinois, as authorized by "the Acts of Congress relative to the disposal of the public Lands in ILLINOIS..." Two light stains in blank lower margin, else quite fine. Monroe's signature is very nice. With engraved portrait. 450.00

508. ROOSEVELT, THEODORE. President and Vice President. Typed Letter Signed, heavily corrected by Roosevelt. 2 full separate pages, 4to. Oyster Bay, Long Island, New York, May 27, 1916. To Mrs. A. W. Nicholson, Portland, Oregon. TR explains that his mail has been very heavy, and that it is "utterly out of the question for me to answer the letters I prize the most with more than a few lines." He continues: "Your letter has only just been brought before me, but not the story of Adison Bennet's to which you referred. I fear it has gone astray. I am happy to say I was of a little assistance in getting Homer's son a place on a railroad where, when I last heard from him, he was doing well. My dear Mrs. Nicholson, if I start a movement to give a stone to Homer, you have no conception of the multitude of similar movements I would have to go into. It seems churlish not to do as you request, but if you were in my place you would understand I simply can't undertake one such matter, without inviting like demands in hundreds of other cases. By George, I wish I had met your boy so as to recognize him. If I had realised who he was, when he was playing polo on Lond Island, I would have gotten him to come over to lunch. I understand exactly how you feel...in having him among those men, the men with whom he is entitled to associate as a gentleman -- and I never met a more typical gentlwoman (one whom Mrs. Roosevelt and I both felt in the same way about!) than a certain gentlewoman who brought her boys up on a ranch! That was a striking experience you touched on in your letter. Of course, my experience has been exactly like yours as to the cowardice and hypocrisy of so very many of the professional uplifters with whom we are dealing...." Highly unusual and personal letter, obviously written under great strain, as evidenced both by the content and the number of holograph corrections in Roosevelt's hand. Fine. 750.00

RARE LETTER SIGNED AS VICE PRESIDENT

509. ARTHUR, CHESTER A. President and Vice President. Manuscript Letter Signed, as Vice President, just two days before the death of President Garfield. 1 page, 8vo. New York, September 17, 1881. To Harrison Millard, New York City, thanking for for his letter and the gift of the "beautiful copy of your National Anthem." Fine condition. 575.00

510. TRUMAN, HARRY S. President and Vice President. Typed Letter Signed, on his imprinted letterhead. 1 page, 4to. Independence, April 5, 1962. To Hon. Homer C. Eberhardt, Atlanta, Ga. Truman had hoped to clear his schedule so as to be present for the annual Spring Banquet of the Demosthenian Literary Society of the University of Georgia, but "due to circumstanes which I did not anticipate it will not be possible...I am as sorry as I can be...." 125.00

511. HOOVER, HERBERT. President. Typed Letter Signed, as President, on imprinted White House letterhead. 1 page, 4to. Washington, June 8, 1931. To Hon. Walter F. George, U.S. Senator from Georgia. Hoover acknowledges Senator George's letter "...in which you ask that consideration be given to the name of Dr. Tait Butler for appointment on the Federal Farm Board. Thank you for writing me about Dr. Butler...." Fine example, and a nice association. 350.00

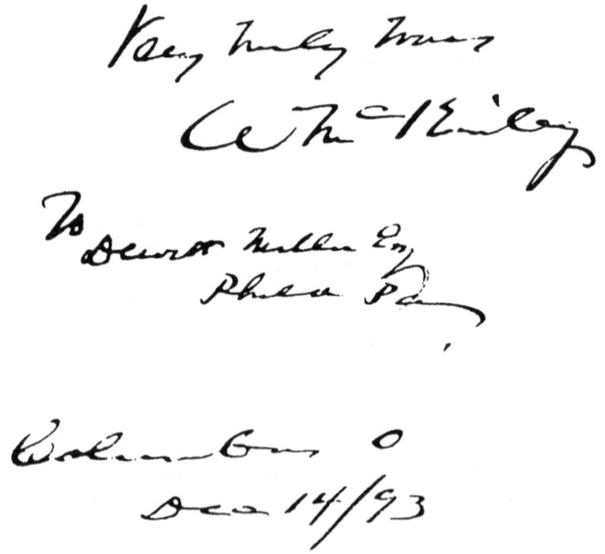

MC KINLEY'S COLLECTED SPEECHES THRU 1893

512. MC KINLEY, WILLIAM. President. Printed book: Speeches and Addresses of William McKinley from His Election to Congress to the Present Time. Gilt-lettered blue cloth. D. Appleton & Co., New York, 1893. First edition. Boldly inscribed on a blank preliminary leaf: "Very truly yours / W. Mc Kinley / To Dewitt Miller Esq. / Phila. Pa. / Columbus O / Dec 14/93". Frontisportrait. Fine copy of a very scarce signed presidential book. 950.00

EXTRAORDINARY COMMENTARY ON THEODORE ROOSEVELT'S RESOUNDING ELECTION VICTORY DAYS EARLIER, WITH THE ADDITIONAL NOTE THAT THE SOUTH "... COULD WORK OUT THE PROBLEM THEMSELVES IF THEY REALLY HOLD TOWARD THE NEGRO THE EARNEST DESIRE TO BETTER THE RACE."

513. TAFT, WILLIAM H. President; Chief Justice, U.S. Supreme Court. Remarkable Typed Letter Signed "Affectionately yours / Bill", as Secretary of War in Roosevelt's cabinet, on imprinted War Department letterhead. 2 separate pages, small 4to. Washington, November 13, 1904. To Hon. Howard C. Hollister, Cincinnati, Ohio. Original stamped, postmarked envelope. He writes:

> "...I agree with you that the victory is so great as to be almost alarming. We need to keep our heads and see that our house is put in order. This is no judgment in favor of a reckless government. It is only a vote of confidence which it is our duty to show that we deserve. The victory is so overwhelming that I cannot think that anything that was done in the way of speaking had any particular effect. The motions had to be gone through with, and we went through them, but the victory is a tribute to the personal popularity of the President.
>
> The Question in the South makes one pause. There are many difficulties connected with it, and yet if some of the leaders would assume a heroic attitude and be willing to give up their representation, which they now unfairly hold, they could work out the problem themselves if they really hold toward the negro the earnest desire to better the race. Perhaps that is what will come out of this victory. Let us hope so...."

One of the most thought-provoking Taft letters we have encountered. Very fine. 750.00

COMPLETION OF NEW MODELS FOR HARPERS FERRY

514. DAVIS, JEFFERSON. President, Confederate States of America. Manuscript Letter Signed, as Secretary of War. 2 pages, 4to. War Department [Washington], January 17, 1856. To Hon. C. J. Faulkner. Davis writes: "I find an unexpected delay has occurred in the completion of the new models; but have assurance that they will be finished this week, so as to be ready for inspection at the beginning of next week when those designed for Harper's Ferry will be sent thither -- after which we shall be able to resume full work at that Armory. That class of the community who have been for a time suspended from employment will I hope then be relieved from their embarrasment...." Davis then goes on at some length to discuss the employment situation at the Armory, saying that he thinks there will be a need for three new clerks. It was at this same Government Arsenal that John Brown led his raid three years later. Fine. 500.00

515. HOOVER, HERBERT. President. Handsome imprinted White House card, boldly signed, as President. Washington, no date. Mint! One of the scarcer presidents to find in this format. 250.00

HAND-COLORED WATERCOLOR OF THE WHITE HOUSE

516. ROOSEVELT, FRANKLIN D. President. Strikingly beautiful hand-colored watercolor vignette of the front approach to the White House. Quarto. Boldly signed, as President, by Roosevelt in bright blue ink on the wide lower white margin. Pristine condition. Handsomely matted and framed under glass in a new frame. Spectacular display piece!! 450.00

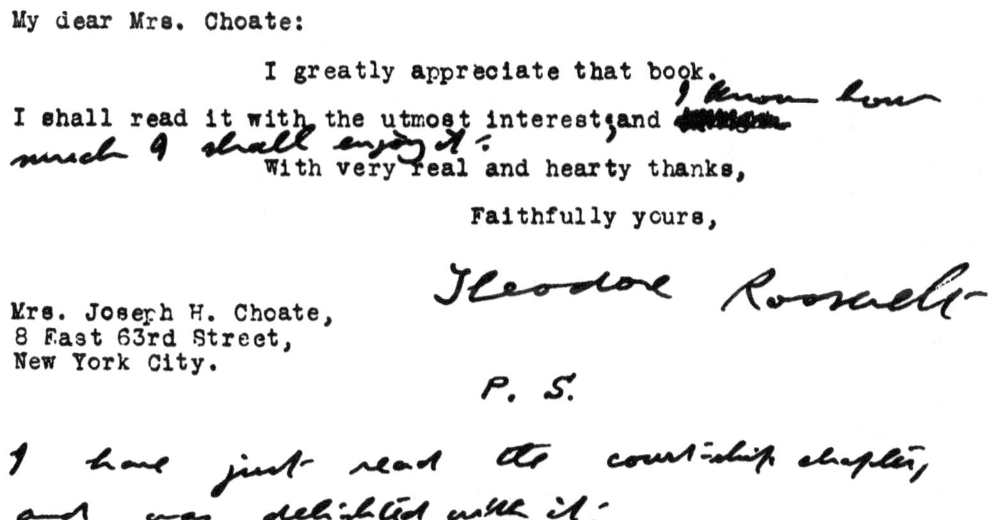

My dear Mrs. Choate:

I greatly appreciate that book. I shall read it with the utmost interest; and I know how much I shall enjoy it:

With very real and hearty thanks,

Faithfully yours,

Theodore Roosevelt

Mrs. Joseph H. Choate,
8 East 63rd Street,
New York City.

P. S.

I have just read the court-ship chapter, and was delighted with it:

517. ROOSEVELT, THEODORE. President and Vice President. Typed Letter Signed, on the imprinted letterhead of the Metropolitan. 2/3 page, 4to. New York, December 27, 1917. To Mrs. Joseph H. Choate, New York City, acknowledging receipt of a book. He writes: "...I shall read it with the utmost interest; and I know how much I shall enjoy it...I have just read the court-ship chapter, and was delighted with it." As illustrated above, Roosevelt has "personalized" this typed letter with several holograph additions in his own hand. Fine. 295.00

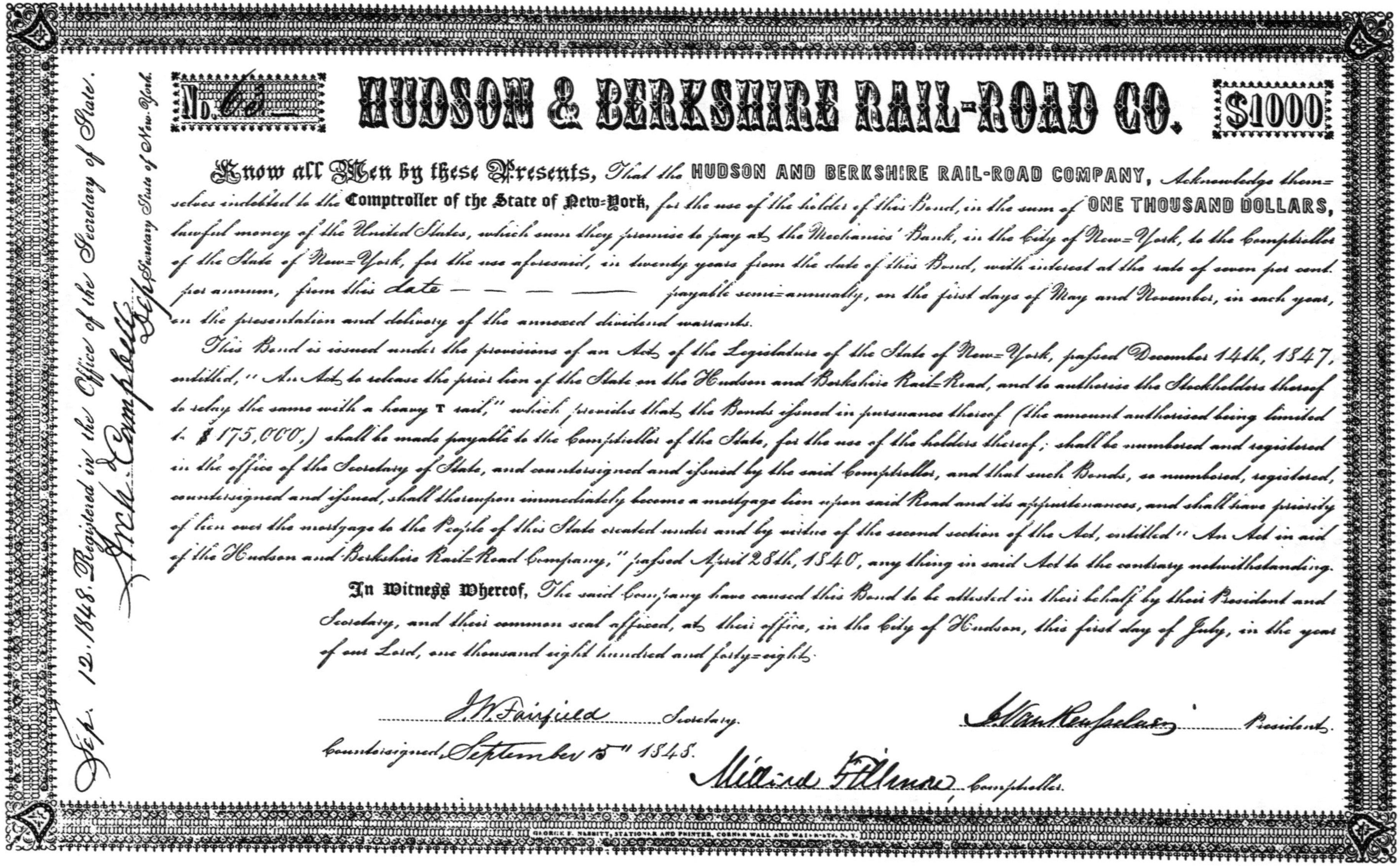

No. 63

HUDSON & BERKSHIRE RAIL-ROAD CO.

$1000

Know all Men by these Presents, That the HUDSON AND BERKSHIRE RAIL-ROAD COMPANY, Acknowledge themselves indebted to the Comptroller of the State of New-York, for the use of the holder of this Bond, in the sum of ONE THOUSAND DOLLARS, lawful money of the United States, which sum they promise to pay at the Mechanics' Bank, in the City of New-York, to the Comptroller of the State of New-York, for the use aforesaid, in twenty years from the date of this Bond, with interest at the rate of seven per cent. per annum, from this date — — — —— payable semi-annually, on the first days of May and November, in each year, on the presentation and delivery of the annexed dividend warrants.

This Bond is issued under the provisions of an Act of the Legislature of the State of New-York, passed December 14th, 1847, entitled, "An Act to release the prior lien of the State on the Hudson and Berkshire Rail-Road, and to authorise the Stockholders thereof to relay the same with a heavy T rail," which provides that the Bonds issued in pursuance thereof (the amount authorised being limited to $175,000,) shall be made payable to the Comptroller of the State, for the use of the holders thereof; shall be numbered and registered in the office of the Secretary of State, and countersigned and issued by the said Comptroller, and that such Bonds, so numbered, registered, countersigned and issued, shall thereupon immediately become a mortgage lien upon said Road and its appurtenances, and shall have priority of lien over the mortgage to the People of this State created under and by virtue of the second section of the Act, entitled "An Act in aid of the Hudson and Berkshire Rail-Road Company," passed April 28th, 1840, any thing in said Act to the contrary notwithstanding.

In Witness Whereof, The said Company have caused this Bond to be attested in their behalf by their President and Secretary, and their common seal affixed, at their office, in the City of Hudson, this first day of July, in the year of our Lord, one thousand eight hundred and forty-eight.

J. W. Fairfield, Secretary.

A. Van Rensselaer, President.

Countersigned, September 5th 1848.

Millard Fillmore, Comptroller.

Sep. 12. 1848. Registered in the Office of the Secretary of State.

Arch. Campbell, Dep. Secretary State of New-York.

[Item No. 518]

HUDSON & BERKSHIRE RAIL-ROAD CO. $1000 COUPON BOND

518. FILLMORE, MILLARD. President and Vice President. Unusual partly printed Document Signed, as Comptroller of the State of New York. One page, folio. September 15, 1848. Coupon Bond for $1000 issued by the Hudson & Berkshire Rail-Road Co., and guaranteed by the State of New York (hence Fillmore's signature as Comptroller). One of a series of 175 bonds issued. Also signed by the President and Secretary of the Rail-Road. Blind-stamped seal of the company with a vignette of an early engine. Seven rows of coupons printed beneath (not shown in the illustration on opposite page). Several tiny punch-cancellation holes ever so slightly affect Fillmore's signature. Ornate ruled border. At this time Fillmore was a candidate for Vice President. Choice financial document, once fairly plentiful, now quite rare!! 950.00

RARE HOLOGRAPH LETTER AS PRESIDENT

519. TAFT, WILLIAM H. President; Chief Justice, U.S. Supreme Court. Autograph Letter Signed, as President, on imprinted White House stationery. 2 separate pages, 8vo. Washington, December 4, 1912. To Colonel Archibald Gracie, New York City. Taft, who had recently been defeated for re-election, writes: "I am very sorry to hear that you are not well and that you are heavy hearted with the prospect. I beg of you to take heart. Your note was written at three in the morning and that is always a mournful time but it comes only a short time before sunrise and the morning. With the earnest hope that I may see you up and about again and with my compliments and good wishes to your family..." Excellent! 1750.00

520. ADAMS, JOHN QUINCY. President. Attractive, partly printed Document Signed, as President. Oblong folio, vellum. Washington, April 1, 1825. Countersigned by GEO. GRAHAM, Commissioner of the General Land Office. Embossed wafer seal of the Land Office affixed with red wax. Grant of 162 and 36/100 acres of land in the area of Cincinnati, as authorized by "the Act of Congress, entitled An Act providing for the sale of the Lands of the United States, in the Territory north west of the OHIO, and above the mouth of Kentucky River..." Clean and fresh, with a choice bold signature of Adams. Engraved portrait accompanies. 475.00

521. MONROE, JAMES. President. Choice signature and several words in his hand cut from a letter. Handsome steel-engraved portrait. Ideal pair for framing or display. 150.00

522. HOOVER, HERBERT. President. His book: A Cause to Win / Five Speeches...on American Foreign Policy in Relation to Soviet Russia. Stiff printed wrappers bound in red cloth. New York, no date. Inscribed on early flyleaf above a printed Hoover quotation: "To Margaret F. Shattuck / With the Good Wishes / of / Herbert Hoover". Probably a First Edition. Very scarce title which we have never seen before. Excellent condition. 195.00

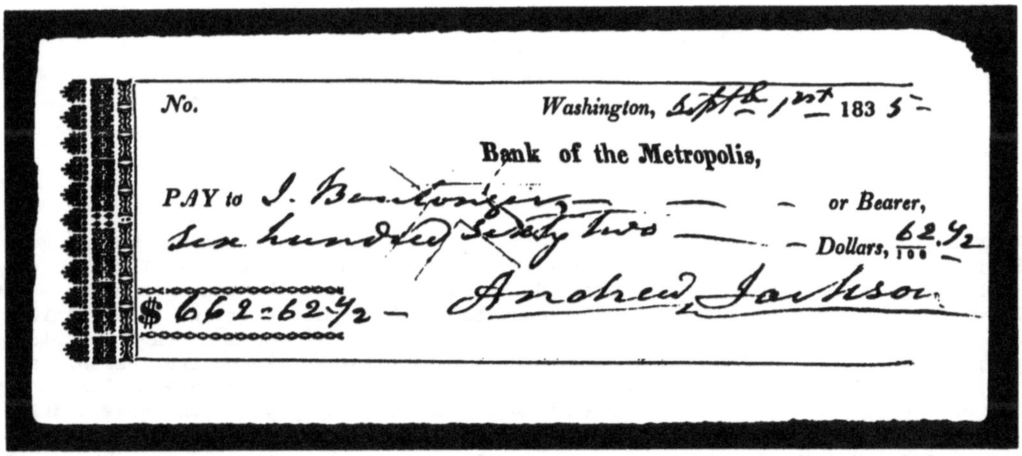

CHECK SIGNED AS PRESIDENT

523. JACKSON, ANDREW. President. Partly printed Signed Bank Check, as President, accomplished in his hand. Oblong 12mo. Washington, September 1, 1835. Drawn on the Bank of the Metropolis, Jackson has made this check payable to I. Bantonger in the amount of $666.62½ (at that time the U.S. Mint made half-cents!). Cancellation slashes (nothing missing) do not affect Jackson's bold signature. With handsome steel-engraved portrait. 1500.00

THE AMERICAN AMBASSADOR TO RUSSIA IS RECALLED

524. BUCHANAN, JAMES. President. Interesting partly printed Document Signed, as President. One page, 4to. Washington, March 30, 1858. President Buchanan authorizes the Secretary of State to affix the Seal of the United States to "the envelope of a letter addressed to His Majesty the Emperor of Russia (Mr. Seymour's recall)..." Choice condition. 675.00

525. CLEVELAND, GROVER. President. Printed book containing the papers of his first presidential term: The Public Papers of Grover Cleveland...March 4, 1885, to March 4, 1889. Deep maroon cloth, gilt-lettered spine. Government Printing Office: Washington, 1889. First edition. Inscribed by Cleveland between his presidential terms on the front endpaper: "Matt H. Ellis Esq. / With the compliments / of / Grover Cleveland / New York February 3d 1891." Some binding wear from rubbing, else a very good copy. 500.00

526. TAFT, WILLIAM H. President; Chief Justice, U.S. Supreme Court. Choice engraved vignette of the White House, by the Bureau of Engraving and Printing, showing the wide driveway to the front entrance. Oblong 12mo. Signed by Taft, probably as President, on the lower white margin. Taft is very scarce in signed White House vignettes. Fine. 375.00

527. ARTHUR, CHESTER A. President and Vice President. Manuscript Letter Signed, as President, on imprinted Executive Mansion stationery. 1 1/2 separate pages, 8vo. Washington, February 25, 1885. To Hon. G. A. Pierce, Territorial Governor, Bismarck, Dakota. Writing at the close of his presidency, Arthur acknowledges the Governor's personal note and states that he fully appreciates "all the friendly expressions it contains." Arthur continues: "In congratulating you upon the successful administration of your office, permit me to reciprocate your kind wishes..." Territorial Governors are appointed by the President and hold their office at his pleasure. Some very light browning on the first page, else quite fine. Arthur is difficult to find in letters of presidential date. 650.00

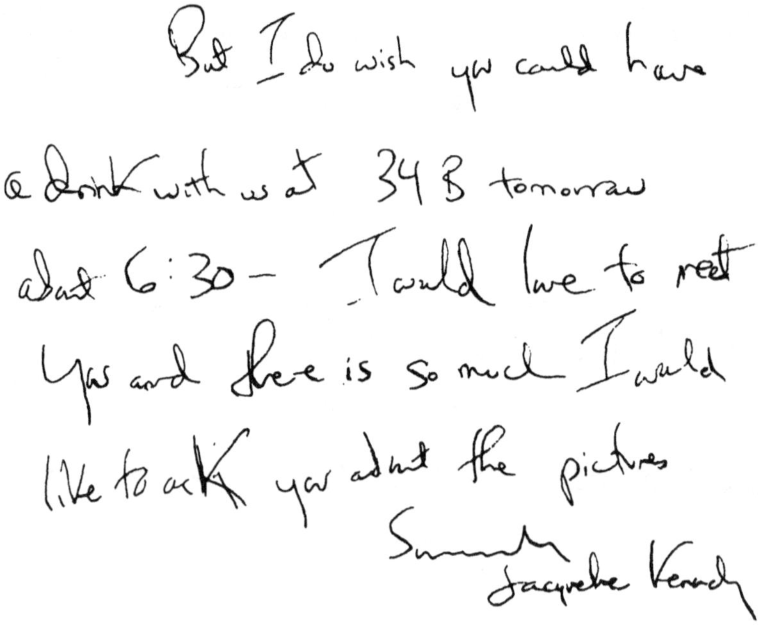
But I do wish you could have
a drink with us at 34 B tomorrow
about 6:30 — I would love to meet
you and there is so much I would
like to ask you about the pictures
Sincerely
Jacqueline Kennedy

528. KENNEDY, JACQUELINE [MRS. JOHN F.] First Lady. Autograph Letter Signed, on the gilt-crested imprinted stationery of the Carlyle Hotel. 3 full pp., 8vo. New York, no date. To Mr. Dowling, owner-manager of the famed New York hotel where the Kennedys often stayed. She writes: "I could not reach you yesterday to thank you for putting the so familiar and much loved Penthouse at our disposal and for filling it with the most fabulous pictures. My breath was taken away when I went to look. As I think you know, the reason I am not staying in it is that my sister really does have vertigo & as these are my last 3 days with her, of course I wanted to stay where she did. But I do wish you could have a drink with us at 34B tomorrow about 6:30 -- I would love to meet you and there is so much I would like to ask you about the pictures..." Probably written between 1957 and 1960. Fine and choice! 750.00

"THE GREAT WHITE FATHER" APPROVES AN ACT OF THE CHICKASAW NATION

529. MC KINLEY, WILLIAM. President. Partly printed Document Signed, as President. 1 page, legal folio. Executive Mansion, Washington, December 5, 1898. Also signed by C. D. Carter, National Secretary of the Chickasaw Nation. Attached to a two-page original Act of the Chickasaw Indian Nation authorizing Lewis V. Colbert to establish and maintain a ferry at the Mannsville Crossing on the Washita River. Under the terms of this Act, Indians could use the ferry toll free, and whites had to pay. The toll fees are specified in the Act. Mc Kinley approves this Act. Choice presidential document relating to American Indians, and a splendid example of a presidential duty one hears and sees little about. Fine condition. [A document similar to this is illustrated on page 123 of our large Presidential Catalogue]. 850.00

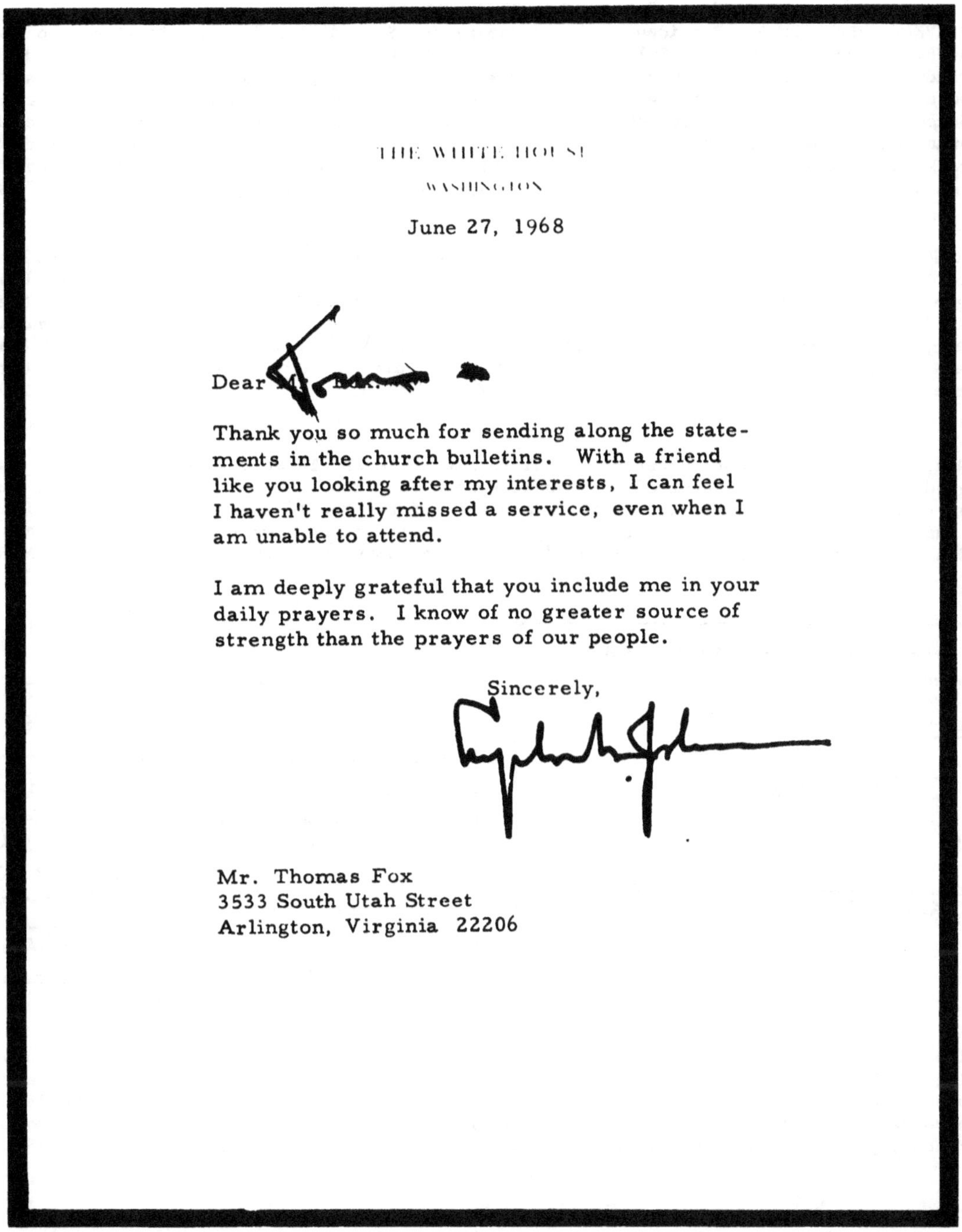

THE WHITE HOUSE

WASHINGTON

June 27, 1968

Dear Tom

Thank you so much for sending along the statements in the church bulletins. With a friend like you looking after my interests, I can feel I haven't really missed a service, even when I am unable to attend.

I am deeply grateful that you include me in your daily prayers. I know of no greater source of strength than the prayers of our people.

Sincerely,

Mr. Thomas Fox
3533 South Utah Street
Arlington, Virginia 22206

530. JOHNSON, LYNDON B. President and Vice President. Excessive rare Typed Letter Signed "Lyndon B. Johnson", as President, on imprinted White House stationery. 1 page, 4to. Washington, June 27, 1968. To Mr. Thomas Fox, Arlington, Virginia. Johnson has boldly penned "Tom" over the typed salutation "Mr. Fox". Fox had served as Head Usher at the White House and had interested President Johnson in attending The National City Christian Church in Washington. In this letter he thanks Fox for "sending along the statements in the church bulletins." Accompanying this fine letter is one of the Church Bulletins, this one dated June 30, 1968. Because of the extensive use of the autopen it is extremely difficult to find authentically signed Johnson letters as President. Fine condition. 1500.00

AVIATION CONFERENCE APPOINTMENT

531. ROOSEVELT, FRANKLIN D. President. Unusual Typed Document Signed, as President. 1 page, small folio. Washington, August 31, 1938. Countersigned by CORDELL HULL, Secretary of State. With white wafer embossed State Department seal. Roosevelt appoints G. Grant Mason, Jr., then serving as a member of the Civil Aeronautics Authority, Chairman of the Delegation of the United States of America to the Fourth International Conference on Private Air Law to be held at Brussels, Belgium. The document has been pressure-mounted on heavy backing, but is otherwise in fine condition. An unusual presidential appointment. 375.00

TO JAMES A. FARLEY, TRACKING DOWN LOST HEIRS!!

532. ROOSEVELT, FRANKLIN D. President. Typed Memorandum Signed "F.D.R.", as President, on imprinted White House stationery. Full page, 8vo. Hyde Park, N.Y., October 6, 1938. Headed: "Memorandum for the Postmaster General", who was his former campaign manager, James A. Farley. Roosevelt writes: "I am trying to find some lost heirs and all efforts so far have been unsuccessful. I wonder if you would see if the Postmaster at Yonkers, New York, can get any information on the following: The people in question are Sarah DeWitt Lent, first wife of Franklin T. Lent, who, in 1903, was living with her five children at 104 Waring Place, Yonkers, N.Y. ..." Fine condition, and a highly unusual communication! 575.00

533. HARRISON, BENJAMIN. President. Typed Letter Signed, on his imprinted stationery. 1/2 page, 4to. Indianapolis, March 4, 1901. To David A. Munro, New York. The former president acknowleges his correspondent's letter "...with the enclosed check for $500 honorarium for the article in your March number. You did not need to make any apology for the delay in sending it. I enclose a receipt...." In an initialed note by Harrison's secretary at the bottom, she says that "General Harrison asks if you will kindly send him an extra copy of each of the three numbers in which his articles appeared." Fine condition. 225.00

534. REAGAN, RONALD. President; Governor of California; film and TV actor. Partly printed Document Signed, as Honorary President of the Ronald Reagan Fan Club. Oblong 16mo. No place, June 1948. Certifies that Darletta Gimpel is a member of the Ronald Reagan Fan Club from June 1948 to June 1949. Also signed by Terry Sevigny, Active President. On the verso, Reagan has penned a charming Autograph Letter Signed "Ronald", welcoming his new fan. He writes: "A hearty

OFFICIAL MEMBERSHIP CARD
THIS CERTIFIES THAT
Darletta Gimpel
IS A MEMBER OF THE
Ronald Reagan Fan Club
FROM June 1948 TO June 1949
Ronald Reagan Terry Sevigny
HONORARY PRESIDENT ACTIVE PRESIDENT
(over)

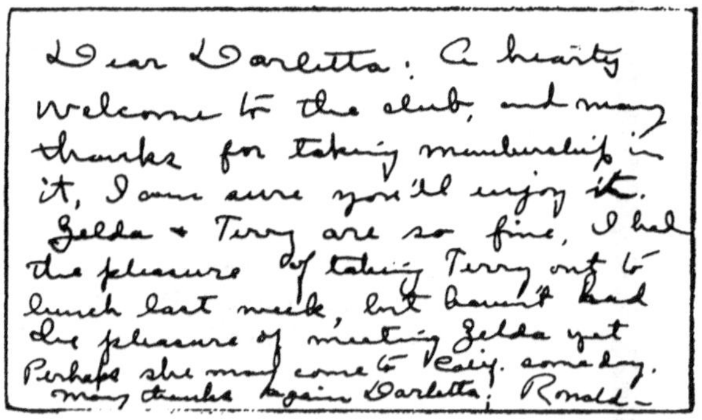
Dear Darletta: A hearty welcome to the club, and many thanks for taking membership in it, I am sure you'll enjoy it. Zelda & Terry are so fine, I had the pleasure of taking Terry out to lunch last week, but haven't had the pleasure of meeting Zelda yet Perhaps she may come to Calif. some day. Many thanks again Darletta! Ronald

welcome to the club, and many thanks for taking membership in it. I am sure you'll enjoy it. Zelda and Terry are so fine. I had the pleasure of taking Terry out to lunch last week, but haven't had the pleasure of meeting Zelda yet. Perhaps she may come to Calif. some day. Many thanks again Darletta! Ronald" An interesting and uncommon souvenir from Reagan's movie career, dating from the year of his break-up with wife Jane Wyman. Choice! 750.00

535. HAYES, RUTHERFORD B. President; Governor of Ohio; Union General in Civil War. Strikingly handsome partly engraved Document Signed, as Commander in Chief of the Military Order of the Loyal Legion of the United States. 1 page, large oblong folio. Philadelphia, December 5, 1891. Countersigned by John P. Nicholson, Recorder in Chief. Embossed orange wafer seal at lower left. Certifies that Second Lieutenant Charles Francis Luther formerly of the 82nd U.S. Colored Infantry is a Companion of the First Class of the Military Order of the Loyal Legion. Ornately engraved, containing the Legion Seal at top center. Military awards and decorations for colored officers are seldom seen. Excellent condition. 395.00

536. MADISON, DOLLY P. 1768-1849. First Lady; celebrated hostess at the Executive Mansion. Manuscript Letter Signed "D. P. Madison". 1p., 4to. Montpellier, August 20, 1839. To Mr. Smith, Cashier of the Bank of the Metropolis, concerning the renewal of her note with that bank. She acknowledges receipt of the renewed note, and states: "...I did not take a note of the exact day and am therefore obliged to ask the favor of your enquiring of Mr. Nourse the date to be inserted.... Altho' I have generally paid the Bank the notes & drafts without renewal, yet in the present instance I have continued it longer on account of not having made dispositions, the prices being a bar, of what has been some time intended. This induces me to deposit the two notes enclosed...." Following the death of her husband, James Madison, in 1836, Mrs. Madison entered into negotiation with the Government for the purchase of her late husband's papers. It was not until this was accomplished that she became free of debt. With engraved portrait. Fine condition, and a revealing financial letter. 850.00

537. ARTHUR, CHESTER A. President and Vice President. Manuscript Order Signed, as Collector of Customs for the Port of New York, on the imprinted stationery of that office. Full page, 4to. Collector's Office, September 25, 1873. Interesting document concerning postal regulations governing the importation of goods sent through the mails. "Books and other printed matter and samples of merchandise, the importation of which through the mail, is allowed by the Postal Convention with Great Britain of June 18, 1867, will, on being transmitted to this office by the Postmaster, be received and held...for the payment of duties thereon. Merchandise the introduction of which into the U. States through the mail is illegal will ...be taken possession of by the Customs Officer...after the prescribed examination thereof at the Post Office, and lodged with the 9th or Seizure Division..." Unusual specimen, in excellent condition. Arthur went from the corrupt Customs House of New York to the Vice Presidency, and following Garfield's assassination and death, was sworn in as President. Attractive item. 575.00

538. EISENHOWER, MAMIE DAUD. First Lady. Typed Letter Signed, as First Lady, on gilt-imprinted White House stationery. Full page, small 4to. Washington, June 1, 1959. To Meredith Johnson, Director of Woodlawn Plantation, Mount Vernon, Virginia. Original envelope. Expresses her gratitude "...for making my recent trip to Woodlawn Plantation such a pleasant one. Not only did I enjoy seeing this historic home and all its lovely antiques, but how exquisite all the flower arrangements were! It was almost like actually spending an hour or so in the past, and I shall long remember my visit there...." In the concluding paragraph she expresses her thanks for the Woodlawn mementos and for remembering her grandchildren. Very slight browning on top third of the letter, mentioned for accuracy only. Fine. 75.00

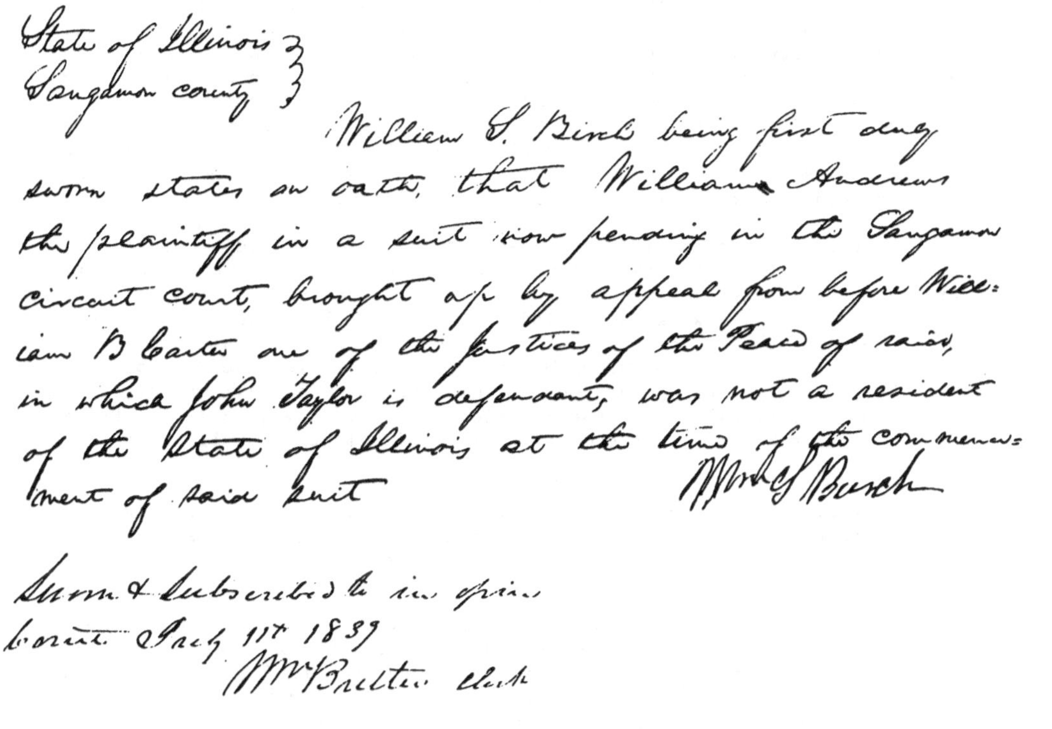
State of Illinois }
Sangamon county }
William S. Birch being first duly sworn states on oath, that William Andrews the plaintiff in a suit now pending in the Sangamon circuit court, brought up by appeal from before William B Carter one of the Justices of the Peace of said, in which John Taylor is defendant, was not a resident of the State of Illinois at the time of the commencement of said suit

Wm S Birch

Sworn & Subscribed to in open court July 11th 1839
Wm Butler clerk

539. LINCOLN, ABRAHAM. President. Early Autograph Manuscript Legal Affidavit, unsigned. 1 page, small 4to. Sangamon County, Illinois, July 11, 1839. Completely in Lincoln's hand, this affidavit bears the signature of William S. Birch; it is also signed by William Butler, Clerk and friend of Lincoln's. There is also a two-line docket in Lincoln's hand on the verso. With a fine engraved portrait of Lincoln. Nice ensemble for framing, and an ideal decoration for a lawyer's office. Excellent condition. 750.00

540. EISENHOWER, DWIGHT D. President and General. Typed Letter Signed "D E", as President of Columbia University, on blue imprinted stationery. 1 page, 8vo. Denver, Colorado, August 31, 1950. To Robert Woodruff, President of Coca-Cola, Atlanta, Georgia. Ike writes: "Thanks for sending along the little notation from QUICK. I most certainly hope that I will not be tagged for that one. Incidentally, I have some interesting things to tell you that have come out of Washington. I shall hope to see you as soon as I get back...." Fine. 150.00

541. TRUMAN, HARRY S. President and Vice President. Striking 8 x 10 photograph showing the full-face smiling portrait of Truman seated at his desk, reading a book. Photograph is from the U.S. Army files, and was taken while President in 1952. Inscribed and signed by Truman, late in life, against the light foreground. Stunning pose! 150.00

542. ADAMS, JOHN. 1735-1826. President of the United States. Autograph Letter Signed. 3pp., 4to. Quincy, January 10, 1813. To [William] Plumer, Governor of New Hampshire. Most amazing and fascinating letter written by the ex-President in what he terms his garrulous old age, covering bits of New England politics, the Clintons of New York, the War of 1812, the American clergy, and the strength of minority factions in the government. Like Adams we "find nothing so difficult as to abridge and compress." In part:

"Our two great Parties have crossed over the Valley and taken Possession of each others Mountain. The Coalition of North and Fox in 1783 was modest in comparison with that between Clinton and the Federalists. To Jay, King, Ross, and Pinkney the Pill was too bitter. A gentleman of greater Talents and higher rank than Rufus King, asked him, at N.York 'Do you intend to vote for De Witt?' Rufus answered 'No. Would you vote for Ben. Austin?'

"I can say little of Mr. Clinton for I know nothing but by hearsay, having never seen him. Of his Ambition, his Avarice, his Intrigues and those of his uncle George, I have heard enough, but know very little. But one thing I know. The State of New York has become a great State: and De Witt Clinton a great Man, good, bad, or indifferent. The Clintons are a Phenomenon in this Nation. No Governor, but George was ever Supported 25 Years. Was this Talent? Was this Virtue? Was this Policy? It was a Union of Interests, that was neither formed or cemented by him, any more than his formation in his Mother's Womb was his Work. A coincidence of Irish, Scotch, Dutch, and Presbyterian Parties, which he, himself never understood supported him in Spight of the clumsy Ambition and gross Avarice, with which he is charged. To account for this combination of Interests in favour of George we must search, thoroughly search the History of the Episcopal Church, and the Great Manors, the Livingstons, the Phillipses and the Vanranselaers in New York. The Schylers, the Hamiltons and the Burrs, and the DeLanceys, have been but temporary Comets in this Planitary System of New York. DeWitt, then is founded on a Rock. The combination of Irish, Dutch, Presbyterians and all other Dissenters will support him against the Church and the Manors: and the generous Horse New England will be ridden as hard as it ever has been by Virginia.

"Was there ever a popular war in any Nation? I was told by wise men in France, that our American Revolutionary War was the first and only popular War that a King of France ever waged. The present War has been unpopular in England for twenty years. The Wars of the Indians are commonly begun against the advice of the oldest and wisest Sachems, and the common People are averse, but War is urged on by ambitious young Warriours. The People, the Bulk of Nations, are unhappily always jealous and envious of Government and all who are concerned in it. They impute all War to the Ambition, Avarice, Envy, Jealousy, Pride and Revenge in their Rulers, in the most popular Governments as well as in the most absolute.

"The Clergy of the Country are growing more and more like the Clergy of all other Countries. Osgood, Parish, Gardiner are but Miniatures of South Sacheverel Land and Lorain, and in that rank I leave them.

"It is the destiny of our Country to be divided. I shall not be credited by any but Governor Langdon and Governor Gerry, Dr. Rush and George Clymer when I assure you that almost every essential Question from 1774 to 1813 has been determined by very Small Majorities. Majorities for the last twelve years have been greater than they ever were before: and perhaps than they ever will be again. I agree with you that the change in New England is more in Appearance than in reality. But the Taxes! the Taxes! The Administration of the Nineteenth Century have conjured up the Hobgoblin and they must exorcise the Fiend if they can.

"Vermont is apparently in opposition to all the rest of New England. New York was sold for a valuable consideration. I suspect you have not been informed of the Analysis of their Election. If I am not misinformed, you will find Rufus King a Senator of U.S.

"You ask why my Letters do not continue in the Patriot? My answer is 1st: I had finished my Plan, which was to deposit in Print, where some curious Antiquarian might hereafter find them, certain Documents explanatory of my Quasi War, and final Peace with France in the last Century: and of my Peace with Great Britain in 1782 & 1783; both of which had been misrepresented, libeled and belied. 2nd: I had exhausted the Patience of all Parties."

Choice historical letter of fine content, and neatly inlaid. 7500.00

543. ROOSEVELT, FRANKLIN D. President. Brief Typed Letter Signed, as Governor of New York, on the blue and gilt-imprinted stationery of the governorship. 1 page, 4to. Warm Springs, Georgia, November 22, 1930. To Frank S. Cummings, Ansonia, Connecticut. Full text reads: "I am very grateful for your letter of November tenth. It was good of you to think of me and I appreciate it...." FDR had just been elected to his second term as Governor, and was on vacation at Warm Springs following his victory. Fine example. 150.00

Dear Bob:

Thank you for your heart-warming remembrance on my birthday; hereafter, I shall certainly know where to go for poetry--made to order.

With warm regard,

Sincerely,

Ike

Mr. Robert Woodruff
P. O. Box 1734
Atlanta, Ga.

I'm filing the poem under the authorship of Jones, Woodruff and Jones! Correct? D

544. EISENHOWER, DWIGHT D. President; General in World War II; planned Allied Invasion of Europe. Typed Letter Signed "Ike", as President of Columbia University, on blue imprinted University stationery. Full page, 8vo. New York, October 21, 1950. To Robert Woodruff, President of the Coca-Cola Co., Atlanta, Georgia. Ike sends his friend thanks for a poem sent to him on his birthday, and in a four-line holograph initialed postscript, adds: "I'm filing the poem under the authorship of Jones, Woodruff and Jones! Correct? D." This may possibly be a reference to Bobby Jones, the great golfer. Ike is scarce in holograph material. 575.00

545. TAFT, WILLIAM H. President; Chief Justice, U.S. Supreme Court. Typed Letter Signed, as Chief Justice, on imprinted Supreme Court stationery. 1/2 page, 4to. Washington, December 14, 1927. To Frank B. Steele, National Society of the Sons of the American Revolution, Washington. Taft regrets that it will not be possible to attend a reception for Mr. & Mrs. Rogers at National Headquarters. Nice example. 150.00

COMMUTATION OF THE DEATH SENTENCE FOR A NOTORIOUS CRIMINAL

546. HAYES, RUTHERFORD B. President. Manuscript Document Signed, as Governor of Ohio. Ornate engraved heading which features a marvellous vignette of the Ohio State Seal. 1 page, folio. Columbus, Ohio, April 27, 1870. To the Sheriff of Adams County, stating that Frank Hardy, who was convicted of Murder in the First Degree and sentenced to be hanged on the 6th day of May, 1870, has his sentence commuted to imprisonment for life. On the verso Hardy has signed a statement in which he accepts the commutation. Unusual, and most attractive! 250.00

547. MC KINLEY, WILLIAM. President; Governor of Ohio; assassinated (1901). Strikingly handsome cabinet photograph by Courtney, located in the McKinley Block, Canton, Ohio. Shows a very dignified formal profile bust pose of the president. Boldly signed in jet-black ink "Cordially Yours / Wm Mc Kinley". All of the signature, with the exception of the lower stroke of the "y" is on the surface of the photograph. The contrast is excellent. An outstanding presidential photograph! 750.00

548. HARRISON, BENJAMIN. President. Manuscript Letter Signed, on his imprinted Berkeley Lodge letterhead. 1 page, 8vo. Old Forge, N.Y., August 10, 1896. To Ruth Sadler, Alameda, California. Expresses thanks for a picture. Nice clean specimen. 225.00

IMPORTANT WAR-DATED LETTER IN SUPPORT OF THE Y. M. C. A.

549. TAFT, WILLIAM H. President; Chief Justice, U.S. Supreme Court. Choice Typed Letter Signed, on his imprinted letterhead. 2 full separate pages, 4to. New Haven, Conn., October 17, 1917. To Mr. Fessenden. Taft writes:

> "Experience fully adequate for knowing what is needed has convinced Dr. John R. Mott, and all others connected with the Young Men's Christian Association, that the $4,000,000 already raised for war work to help our soldiers in their camps in this country and overseas, will have to be supplemented by $35,000,000 more to accomplish the valuable and indispensable objects of the Young Men's Christian Association. Everyone, without exception, testifies in superlative language to the good which the Y.M.C.A. is doing in the British Army, in the French Army, and now among our own boys.
>
> Every father and mother who have a boy at the front, or in the cantonments, know through the boy that except for the Y.M.C.A., life in the ranks would be intolerable. The Government furnishes all that it can, but the Y.M.C.A., with its executive experience in this and other wars, and with its elasticity, is able to do what the Government cannot do.
>
> The Red Cross attends to the wounded men and the sick men, the Y.M.C.A. to the unwounded, the men who are on duty or who are serving by waiting. The people of the United States have tried the Young Men's Christian Association, and know it. They know that Dr. Mott never attempts anything that he does not succeed in; that he never asks for money that he does not know where every dollar is to go and to effect the purpose which he declares. It is really a great opportunity for those who are not able to serve in the trenches to do something that will directly contribute to winning this war...."

In the concluding paragraph Taft invites his correspondent to a luncheon at the Hotel Taft in New Haven, where the campaign for Connecticut will be launched. A most interesting letter showing Taft's eagerness to assist in the war effort by raising funds for Dr. Mott and the Y.M.C.A. Mott was later to receive the Nobel Peace Prize. Very fine. 575.00

550. ROOSEVELT, FRANKLIN D. President. Typed Letter Signed, as Assistant Secretary of the Navy, on imprinted stationery of that office. 1 page, large 4to. Washington, February 2, 1918. To Hon. Clayton L. Wheeler, United States Marshal, Utica, New York, explaining the procedure a soldier stationed at Camp Wadsworth, South Carolina, should follow to secure an appointment to the Naval Academy at Annapolis. In part: "...it is necessary to be nominated by either his Senator or Representative in Congress....As to West Point, the only way he can be appointed to that institution would be to make known his desire to his commanding officer. In this way, provided he possesses the proper qualifications, his name will be forwarded to the proper officials in Washington for consideration. I am sincerely sorry there is nothing I can do for him at this end..." Interesting letter written during World War 1. 275.00

551. HARRISON, MARY LORD. Second wife of Benjamin Harrison, whom she married after his departure from the White House. Autograph Letter Signed "Mary Lord Harrison", on her imprinted stationery. 3 1/2 pages, 8vo. New York, February 11, 1935. To Mr. Roppert, enclosing "a letter to me from Richard Mansfield for your collection, if you would be willing to take this in return for the Harrison pictures you sent me. At present I cannot buy them, but am greatly interested in the group picture and the one of Wm. Henry Harrison and my husband speaking on the Treasury steps in New York at the Washington Centennial. The others are also interesting to me, but these are the special ones...." Interesting association. Fine. 125.00

SEEKING THE ARMY'S ADOPTION OF A VETERINARIAN'S DISCOVERY OF "HIS METHOD OF TREATING THE HORSES FOOT"

552. GRANT, ULYSSES S. President and Union General. Superb Autograph Letter Signed "U. S. Grant / Gen'l". 4 full pages, 8vo. Washington, March 27, 1867. To General Montgomery C. Meigs, Quartermaster General of the U.S. Army. Grant writes: "Dr. Dunbar, who has spent the Winter here in the hope of having his method of treating the horses foot adopted by the Govenemnt, under the resolution of Congress authorizing the Sec. of War to appropriate money for that purpose, has met with no success so far. My own opinion is that this method has so much merit in it as to make it a matter of National importance, not that the government alone should be in possession of it, but that it become generally taught, so that wherever the horse is used the benefit of this treatment may be applied in case of need. How to secure this becomes the question! I would myself favor the establishment of a Veterinary College, under the patronage of government, where Army farriers could be taught, free, the whole secret and treatment, leaving the question of compensation to be made by outside persons wishing instruction in it, to be settled by the discoverer. It is not to be expected that any such measure as this will be adopted under present authority given to the Sec. of War, but if you feel the interest in this matter that I do, and can make any suggestion how to get this treatment adopted, either under present authority, or by asking further legislation, I will be obliged to you...." Interesting letter on an uncommon subject. Excellent! 875.00

HANDSOME SIGNED CABINET PHOTOGRAPH

553. CLEVELAND, GROVER. President; Governor of New York. Superb cabinet photograph of Cleveland, profile bust pose, by McDonald & Sterry, Albany, N.Y. Boldly signed in full by Cleveland, probably while Governor, on the bottom portion of the photographer's mount. Large imprint of the photographer on verso, with the year 1884 written in another hand. Pristine! 500.00

554. TRUMAN, HARRY S. President and Vice President. Typed Letter Signed "Harry", on his imprinted stationery. 1 page, 4to. Independence, Missouri, January 12, 1961. To his old friend David Morgan, then hospitalised in Los Angeles. Original postmarked envelope bearing Truman's printed franking signature. Truman acknowledges Morgan's card, saying "...I am as sorry as I can be that you had to go back to the hospital. I sincerely hope that it is only temporary..." Then, writing just eight days prior the inauguration of John F. Kennedy as President, Truman quips "I think we are on the way to recovery with the new President." An interesting letter, as Truman and Kennedy did not always get along well. Fine. 175.00

555. FORD, GERALD R. President and Vice President. Important Typed Letter Signed "Jerry Ford", as Minority Leader of the House of Representatives, on imprinted letterhead. Full page, 4to. Washington, Sept. 23, 1965. To Howard Barker, Belmont, Michigan. "...The consular convention with Russia is before the Senate only because that body has sole jurisdiction over the ratification of treaties and other international agreements....Senator Hickenlooper, senior Republican on the Committee on Foreign Relations, has voted against ratification and has pointed out the dangers involved. But the committee...is dominated by a 2 to 1 Democratic majority and they have voted to approve President Johnson's recommendations....Recently the Senate decided not to attempt approval of the treaty...because of wide-spread opposition." 225.00

556. HARDING, FLORENCE KLING. First Lady. Typed Letter Signed, as First Lady, on gilt-crested (presidential eagle) White House stationery. 1 page, 8vo. Washington, June 10, 1921. To Mrs. C. W. Parks, Washington, D.C. Original stamped, postmarked envelope. Sends thanks for "the beautiful roses...from you and Admiral Parks", saying that engagements out of town had prevented her from writing sooner. She concludes: "The roses kept their beauty for days as a reminder of your charming Hawaiian (sic) greeting...." Fine example. 150.00

557. MONROE, JAMES. President. Scarce, partly-printed Document Signed, as President. Tall folio, vellum. Washington, July 25, 1823. Countersigned by GEO. GRAHAM, Commissioner of the General Land Office. Embossed wafer seal of the Land Office at lower left. Grant of land to John Fezvant, a Surgeon for the War, "to the United States, in the VIRGINIA LINE on Continental Establishment, and in pursuance of an act of the Congress...intitled An Act to enable the Officers and Soldiers of the VIRGINIA LINE...to obtain titles to certain LANDS lying northwest of the river OHIO, between the Little Miami and Sciota..." The land is very fully described as to location. Fine signature of Monroe, and the document itself is in very fine condition. A much less frequently found format for Monroe land grants. With portrait. 495.00

ORNATE CANAL DEPARTMENT CERTIFICATE SIGNED AS COMPTROLLER

558. FILLMORE, MILLARD. President and Vice President. Handsome, ornately engraved Document Signed, as Comptroller of New York. 1 page, oblong 4to. Albany, April 26, 1848. Certifies that $250 has been borrowed by the Canal Department, State of New-York, being a LOAN for the ENLARGEMENT of the ERIE CANAL. Extremely ornate with multiple engraved vignettes, one of a factory scene, another a handsome allegorical representation of the New York State Seal, and a tiny portrait of DeWitt Clinton, father of the New York Canal System. Engraved by Rawdon, Wright & Hatch, New York. Cancelled by three dime-size holes at the bottom of the certificate, one of which obliterates most of Fillmore's last name. Documents of this type signed by Fillmore are very rare, and all those known have the same type of cancellation. 750.00

MOBILIZING THE COUNTRY FOR THE KOREAN WAR

559. TRUMAN, HARRY S. President and Vice President. Important Typed Letter Signed, as President, on imprinted White House stationery. 1 page, 4to. Washington, January 2, 1951. To Hon. Justin Miller, President, National Association of Broadcasters, Washington. Truman writes: "I appreciate your letter of December fifteenth on behalf of the National Association of Broadcasters. This assurance of support and cooperation in our mobilization program is indeed helpful to me. Many, many thanks for writing...." Pristine condition. 525.00

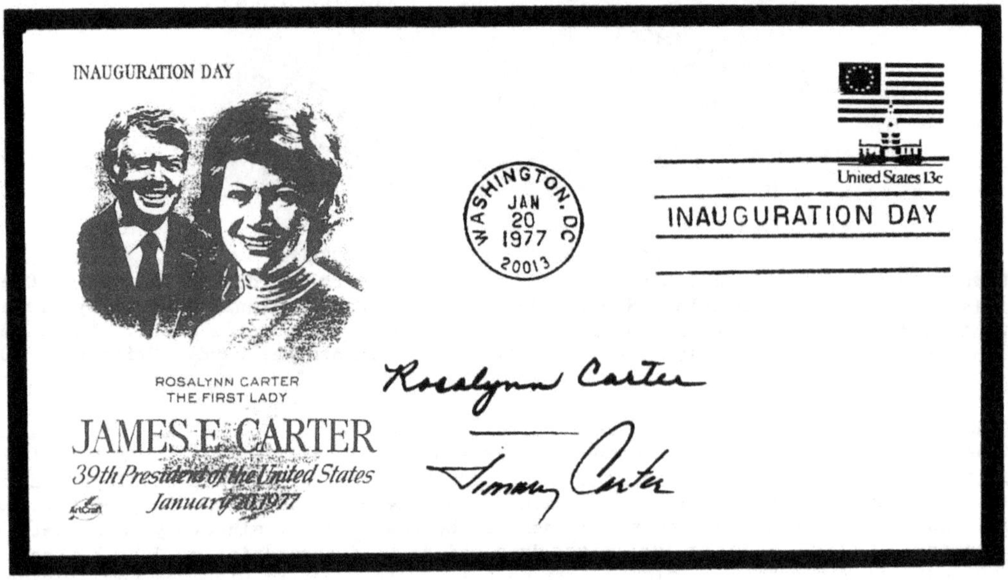

560. CARTER, JIMMY AND ROSALYNN. President and First Lady. Ornate cacheted (Artcraft) cover honoring Inauguration Day, Washington, January 20, 1977. Signed by both President and Mrs. Carter on the face of the envelope, to the right of the handsome cachet featuring their portraits. Pristine condition, and an outstanding item. 250.00

THE GREAT WHITE FATHER COMMUTES THE SENTENCE OF AN INDIAN

561. CLEVELAND, GROVER. President. Unusual partly printed Document Signed, as President. Full page, 4to. Washington, February 26, 1889. President Cleveland authorizes the Secretary of State to affix the Seal of the United States to "warrants for the commutation of the sentences of Kis-ku-da, alias Socate, and Daniel Carrigan...." Seldom does one encounter documents of this type pertaining to Indians. Boldly signed. Handsomely preserved. 495.00

HOOVER'S ADDRESS TO THE 1956 REPUBLICAN NATIONAL CONVENTION

562. HOOVER, HERBERT. President. Printed pamphlet containing his Address...before the Centennial Convention of the Republican Party / San Francisco / August 21, 1956. Self-covered printed wrappers. 11 pages, narrow 8vo. Signed by Hoover on the front wrapper beneath the title. Pristine condition. 150.00

FROM THE ARMY OF OCCUPATION IN MEXICO, TO PRESIDENT JAMES K. POLK

563. TAYLOR, ZACHARY. President; General in Mexican War, where he achieved hero-status, allowing him to be elected President in 1848. Manuscript Letter Signed "Z. Taylor, Majr. Genl. / U. S. Army." Very full page, 4to. Head Quarters, Army of Occupation, Camp near Victorial, Mexico, January 14, 1847. To His Ex. James K. Polk, President of the United States. Docketed integral leaf. General Taylor calls Polk's attention to the name of "Mr. Satterlee Hoffman as an applicant for a Subaltern's Commission in any new regiment which Congress may think proper to raise....Mr. Hoffman is a son of the late Lieut. Colonel Hoffman who died at Corpus Christi in November 1845....He is a young man...of fair talents, good education and unexceptionable character, and...would discharge his duties with credit to himself and the service. I beg leave to recommend him strongly to your favor and to state that I should be much gratified should you think proper to confer the desired appointment upon him...." Pristine condition. With a fine steel-engraved portrait. Wonderful association!! 1500.00

564. ADAMS, ABIGAIL. 1744-1818. First Lady (wife of John Adams); first First Lady to live in the White House. Autograph Document, with her full signature in the first line of text. 1 page, narrow oblong 12mo. Braintree [Mass.], May 23, 1765. Full text reads: "Received of Abigail Adams one pound Six Shillings and eight pence Lawful Money for a quarters wages. I say received by / [signed] Rachel Marsh". Newly mounted with acid-free board and framed under glass with a handsome steel-engraved portrait of our second First Lady. Striking ensemble. 750.00

565. VAN BUREN, MARTIN. President and Vice President; Secretary of State; Governor of New York. Autograph Letter Signed. 2 full pages, legal folio. Hudson [New York], August 2, 1832. To B[enjamin] F. Butler, his close friend and advisor, and later a member of his cabinet. He writes: "I regretted soon after my letter had gone that I had made any suggestion about your coming down, for fear there might be some difficulty or possible objection to your doing so... I shall go to Kinderhook tomorrow, & according to my present impression to Lebanon on Tuesday ...of which latter movement I have promised to advise Gov. Throop...If I can get well fixed at Lebanon I shall remain there until Albany is free from Cholera....From that place I can be in constant communication with you....I send you the letter of the Committee, with a sketch of my reply, drawn up in the midst of company, which I wish to submit to you for criticism. Say in your own words what you would say in my situation....I shall wait at Kinderhook...for the first mail from Albany in the next week, in hopes of hearing from you. Martin [his son] is not very well...Your affectionate & devoted friend..." Fine condition. 575.00

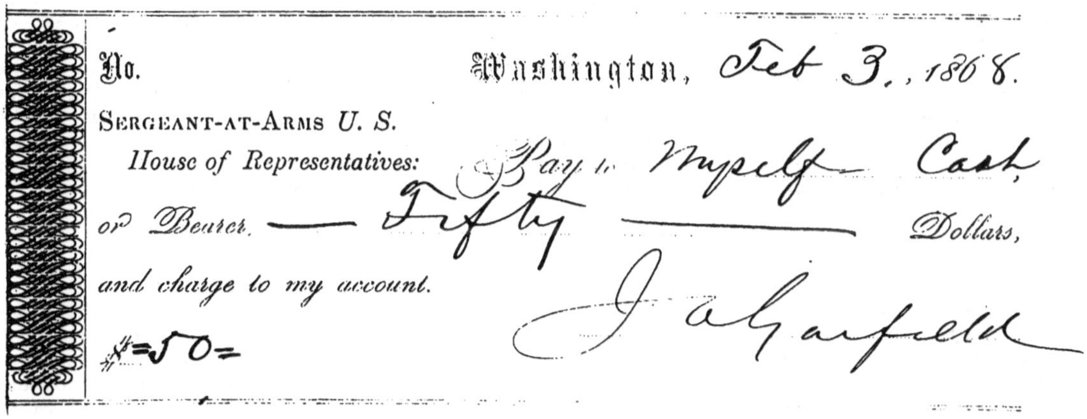
No. Washington, Feb 3., 1868.
Sergeant-at-Arms U. S.
House of Representatives: Pay to Myself Cash,
or Bearer. — Fifty — Dollars,
and charge to my account.
$=50= J A Garfield

566. GARFIELD, JAMES A. President. Partly printed Signed Counter Check, accomplished in his hand. Oblong 12mo. Washington, February 3, 1868. Drawn on the Sergeant-at-Arms of the U.S. House of Representatives. Payable to "Myself" for "Cash". Cut-cancelled (nothing missing). Choice specimen. With handsome steel-engraved portrait. 475.00

567. BUCHANAN, JAMES. President. Autograph Letter Signed. ½ page, 4to. Wheatland, near Lancaster [Penn.], July 26, 1852. To A. A. Mayer. Attractive letter, boldly penned on blue paper, sending his autograph to an admirer. With steel-engraved portrait. 325.00

568. ROOSEVELT, ELEANOR. First Lady. Typed Letter Signed, as First Lady, on gilt-imprinted White House stationery. 2/3 page, tall 8vo. Washington, September 25, 1936. To "Dear Barbara (Mrs. Harry Hopkins)", sending thanks "for the yellow roses. They are very lovely and it was more than kind of all of you to think of sending them to me. I am feeling fine once more and will soon be back in my usual stride. Affectionately..." Nice association! 95.00

COMMENTING ON THE BALTIMORE RIOTS OF 1812, MONROE WRITES:
"...MOBS OUGHT NOT TO EXIST, AND SHOULD BE SUPPRESSED."

569. MONROE, JAMES. President; Secretary of War and State; Minister to England. Remarkable, and highly important Autograph Letter Signed, as Secretary of State in Madison's cabinet. Full page, 4to. Albemarle [his home in Virginia], August 5, 1812. To an unknown recipient. In this outspoken letter on terrorism and mob violence, Monrpe writes in part: "...We hear nothing of Com: Rogers, and am much in the dark respecting the character, the causes, and consequences of the late movement at Baltimore. Altho' a combination of men, unknown to the law, without notice to the constituted authorities, to support a measure, even legal in itself, tending to excite a popular feeling, and raise a mob, for the purpose of suppressing it, can not be commended, yet mobs ought not to exist, and should be suppressed...."

Beginning with the first day of hostilities of the War of 1812, on June 18, 1812, the war provoked passionate pro and anti British sentiments in the hearts of Americans. The government's position, represented here by Monroe as Secretary of State, was vociferously opposed by the Federalists and their viewpoint was espoused by the newspaper The Federalist Republican, published in Baltimore by Alexander C. Hanson, the grandson of John Hanson, and by Henry Lee, noted Revolutionary War general. Their position, clearly supporting Great Britain, was published in the issue of July 27, 1812. On the following day, July 28, an unruly mob, crying out that Hanson and his supporters were traitors, attacked the newspaper office. Hanson, Lee and their few adherents were rushed to a local jail for their own protection, but the next day the mob prevailed and broke into the jail, killing one of the newspaper employees, and injuring Hanson and severely and permanently injuring General Lee.

A remarkable dichotomy reflecting Monroe's considered conviction that terrorism, even in the right or legal cause, cannot be condoned. Fine condition. 2500.00

570. COOLIDGE, CALVIN. President and Vice President. Typed Letter Signed, as President, on imprinted White House stationery. 1 page, 4to. Washington, June 5, 1924. To Victor P. Laning, Hudson, New York, expressing his thanks for sending "the extremely interesting remembrance of the early days in Vermont. I shall prize it and the kind thought which prompted the gift..." Coolidge was born in Plymouth, Vermont, and spent his childhood there. Fine. 350.00

571. PIERCE, FRANKLIN. President; General in Mexican War; lawyer and Congressman. Autograph Letter Signed. 2 full pages, 8vo. Keene [N.H.], October 31, 1861. To F. W. Blood, Hillsboro, N.H. Docketed integral leaf. The ex-President writes: "I can see why my presence the last of the week might seem desirable, but there seems to be little hope that the line of business can be radically changed or that the leeches can be shaken off....Let me know whether my Brother has returned from Lowell -- whether he has paid over any money to you or said anything about it -- when he proposes...to drive the rest of the cattle, &c. I should prefer to be at H. when the animals are brought down from Goshen and Washington....I may conclude to go to H. on Monday but this will depend perhaps upon what I may hear from you on Saturday night...." Interesting letter, as Pierce's brother always presented somewhat of a problem. Fine. 575.00

PRESIDENT HARDING REMEMBERS THE FAMED CIVIL WAR NAVAL BATTLE

572. HARDING, WARREN G. President. Typed Letter Signed, as President, on imprinted White House stationery. Very full page, 4to. Washington, February 3, 1922. To H.F.J. Porter, Chairman, DeLamater Ericsson Commemoration, New York. Harding writes that "owing to the pressure of public duties here in Washington", he will be unable to accept an invitation for commemorating the Sixtieth anniversary of the Battle of the Monitor and Merrimac. He continues: "I would be glad to have you express...my sense of the great debt which the American Nation owes to Captain John Ericsson. In recent years a more adequate appreciation has been developing, of the scope and range of his work for humanity. It is coming to be realized...that he was one of the foremost among American inventors in many departments. I am glad to know that this occasion is to be commemorated not only in this country but in his native...Sweden. Ericsson's work has been one of the potent ties between our own country and his native land, from which so large an element of our best American citizenship is derived...." Choice! 795.00

WITH A HOLOGRAPH POSTSCRIPT

573. TRUMAN, HARRY S. President and Vice President; Senator from Missouri. Typed Letter Signed "Harry", on the imprinted stationery of the United States Senate. 1 page, 4to. Kansas City August 26, 1944. To his old friend, David H. Morgan. Original postmarked envelope bearing Truman's imprinted franking signature over which he has placed a stamp. Writing after being nominated by the Democrats for Vice President, Truman acknowledges his friend's letter received at Independence. He adds: "I do appreciate most sincerely your offer to help in the coming campaign. Also, the wonderful picture of the B-29 in flight...." And in the two-line holograph postscript, Truman writes: "Hope everything works out all right with the family." Excellent condition, and scarce from this period. 350.00

THE SOUTHERN ARMY'S DEPENDENCE ON VIRGINIA

574. **JEFFERSON, THOMAS.** President and Vice President; Signer of Delaration of Independence; Secretary of State. Manuscript Letter Signed, as Governor of Virginia. Full p., 4to. In Council, November 21, 1780. To Colonel [Timothy] Pickering, Quartermaster General of the Continental Army, re the selection of a Deputy Quartermaster General. Jefferson states

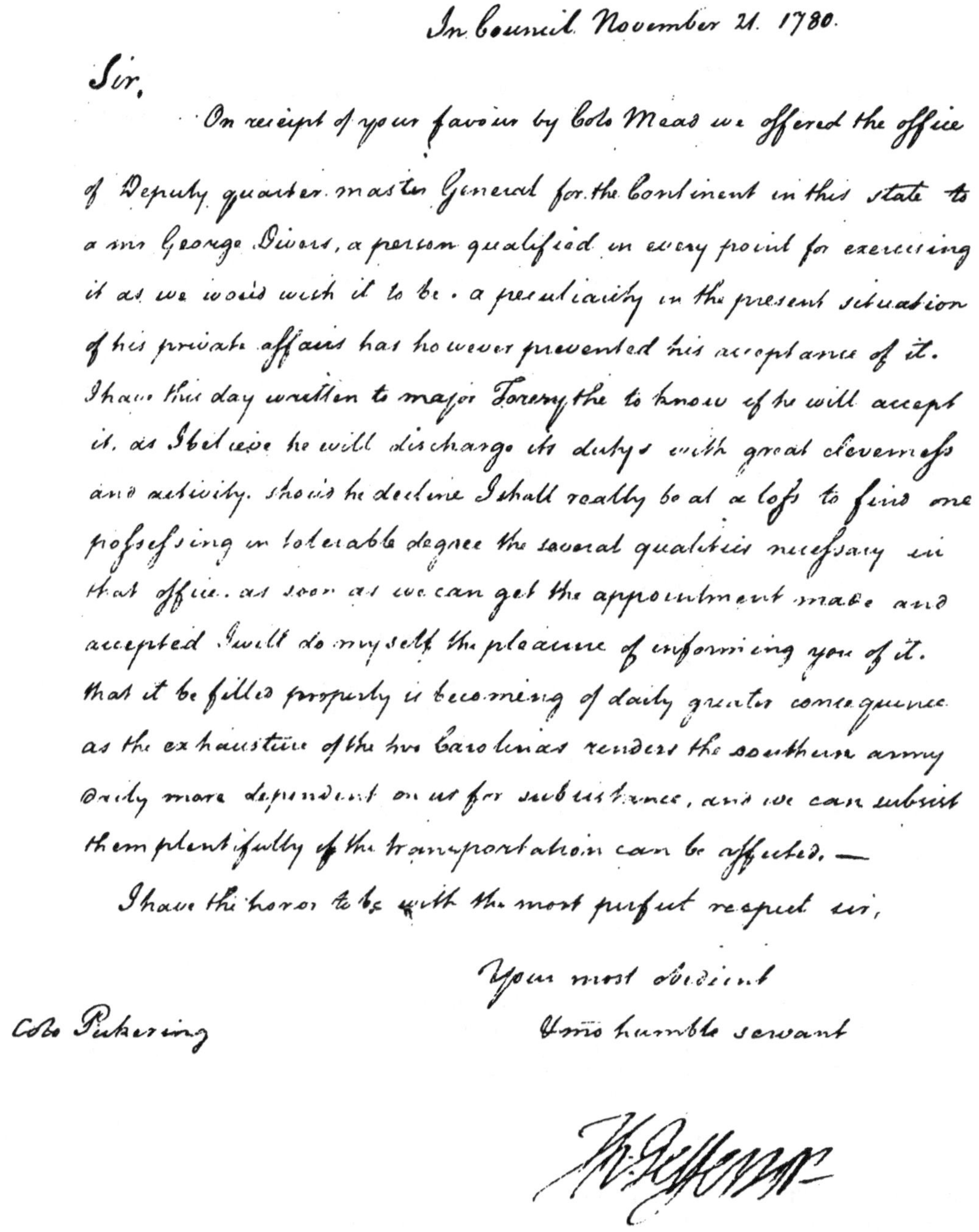

In Council November 21. 1780.

Sir,

On receipt of your favour by Colo. Mead we offered the office of Deputy quarter master General for the Continent in this state to a mr George Divers, a person qualified in every point for exercising it as we wou'd wish it to be. a peculiarity in the present situation of his private affairs has however prevented his acceptance of it. I have this day written to major Foresythe to know if he will accept it. as I believe he will discharge its dutys with great cleverness and activity. shou'd he decline I shall really be at a loss to find one possessing in tolerable degree the several qualities necessary in that office. as soon as we can get the appointment made and accepted I will do myself the pleasure of informing you of it. that it be filled properly is becoming of daily greater consequence as the exhausture of the two Carolinas renders the southern army daily more dependent on us for subsistance, and we can subsist them plentifully if the transportation can be affected. —

I have the honor to be with the most perfect respect sir,

Your most obedient

Colo. Pickering

Humble servant

Th: Jefferson

that the post was offered to George Divers, "a person qualified in every point for exercising it as we wou'd wish it to be. A peculiarity in the present situation of his private affairs has however prevented his acceptance of it. I have this day written to Major Foresythe to know if he will accept it, as I believe he will discharge its dutys with great cleverness and activity. Shou'd he decline I shall really be at a loss to find one possessing in tolerable degree the several qualities necessary in that office. As soon as we can get the appointment made and accepted I will do myself the pleasure of informing you of it. That it be filled properly is becoming of daily greater consequence as the exhausture of the two Carolinas renders the southern army daily more dependent on us for subsistance, and we can subsist them plentifully if the transportation can be affected...." Fine condition, and bearing Jefferson's customary bold signature. With engraved portrait. 4,500.00

RARE EARLY REPORT CARD SIGNED AS PRINCIPAL OF THE ECLECTIC INSTITUTE

575. GARFIELD, JAMES A. President. Partly printed Document Signed, as Principal of the Eclectic Institute. Full page, 4to. Hiram, Ohio, October 26, 1860. Term report of Mary P. Hatfield for the Fall Term of 1860, giving her "General Deportment and Class Merit...marked on a scale of 10". This Report was sent to the girl's father. This is the first Garfield document of this type we have encountered. He was at the Eclectic Institute for only a brief time before volunteering his services to the Union Army. Excellent condition. With portrait. 575.00

THE FOURTH TERM VICTORY

576. ROOSEVELT, FRANKLIN D. President. Typed Letter Signed, as President, on imprinted White House stationery. 1 page, 4to. Washington, November 14, 1944. To Brigadier General Frank T. Hines, Administrator of Veterans' Affairs, Washington. Roosevelt writes: "My dear Frank: I am deeply touched by the warmth of your congratulations and your very generous words. My heartfelt thanks to you and Mrs. Hines for your prayerful wishes...." FDR had just been elected to an unprecedented fourth term. The deterioration in his health is evident from the small signature on this letter, so uncharacteristic of former years. Choice!! 575.00

577. PIERCE, FRANKLIN. President. On a 24mo leaf he has written: "Very respectfully / Yr. friend & Servt. / Franklin Pierce". Ca. 1865. With engraved portrait. Very fine. 150.00

JACKIE HAS TO SAY "NO" TO AN OLD FRIEND

578. KENNEDY, JACQUELINE. First Lady. Typed Letter Signed "Jackie", as First Lady, on the gilt-imprinted stationery of The White House. 2/3 page, small 4to. Hyannis Port, September 24, 1961. To Igor Cassini, 500 Park Avenue, New York City. She writes: "Dear Ghi Ghi: Thank you so much for writing me about the proposed book on the White House. I do wish I could say that I would participate in this, but I'm sure that you can understand that there will be only one official book on the White House, and that project has already been assigned. Affectionately..." With original stamped White House envelope, postmarked Hyannis Port. Also present is the two-page typed carbon copy of Cassini's letter to Mrs. Kennedy, dated September 20, 1961, explaining that he wishes to do a picture book about the White House and asking for her assistance. Excellent condition. 350.00

WAR OF 1812 MILITARY COMMISSION

579. MADISON, JAMES. President. Handsome partly printed Document Signed, as President. One page, oblong legal folio. Washington, November 20, 1812. Countersigned by WILLIAM EUSTIS, Secretary of War. Embossed, perforated seal of the War Department affixed with red wax at bottom left. President Madison appoints Alexander Erskins a Second Lieutenant of Volunteers. Clean and fresh, with all the writing exceptionally bold and clear. Very choice!! 750.00

580. MC KINLEY, WILLIAM. President. Lower fragment, complete in itself, of a partly printed Document Signed, as Governor of Ohio. Oblong 4to. Columbus, May 26, 1894. Large gilt-embossed wafer seal with blue silk ties. Also signed by the Ohio Secretary of State. Handsome, colorful specimen. 150.00

"I AM VERY MUCH GIVEN TO BOATING AND FISHING..."

581. CLEVELAND, GROVER. President. Autograph Letter Signed, in between presidential terms, on stationery imprinted "Marion, Massachusetts". 2 1/2 pages, 8vo. August 16, 1890. To F. W. Bird, prominent Massachusetts Democrat. Cleveland hopes to be able to meet with his correspondent before his vacation is over, and gives a bit of his upcoming schedule. He adds: "We have company to entertain and as I am very much given to boating and fishing I am apt to be on the water much of the time. I wish you would write me as much in advance as possible appointing a day and hour when you would be glad to call and I will be at home. I don't know where you are located; but if it is not far away and near the water I might sail to you some day...." Pristine condition. 350.00

582. MADISON, DOLLY P. First Lady. Complete address-leaf, addressed in her hand, and franked <u>Free D. P. Madison</u> in the top right corner. The recipient was Miss Mary Stevens Lands, St. Mary's Hall, Burlington, New Jersey. No postal markings or docket. No date, but a fine widow's frank. With handsome steel-engraved portrait. 475.00

583. GRANT, JULIA DENT. First Lady. Full signature, boldly penned on a small card, and dated in her hand "Nov. 20th 90". Seldom available in this format. Fine. 75.00

584. TRUMAN, HARRY S. President and Vice President. Typed Letter Signed, on his imprinted letterhead. Full page, 4to. Independence, Missouri, November 5, 1960. To Don Gibson, Hamilton, Ohio, acknowledging his letter and several interesting gifts, including a picture of Andrew Johnson mounted with his original signature; two volumes of <u>Teach the Freeman</u> by Louis Rubin, Jr.; <u>Messages of the Presidents of the United States</u>; and <u>Address of President Harrison</u>, published by Jonathan Phillips, Columbus, Ohio, 1841. Truman continues: "These are all very welcome additions to our Library collection...." Nice association!! 250.00

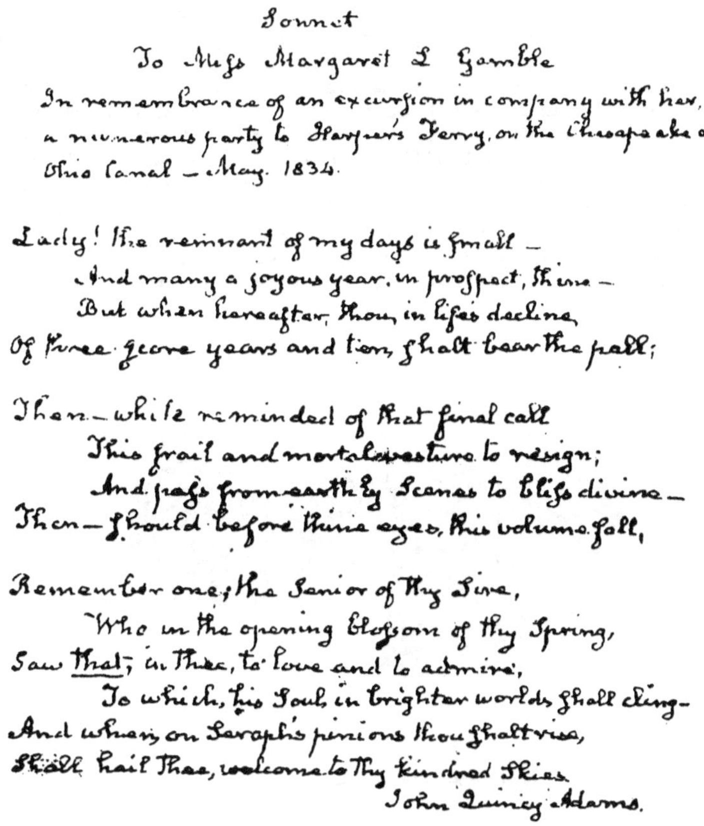

Sonnet
To Miss Margaret L Gamble
In remembrance of an excursion in company with her, and
a numerous party to Harper's Ferry, on the Chesapeake and
Ohio Canal – May. 1834.

Lady! the remnant of my days is small –
And many a joyous year, in prospect, thine –
But when hereafter, thou in life's decline
Of three score years and ten, shalt bear the pall;

Then – while reminded of that final call
This frail and mortal vesture to resign;
And pass from earthly Scenes to bliss divine –
Then – should before thine eyes, this volume fall,

Remember one, the Senior of thy Sire,
Who in the opening blossom of thy Spring,
Saw that, in thee, to love and to admire,
To which, his Soul, in brighter worlds shall cling –
And when, on Seraph's pinions thou shalt rise,
Shall hail thee, welcome to thy kindred Skies.
John Quincy Adams.

THE POET-PRESIDENT PENS A SONNET FOR A YOUNG FEMALE FRIEND

585. ADAMS, JOHN QUINCY. President; Secretary of State and diplomat; elected to Congress from his home district in Massachusetts following his presidency; only president to have a volume of his poetry published. Remarkable Autograph Manuscript Poem Signed, penned on a small quarto album leaf bearing a printed vignette at top. 1 page, circa 1834. Adams writes:

Sonnet
To Miss Margaret L. Gamble

In remembrance of an excursion in company with her, and a numerous party to Harper's Ferry, on the Chesapeake and Ohio Canal -- May 1834.

Lady! The remnant of my days is small --
And many a joyous year, in prospect, thine --
But when hereafter, thou in life's decline
Of three score years and ten, shalt bear the pall;

Then -- while reminded of that final call
This frail and mortal vesture to resign;
And pass from earth by Scenes to bliss divine --
Then -- Should before thine eyes, this volume fall,

Remember one, the Senior of thy Sire,
Who in opening blossom of thy Spring,
Saw <u>that</u>, in thee, to love and to admire,
To which, his Soul in brighter worlds shall cling --
And when, on Seraph's pinions thou shalt rise,
Shall hail thee, welcome to thy kindred Skies.

John Quincy Adams.

An exquisite and charming manuscript poem written by the venerable former president. Very fine condition. With engraved portrait. 2500.00

586. WILSON, WOODROW. President. Imprinted White House Card, boldly signed by Wilson as President. Washington, no date. Pristine condition, with no mounting traces. Choice! 275.00

587. ROOSEVELT, ELEANOR. First Lady. Typed Letter Signed, as First Lady, on imprinted White House stationery. 1 page, 4to. Washington, September 5, 1939. To Harry [L. Hopkins], then serving as Secretary of Commerce. She writes: "It was very nice to get your letter and I would love to have Diana here, but, unfortunately, I am leaving on a lecture trip on the 11th of September and Franklin has been so uncertain that I have not been able to make any definite dates this week, as I may go back to Washington if he does not get up here. Why not plan to have Diana spend the 16th and 17th, when I will be in Washington, with me? Perhaps you can come with her and we can plan some kind of a spree. I shall be anxious to see you and have a long talk with you as soon as you get back...Affectionately..." Accompanied by two retained copies of letters from Hopkins to Mrs. Roosevelt concerning the proposed visit of his daughter, and a humorous TLS of Tommy, Mrs. Roosevelt's devoted secretary, picking up on a comment made by Hopkins in one of his letters to Eleanor. At the time Hopkins was in the hospital for tests. A very interesting group! 150.00

588. HARRISON, BENJAMIN. President. Handsome engraved vignette of the White House showing three children playing on the spacious lawn. Boldly signed by Harrison in jet-black ink on the wide lower white margin. Probably signed as President. Choice! 450.00

589. COOLIDGE, CALVIN. President and Vice President. Handsome partly engraved Document Signed, as Governor of Massachusetts. 1 page, small oblong folio, vellum. Amherst, Mass., June 24, 1919. Countersigned by Edward M. Lewis, Acting President of the Faculty of the Massachusetts Agricultural College. Governor Coolidge, acting in his capacity as President of the Corporation, confers the degree of Bachelor of Science on Gunnar Emmannuel Erickson. Lovely engraved allegorical vignette, incorporating the Mass. state seal, at top center. We have never seen another example of this type of Coolidge document. Highly attractive! 225.00

"IS THAT THE BEST POSSIBLE PRICE[?]"

590. KENNEDY, JACQUELINE. First Lady. Amazing Autograph Letter Signed "Jacqueline Kennedy", on the imprinted stationery of the Carlyle Hotel. 2 full pp., narrow 8vo. New York, no date. Ca. 1957-60. To Mr. Alvaro, a jeweler. The wife of the Massachusetts Senator, and future First Lady writes: "I am interested only in the gold & diamond one. Perhaps I can persuade someone to give it to me for Xmas, baby etc. I will try. Is that the best possible price -- it is so expensive. I will let you know later -- & hope it will be the pretty one -- & not the gold links -- though they are nice too -- but not after you've seen the other!..." At the bottom of the second page, beneath her written signature, she has printed "Mrs John F. Kennedy / 3307 N St. N.W. Washington DC". We do not know if Mrs. Kennedy obtained a "better" price in making her purchase. We do know that our price is firm at: 750.00

591. TRUMAN, HARRY S. President and Vice President. Printed Menu and Programme for the "Dinner in honor of our fellow member The President of the United States Harry S. Truman given by the National Press Club...January 11, 1947. Quarto. Inscribed by Truman on the announcement page (from which the previous text was taken): "To Paul Wooton, who has always been my friend, best wishes from a friend of his Harry S Truman". Fine and unusual! 250.00

592. WILSON, WOODROW. President; Governor of New Jersey; President of Princeton University; historian and lecturer. Typed Letter Signed, as Governor of New Jersey, on the gilt and black imprinted stationery of that office. 1 page, 4to. Executive Department, March 17, 1911. To Rev. Edward P. Drew, Worcester, Mass. In part: "...I am very much complimented that the Worcester Congregational Club should desire me to speak before them...but unhappily I have gone the limit of my strength and of my official liberty in the matter of speaking engagements and simply dare not add any more...." Original stamped and addressed envelope. Choice! 250.00

593. TAFT, WILLIAM H. President; Chief Justice. His book: Political Issues and Outlooks / Speeches Delivered Between August, 1908, and February, 1909. Gilt-lettered blue cloth. New York, 1909. First edition. Boldly signed by Taft on the front endpaper above his personal imprinted bookplate. Fine copy of a very scarce Taft title. 295.00

594. VAN BUREN, MARTIN. President and Vice President. Autograph Letter Signed. 1/2 page, small 4to. Lindenwald, September 20, 1852. To G. W. Ludlow. Entire message reads: "I have your letter and it will not be my fault if I am not at the appointed time & place. With kind regards to Mrs. Ludlow...." With engraved portrait. Fine specimen. 250.00

595. CARTER, ROSALYNN. First Lady. Typed Letter Signed, on her imprinted stationery. 1 page, 8vo. No place, July 23, 1982. To Bill Baxter, thanking him for his letter and kind words. "Your friendship and support mean a great deal to Jimmy and me, and he joins me in sending you and your mother our best wishes...." Fine. 45.00

596. COOLIDGE, CALVIN. President and Vice President; Governor of Massachusetts. His book: Have Faith in Massachusetts. Speeches and Addresses of Calvin Coolidge, elected Governor...on a platform of Law and Order. Gilt-lettered blue cloth. Second edition enlarged. Boston, 1919. Boldly inscribed on the front endpaper: "To Irwin L. Lindabury / With regards / Calvin Coolidge / 1920". Bookplate of Mr. Lindabury. Fine copy in worn dust-jacket. 150.00

597. PIERCE, FRANKLIN. President. Autograph Letter Signed. 4 very closely penned pages, 8vo. Andover, Mass., October 15, 1859. To Hon. J. M. Wilson, Chicago, Illinois. Friendly letter to a former congressional colleague. In part: "Altho' our correspondence has been long interupted, I have cherished pleasant memories of the intimacy which existed between us for so many years and have heard...of your prosperous and useful career...My nephew, Mr. William A. Aiken...has been for some time in business in Chicago and I hope that he will make your acquaintance....His brother John F. proposes to go out with him, with the view of pursuing the study of law...in your City. They are both young men of sound principles, and estimable character in all respects....Their mother and Mrs. Pierce are, as you may know the only surviving members of Dr. Appleton's family. I was at Hillsboro last week and passed several hours with your Uncle, Gen'l McNiel. I think he is the oldest man now living in that Town, but he is bright, vivacious and retains his vigor mentally and physically wonderfully....Mrs. Pierce's health I regret to say is still too delicate to encounter the rigor of a New England winter and we propose to leave in a few weeks for Bermuda...." Docketed at head of first page, and neatly inlaid. An interesting, lengthy letter. 850.00

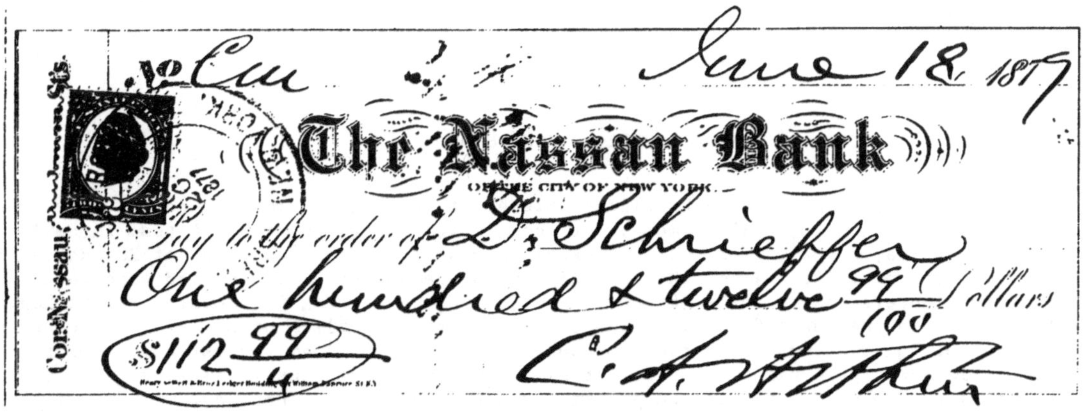

598. ARTHUR, CHESTER A. President and Vice President; Collector of Customs for the Port of New York. Partly printed Signed Bank Check, accomplished in his hand. Oblong 8vo. New York, June 18, 1879. Drawn on the Nassau Bank of New York City in favor of D. Schrieffer in the amount of $112.99 Blue U.S. Revenue stamp affixed at right. Small tear neatly repaired on verso. Very fine appearance. With engraved portrait. 500.00

599. MC KINLEY, WILLIAM. President; Governor of Ohio; assassinated. Manuscript Letter Signed, as Governor of Ohio, on imprinted Executive Department stationery. Full page, 4to. Columbus, April 21, 1892. A "To Whom it may Concern" letter introducing Wade Chance of Canton, Ohio "whom I have known since boyhood. He is a young man of good address, sustaining the highest personal character at home..." Some fold wear, else very good. 150.00

600. TRUMAN, BESS W. First Lady. Typed Letter Signed, as First Lady, on gilt-imprinted White House stationery. 1 page, 4to. Washington, January 27, 1948. To [Paul] Wooten, the journalist, sending thanks for his note and attached clipping. "You were thoughtful to send it. Of course I am glad to learn you did not select the picture! Margaret and I are looking forward to our visit to New Orleans, even though it will be a brief one...." Fine example. 75.00

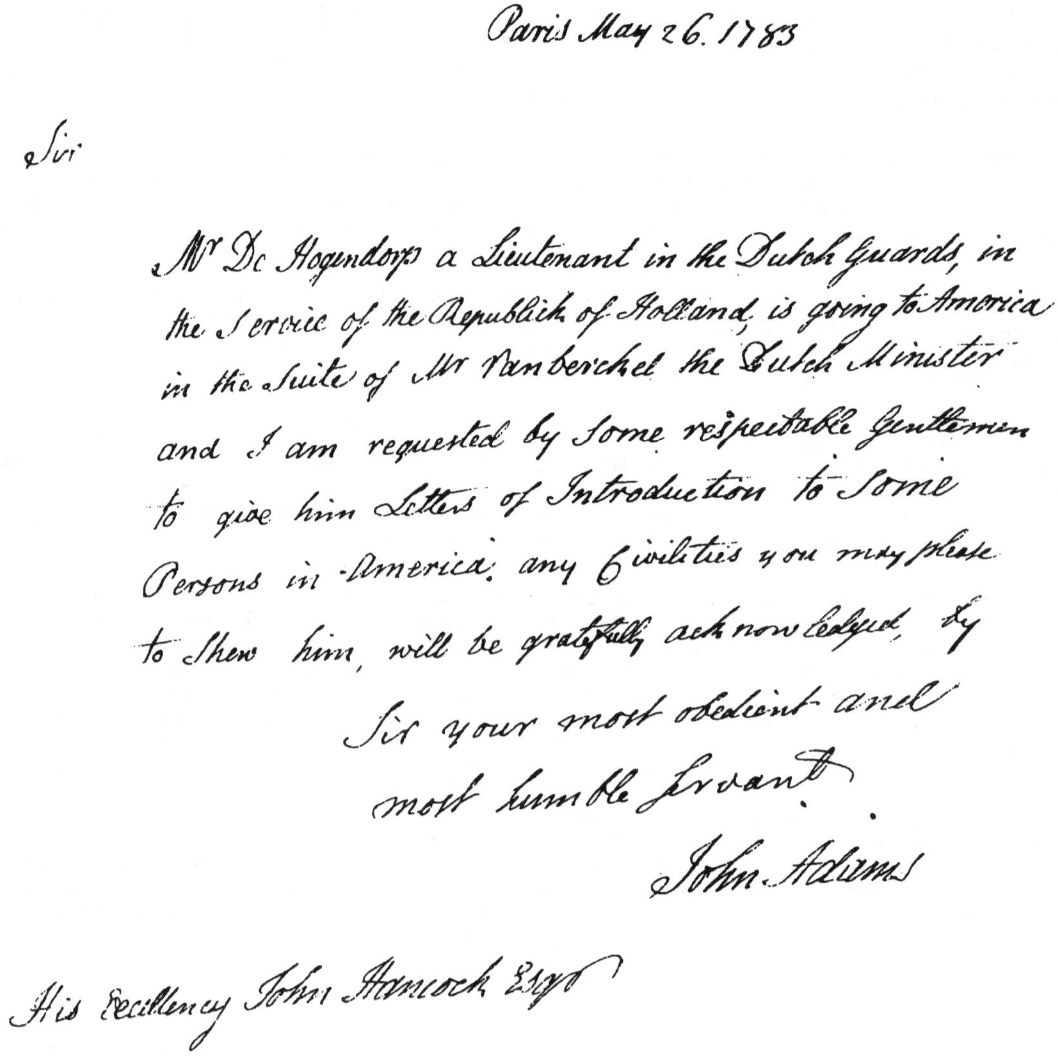

Paris May 26. 1783

Sir

Mr De Hogendorp a Lieutenant in the Dutch Guards, in the Service of the Republick of Holland, is going to America in the Suite of Mr Vanberckel the Dutch Minister and I am requested by Some respectable Gentlemen to give him Letters of Introduction to Some Persons in America: any Civilities you may please to Shew him, will be gratefully acknowledged, by

Sir your most obedient and most humble Servant.

John Adams

His Excellency John Hancock Esqr

FINE LETTER TO JOHN HANCOCK

601. ADAMS, JOHN. President and Vice President; Signer of the Declaration of Independence. Superb Autograph Letter Signed, while a member of the American peace negotiating team in Paris. One page, 4to. Paris, May 26, 1783. To His Excellency John Hancock [Governor of Massachusetts]. Docketed integral leaf. Adams, who as Minister to the United Provinces had negotiated a loan from Dutch bankers to the United States, here introduces a young Dutchman. "Mr. De Hogendorp a Lieutenant in the Dutch Guards, in the Service of the Republick of Holland, is going to America in the Suite of Mr. Vanberckel the Dutch Minister, and I am requested by some respectable Gentlemen to give him Letters of Introduction to some Persons in America. Any Civilities you may please to shew him, will be gratefully acknowledged..." Hancock, whom it will be remembered was a fellow Signer of the Declaration of Independence and past-President of the Continental Congress, received this letter from his colleague while serving as Governor of Massachusetts. Choice association. Excellent condition. With matching portraits of both Adams and Hancock. 7500.00

602. TYLER, JOHN. President and Vice President. Complete address-leaf, addressed and franked by Tyler as President. Quarto. Addressed to "Judge [John Y.] Mason / Sec. of the Navy" and franked "J. Tyler" in the top right corner. Mason's initialed endorsement, dated Dec. 5th 1844, appears in the margin. With engraved portrait. Nice presidential frank! 350.00

603. PIERCE, FRANKLIN. President; General in Mexican War. Autograph Letter Signed, undated, but as President. Full page, small 4to. Washington, Tuesday Morning, no date. To Governor [W.L.] Marcy, then serving as Secretary of State in Pierce's cabinet. Pierce writes: "Dr. Whitman will with the despatches hand you a letter from Mr. Clay addressed to me. Besides Dr. W's private business he would like to converse with you upon a subject of public interest...." With handsome steel-engraved portrait. Uncommon in ALS of presidential date. 650.00

604. GRANT, ULYSSES S. President; Union General; accepted Lee's surrender. Handsome albumin cabinet photograph of Grant by Taber of San Francisco. Full-face bust pose, undoubtedly taken as President. Boldly signed "U. S. Grant" on the lower white margin of the photographic surface, above the photographer's imprint. Pristine condition, and a seldom-seen photograph. 950.00

NEW YORK CUSTOMS DOCUMENT SIGNED TWICE BY THE FUTURE PRESIDENT AS COLLECTOR OF THE PORT OF NEW YORK

605. ARTHUR, CHESTER A. President and Vice President. Partly printed Document Signed, twice, as Collector of the Port of New York. Full page, legal folio. [New York] March 11, 1875. Headed "OATH OF OFFICE". States that B. Mayereau has been appointed Storekeeper of Private Bonded Stores at the New York Customs' House, and that he has sworn to "faithfully execute the duties ...and will use the best of my endeavors to prevent and detect frauds in relation to the duties imposed by the laws of the United States..." In the second part of this document, Mayereau swears that he has "never voluntarily borne arms against the United States..." Both these oaths appear on the same side of the page within a framed border, and both are separately signed by Arthur and Mayereau. Attractive, and unusual document. 350.00

606. EISENHOWER, DWIGHT D. President; General in World War II. Typed Letter Signed, as President, on imprinted White House stationery. 1 page, 4to. Gettysburg, December 27, 1958. To His Excellency Mongi Slim, Ambassador of Tunisia, Washington, D.C. Original postmarked envelope. Eisenhower writes: "Thank you so much for the fine wicker box of dates that you sent to me as a Christmas remembrance. I am truly grateful to you for thinking of me, and delighted to have one of the fine products of your country. With best wishes for a fine New Year..." Pristine condition. 450.00

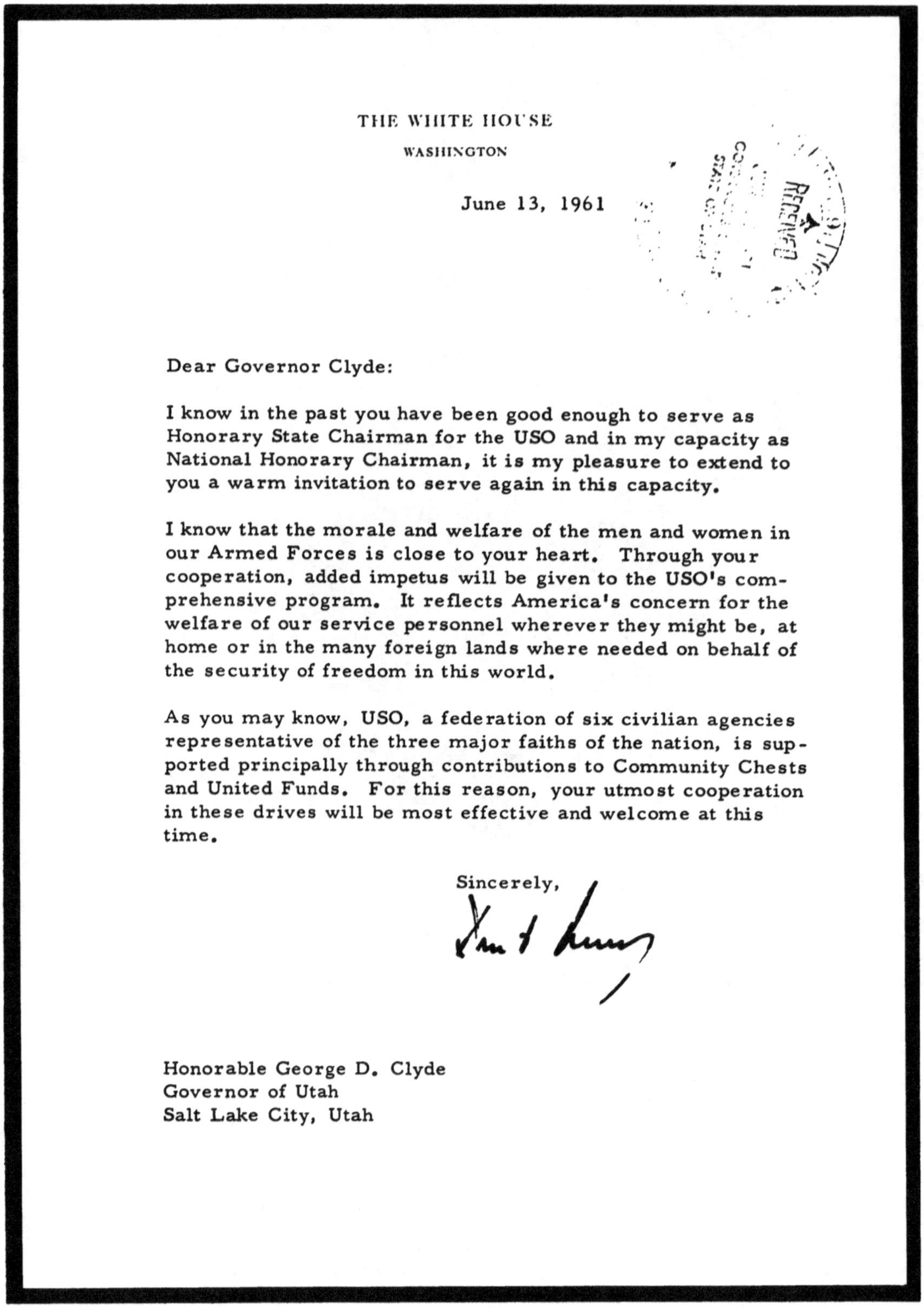

THE WHITE HOUSE

WASHINGTON

June 13, 1961

Dear Governor Clyde:

I know in the past you have been good enough to serve as Honorary State Chairman for the USO and in my capacity as National Honorary Chairman, it is my pleasure to extend to you a warm invitation to serve again in this capacity.

I know that the morale and welfare of the men and women in our Armed Forces is close to your heart. Through your cooperation, added impetus will be given to the USO's comprehensive program. It reflects America's concern for the welfare of our service personnel wherever they might be, at home or in the many foreign lands where needed on behalf of the security of freedom in this world.

As you may know, USO, a federation of six civilian agencies representative of the three major faiths of the nation, is supported principally through contributions to Community Chests and United Funds. For this reason, your utmost cooperation in these drives will be most effective and welcome at this time.

Sincerely,

Honorable George D. Clyde
Governor of Utah
Salt Lake City, Utah

RARE WHITE HOUSE LETTER TO THE GOVERNOR OF UTAH

607. KENNEDY, JOHN F. President; assassinated. Magnificent Typed Letter Signed "John F. Kennedy", as President, on imprinted White House stationery. Full page, 4to. Washington, June 13, 1961. To Honorable George D. Clyde, Governor of Utah, Salt Lake City. Kennedy, in his capacity as National Honorary Chairman for the USO, asks Governor Clyde to serve again as Honorary State Chairman. [See illustration above for full text]. Stamped docket of the Governor's Office at upper right. Pristine condition, and a real presidential gem!! 3500.00

GRANT TO STANTON ABOUT THE ALLEGED ILL-TREATMENT OF REBEL PRISONERS

608. GRANT, ULYSSES S. President; Union General; accepted Lee's surrender. Autograph Telegram Signed "U. S. Grant / Lt. Gen.". Full page, small 4to. City Point, Virginia, February 15, 1865. To Hon. E. M. Stanton, Secretary of War, Washington. Penned on the verso of stationery imprinted "Head Quarters Armies of the United States". Full text reads: "The rebel Agt. of Exchange says he understands that Campbell Mars and others are still in irons at Johnson's Island. Will you please direct Gen. Hoffman to furnish me a list of rebel prisoners who are still so confined and under what orders so that I may know whether such complaints are well founded...." An important and dramatic war communication. Fine. 2750.00

609. LINCOLN, ABRAHAM. President. Partly printed Document Signed "Abraham Lincoln". 1 page, 4to. Washington, May 19, 1863. President Lincoln authorizes the Secretary of State [Seward] to affix the Seal of the United States to "my Proclamation of the Convention between the United States and Peru concluded and signed at Lima on the 12 January 1863..." Attractive quarto-size document, bearing Lincoln's full signature, and in fine condition. With a fine engraved portrait of Lincoln. 2750.00

610. JACKSON, ANDREW. President and General in War of 1812. Partly printed Document Signed, as President. Oblong 4to. Washington, May 20, 1829. Countersigned by John Branch, Secretary of the Navy. Blind-stamped seal in upper left corner. Appointment of R.H.S. Peterson to be a Midshipman in the United States Navy. Vellum. Fine bold signature of Jackson, and an exceptionally bright fresh document. There are, however, several minute holes in one of the folds, which are hardly noticeable. With engraved portrait. 750.00

611. NIXON, RICHARD. President and Vice President. His book: The Real War. Silver-lettered crimson cloth. New York, 1980. First edition. One of an unspecified number of copies of a limited edition signed by Nixon on the colophon leaf. Publishers box. Mint. 225.00

612. CLEVELAND, FRANCES FOLSOM. First Lady. Autograph Letter Signed, as First Lady, on silver-imprinted Executive Mansion social stationery. 2 full separate pages, 12mo. Washington, no date. To Mrs. Farnsworth, staying at The Arlington. Original envelope addressed by the First Lady. She writes: "I thank you very much for letting me see those charming photographs of your daughters. You must be very proud of her. Her work is really remarkable. Please congratulate her for me upon her great success -- and remember me most cordially to her and to General Farnsworth...." Pristine condition. 125.00

613. TRUMAN, HARRY S. President and Vice President. Choice oblong quarto group photograph showing President Truman receiving his membership card for the National Press Club from Paul Wooton. Inscribed on the photographer's mount (mat) at bottom: "To my friend, neighbor, Paul Wooton with / kindest regards & best wishes / Harry S Truman". Mounted and matted. Ideal for framing or display. 225.00

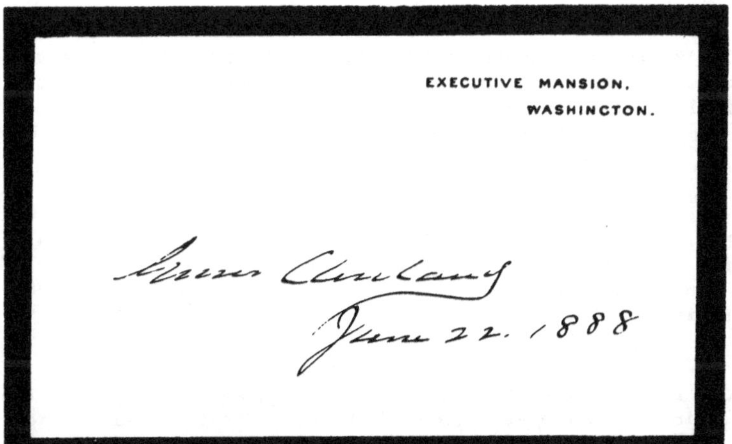

614. CLEVELAND, GROVER. President. Blue-imprinted Executive Mansion card boldly signed and dated "June 22, 1888", as President. Quite fine save for mounting traces on verso. Cleveland rarely dated these signature cards. This one is dated during his first term. 250.00

615. FILLMORE, MILLARD. President and Vice President. Manuscript Letter Signed, as Comptroller of New York State. 1/2 page, 4to. Albany, March 17, 1848. To Ransom Cook, Dunnemasa, Clinton County, New York. With the postmarked integral address-leaf. Fillmore, who later the same year was elected Vice President of the United States, writes that he has "seen Mr. Comstock relative to the purchase of your machinery. He informed me that he would, in a few days, present a report to the state officers...When the report has been received and considered, action will be taken upon your matter...." Fine condition. With portrait. 295.00

616. FORD, GERALD R. President and Vice President (not popularly elected to either office). Striking gilt-imprinted bookplate bearing the Presidential Seal and "GERALD R. FORD / 38th President of the United States of America", enclosed within a ruled border. Boldly signed by Ford in jet-black ink. Pristine condition, and ideal for framing or display. 65.00

617. CARTER, JIMMY. President. Handsome quarto reproduction of an etched portrait by C. Plant, showing two different bust poses of Carter. Boldly signed "Jimmy Carter" in bright blue ink on the lower white margin. Although undated, signed as President, in person for a Senate Page. Pristine condition. Wonderful item for framing or display. 200.00

618. JACKSON, ANDREW. President; General in War of 1812, and hero of Battle of New Orleans. Complete address-leaf franked "Free Andrew Jackson" across the entire top of the address panel, as President. Clear circular Washington postmark. January 2 [1834]. Addressed in a secretarial hand to James K. Paulding, Navy Agent, City of New York. Paulding, a writer, later served as Secretary of the Navy. Some very minor faults at top margin, else quite fine. Also stamped FREE. Presidential franks of Jackson are very scarce. 950.00

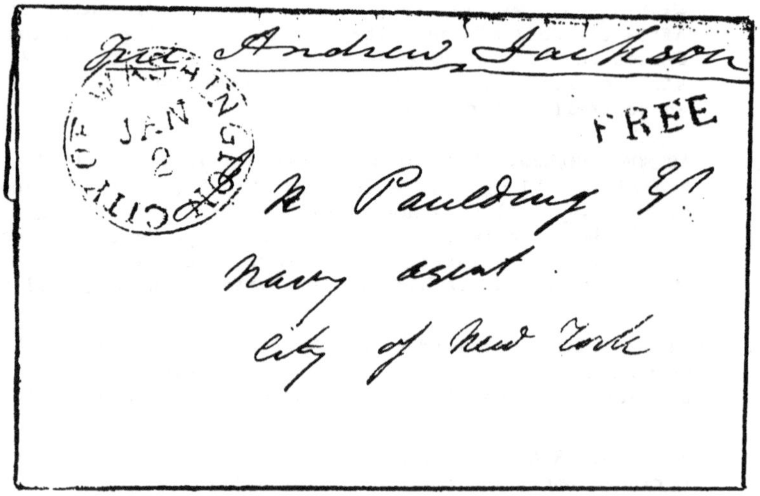

619. COOLIDGE, CALVIN. President and Vice President. Printed book: The Autobiography of Calvin Coolidge. Grey boards, blue cloth back, gilt lettered. New York, 1929. First edition. Limited to 1000 numbered copies boldly signed by Coolidge on the colophon page. Virtually mint, in original publishers box (also mint). Just like new!! Really choice! 225.00

620. HARRISON, BENJAMIN. President. Partly printed Document Signed, as President. 1 page, 4to. Washington, May 12, 1890. Authorizes the Secretary of State to affix the Seal to an envelope "containing my letter addressed to His Majesty Alexander III Emperor of Russia, on the birth of a daughter of the Grand Duchess Mavrikievna, Consort of his cousin the Grand Duke Constantinovich." Excellent condition, and a nice souvenir of Russo-American relations from the Czarist era. 475.00

621. HOOVER, HERBERT. President. Typed Letter Signed, on his imprinted stationery. 1 page, 4to. New York, December 30, 1962. To Mr. & Mrs. Harry Bruno. "What a cheerful New Year greeting is that beautiful white azalea plant -- and more just another indication of the devotion of long-time friends. I hope that the New Year will bring you both many blessings and many satisfactions...." Fine example. 125.00

TO PEARL S. BUCK

622. ROOSEVELT, ELEANOR. First Lady. Typed Letter Signed, as First Lady, on gilt-imprinted White House stationery. 1/2 page, 4to. Washington, October 21, 1943. To Miss [Pearl S.] Buck. She writes: "Thank you for writing to me about the books written by the daughters of Lin Yutang. I will gladly review the books when I receive them...." Nice association. 95.00

PICTORIAL CAMPAIGN SHEET MUSIC

623. [HAYES, RUTHERFORD B.] Printed Sheet Music: Grand Centennial March, by E. Mack. Folio, 1876. "Respectfully dedicated to the Republican Centennial Presidential Candidate, Hon. Rutherford B. Hayes, of Ohio." Large printed portrait of Hayes from a drawing by J. E. Baker. Published by John P. Perry & Co., Boston. Fine condition, and a dramatic display piece! 75.00

624. ADAMS, JOHN QUINCY. President; Secretary of State. His book: Oration on the Life and Character of Gilbert Motier de Lafayette. Delivered at the request of both Houses of the Congress of the United States...at Washington, on the 31st December, 1834. By John Quincy Adams, a member of the House. Presentation red leather binding, gilt-ruled. Gales & Seaton: Washington, 1835. Leaf tipped to title-page has signed presentation inscription by the former president: "Gayton P. Osgood / from / John Quincy Adams". Very rare in this format. Fine condition. 1250.00

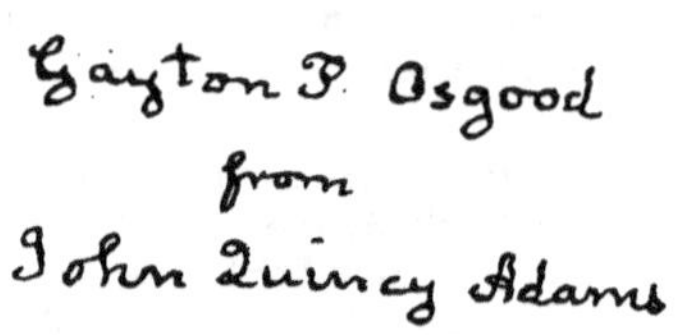

LINCOLN AUTHORIZES AN APPOINTED FEDERAL AGENT TO TRANSPORT CONTRABAND REBEL COTTON

625. LINCOLN, ABRAHAM. 1809-1865. President. Manuscript Document Signed "Abraham Lincoln", as President. One page, legal folio. Executive Mansion, November 29, 1864. Penned on the verso of a partly printed form executed and signed by H. A. Risley, Supply Agent, for the purchase of products of insurrectionary States, on behalf of the Government of the United States, at Norfolk, Virginia. Risley states that he has agreed to purchase 2500 bales of cotton that will be transported "at points on or near the National Military Lines in the Parishes of Madison, Tensas, and those north in the State of Louisiana...to Memphis, Tennessee..." Lincoln orders: "...that the Cotton moving in compliance with, and for fulfilment of said contract,

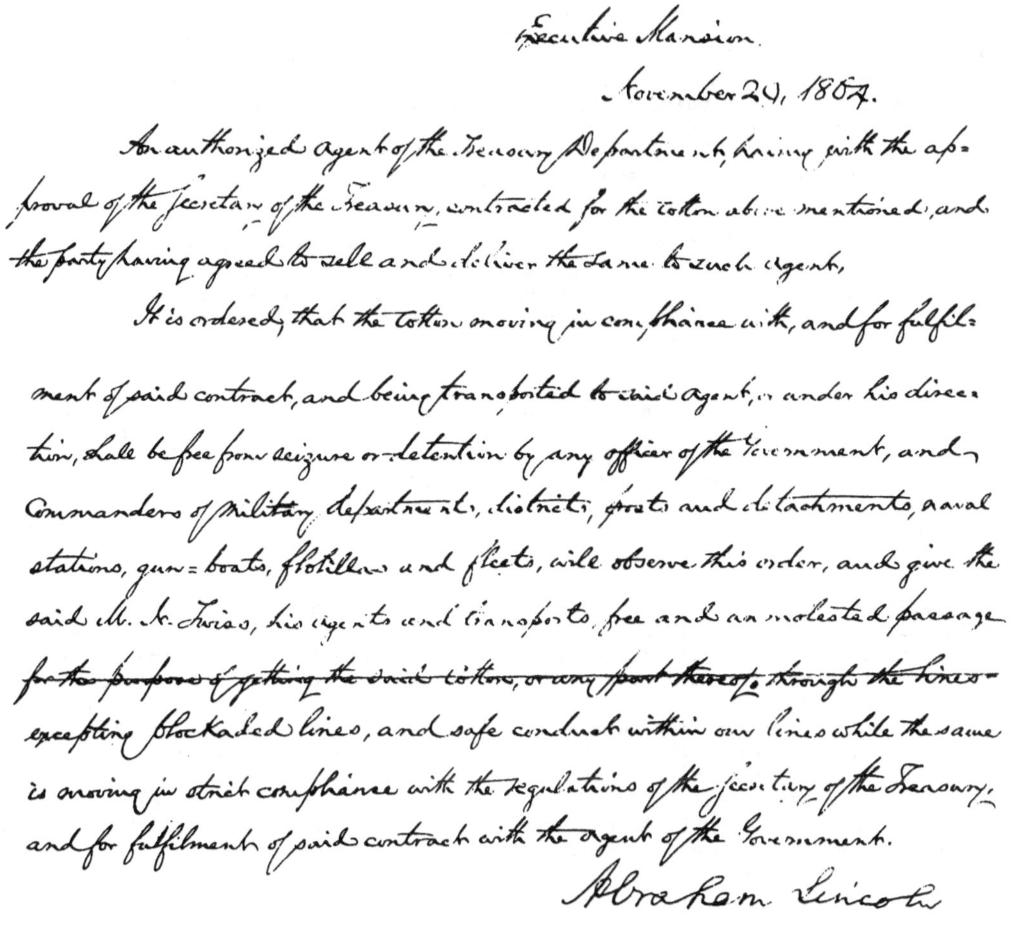
Executive Mansion.

November 24, 1864.

An authorized agent of the Treasury Department, having with the approval of the Secretary of the Treasury, contracted for the cotton above mentioned, and the party having agreed to sell and deliver the same to such agent,

It is ordered, that the cotton moving in compliance with, and for fulfilment of said contract, and being transported to said agent, or under his direction, shall be free from seizure or detention by any officer of the Government, and Commanders of Military departments, districts, posts and detachments, naval stations, gun-boats, flotillas and fleets, will observe this order, and give the said H. A. Risley, his agents and transports, free and unmolested passage ~~for the purpose of getting the said cotton, or any part thereof, through the lines~~ excepting blockaded lines, and safe conduct within our lines while the same is moving in strict compliance with the regulations of the Secretary of the Treasury, and for fulfilment of said contract with the agent of the Government.

Abraham Lincoln

and being transported to said Agent...shall be free from seizure or detention by any officer of the Government, and Commanders of Military Departments, districts, posts and detachments, naval stations, gun-boats, flotillas and fleets, will observe this order, and give...free and unmolested passage for the purpose of getting the said cotton...through the lines, excepting blockaded lines, and safe conduct within our lines while the same is moving in strict compliance with the regulations of the Secretary of the Treasury...." An unusual Civil War document. Some slight wear in the folds, else fine. Lincoln's signature is choice. 4000.00

626. BUCHANAN, JAMES. President; Secretary of State; Minister to England; Pennsylvania statesman. Manuscript Petition Signed, together with the signatures of 25 other members of the Pennsylvania Delegation in Congress. No place or date [1829-1831]. To John Branch, Secretary of the Navy, urging the appointment of Henry Pawling, "a graduate of the University of Pennsylvania, and a Citizen of Montgomery County" to be Assistant Surgeon in the U.S. Navy. The signatures on the first page are in two columns, and Buchanan signed at the bottom left, thus giving visability to his signature. Docketed integral leaf present. Fine example. 200.00

THE BURNING OF THE HERMITAGE AND THE LOSS
OF HIS BELOVED RACHEL'S LETTERS

627. JACKSON, ANDREW. President and General. Important Autograph Letter Signed, penned three months after leaving the presidency. 1 2/3 pages, 4to. Hermitage, June 24, 1837. To Harriet Butler, wife of Benjamin F. Butler (Attorney General under Jackson and Van Buren). With the integral address-leaf. After acknowledging letters from both Butlers, Jackson continues: "I assure you my dear madam, that the promise I made you of the autograph of my dear deceased wife was not forgotten. The act of Providence -- the burning of my house, I fear has put it out of my power to comply with my promise in this particular. I have, from the search made, a right to conclude that all her letters were destroyed with the Bureau that contained them -- none as yet can be found. Mrs. Watson told me she had one of her letters, and if I should fail on my return home in finding Mrs. J's letters and be unable to comply with my promise to you, she would resign to you the letter to comply with my promise. I had no idea of the extent of injury I had sustained by the burning -- all my bureaus and papers up stairs, it appears, are missing -- two bureaus with papers, one of which contained my dear wife's letters...." In spite of the fire, Jackson was still able to report: "I feel happy at the Hermitage, and return to you my grateful feelings for your congratulations for my increasing health and long life....I am truly grateful to Providence for restoring me to my peaceful Hermitage; and thankful to Him for the chekered health which I enjoy -- it is very far from being perfect. I have long since learned to be content with my lott, and always submit with cheerfulness to the will of heaven. My daughter has presented me with a fine son...." Small ink-burn in the "A" of Jackson's first name, and small seal tear in the blank area of the address-leaf, else generally fine. 4975.00

628. EISENHOWER, DWIGHT D. President and General. Partly printed Document Signed "D.D. Eisenhower" as Captain of Infantry, U.S.A. Commanding. 1 page, oblong 4to. Camp Colt, Gettysburg, Penn., April 13, 1918. Appointment of James C. Beene to the rank of Sergeant, First Class. Small eagle vignette at top center. Marginal tape stain. Very scarce from this early period in the future president's military career. 350.00

629. TRUMAN, HARRY S. President and Vice President. Typed Letter Signed, as President, on imprinted White House stationery. 1 page, 4to. Washington, June 18, 1945. To David Stern, Publisher, Philadelphia Record, Philadelphia, Pa. Original mailing envelope. Truman writes: "I hope that the next time you are in Washington you will drop in and see me. You might give Matt Connelly, my appointment secretary, a ring and he will set a convenient time...." Excellent condition. 350.00

630. HARRISON, BENJAMIN. President. Typed Letter Signed, on his imprinted letterhead. 1 page, 4to. Indianapolis, January 16, 1901. To David A. Munro, the publisher, in New York. The former President writes: "...The manuscript of my second article is by this time in your hands. The suggestion of Messrs Crowell & Co. attracted me only because their publications were of a small and unpretentious sort. Perhaps when I complete the three articles promised you I may not be so much out of conceit with them as to consider the matter of giving them a more permanent form -- perhaps with another address or two that I have made before upon public topics. I enclose you a letter [present] from the Secretary of the Editorial Board of the Columbia Law Review. It seems strange that it should not have been known to these people that the article had appeared in the North American Review...." The letter referred to, addressed to Harrison, has reference to obtaining a copy of his speech on the Phillippine question. The two letters, both in fine condition. 325.00

631. HOOVER, HERBERT. President. Typed Letter Signed, as President, on imprinted White House letterhead. 1 page, 4to. Washington, January 23, 1932. To Senator Walter F. George, Washington, D.C. The Republican president writes the Democratic senator that he has received from him "the name of Honorable Norval Richardson for consideration in connection with an appointment to one of the ministerial posts in Europe...." Fine. 325.00

632. GARFIELD, LUCRETIA R. First Lady. Autograph Letter Signed, on her monogrammed, black-bordered stationery. 1 1/2 separate pages, 12mo. Mentor, Ohio, May 17, 1895. To Mrs. Lincoln. "Your invitation to contribute to your Newspaper issue is received. I thank you for the thought of me, but can send you only a little check to be applied to your charity. My kind remembrance to Doctor Lincoln..." Fine example. 125.00

SCARCE BLACK-BORDERED IMPRINTED EXECUTIVE MANSION CARD

633. ARTHUR, CHESTER A. President and Vice President; became President upon the death of James A. Garfield, September 17, 1881. Choice black-bordered, imprinted "Executive Mansion" card, boldly signed by Arthur as President. Washington, no date. This type of mourning card was used only for about a month after Garfield's tragic death at the hand of an assassin, and is indeed very scarce. Pristine condition. 350.00

THURLOW WEED AND LINCOLN'S ELECTION TO THE PRESIDENCY IN 1860

634. FILLMORE, MILLARD. President and Vice President. Magnificent Autograph Letter Signed. 4 full pages, 8vo. Buffalo, March 12, 1862. To J. Chamberlain, New York. Fillmore writes:

> "...It is a gratification to know the secret springs by which certain public results are worked out. I have always suspected that there might be some truth in the report that T[hurlow] W[eed] found it convenient to show his patriotism by visiting Europe ostensibly to prevent recognition of Confederate Independence, but really to avoid being called as a witness before Van Wyck's investigating committee. May not this have suddenly terminated the negotiation to take charge of the Editorial department of the World? Still you might do much worse than to have W[eed]. He is a sagacious, cunning politician, and was the first among his friends to see and admit the danger to the Country from Lincoln's election, and he had courage and honesty enough to make an effort to settle matters by some compromise after Lincoln's election and before his inauguration. But unfortunately he was powerless for good, though he had been omnipotent for evil. His position was that of a leader of a mob who controlls its actions while he leads, but the moment he hesitates or turns back he is trodden down and crushed....
>
> I cordially approve of your idea of writing the history of this country from the annexation of Texas to the close of the present war. God grant that it may close soon and that your life and strength may be spared to accomplish so great a work, and that you may be abundantly rewarded for your labors, in money and fame.
>
> You expressed a desire to see again the Suppressed portion of my Annual Message in December 1852. I had only the copy preserved in my scrap book, and concluded to have a few copies printed in Confidence as well to prevent its accidental loss, as to consult some friends about the propriety of publishing it. I have submitted it to Mr. [Edward] Everett only, and he advises against its publication, for the same reasons that he advised to strike it out of the Message, viz. for fear the agita[tion] of the question of Slavery might do more harm than good. I have therefore concluded for the present to withhold it, but I enclose you a copy as a friend, and would like to know how it strikes you...."

Handsomely preserved, and without question one of the finest content Fillmore letters to come our way in years. 3500.00

GERALD R. FORD

Warmest best wishes,

Gerald R. Ford

Mr. Jerry Hisley
604 Woodside Road
Pikesville, Maryland 21208

QUOTING FROM ONE OF HIS FAVORITE BIBLE PASSAGES

635. FORD, GERALD R. President and Vice President; not elected by the people to either office; sworn in as President after Nixon's resignation. Remarkable Typed Letter Signed "Gerald R. Ford" on his imprinted gilt-crested (Presidential Seal) stationery. 1 page, small 4to. [Rancho Mirage, California] June 12, 1981. To Jerry Hisley congratulating him on his 10th Birthday. Ford continues: "One of my favorite Bible passages is the one I had the Bible opened to when I took the Oath of Office as President. It is Proverbs 3:5-6: Trust in the Lord with all thine heart; and lean not unto thine own understanding. In all thy ways acknowledge Him and He shall direct thy paths. Have a wonderful day...May you be successful in all your future endeavors." With original envelope bearing Ford's facsimile franking signature. Pristine. 450.00

PATENT SIGNED BY TWO PRESIDENTS

636. JACKSON, ANDREW. President and General. Partly engraved Document Signed, as President. 1 page, tall folio, vellum. Washington, June 16, 1830. Countersigned by MARTIN VAN BUREN, Secretary of State, and also by John Macpherson Berrien, Attorney General. Handsome blind-stamped perforated seal with spread-eagle design affixed with red wax. Three-page holograph description of the invention attached with silk ties. Letters Patent granted to John Pool, Jr. for his improvement in or application of mathematical instruments, designed for the practical surveyor, navigator, geometrician, or draftsmen generally, called the Geometrical Protractor and Tablet. Attractive document, with fine signatures. 1750.00

THE MONROES HELP THE MADISONS TO FURNISH THEIR NEW HOME IN VIRGINIA

637. MONROE, JAMES. President. Remarkable Autograph Letter Signed. Very full page, small quarto. Alb[emarle], February 6, 1798. [To James Madison, his new neighbour]. Monroe writes:

> "We are very thankful for the articles yr. self & Mrs. M. were so good as [to] send us. They are really rarities and of importance in our present situation. We sho'd however be very sorry if you reduced yr. own stock so as to feel the want of them.
>
> We send you two mattresses -- one of hair & another of wool, 4 dozen of the better kind of diaper napkins & 2 of inf[erio]r, very useful for common purposes; 4 table cloths, 2 of the size for a room of 18 feet, 2 others of great length wh. may each be cut either in two or three -- new. We wo'd add many more if you had desired, but that may still be done at another time. We have not more of kitchen furniture that will be sufficient for two families. I shall not dispose of any p[ar]t for the present so that you may have what you want. The waggon is in great haste so that I have only time to request our best regards to Mrs. M., yr. father & family. Sincerely yr. friend & servant / Jas. Monroe".

Truly, a letter of great historical association! Monroe was later to serve as Secretary of State and War in Madison's presidential cabinet. Irregularly trimmed at top, and the right third of the letter lightly water-stained; paper strips strengthen folds on verso. While not be any means mint, still in very satisfactory condition. For additional information on this period we refer you to pp. 237-39 in Gay's Life of Madison. 2000.00

"TOWARD UNITED NATIONS" CACHETED FIRST DAY COVER

638. ROOSEVELT, ELEANOR. First Lady. Scarce colorful cacheted Toward United Nations / April 25, 1945 / Franklin D. Roosevelt U.S. First Day Cover, bearing a Plate No. Bloc of four of the commemorative stamps. Postmarked San Francisco, April 25, 1945 (two weeks after FDR's death). Signed on the lower blank margin, beneath the postmark, by Mrs. Roosevelt. Choice! 95.00

UNUSUAL GROUP PHOTOGRAPH OF WILSON AND THE WHITE HOUSE PRESS

639. WILSON, WOODROW. President. Oblong studio photograph by Harris & Ewing depicting President Wilson seated alone on the arm of a small lawn bench with the members of the White House Press Corps gathered about. Taken on the White House lawn. On the lower wide margin Wilson has placed his signature and about thirty of the reporters have also signed, including JAMES P. TUMULTY, Wilson Private Secretary. Of the reporters we recognize only the name of David Lawrence, but all the others were probably very well known in their time. Choice! 450.00

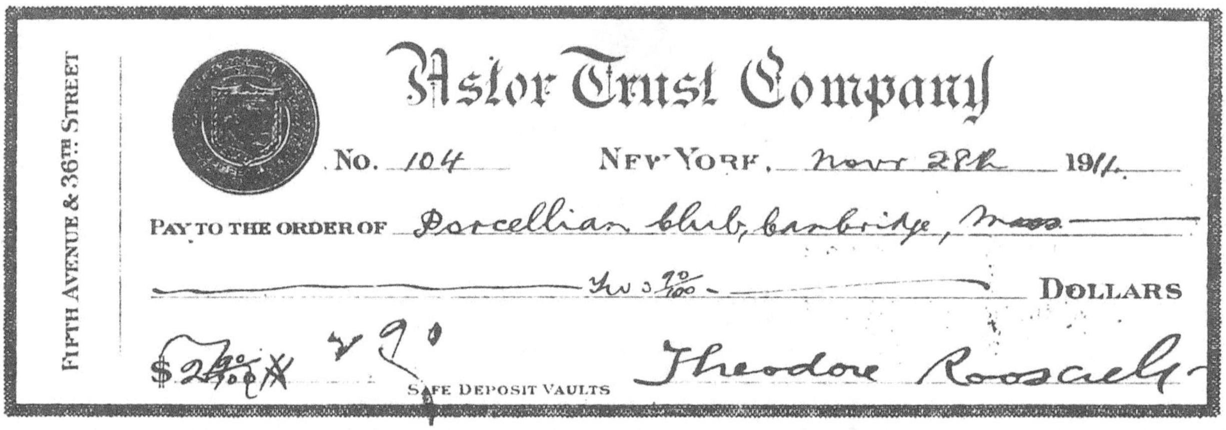
Astor Trust Company

FIFTH AVENUE & 36TH STREET

No. 104 New York, Novr 28th 1911

Pay to the order of Porcellian Club, Cambridge, Mass.

Two 90/100 Dollars

$2.90/100

Safe Deposit Vaults

Theodore Roosevelt

640. ROOSEVELT, THEODORE. President and Vice President. Partly printed Signed Bank Check, accomplished in the hand of a secretary. Oblong 8vo. New York, November 28, 1911. Drawn on the Astor Trust Company. Payable to the Porcellian Club, Cambridge, Mass. Punch-cancellation holes do not affect Roosevelt's fine signature. Very fine specimen. 350.00

SIGNATURES OF THE PRESIDENT, FIRST LADY, VICE PRESIDENT,
AND ALL THE MEMBERS OF HAYES' CABINET

641. HAYES, RUTHERFORD B. President. Oblong 8vo album leaf signed and dated, January 11, 1879, by Hayes as President. He has also penned "Fremont, O." On another matching album leaf may be found the signature of First Lady Lucy W. Hayes, and on subsequent leaves Vice President W.A. WHEELER, and cabinet members: WM. M. EVARTS, JOHN SHERMAN, GEO. W. MC CRARY, R.W. THOMPSON, CARL SCHURZ, CHARLES DEVENS, and D. M. KEY. The cabinet members have also penned the names of the various departments they headed. Nice grouping!! 250.00

642. CLEVELAND, GROVER. President. Boldly-penned signature, dated as President, February 1, 1896. Well-centered on an oblong octavo album leaf. Choice. 125.00

"THE WORLD FORGETTING BY THE WORLD FORGOT"

643. ADAMS, JOHN. 1735-1826. Second President of the United States; Signer of Declaration of Independence; U.S. Minister to Holland, France and England. Magnificent Autograph Letter Signed, as Minister to France. 10 1/2 pages, 4to. Auteuil near Paris, April 25, 1785. To Elbridge Gerry, fellow Signer and patriot from Massachusetts, then a member of the Continental Congress. Docketed by Gerry on the integral leaf. A letter of such importance, we are pleased to give an extensive quotation.

"I have rec'd...the Ratification of my Loan. In all that I said of Separating the foreign from the Domestic Debt, and in every Thing I may write about our affairs at Home, I always mean to submit my Guesses to the Superior Lights and better Judgments of those who are at home. When I was with you in Congress, I frequently found myself at a Loss to judge of the State of Things and the Sentiments of Persons in our own State, which obliged me to make it a Rule to go home once a year. I wish I could observe the same Rule now....It is now Seven Years and a half, since I left you at York Town, and the first of this Month completed Seven Years, since I landed at Bordeaux. The Chain of my Intelligence has been frequently interrupted and always imperfect. So that I frequently feel the Want of the Society of my Countrymen. It is really high Time for me to come home....I am really weary of the insipid Life I lead, and that Nullity and Annihilation to which we are reduced.

You say that a Report is before Congress to send Ministers to Spain and England, and Mr. Jay informs me that Congress have resolved to send one to London. These, if I have any Judgment are right Measures. Both of you hint that I may possibly be sent to London. If this should happen, although I know it will be the most stormy, perplexing and distressing Errand upon which any man can be sent, I will not refuse, but I shall expect however to be allowed to come home after a year, whether I succeed in any measure or not....I don't contend for the Necessity of having Ministers perpetually at the Courts of Europe: But untill your affairs are settled with Spain and England, I think it will be unavoidable. I wish We could do without them from this moment. It is a Life that I abhor. It is either Agony or Insipidity. Never pleasant. I take no more interest in any Thing about me, except the Business I have to do, than if I were dead.

I beg you would give your self no Anxiety about any Thing I say respecting Salaries. I think the Reduction of them wrong. I don't find that Articles of Subsistence are cheaper since the Peace...and We are more taken Notice of by foreign Ministers and have much more to do with them. Upon the present allowance We can keep no Tables nor see any company....Retirement is more agreeable to me than Company, but is not for the Interest of the public. Mr. Laurens or Mr. Bingham with their Fortunes...might spend three or four Thousands a Year of their own Incomes added to what you allow. But you know I cannot. I am told it is reported, that I have one Per Cent allowed me upon the Loan in Holland, and that a Sum of Money is always given upon the Signature of a Treaty. This upon my Honour is totally false. Of all the immense Sums that have been borrowed under my Name, not one farthing has ever come to my Benefit nor have I ever received a Farthing on the Signature of any Treaty, or made a farthing for my self in any way but the Salary you have allowed me. Many will call me a Fool, because all know I have been in a Situation where I might have made Profits, and where many others would. But such are my Sentiments, and my Head and Heart have been too full of the Public to think much of myself or my Children.

Mr. Jefferson has rec'd and answered your Letter and returns his Regards to you. He is an excellent Hand.

My Son, John Quincy Adams, will deliver you this. I don't know how to do without him. But he must qualify himself to get his Bread, for I have not the Means to provide for him, and to bring him up in a State of Dependence upon the Public or me, is not agreeable to his feelings or mine. So I send him to College and the Bar, where if I had persevered myself, it would have been much better for him and for two other fine Boys and one charming Girl...

What is to be done with the Cincinnati: is that order of Chivalry, that Inroad upon our first Principle, Equality, to be connived at? It is the deepest Piece of Cunning yet attempted. It is sowing the Seeds of all that European Courts wish to grow up among us, viz of Vanity, Ambition, Corruption, Discord, & Sedition. Are we so dim Sighted as to not see, that the taking away [of] the hereditary descent of it, will not prevent its banefull Influence? Who will think of preventing the Son from wearing a Ribbon and a bit of Gold that his Father wore. Mankind love to see one Child at least of every beloved and respected Father possessed of his Estate, his office &c after his Decease. Besides, when once the People begin to think these Marks Rewards, these Marks are soon considered as the only Proofs of Merit. Such Marks should not be adopted in any Country where there is Virtue, Love of Country, Love of Labour. -- When Virtue is lost Ambition succeeds. Then, indeed, Ribbons & Garters become necessary: but never till then. Then indeed, these should be public Rewards conferred by the State, the civil Sovereign, not private Men or Bodies.

I have been asked why I have not written against it. Can it be necessary for me to write upon such a Thing. I wrote twenty Years ago some Papers which have been called an Essay on the Feudal Law in which my sentiments...are sufficiently expressed, concerning all such Distinctions and all Orders of Chivalry and Nobility. But Sir, while Reputations are so indiscreetly puffed, while Thanks and Statues are so childishly awarded, and the greatest real services are so coldly received, I had almost said censured, We are on the high Road to have no Virtues left, and nothing but ambition to reward. Ribbons are not the only reward of Ambition. Wealth and Power must keep them Company. My Countrymen give Reputations to Individuals that are real Tyrannies. No Man dare resist or oppose them. No wonder then that such Reputations introduce Chivalry &c without opposition tho' without Authority. The Cry of Gratitude Gratitude is Animal Magnetism: it bewitches all Mankind and has established every Tyranny, Imposture & Usurpation that ever existed upon Earth....I could not have believed, if I had not seen it, that our officers could have adopted such a scheme, or the People, the Legislatures, or Congress have submitted to it...I don't wonder at a Marquis de la Fayette or a Baron Steuben. They were born and bred to such Decorations and the Taste for them. From the Moment that Captain [John Paul] Jones had his Cross of Merit bestowed by the King and consented to by Congress, I suspected that some such Project was in contemplation. Awefull, my Friend, is the Task of the intelligent Advocate for Liberty. The Military Spirit, the Ecclesiastical Spirit, the Commercial Spirit, and innumerable other evil Spirits are eternally devising Mischief to his Cause and disturbing his repose. It is a constant Warfare from the Cradle to the Grave, without Comfort, Thanks, or Rewards, and is always overcome at last.

Is not this Institution against our Confederation? Is it not against the Declarations of Rights in several of the States? Is it not an Act of Sovereignty disposing and creating of publick Rewards, presumptuously enterprised by private Gentlemen? Is the Assembly a lawfull Assembly? Is it not cruel to call this a Club for private Friendship, or a Society for Charity for Officers, Widows & Children. Would even such a Society be lawfull without the Permission of the Legislature? Is it not Substituting Honour for Virtue in the infancy of a Republic? Must it not introduce and perpetuate Contents and Dissentions pernicious in all governments but especially in ours? Is it not an effectual Subversion of our Equality. Inequalities of Riches cannot be avoided as long as Nature gives Inequality of Understanding and Activity, and these Inequalities are not unusefull. But artificial Inequalities of Decorations, Birth and Title, not accompanying public Trusts, are those very Inequalities which have exterminated Virtue and Liberty and substituted Ambition and Slavery in all ages and countries.

if this appears to be their determination, it is not worth the while of you and me to die Martyrs to Singular Notions. You are young and may turn fine Gentleman yet — I am too old, and therefore will retire to Pens Hill,

The World forgetting by the World forgot.

I am my dear Sir your
Sincere Friend
John Adams

I don't wonder that the Word Republican is odious and unpopular throughout the World. I don't wonder that so fine, even of the great Writers, have admired this Form of Government. Plato himself, I am fully persuaded from his Writings, was not a Republican. It is the best of Governments, while the People are Republicans, i.e. virtuous, simple and of independent Spirit. But when the People are avaricious, ambitious and vain, instead of being virtuous, poor and proud, it is not. A Republican is an equivocal Character. A Dutchman, a Genoese, a Venetian, a Swiss, a Genevan and an Englishman are all called Republicans. -- Among all these shades you will scarcely find the true Colour. Our Countrymen, may be the nearest, but there is so much Wealth among them and such an universal Rage of avarice, that I often fear they will only make their real Republicans miserable for a few Years, and then become like the rest of the World. If this appears to be their determination, it is not worth the while of you and me to die Martyrs to Singular Notions. You are young and may turn [a] fine gentleman yet. -- I am too old, and therefore will retire to Pens Hill,

The World forgetting by the World forgot...."

Well, if you read through all that you know how Adams felt about the founding of the Society of the Cincinnati by George Washington and Henry Knox! Truly, a magnificent letter, and one of the longest from Adams' brilliant pen to appear on the market. Fine condition.
15,000.00

644. GARFIELD, JAMES A. President; assassinated after serving just four months in office; Union General in Civil War; Congressman from Ohio. Choice albumin carte-de-visit photograph by Brady's National Photographic Portrait Galleries, New York and Washington. Boldly signed on the photographic surface beneath Garfield's image: "J. A. Garfield / Ohio". Photographer's gilt imprint on lower mount: "Brady / Washington". Also imprinted in black on verso. An outstanding photograph dating from Garfield's early years in Congress [ca. 1865-1868]. Insignificant mounting traces on verso, else fine. 1750.00

645. POLK, SARAH K. First Lady. Her signature as "Mrs. James K. Polk / Polk place / Nashville, Tennessee / Age 87" boldly penned on an octavo leaf. Fine and scarce. 125.00

646. TRUMAN, HARRY S President and Vice President. His book describing life as a private citizen following his presidency: Mr. Citizen. Cloth. [New York] 1960. First edition. Inscribed on the half-title page: "To Harry N. Burgess / from / Harry S Truman / kind regards / 2-8-61" Original pictorial dust-jacket featuring Truman's portrait. Fine. 150.00

647. FILLMORE, MILLARD. President and Vice President. Complete address-leaf, franked by then Congressman Fillmore in the upper right corner: "M. Fillmore / M.C." Addressed by Fillmore to his law partner, S. H. Haven, Buffalo, New York. Clear circular WASHINGTON CITY postmark, and "FREE" on face of the cover. Attractive franked address-leaf. 250.00

648. HARDING, WARREN G. President. Attractive full signature, "Warren G. Harding", penned on a slip of paper with ample margins for framing. With portrait. Pristine! 125.00

649. BUCHANAN, JAMES. President. Attractive full signature, newly matted and framed with a fine engraved portrait. Ready for your wall! Nice specimen. 150.00

650. HOOVER, HERBERT. President. His book: America's First Crusade. Lettered gray cloth. New York, 1942. First edition. Inscribed on the front endpaper: "To Everett Colby / With the Kind Regards / of Herbert Hoover". Fine.
150.00

A NEEDED CHANGE IN THE MISSION TO GUATEMALA

651. CLEVELAND, GROVER. President. Interesting Autograph Letter Signed, as President, on imprinted Executive Mansion stationery. 3 full pages, 8vo. Washington, January 23, 1888. To "Dear Mary". He writes: "It may be that the good of the public service will necessitate a change in the Diplomatic Representation at Guatemala where Mr. Hall is now located. You have done much to keep him in office this long and if I conclude that another should go there I want to send a man who will attend to the interests which the good people for whom you have spoken have at heart. I should like to know who these people are and Chief one among them, so that if I think best I can communicate with them. Will you tell me all you know about it? Charley is here and spent a part of Saturday and yesterday with us. He talked a little about coming in again to-day but he is apt to slip away upon such a half promise and I suspect he will do so in this case. We were glad to know through him that you were very well and had an opportunity to see Sue. You know we want you here as soon as you can come to us. With love to Will and a great deal from Frank, I am, Yours affectionately..." It would almost seem that this interesting presidential letter was written to a family member. In his closing, "Frank", undoubtedly refers to his wife, Frances Folsom Cleveland. First page very lightly and uniformly tanned, else fine. 750.00

DOWN-TO-EARTH, HOMEY, ADVICE FROM THE VICE PRESIDENT-ELECT

652. COOLIDGE, CALVIN. President and Vice President. Exquisite Autograph Letter Signed, as Governor of Massachusetts and Vice President-elect, on the gilt and blue crested stationery of the Governor's Office. Full page, 8vo. State House, Boston, November 28, 1920. To "My dear Allan". Complete message to this young admirer reads: "Thank you for your note. Always find out what your mother thinks is right and then do it. Yrs..." Very rare in full holograph, and highly unusual in content! Pristine condition. 950.00

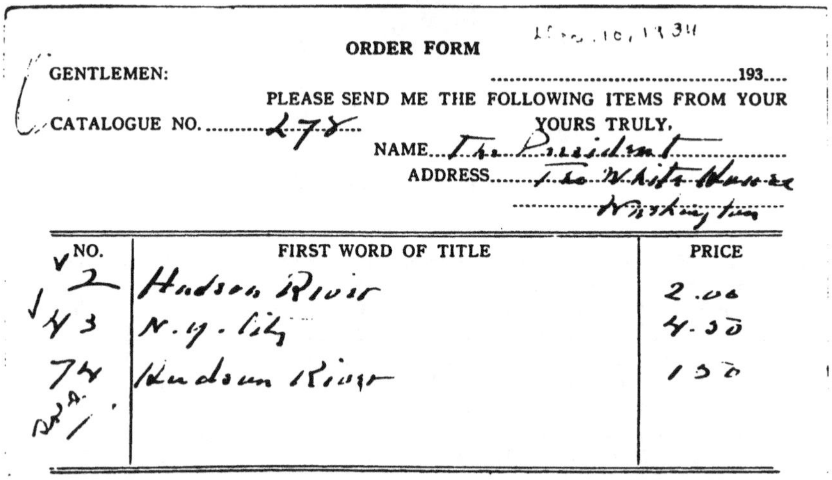
ORDER FORM

GENTLEMEN: ....193....

PLEASE SEND ME THE FOLLOWING ITEMS FROM YOUR CATALOGUE NO. 278

YOURS TRULY,

NAME The President

ADDRESS The White House

Washington

NO.	FIRST WORD OF TITLE	PRICE
2	Hudson River	2.00
43	N.Y. City	4.50
74	Hudson River	1.50

THE PRESIDENT ORDERS BOOKS

653. ROOSEVELT, FRANKLIN D. President. Partly printed Order Form from John E. Scopes & Co., the Albany booksellers, accomplished in Roosevelt's hand. Oblong 12mo [December 10, 1934]. With original addressed, imprinted, cancelled and stamped White House envelope. Roosevelt orders three books from Scopes' Catalogue 278, two on the Hudson River and one on New York City. Under name and address he has written: "The President / The White House / Washington". Highly unusual presidential item! Fine. 350.00

THE PATENT RIGHTS CONGRESS IN VIENNA

654. GRANT, ULYSSES S. President. Choice partly printed Document Signed, as President. One page, 4to. Washington, June 7, 1873. President Grant authorizes the Secretary of State to affix the Seal of the United States to "a Full Power authorizing Hon. J. M. Thacker to represent the United States at the International Congress to be held at Vienna relating to Patent Rights ..." Excellent condition, and a wonderful gift for a patent attorney! 525.00

WILSON'S ADDRESS TO CONGRESS ON THE RAILROAD CRISIS

655. WILSON, WOODROW. President. Printed speech: Address...delivered at a Joint Session of the Two Houses of Congress / August 29, 1916. Self-covered printed wrappers. Government Printing Office: Washington, 1916. 8 pages, small 4to. Signed by President Wilson on the last page beneath the concluding line of text. Lightly folded for mailing in an envelope, else very fine. Laid in a cloth case with gilt-lettered spine. The threat of a national railroad strike in 1916 necessitated Wilson's delivering this "crisis" speech to the Congress. Scarce. 450.00

656. HOOVER, HERBERT. President. Handsome large quarto bust portrait by the Bureau of Engraving & Printing. Boldly signed in bright blue ink by Hoover beneath his likeness. Pristine condition, and rarely available in this larger size. Striking display piece!! 325.00

GRANT EXPRESSES HIS RELUCTANCE TO REMOVE GENERAL THOMAS

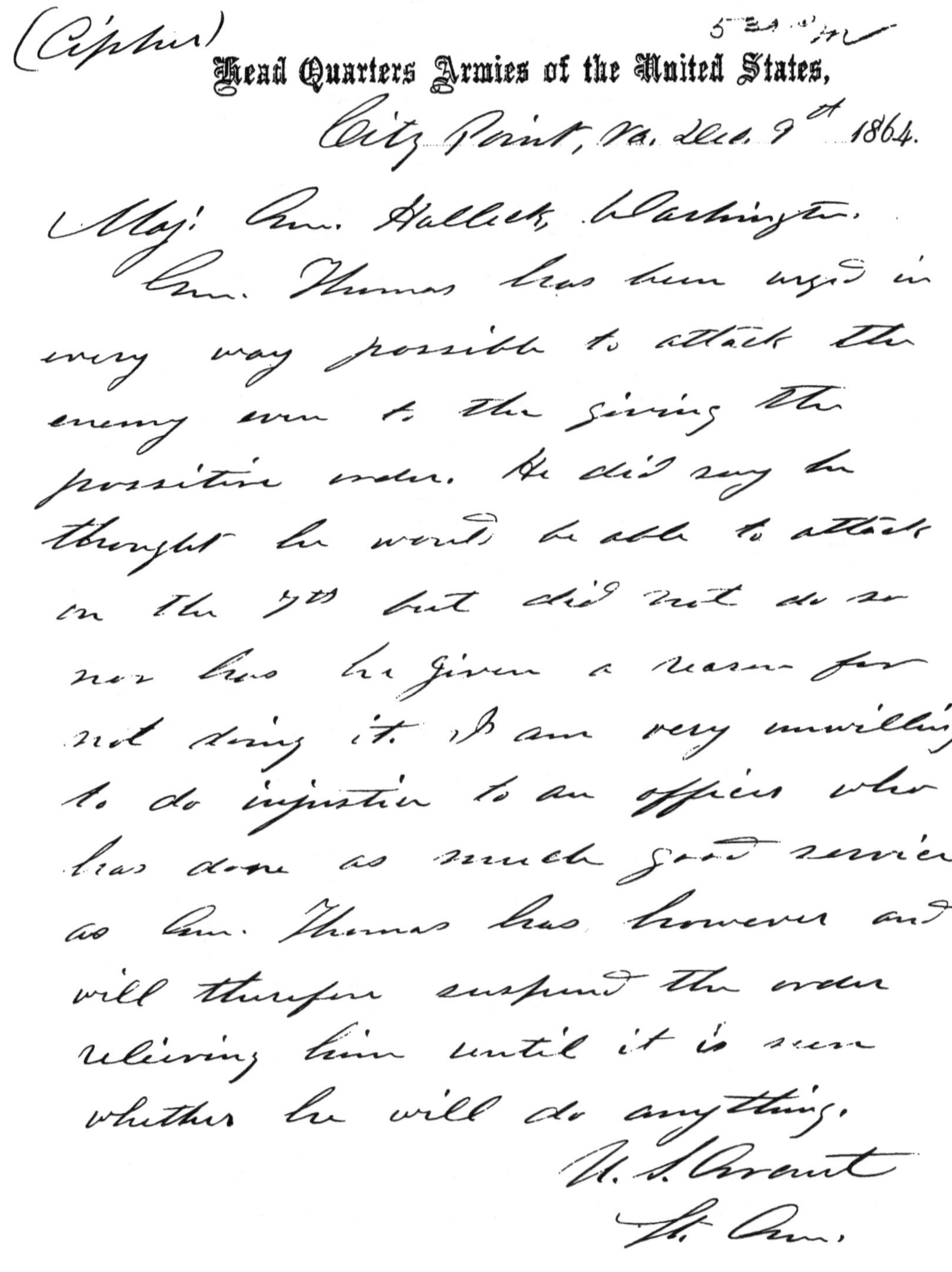
(Cipher)
Head Quarters Armies of the United States,
City Point, Va. Dec. 9th 1864.
Maj. Gen. Halleck, Washington.
Gen. Thomas has been urged in every way possible to attack the enemy even to the giving the possitive order. He did say he thought he would be able to attack on the 7th but did not do so nor has he given a reason for not doing it. I am very unwilling to do injustice to an officer who has done as much good service as Gen. Thomas has however and will therefore suspend the order relieving him until it is seen whether he will do anything.
U. S. Grant
Lt. Gen.

657. GRANT, ULYSSES S. President; Union General; accepted Lee's surrender. Autograph Telegraph Message Signed "U. S. Grant / Lt. Gen.", on imprinted Army stationery. Full page, 4to. City Point, Virginia, December 9, 1864. To Major General [Henry W.] Halleck, Washington. Grant writes: "Gen. Thomas has been urged in every way possible to attack the enemy even to the giving the possitive order. He did say he thought he would be able to attack on the 7th but did not do so nor has he given a reason for not doing it. I am very unwilling to do injustice to an officer who has done as much good service as Gen. Thomas has...and will therefore suspend the order relieving him until it is seen whether he will do anything...." General George H. Thomas accompanied Sherman in his Atlanta campaign. He was sent to Tennessee to repel Hood's army (Sept. 1864), and five days after Grant sent the above message, he did indeed act decisively, winning the Battle of Nashville (December 15-16, 1864). A dramatic war message of the great Union general. Pristine condition. 3500.00

PRESIDENT DAVIS EXPLAINS THE DISPOSITION OF CONFEDERATE TROOPS TO THE GOVERNOR AND CITIZENS OF NORTH EAST MISSISSIPPI

658. DAVIS, JEFFERSON. President, Confederate States of America. Fascinating, lengthy Manuscript Letter Signed, as President. 5 1/4 pages, 4to. Richmond, Virginia, May 8, 1863. To Governor James Whitefield and three other Mississippi citizens, in part discussing the removal of troops from Mississippi and Alabama. Davis writes:

> "I have duly reflected on the important matters presented by you in our interview...and the report of the Committee appointed to consider the means for defence of the City of Columbus and Valley of Tombighee, as well as...the number, condition, and disposition of the troops in North Eastern Mississippi. The subject had not failed previously to command my attention and I had already striven better to provide for the defence of a section important to the wellbeing of the Confederacy and from many personal considerations deeply interesting to me. It would be needless to explain to you how far my ability falls short of my earnest desire or to recount the causes which so often prevent me from affording that full protection to various portions of our common country which is called for by every consideration that can animate manly and patriotic breasts or excite a public officer to greatest exertion.
>
> To supply...the want created by the transfer of Gen'l Van Dorn's cavalry to the field of operations in Tennessee all the disposable mounted force in South Alabama was ordered up and inquiry was instituted to ascertain whether Gen'l Van Dorn with his command could not be consistently returned to the Department from which he had been withdrawn.
>
> The repulse of the enemy at Charleston relieving our immediate necessities at that place, call was made for eight or ten thousand troops to be sent to reinforce Gen'l Pemberton....To arm the Militia called out by the Governor of Mississippi, four thousand small arms...have been sent forward with an assurance that more would be furnished, if more men could be raised to bear them....The prisoners captured at the Post of Arkansas, say 3000 in number, have been ordered...to proceed to the command of Gen'l Pemberton....
>
> What else it may be possible for me to do, depends upon the fluctuating tide of War....General Forrest with his brigade cannot be detached from the Army of Tennessee and assigned to duty in North Mississippi. You can however assure our fellow citizens...that their condition has not been overlooked, that their sufferings have been fully sympathized with and that their necessities will be ever remembered. Gen'l Pemberton, commanding the Department, has my full confidence and will I think...entirely justify the faith with which he has been regarded by the People of Mississippi.
>
> Allow me to suggest the propriety of organizing all those who cannot take the field either as Militia or Confederate troops, for such defence of towns and bridges, as may be afforded by men who are only able on an emergency to go out for a few hours or days to repell plundering and devastating parties who may attempt raids upon their respective localities. Without such previous organization there will be confusion and delay, if not want of concert, fatal to any effective action and the troops must either be so dispersed as to destroy their strength or important places be exposed to destruction by small bands of mounted marauders...."

Truly a marvellous war-date letter in very choice state of preservation. Letters of this importance and candor written by President Davis during the War seldom find their way on to the market. 3000.00

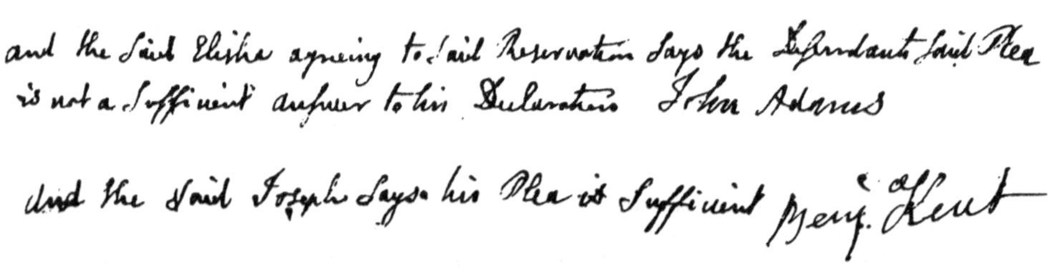
and the Said Elisha agreeing to Said Reservation Says the Defendants Said Plea is not a Sufficient answer to his Declaration John Adams

And the Said Joseph Says his Plea is Sufficient Benj. Kent

659. ADAMS, JOHN. President and Vice President. Early Autograph Document Signed. Oblong 12mo. No place or date. Three lines in Adams' holograph, written ca. 1767, while a young practicing attorney. With engraved portrait. Nice example. 750.00

A TREATY WITH THE RUSSIANS

660. PIERCE, FRANKLIN. President. Handsome partly printed Document Signed, as President. Full page, 4to. Washington, July 21, 1854. President Pierce authorizes the Secretary of State to affix the Seal of the United States to "a full power authorizing him to treat with Russia on the subject of the rights of neutrals...." William L. Marcy served as Pierce's Secretary of State. Clean and fresh specimen. With handsome steel-engraved portrait. 750.00

National Inauguration Ball
MARCH 4th 1865.
PRESIDENT OF THE U.S.
ABRAHAM LINCOLN.
VICE PRESIDENT OF THE U.S.
ANDREW JOHNSON.
The Honor of
Company is requested
Managers
E PLURIBUS UNUM
WE ARE ONE AND INDISSOLUBLE
1860-65
1812-15
1777-83

661. [LINCOLN, ABRAHAM]. President of the United States. Handsome engraved invitation to attend Lincoln's Second Inauguration Ball. Quarto. Headed: "National Inauguration Ball / March 4th 1865." Portraits of Lincoln and Vice President Andrew Johnson at top center. In three columns are listed the names of the Managers, including Hannibal Hamlin, Schuyler Colfax, John Sherman, Henry Wilson, E. D. Morgan, E. B. Washburn; Generals Grant, Sherman, Sheridan, Holt, Augur, Hancock, Doubleday; Admirals Farragut and Porter; F. E. Spinner, S. B. Colby, Hugh McCulloch and John G. Nicolay. At bottom the following imprints appear: "Designed & Drawn by Bruff / Engraved by Dempsey & O'Toole." Undoubtedly Bruff was J. Goldsborough Bruff, the artist who is best remembered for his illustrative maps and illustrations that appeared in western overland narratives. Printed on stiff paper. Pristine condition. Very rare and desireable piece of Lincoln memorabilia. 750.00

662. HOOVER, HERBERT. President. His book: An American Epic / Famine in Forty-Five Nations / Organization Behind the Front 1914 - 1923. Volume Two. Silver-lettered blue cloth. Chicago, 1960. First edition. Boldly inscribed in jet-black ink on the front endpaper: "To the Capitol Hill Club / With the Good Wishes / of / Herbert Hoover." Dust-jacket. Fine. 150.00

663. KENNEDY, JACQUELINE BOUVIER. First Lady. Her book: One Special Summer. Co-authored and illustrated with her sister, Lee Bouvier [Princess Lee Radziwill]. Large quarto. Decorated blue boards. Delacorte Press: New York, 1974. First edition. Limited to 500 copies signed by the sisters with their maiden names on the colophon page: "JACQUELINE BOUVIER and LEE BOUVIER." The book tells in original illustrations and facsimile script of a trip to Europe taken by the two sisters in 1951. Original publishers' box. An interesting book! 225.00

664. MC KINLEY, WILLIAM. President; Governor of Ohio. Typed Letter Signed, on the imprinted letterhead of the U.S. House of Representatives, where he was serving as Congressman from Ohio. 1 page, 4to. Washington, July 2, 1888. To Hon. J. Park Alexander, Akron, Ohio. Writing on his return from the Republican National Convention which nominated Benjamin Harrison for its presidential candidate, McKinley writes that of "the many letters received commending my course at Chicago, none have given me greater satisfaction than yours. Please give my kind regards to your family, and convey to them my thanks for their generous friendship for me...." Attractive example. 250.00

MUSTER ROLL SIGNED AS THE COMMANDER OF FORT CRAWFORD

665. TAYLOR, ZACHARY. President; General in Mexican War; spent most of his military career at forts on the western frontier. Partly printed Document Signed "Z. Taylor, Col. / Comdg". One page, large oblong folio [20 3/4 x 16 3/4 inches]. Fort Crawford, Prairie du Chien [Michigan Territory, now in the State of Wisconsin], October 1832. A muster roll of non-commissioned officers and privates employed on extra duty, by Colonel Taylor, as mechanics and laborers at the saw mill, near Fort Crawford, during the month of October, 1832. Signed by Taylor as commanding officer of the fort, a post he held from August 1832 to November 1836. Very fine condition, and a most unusual form of document for a presidential collection. 950.00

666. GRANT, ULYSSES S. President and General. Handsome proof engraved portrait of President Grant, in formal civilian attire. Bust profile likeness by the Bureau of Engraving and Printing, and showing their imprint. Boldly signed by Grant, probably while President, in bright violet ink beneath his image. Small 8vo. Very fine specimen, and rather scarce in this format. 750.00

667. ROOSEVELT, FRANKLIN D. President. Typed Letter Signed, as Assistant Secretary of the Navy, on imprinted stationery of that office. Full page, large 4to. Washington, November 1, 1917. To Hon. John J. Mattison, Postmaster, Canandaigua, New York. Roosevelt asks pardon for his delay in writing his correspondent about an appointment, saying "...I have to let the Department work take precedence over everything else." The appointment concerns a man who wished to be promoted from a substitute clerk to a regular clerk. Fine. 225.00

ACKNOWLEDGING CONGRATULATIONS ON HIS PRESIDENTIAL NOMINATION

668. GARFIELD, JAMES A. President; assassinated after serving just four months in office. Manuscript Letter Signed. Full page, 8vo. Mentor, Ohio, June 22, 1880. To Abraham Payne, Providence, Rhode Island. The future president writes: "The enormous press of business during the last two weeks has prevented my replying sooner...and even now I can but take time to thank you for the kind congratulations..." Fine specimen. With engraved portrait. 350.00

669. CLEVELAND, GROVER. President. Autograph Letter Signed. 2 full pages, 8vo. New York, October 14, 1892. To W. Bayard Cutting. Interesting letter written during the presidential campaign in which Cleveland was successful in regaining the White House from Benjamin Harrison who had defeated him four years earlier. Cleveland writes: "I was exceedingly touched by your kind letter...and its enclosure. The latter I have delivered to the Campaign Committee. It will gratify you to know that it was very opportune and much appreciated. I am deeply grateful for your personal friendliness and I assure you that I find in the commendation of such disinterested and patriotic men as I know you to be, the best recompense for laborious effort in the discharge of public duty. I read your letter to Mrs. Cleveland; and I beg you to receive with my thanks, the gratitude of a loving wife...." Fine. 350.00

670. BUCHANAN, JAMES. President. Autograph Letter Signed, while representing Pennsylvania in the United States Senate. 1/2 page, 4to. Senate Chamber [Washington], December 29, 1841. To Mr. Stansbury. Integral address-leaf. Buchanan writes: "I am anxious that you should write out my speech as soon as possible, consistently with your usual care & ability: and I want to see it before its publication...." Fine example. With engraved portrait. 450.00

PRAISING AN ARTIST FOR AN ENGRAVED PORTRAIT OF HER HUSBAND

671. GRANT, JULIA DENT. First Lady. Autograph Letter Signed, in pencil, on her imprinted monogrammed note paper. One and a fraction pages, 12mo. Washington, February 24, 1868. To William E. Marshall. She writes: "I am delighted with your splendid engraving of my husband. I can not say too much in its praise. As a likeness I do not think it could be better and I shall always prize your elegant gift...." General Grant was nominated and elected president later the same year. Scarce! 225.00

RARE HOLOGRAPH LETTER AS FIRST LADY

672. HOOVER, LOU HENRY. First Lady. Autograph Letter Signed, as First Lady, on silver-imprinted stationery "The President's Camp / On the Rapidan". 3 full pages, 8vo. June 9, no year. To Miss Nicolay, apparently a young artist. She writes: "I am very sad that I have not been able to see your picture, whose description interested me so very much. But I deliberately postponed going to see it for two or three weeks after your pleasant invitation was received, as I wanted to take my son with me when he was in Washington during the spring holidays. And then I had the accident which has prevented my going out at all! I hope that you will not have left for the summer when I return to town and that we will be able to arrange a time when...I may call to see the picture...." This is the first holograph letter of Mrs. Hoover penned as First Lady that we can recall, and we have never seen presidential stationery with this imprint. Excellent condition, and very, very choice!! 350.00

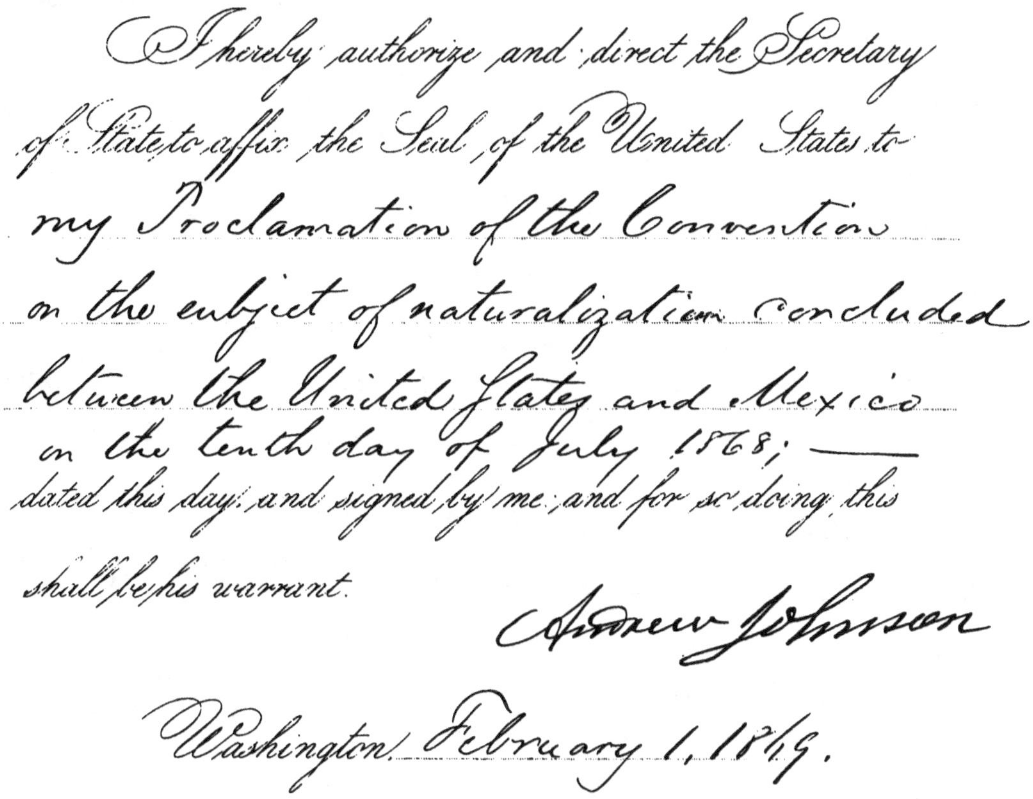
I hereby authorize and direct the Secretary of State to affix the Seal of the United States to my Proclamation of the Convention on the subject of naturalization concluded between the United States and Mexico on the tenth day of July 1868; — dated this day, and signed by me; and for so doing this shall be his warrant.

Andrew Johnson

Washington, February 1, 1869.

NATURALIZATION TREATY WITH MEXICO

673. JOHNSON, ANDREW. President and Vice President. Important partly printed Document Signed, as President. 1 page, 4to. Washington, February 1, 1869. President Johnson authorizes the Secretary of State to affix the Seal of the United States to "my Proclamation of the Convention on the subject of naturalization concluded between the United States and Mexico on the tenth day of July 1868...." Excellent condition. With engraved portrait. 650.00

674. CLEVELAND, FRANCIS FOLSOM. First Lady. Magnificent sepia cabinet photograph, profile bust pose, by C. M. Bell, Washington (imprint on the lower mount). Signed by the young Mrs. Cleveland, who married her husband in the White House, on the photographic surface beneath her image. Last two letters of "Cleveland" slightly smudged, else quite fine. 225.00

"I SHALL REAPPOINT YOU AS SOON AS CONGRESS ADJOURNS"

675. TAFT, WILLIAM H. President; Chief Justice, U.S. Supreme Court. Most interesting and curious Typed Letter Signed, as President, on imprinted White House stationery. 1 page, 4to. Washington, February 28, 1911. To Hon. Hy D. Davis, United States Marshal, Cleveland, Ohio. Taft writes: "...If you are not confirmed I shall reappoint you as soon as Congress adjourns. I cannot bother with the Senator. You will have to do that yourself...." This refers to an effort by Senator Burton of Ohio to block Davis's reappointment. Pristine condition. 450.00

676. GRANT, ULYSSES S. President; Union General. Autograph Letter Signed. 1 page, 8vo. New York City, April 18, 1882. To Mrs. [Norman B.] Judd, widow of Lincoln's friend, campaign manager and early political advisor. Grant writes: "I have forwarded your letter of the 15th inst. with indorsement, to the Sec. of State calling his attention to your husband's services which I know -- with your husband himself -- he will remember...." Fine condition, and a choice association. With engraved portrait. 450.00

Sir

The ungentlemany Expressions, and gasconading conduct of yours relative to me on yesterday was in true charecter of your self, and unmask you to the world, and plainly shews that they were the ebulitions of a base mind goaded with stubborn prooffs of fraud, and flowing from a source devoid of every refined senti-ment, or delicate sensation — But sir the voice of the people has made you a Governor — this alone makes you worthy of my notice, or the notice of any Gentleman — To the office I bear respect, to the voice of the people who placed it on you I pay respect, and as such I only deign to notice you, and call upon you for that satisfaction and explanation that your ungentlemany conduct & expressions require, for this purpose I request an interview, and my friend who will hand you this will point out the time and place, when and where I shall expect to see you with your friend and no other person — my friend and myself will be armed with pistols — you cannot mistake me, or my meaning. I am &c &c

Andrew Jackson

1803 To John Sevier. Esqr.
Governor.

[Item No. 677]

CHALLENGING GOVERNOR SEVIER TO A DUEL

677. JACKSON, ANDREW. 1767-1845. President and General. Remarkable historic Autograph Letter Signed "Andrew Jackson". Full page, 4to. No place or date [1803]. To "His Excellency / John Sevier", Governor of Tennessee. Detached address-leaf present. Jackson writes:

Sir

The ungentlemany (sic) expressions, and gasganading conduct of yours relative to me yesterday was in true character of your self, and unmasks you to the world, and plainly shews that they were the charletons of a base mind goaded with stubborn prooffs (sic) of fraud, and flowing from a source devoid of every refined sentiment, or delicate sensation. But Sir the Voice of the people has made you a Governor -- this alone makes you worthy of my notice or the notice of any Gentleman. To the office I bear respect, to the voice of the people who placed it on you I pay respect, and as such I only deign to notice you, and call upon you for that Satisfaction and explanation that your ungentlemany (sic) conduct & expressions require. For this purpose I request an interview, and my friend who will hand you this will point out the time and place, when and where I shall expect to see you with your friend and no other person. My friend and myself will be armed with pistols. You cannot mistake me, or my meaning. I am &c &c

Andrew Jackson

In 1801 Governor Sevier, being ineligible for a fourth successive term, gave way to Archibald Roane, a young lawyer who had come out to the wilderness with Jackson in the early days. Sevier now ran against Jackson for the generalship, and when the vote was found to be tied, Roane cast his deciding ballot for his friend, Jackson, who was thus elected [1802]. In 1803 Jackson supported Roane for the governorship against Sevier, who was now eligible. The quarrel between Sevier and Jackson, which had begun in 1796, developed into bitter enmity and all but led to a serious personal encounter. Sevier, however, was successful in the election and Jackson gained no advantage. Though their encounter in 1803, in which the affair culminated, was farcical, it left a deep impression upon Sevier, who dreamed that his father appeared to him to assure him that Jackson was "a very wicked base man, and a very improper person for a judge."

This choice ALS has been expertly laminated with fine silk on the verso, and is in otherwise fine condition. The writing is dark and unfaded. A wonderful conversation item for any outstanding set of presidential letters, or for the Jackson specialist. 12,500.00

WARM HOLOGRAPH LETTER TO A FORMER PRESIDENTIAL ADVISOR

678. EISENHOWER, MAMIE DAUD. First Lady. Autograph Letter Signed "Mamie E -", on her imprinted stationery. 2 full separate pages, large 8vo. Gettysburg, Penn., July 4, 1964. To "Dear Bobby" [Robert Cutler, who served as Ike's representative on the National Security Council. She writes: "Ike and I were so pleased to receive your letter and the beautiful poem on genuine Sheepskin for our 48th Wedding Aniv. Only wish you had been here to read it aloud like you did at the White House parties. You certainly are a new 70 year Cupid. Mr. Goodman did a masterpiece of script writing. Thank him for us. We spent night of 30th with General and Mrs. Heaton celebrating their 38th. Luncheon with the Strauss, then home for a dinner with John and Barbie. Lots of Champagne Toasts....We hope to be off for S.F. on the 9th. We expect to be home all of August so if your (sic) near, come by. Sept. in Wisconcin. Much love -- Mamie E." Choice letter! 200.00

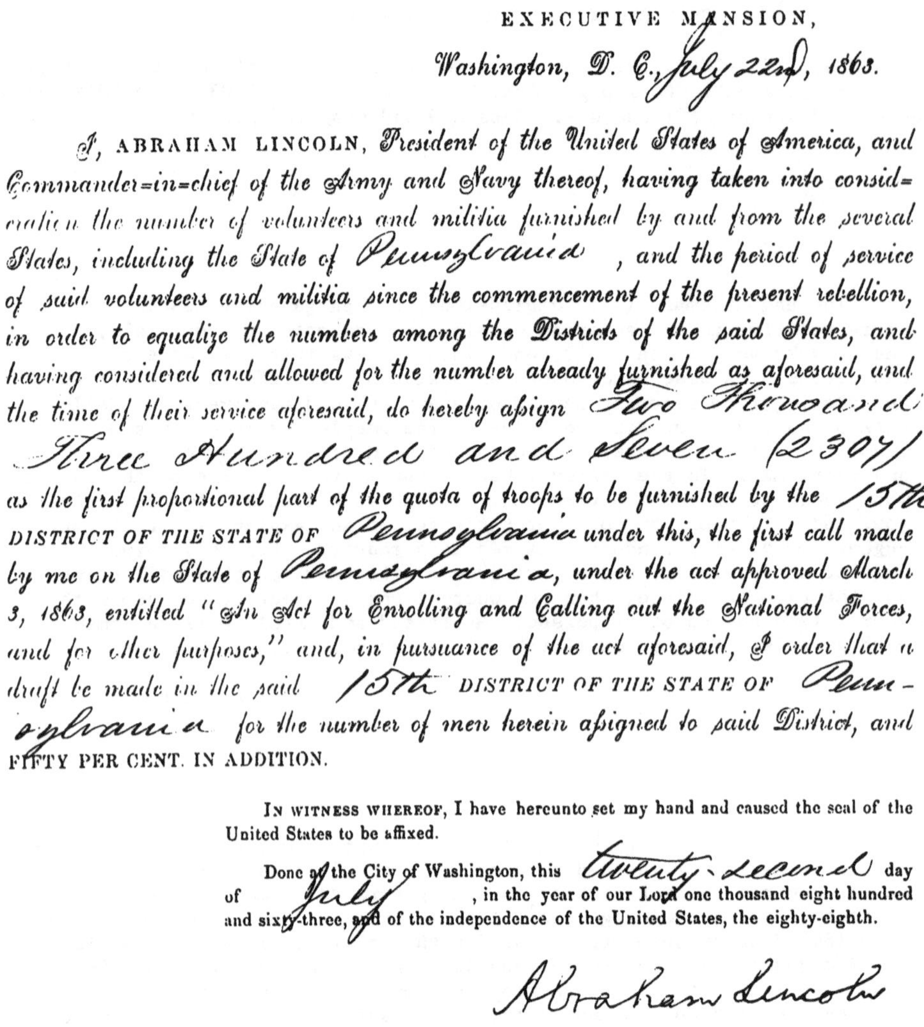

EXECUTIVE MANSION,

Washington, D. C., July 22nd, 1863.

I, ABRAHAM LINCOLN, *President of the United States of America, and Commander-in-chief of the Army and Navy thereof, having taken into consideration the number of volunteers and militia furnished by and from the several States, including the State of* Pennsylvania *, and the period of service of said volunteers and militia since the commencement of the present rebellion, in order to equalize the numbers among the Districts of the said States, and having considered and allowed for the number already furnished as aforesaid, and the time of their service aforesaid, do hereby assign* Two Thousand Three Hundred and Seven (2307) *as the first proportional part of the quota of troops to be furnished by the* 15th DISTRICT OF THE STATE OF Pennsylvania *under this, the first call made by me on the State of* Pennsylvania*, under the act approved March 3, 1863, entitled "An Act for Enrolling and Calling out the National Forces, and for other purposes," and, in pursuance of the act aforesaid, I order that a draft be made in the said* 15th DISTRICT OF THE STATE OF Pennsylvania *for the number of men herein assigned to said District, and* FIFTY PER CENT. IN ADDITION.

IN WITNESS WHEREOF, I have hereunto set my hand and caused the seal of the United States to be affixed.

Done at the City of Washington, this twenty-second day of July, in the year of our Lord one thousand eight hundred and sixty-three, and of the independence of the United States, the eighty-eighth.

Abraham Lincoln

LINCOLN'S DRAFT CALL FOR TROOPS

679\. LINCOLN, ABRAHAM. 1809-1865. President. Historic partly printed Document Signed, as President. Full page, 4to. Executive Mansion, Washington, July 22, 1863. As President and Commander-in-Chief of the Army and Navy, Lincoln calls on the Fifteenth District of Pennsylvania to supply 2307 men as their quota for the national draft. This action by Lincoln met with considerable opposition in some areas, and precipitated riots in some cities, including New York. This document is in extremely fine condition, and bears the scarcer full signature of Lincoln. With handsome portrait. 5000.00

680\. PIERCE, FRANKLIN. President. Autograph Letter Signed. 3½ pages, 8vo. Hillsboro, N.H., August 1, 1866. To his sister-in-law, Mrs. [Mary] Aiken, Andover, Mass., whom he greets as "My dearest Sister". The former president acknowledges her letter received early the previous week, saying: "...[I] should have answered it before if I had been good for much. I was quite prostrated by the extremely hot weather and have not sprung up since. Last Friday I mustered sufficient strength and force to come here where at the old homestead where I was born. I am apparently better, but not strong. My nephew and I have projected a journey to be commenced next week with my horses. We have no definite plans yet, and perhaps may have none. Not intending to limit ourselves with regard to time, distance or direction...." He enquires of other family members and hopes to run down to Andover for a day visit. Interesting family letter penned late in Pierce's life. Excellent condition. 750.00

681\. COOLIDGE, GRACE GOODHUE. First Lady. Autograph Letter Signed, on stationery imprinted "The Narrows". 1 2/3 pages, narrow 4to. Columbus, North Carolina, January 12, 1938. To Mr. Schmid She writes: "You provided us with a great treat in the crate of Florida oranges, grapefruit and marmalade and the mountain family in North Carolina join in the expression of appreciation and thanks....My children and grandchild are going to St. Petersburg with Gov. and Mrs. Trumbull on the 21st....We are planning to leave here on the 20th for home. As we are motoring and therefore dependent upon the condition of the roads we may be delayed...." 75.00

682. TAFT, WILLIAM H. President; Chief Justice, U.S. Supreme Court. Typed Letter Signed, on imprinted Supreme Court stationery. 1/2 page, 4to. Washington, March 26, 1923. To Rev. Paul R. Hickok, Second Presbyterian Church, Troy, N.Y. Taft writes: "...I don't remember making the statement of which you speak. I believe the Silliman Institute was an excellent institution and did good work, but I can not think that I made so sweeping a reference to it as that which you quote...." Fine example. 150.00

683. MC KINLEY, WILLIAM. President; assassinated. Scarce Typed Letter Signed, as President, on imprinted Executive Mansion stationery. 1 page, 4to. Washington, June 26, 1900. To Wayland Hoyt, Philadelphia, Pa., assuring him "...that your words of congratulation are cordially appreciated. Accept my thanks for your kindly expressions..." Mc Kinley had just been nominated by the Republican Party for a second presidential term. His letters written while in the presidential office are quite scarce. Fine. 750.00

ROOSEVELT SEEKS TO HALT THE ILLEGAL DISTRIBUTION OF POSTAGE
STAMPS WHICH DIFFER FROM THE REGULAR ISSUES

684. ROOSEVELT, FRANKLIN D. President. Highly interesting Typed Memorandum Signed "FDR", as President, on imprinted White House stationery. Full page, 8vo. Washington, January 9, 1935. To the Postmaster General [James A. Farley]. Roosevelt, a noted collector of stamps, writes: "Complaint has been made that in several instances a few sheets of new stamp issues have been allowed to get out of the Bureau of Engraving and Printing in some special condition -- different from the type sold to the general public. Such cases relate to unperforated or ungummed sheets. I do not think that this should be continued, even if such sheets are regarded merely as samples and not available for postage in the regular way. Will you, therefore, be good enough to take steps to discontinue the issuance of any stamp or stamps except in the precise condition in which the issue is placed on sale at the post offices?..." Quite a remarkable presidential directive! Choice condition. 1250.00

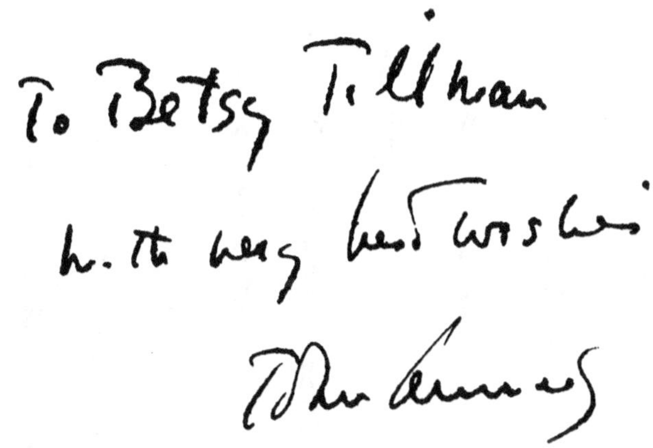

685. KENNEDY, JOHN F. President; assassinated. His Pulitzer Prize-winning book: Profiles in Courage. Cloth. New York, 1955. Inscribed on the front endpaper: "To Betsy Tillman / With very best wishes / John Kennedy". With slightly worn dust-jacket. Fine. 750.00

686. EISENHOWER, DWIGHT D. President and General. Typed Letter Signed, on his gilt "DDE" stationery. 1 page, 4to. Gettysburg, Penn., May 27, 1963. To James T. Handley, North Hollywood, California. Ike expresses his appreciation for "your generous gift of the pictures of General Lee and of Martha and George Washington....They will be sent to the Eisenhower Museum in Abilene inasmuch as we have no proper facilities here for such items....I am, of course, happy to have these two heirlooms from the Handley Family of Missouri...." Fine letter, bearing Ike's full signature. 275.00

687. TRUMAN, HARRY S. President and Vice President. Handsome color postcard printing of Thomas H. Benton's Mural of pioneers and Indians, as depicted on a 1971 U.S. commemorative postage stamp Mounted on a slightly larger card bearing the stamp and a First Day of Issue cancellation. Independence, Missouri, May 8, 1971. Signed by Truman on the lower margin. The ceremonies marking the issuance of this stamp was one of Truman's last public appearances. Pristine condition, and highly decorative. 95.00

688. HOOVER, HERBERT. President. Typed Letter Signed, as Secretary of Commerce, on the imprinted crested stationery of that office. 1 page, 4to. Washington, July 7, 1928. To Walter L. Spaulding, Indian Orchard, Mass., acknowledging his letter of June 30th. "I want you to know how deeply I appreciate the kind note of friendship which it conveys...." Hoover had just been nominated by the Republican Party to run for the presidency. With envelope. Fine. 125.00

"THE POISON OF CRASS MATERIALISM..."

689\. TAFT, WILLIAM H. President; Chief Justice, U.S. Supreme Court. Remarkable Autograph Letter Signed, as Chief Justice, on imprinted Supreme Court stationery. 2 1/2 pages, small 4to. Washington, Thanksgiving Day, November 29, 1923. To the Right Reverend William F. McDowell, Bishop of Washington. Original envelope addressed by Taft. He writes: "I write to tell you how much I admired and felt your sermon. It offered an antidote for the poison of crass materialism and blatant selfishness which exploits itself in our Pharasaical politics and Demagoguery and in the mad chase for physical pleasures and entertainment. It was a most appropriate lesson for the day, pricking the babble of our National self-righteousness and showing in its true light the brutal phase of our cherished isolation. In spite of your disavowal it contained a deep truth for statesmen. Thank you for making provision for Mrs. Taft and me in a pew which enabled us to see and hear..." Really choice!! 1500.00

690. HOOVER, HERBERT. President. Choice engraved vignette of the old front approach to the White House showing two strollers and a horse-drawn carriage. Oblong 8vo. Boldly signed on the wide lower white margin: "The Good Wishes / of / Herbert Hoover". Not inscribed. Engraving is by the Bureau of Engraving and Printing. Pristine condition. 250.00

PRESIDENT HARRISON ACKNOWLEDGES CONGRATULATIONS FROM THE SHAH

691. HARRISON, BENJAMIN. President. Partly printed Document Signed, as President. 1 page, 4to. Washington, June 7, 1889. The President authorizes the Secretary of State to affix the Seal of the United States to an "envelope containing my letter addressed to His Majesty the Shah, Teheran, thanking him for his friendly wishes and congratulations upon my elevation to the Chief Magistracy." Attractive, fresh, clean document. Bold signature. 575.00

SENDING HIS RING TO VARINA, AND SETTING THEIR WEDDING DATE

692. DAVIS, JEFFERSON. 1808 - 1889. President of the Confederate States of America; graduate of West Point; elected to Congress in 1845; Secretary of War in Franklin Pierce's cabinet. Remarkable Autograph Letter Signed "Uncle Jeff", to Varina Howell, care of W. B. Howell, at Natches. 1 2/3 pages, 4to. No place. February 25, 1845. With the integral address-leaf, bearing a two-line initialed postscript by Davis. Davis begins: "My own Varina / Your Father handed me the kind note which showed me that even in this hour which to you must be one of anxiety and apprehension you did not forget my solicitude for you. Sweet harbingers of that sympathy and generous consideration, the mutual existance of which must ensure the happiness of us both. I send you herein a ring, taken of the casket I would present <u>if I could help it</u>...The hour at which the ceremony shall be performed is to me immaterial and I would have preferred that you should have selected it. I will write to the parson asking him to go out at 10 A.M. -- give say one hour to prepare you for execution would bring 11 o'clock -- if less time will serve you please inform me this afternoon -- in all things consult your own conscience and pleasure..." Davis lists a few names of guests he would like invited, and continues: "Pray be calm and meet the contingency of this important change as becomes you, as one who has <u>a hurt for every fate</u>, and be assured, I will try to do better than I have ever promised to fulfil brighter hopes than I have ever inculcated, and failing in this, my sympathy shall pour oil upon your wounds, my heart shall beat warmly to relieve you from the chills of misfortune's winter and my form shall screen you from the lightinings of our angry destiny. Here I got so fine I had to turn back and read, and read but not to finish. I wish you would put in that Lion pawing up the dirt, without which I fear you will find the picture incomplete. Or if you dont sufficiently understand it to do so, all I have to say is that it is the same case with myself. With <u>Trifles light as air</u> I longer wont detain you. Then go where clothes await thee, and things. Farewell my dearest and be prepared soon to take leave of your affectionate <u>Uncle Jeff</u>:" Davis married Varina Howell on the following day, February 26, 1845. Of her, DAB reports: "[She] was a local beauty, a member of the upmost social rank, a high-spirited and accomplished woman. This marriage identified [Davis] conclusively with the local aristocracy." 3000.00

Congreſs of the United States:

AT THE THIRD SESSION,

Begun and held at the City of Philadelphia, on Monday the ſixth of December, one thouſand ſeven hundred and ninety.

An ACT *ſupplementory to the Act, making Proviſion for the Reduction of the* PUBLIC DEBT.

WHEREAS it hath been made known to Congreſs that the Preſident of the United States, in conſequence of " An act making proviſion for the reduction of the public debt," hath cauſed a certain loan to be made in Holland, on account of the United States, to the amount of three millions of florins, bearing an intereſt of five per centum per annum, and reimburſable in ſix yearly inſtalments, commencing in the year one thouſand eight hundred, and ending in the year one thouſand eight hundred and ſix, or at any time ſooner, in whole or in part, at the option of the United States.

And whereas it hath been alſo ſtated to Congreſs, that the charges upon the ſaid loan have amounted to four and a half per centum, whereby a doubt hath ariſen, whether the ſaid loan be within the meaning of the ſaid laſt mentioned act, which limits the rate of intereſt to five per centum per annum ;

And whereas it is expedient that the ſaid doubt be removed ;

BE it enacted and declared by the SENATE *and* HOUSE *of* REPRESENTATIVES *of the United States of America in Congreſs,* That the loan aforeſaid ſhall be deemed and conſtrued to be within the true intent and meaning of the ſaid act, intituled " An act making proviſion for the reduction of the public debt," and that any farther loan, to the extent of the principal ſum authorized to be borrowed by the ſaid act, the intereſt whereof ſhall be five per centum per annum, and the charges whereof ſhall not exceed the ſaid rate of four and a half per centum, ſhall, in like manner, be deemed and conſtrued to be within the true intent and meaning of the ſaid act.

FREDERICK AUGUSTUS MUHLENBERG,
Speaker of the Houſe of Repreſentatives.

JOHN ADAMS, *Vice-Preſident of the United States, and Preſident of the Senate.*

APPROVED, March the third, 1791.

GEORGE WASHINGTON, *Preſident of the United States.*

DEPOSITED among the ROLLS in the OFFICE of the SECRETARY of STATE.

Secretary of State.

RARE FINANCIAL BROADSIDE OF THE FIRST CONGRESS

693. JEFFERSON, THOMAS. President and Vice President; Signer of Declaration of Independence; Minister to France; Governor of Virginia; our first Secretary of State. Superb Printed Broadside Act of the First Congress, boldly signed in ink by Jefferson as Secretary of State. 1 page, tall legal folio (original wide margins on all sides). Philadelphia, March 3, 1791. Signed in type by Frederick Augustus Muhlenberg, Speaker of the House of Representatives; John Adams, Vice-President of the United States and President of the Senate; and George Washington, President of the United States. Printed text of an Act of the First Congress, Third Session, entitled An ACT supplementory to the Act, making Provision for the Reduction of the PUBLIC DEBT. By this piece of legislation Congress gives its consent to the President for borrowing three millions of florins from Holland, bearing an interest of five per centum per annum. Pristine condition, and a superlative piece of financial Americana. With engraved portrait. 4500.00

TO DR. BENJAMIN RUSH

WRITING HIS 1776 COLLEAGUE AT THE CONTINENTAL CONGRESS, AND FELLOW SIGNER OF THE DECLARATION OF INDEPENDENCE: "I REJOICE THAT YOUR SON RICHARD IS BECOMING EMINENT IN HIS PROFESSION. MAY HE BECOME AS RENOUND IN LAW AND STATE AS HIS FATHER IS AND I HOPE HIS BROTHER WILL BE IN MEDICINE..."

694. ADAMS, JOHN. President and Vice President; Signer of the Declaration of Independence; diplomat. Autograph Letter Signed " J. Adams." 1 1/2 pages, 4to. Quincy, June 7, 1809. To Dr. [Benjamin] Rush, of Philadelphia (Signer, physician and philosopher). Adams thanks his former colleague for his various letters, and also for his son's inaugural dissertation. He continues: "I wish him success in his studies, travels and practice. May he become as eminent, as skilful, as humane and as successful as his father. I rejoice that your son Richard is becoming eminent in his profession. May he become as renound in law and State as his father is and I hope his brother will be in medicine..." Turning to other matters: "It would divert you, if I were to amuse myself with writing an answer to the Tory Enemy you mention. That Wretch's father stepped into my Practice in Boston when I was sent to Congress and my Business made a fortune of two or three hundred thousand dollars. Left him a splendid fortune, a Palace in Boston, a superb Country Seat and very large sums in Banks and Stocks. A fortune accumulating now every day whereas I have not added a Shilling to my property these eight years (since leaving the Presidency). He is worth I suppose four times as much as I am. His Uncle by my appointment made as Navy Agent in three or four years more than I am worth. If I was allowed two and a half per cent on a Million Sterling that I borrowed and passed thru my hands in Holland, as he was for 4 or 500 thousand dollars he spent as Navy Agent it would amount to twice the sum I am worth. For this I was never allowed a farthing...." Adams wonders if Mr. Duane will keep his promise of republishing all Adams' letters. "I fear I shall be too voluminous for him. Frederick the Great sent word to the Emperor Joseph... before the War of Bavaria 'To remember that tho he mounted his horse with difficulty, it was with equal difficulty that he dismounted, when once he was on.'" Adams concludes: "I should be glad to know how the British Subjects, the American Oligarchy and the Democratic Republicans judge of my Revelations...." Handsomely preserved, and with the fine content one comes to expect from an Adams letter. 5750.00

695. GARFIELD, JAMES A. President; assassinated. Manuscript Letter Signed, while a member of the House of Representatives. Full page, 4to. Washington, June 6, 1872. To J. H. McCalmont, Pension Office, Washington. Garfield writes: "I called yesterday on the Commissioner of Patents and found him engaged in hearing a case, which several lawyers were arguing before him. I could not therefore get an opportunity to see him. I called again today and found him absent from the City. I thereupon called on the Asst. Comr. and made a request that you be transferred and he promised to lay the matter before General Leggett, as soon as he returns ...." Four very light small tape stains, else quite fine. With portrait. 325.00

INSCRIBED COPY OF CLEVELAND'S FIRST TERM PRESIDENTIAL PAPERS

696. CLEVELAND, GROVER. President. His book: The Public Papers of Grover Cleveland...March 4, 1885 to March 4, 1889. Original decorated deep magenta cloth, gilt-lettered spine. Government Printing Office: Washington, 1889. Inscribed by Cleveland between his presidential terms to: "Hon. Erastus Corning / from Grover Cleveland / May 1, 1892", on early blank flyleaf. Very slight wear to spinal extremities, else quite fine. Scarce in signed books. 500.00

697. PIERCE, FRANKLIN. President; General in War with Mexico; Congressman from New Hampshire. Autograph Letter Signed. 1 1/3 pages, 4to. Hillsboro [N.H.], April 18, 1837. To Hon. Mahlon Dickerson, Secretary of the Navy. Docketed, postmarked integral address-leaf, addressed but not franked by Pierce. In part: "Having been informed that Horatio Bridge Esq. of Augusta, Me. is an applicant for the office of Purser in the U.S. Navy, I cannot but feel much interest in his appointment. It is said, that there is at present no Purser from that State and I am quite sure, that no section of the Country can furnish an individual better qualified for the situation or more deserving than Mr. Bridge From a long acquaintance, which commenced in College, I can recommend him with confidence as a man of talents and integrity and a Gentleman in the broadest acceptation of the term. I need hardly add, that his appointment would prove honorable & advantageous to the Service and afford me great pleasure individually...." Excellent condition. 575.00

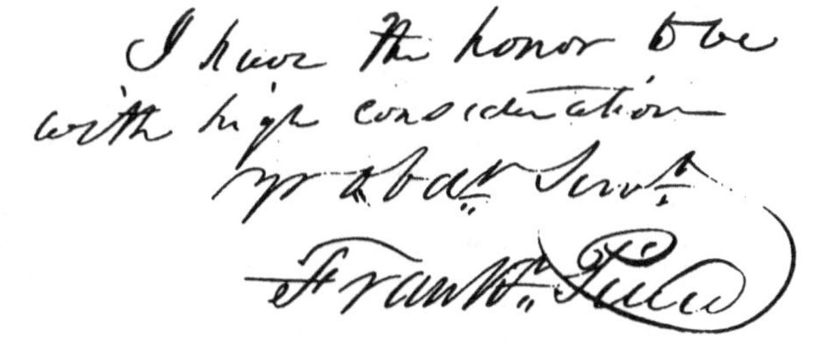

RONALD REAGAN
PACIFIC PALISADES

Dear Don

You have one h-l of a script here and it should be a picture. I dont know how widely you've shown it around but I cant believe there isnt some one in the business who'll go for it. Have you run down the list of the guys over at Universal including their new producers and fellows like Bob Arthur?

One big problem of course is casting and it seems to me you'll have to explore one or two courses and have some suggestions on hand. For example to go the route of some one like Cagney I think you'd have to split the role and play a young man up to adulthood. Failing this it is of course easier to age a young man than it is to make an old one young so you could cast around among the possibilities in the younger set to see who might be capable of making up for the "later years." This was done fairly well in "The Way The West Was Won."

I'll certainly holler about this to all I come in contact with – Thanks for letting me read it.

Ronnie

WONDERFUL THEATRICAL LETTER TO THE COWBOY ACTOR, "RED RYDER"

698. REAGAN, RONALD. Fortieth President of the United States; movie actor, appearing in 53 films; President of Screen Actors' Guild; Governor of California. Autograph Letter Signed "Ronnie" penned in bright red ink on his imprinted stationery. Full page, 4to. Pacific Palisades, no date. Circa 1962. To Don ["Red Ryder" Barry] the cowboy actor. Reagan writes: "You have one h - l of a script here and it should be a picture. I don't know how widely you've shown it around but I cant believe there isn't some one in the business who'll go for it. Have you run down the list of the guys over at Universal including their new producers and fellows like Bob Arthur? One big problem of course is casting and it seems to me you'll have to explore one or two courses and have some suggestions on hand. For example to go the route of some one like Cagney I think you'd have to split the role and play a young man up to adulthood. Failing this it is of course easier to age a young man than it is to make an old one young so you could cast around among the possibilities in the younger set to see who might be capable of making up for the <u>later years</u>. This was done fairly well in <u>The Way the West Was Won</u>. I'll certainly holler about this to all I come in contact with. Thanks for letting me read it." One of a handful of letters in full holograph from Reagan's pen to be offered since his inauguration. Fine condition, and an excellent letter for the collector of modern presidents in full holograph. 2500.00

HOLD FOR RELEASE HOLD FOR RELEASE HOLD FOR RELEASE

CONFIDENTIAL: The President's State of the Union Message is for automatic release at 12:15 p.m., E.S.T., Wednesday, January 7, 1953. No portion, synopsis, or intimation may be published or broadcast before that time.

PLEASE GUARD AGAINST PREMATURE PUBLICATION OR ANNOUNCEMENT.

ROGER W. TUBBY
Secretary to the President

- -

TO THE CONGRESS OF THE UNITED STATES:

I have the honor to report to the Congress on the state of the Union.

This is the eighth such report that, as President, I have been privileged to present to you and to the country. On previous occasions, it has been my custom to set forth proposals for legislative action in the coming year. But that is not my purpose today. The presentation of a legislative program falls properly to my successor, not to me, and I would not infringe upon his responsibility to chart the forward course. Instead, I wish to speak of the course we have been following the past eight years and the position at which we have arrived.

The Nation's business is never finished. The basic questions we have been dealing with, these eight years past, present themselves anew. That is the way of our society. Circumstances change and current questions take on different forms, new complications, year by year. But underneath, the great issues remain the same -- prosperity, welfare, human rights, effective democracy, and above all, peace.

Now we turn to the inaugural of our new President. And in the great work he is called upon to do he will have need for the support of a united people, a confident people, with firm faith in one another and in our common cause. I pledge him my support as a citizen of our Republic, and I ask you to give him yours.

To him, to you, to all my fellow citizens, I say, Godspeed.

May God bless our country and our cause.

HARRY S. TRUMAN

PRESS RELEASE OF TRUMAN'S LAST STATE OF THE UNION ADDRESS

699. TRUMAN, HARRY S. President and Vice President. Mimeographed Press Release of Truman's final State of the Union Message, Signed as President on the concluding page. 16 pages, tall legal folio. The White House, Washington, January 7, 1953. Very fine condition. [See above illustration for first and last portions of this notable speech.] 750.00

EXPLAINING PRESIDENT POLK'S POLICY

700. BUCHANAN, JAMES. President. Autograph Letter Signed, as Secretary of State in Polk's cabinet. Full page, 4to. Washington, July 3, 1846. To Dr. Isaac Z. Coffman. Buchanan writes: "The rule which the President found it necessary to adopt in the appointment of Surgeons for our volunteer forces was to select these officers from the States where troops have been called into actual service. Volunteers going upon a remote service were anxious that their physicians should be selected from among their neighbours & friends & not sent to them from distant States. I regret that it is not in my power to serve you; because to do so would afford me sincere pleasure...." Written during the War with Mexico. Interesting letter! 575.00

FDR RECEIVES INTELLIGENCE ON THE SUPREME COURT FROM HIS ATTORNEY GENERAL

701. ROOSEVELT, FRANKLIN D. President. Interesting Typed Letter Signed, as President, on imprinted White House stationery. 1 page, 4to. Washington, May 24, 1934. To Hon. James Crawford Biggs, Solicitor General, Department of Justice, Washington. Roosevelt writes: "Every week or so Homer [Cummings] sends me the result of the Supreme Court decisions, and this week he tells me you won all five cases. My very warm congratulations!..." In view of the difficulty FDR's New Deal legislation was encountering with the Supreme Court ["The nine old men", as FDR referred to them] this brief letter is of more than passing interest. Very fine! 475.00

RARE AMBROTYPE PHOTOGRAPH OF BUCHANAN

702. [BUCHANAN, JAMES]. President. Excessively rare original ambrotype photograph depicting the half-length image of Buchanan. He is shown seated with his right hand resting on a table. Very little of the chair or table can be seen. Overall size: 2 x 2 1/2 inches. An ambrotype is a picture or positive made from a glass negative by combining it with a dark background. Mounted in the original ornamental gilt-foil frame and set in an old case. Excellent condition, and quite possibly unique. 1500.00

703. MC KINLEY, WILLIAM. President; assassinated. Manuscript Letter Signed, as a Congressman from Ohio, on imprinted House of Representatives stationery. Full page, tall 8vo. Washington, July 17, 1890. To Harvey Slusser, Louisville, Kentucky, asking him to notify McKinley when he wishes to take a leave of absence. Small tear in blank left margin, else fine. Boldly penned on green-imprinted letterhead. 225.00

704. FILLMORE, MILLARD. President and Vice President. Autograph Greeting Signed, penned on a 12mo leaf of black-bordered mourning stationery. "For Edward Goodridge / With the Respects of / Millard Fillmore / Buffalo, N.Y. / Augt. 31, 1857." With engraved portrait. Handsome specimen for framing or display. 150.00

705. WILSON, WOODROW. President. Strikingly handsome large quarto formal photograph by Harris and Ewing, depicting the nearly full-face bust image of Wilson. Boldly signed (not inscribed) by Wilson on the wide lower margin. Striking pose! Excellent condition. 450.00

706. COOLIDGE, CALVIN. President and Vice President; Governor of Mass. Typed Letter Signed, on his imprinted law office stationery. 1 page, 4to. Northampton, Mass., March 6, 1929. To Right Reverend and Mrs. William F. McDowell, Washington, D.C. Writing just two days after retiring from the Presidency, Coolidge states: "Your telegram of March 4th has been received. I want you to know how much I appreciate your writing me...." Fine. 150.00

AN 1848 VIEW OF THE WHITE HOUSE

707. HOOVER, LOU HENRY. First Lady. Handsome oblong quarto photograph of an 1848 lithograph of the White House. Boldly signed in jet-black ink by Mrs. Hoover on the wide lower white margin. Excellent condition, and a most unusual item. 200.00

"THE FATHER OF THE MODERN AMERICAN NAVY"

708. ADAMS, JOHN. 1735-1826. President and Vice President; Signer of Declaration of Independence; negotiated Treaty of Paris ending American Revolution; the cabinet post of Secretary of the Navy established in 1798 under his influence. Remarkable Autograph Letter Signed

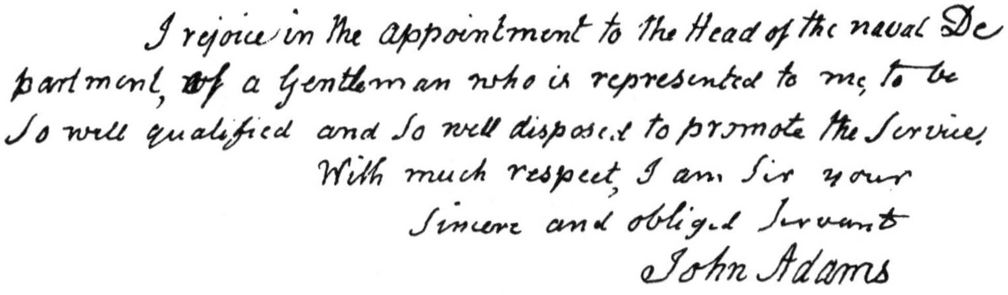
I rejoice in the appointment to the Head of the naval De
partment, of a Gentleman who is represented to me, to be
So well qualified and So well disposed to promote the Service.
With much respect, I am Sir your
Sincere and obliged Servant
John Adams

"John Adams". 1 1/3 pp., 4to. Quincy, April 24, 1813. To Hon. William Jones, Secretary of the Naval Department. Adams writes: "As it ever has been, and forever ought to be, a general Rule of The Presidents and Heads of Departments not to answer Letters soliciting or recommending Appointments to Office: the Exception to the general Rule by your kind Letter of the 13th of this month, lays me under a particular obligation. The Reason you assign, is perfectly satisfactory to me: and I rejoice in it, as it proves the good sense and generous feelings of our American Young Men, which have animated such Numbers, to solicit the Post of danger. Commodore Rodgers has accepted young Marston as a Volunteer, and he is now on board the President below the Castle ready I presume for Sea...Far be from me, any Pride or Vanity, in the recollection of any share I have taken in the Institution of Our American Navy: I am ashamed when I look back and recollect how little I have done, said or written in favour of this Essential Arm of the defence of our Country. I know it to be the Astonishment of every Man of Sense in Europe that We have neglected it so long. In my opinion a compleat History of our military Marine ought to be written...Congress could not appropriate Money, to a purpose more beneficial to the Interest, the Safety, the Independence, the Honour, Power and Glory of their Country, if they should devote to a Man of Letters, who would undertake the Work, four times as large a Sum as the Dutchess of Marlborough bequeathed for the Biography of her Husband..." In the concluding paragraph, illustrated, Adams congratulates Jones on his appointment to head the Navy Department. An important letter in fine condition. 5,000.00

709. ROOSEVELT, ELEANOR. First Lady. Autograph Letter Signed, with initials "E. R.", as First Lady on her imprinted "Washington Square West" stationery. 2 full pages, 8vo. New York, February 22 [1944]. To "Harry dear" [Harry Hooker, formerly in business with FDR, and their accountant]. She writes: "I'm sorry not to see you but if the check up is necessary and gives you more confidence it will be a good thing. I wish I could talk to you by Georgie says you did not want me to call. Let me know when you are back and if you can come to Washington after the 28th. You will find F[ranklin] home, I hope, and full of information...." Scarce in full holograph during the presidential years. Fine. 150.00

PRESIDENT MONROE MAKES PROMISES TO HIS BANKERS

710. MONROE, JAMES. President; Secretary of State and War; Governor of Virginia; Minister to England. Autograph Letter Signed, as President. 1 1/3 pages, 4to. Oak Hill [his estate in Virginia], October 27, 1819. To his banker. Docketed integral leaf. In part: "...I send you, with my signatures, three notes for renewal, at the proper intervals, of my credit with the bank. You will as heretofore desir'd pay to it the amount which you may secure from Mr. Swart. As soon as I get my flour down I shall make a further payment, so that I hope to discharge my debt to the bank, in the course of the ensuing spring. I beg you to make my acknowledgment to the Directors for the great kindness & attention which I have received from them...." Turning to his attempt to collect from the government money due him from the time he was Ambassador to England, Monroe continues: "I meet the Commissioners for the settlement of my administration account on Saturday. I am sorry you did not send me your account...that I might have included it in this settlement, but as it cannot be closed at this meeting, there will be time to provide for it at the next...." Ten years later, in old age and poverty, Monroe was still trying to collect the debt he claimed was owed him by the government. Fine condition, and an interesting financial presidential letter. 2000.00

711. VAN BUREN, MARTIN. President and Vice President; Secretary of State. Partly printed Document Signed, as President. 1 page, 4to. Washington, October 21, 1840. Authorizes and directs the Secretary of State to affix the Seal of the United States "to the order, remitting the fine and costs, in the case of Henry White, in the District of Michigan..." Some light staining on the left side of the document which does not affect Van Buren's fine signature. With a handsome steel-engraved portrait. 325.00

712. HAYES, RUTHERFORD B. President. Handsome cabinet bust photograph of President Hayes, bearing the ornate imprint of G. W. Pach, New York, on the verso. Inscribed by Hayes on the lower surface of the photograph and extending on to the lower mount: "R. B. Hayes / To / C. Messoisier Poissy, France". Excellent condition. 1500.00

DIFFICULTIES IN MAINTAINING THREE PRESIDENTIAL HOMES

713. MONROE, JAMES. President; Governor of Virginia; Minister to England. Autograph Letter Signed, as President. 2 full pages, 4to. Albemarle [Virginia], October 10, 1817. Correspondent unidentified, but apparently the caretaker of his property in Loudoun County. Intriguing letter showing Monroe juggling affairs at three different homes; his two Virginia estates plus the White House. In part: "...I intend to leave this for Washington the latter end of next week, and to visit Loudoun soon after my arrival in the city. I have thought of sending over a small wagon to take from Orange a Carpenter (with his wife) to manage my mill and do work on the estate, to bring back one or two merino rams, and the cloth for my people here...You know what will be sufficient for Loudoun, 160 or 170 yards will do here, tho' 200 might be used. About 30 yards will be necessary for servants at Washington of dark brown, like that I had before...My object [is] to obtain what is necessary for my servants in Washington...& what is necessary for my people in Loudoun & here, & to pay for the same in wool, if Mr. Davenport will take it; and if there should be more wool than will pay for the above, to take the value of it in other cloth, eight or 10 yards in black for my brothers, 3 or 4 in grey...for myself, both the latter of the best quality & the rest in negro cloth. If... better bargains may be had by...paying him in money (which I do not wish however) I would do so...Act as you think best...." An interesting and revealing presidential letter, showing the detail that Monroe gave to domestic affairs. One could just immagine a modern president giving his attention to the ordering of cloth for White House servants! 2,750.00

714. COOLIDGE, CALVIN. President and Vice President. Imprinted White House Card signed as President. Excellent condition. 195.00

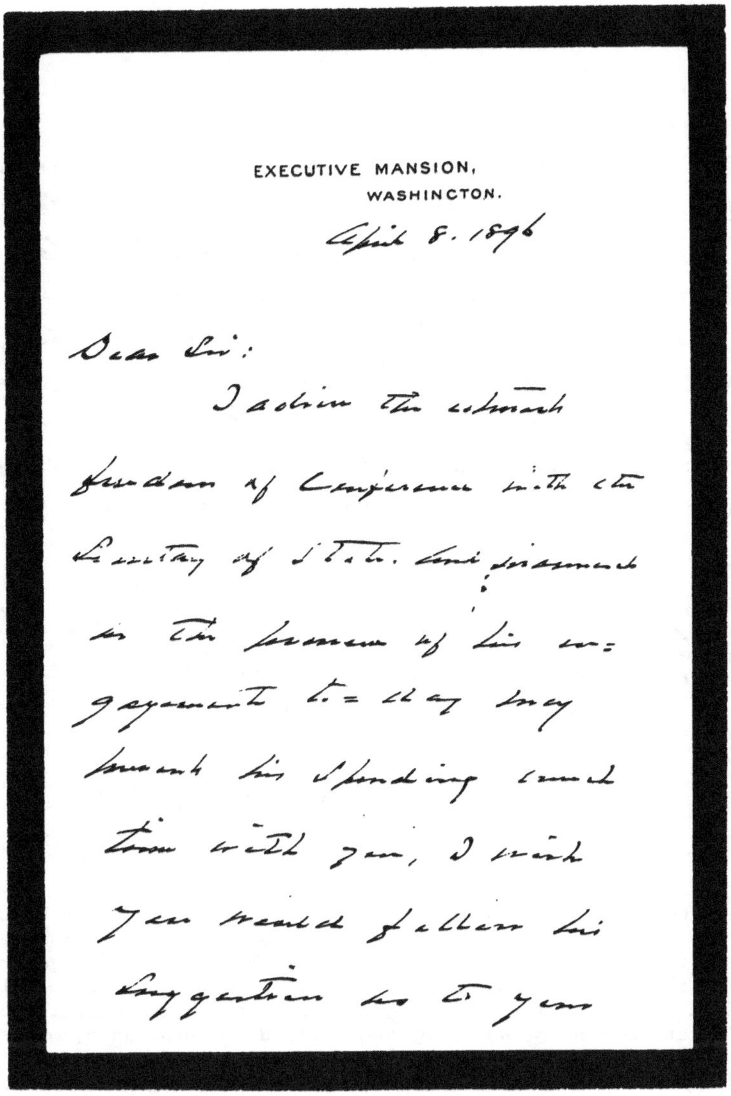
EXECUTIVE MANSION,
WASHINCTON.

April 8. 1896

Dear Sir:

I advise the utmost freedom of conference with the Secretary of State, but in as much as the pressure of his engagements to=day may prevent his spending much time with you, I wish you would follow his suggestion as to your

ALS AS PRESIDENT TO GENERAL FITZHUGH LEE

715. CLEVELAND, GROVER. President; Governor of New York. Autograph Letter Signed, as President, penned on imprinted Executive Mansion stationery. 1 1/2 pages, 8vo. Washington, April 8, 1896. To Hon. Fitzhugh Lee, Care of Commissioner of Internal Revenue, Washington, D. C. Original envelope, marked "Personal", addressed by Cleveland. He writes: "I advise the utmost freedom of conference with the Secretary of State, but in as much as the pressure of his engagements to=day may prevent his spending much time with you, I wish you would follow his suggestion as to your consultation with the First Assistant...." Curious content, and a rather strange letter for a President to write. Fine condition. 650.00

WHILE VACATIONING IN SOUTHERN MASSACHUSETTS

716. ROOSEVELT, FRANKLIN D. President; Governor of New York. Scarce Autograph Letter Signed, on his imprinted Fidelity and Deposit Co. stationery. Full page, 4to. Willowbend Farm, July 6 [1928]. To Bronson Tucker. Original envelope addressed by Roosevelt. Fine letter penned in his humorous way to his summer landlord: "My copy of the lease is Lord knows where in N.Y. -- so I have no idea when the rent is due my very nice landlord! Anyway here is half of it & I will let you have the rest when I get back in two weeks. We love the place & are most comfortable. Hope to see you & your wife soon...." Attractive, full-page holograph letter. Scarce in full holograph. In 1928 FDR made his bid, successfully, for the Governorship of New York. Fine. 1250.00

THE FIRST LADY MEETS WITH WOMEN BROADCASTERS

717. TRUMAN, BESS WALLACE. First Lady. Autograph Letter Signed, as First Lady, on gilt-imprinted White House social stationery. 3 pages, 8vo., Washington, no date. To [Mary Margaret] Mc Bride, well known radio journalist of the 1940's. Mrs. Truman expresses her thanks for her correspondent's note, and continues: "...It gave all three of us much pleasure to meet the women broadcasters and to have them here in the White House. It is a group to be really proud of. Wish I'd had some time to chat with you. Do you ever see Katie Accala? When you get down to Washington on your own, let me know...." Fine condition. 250.00

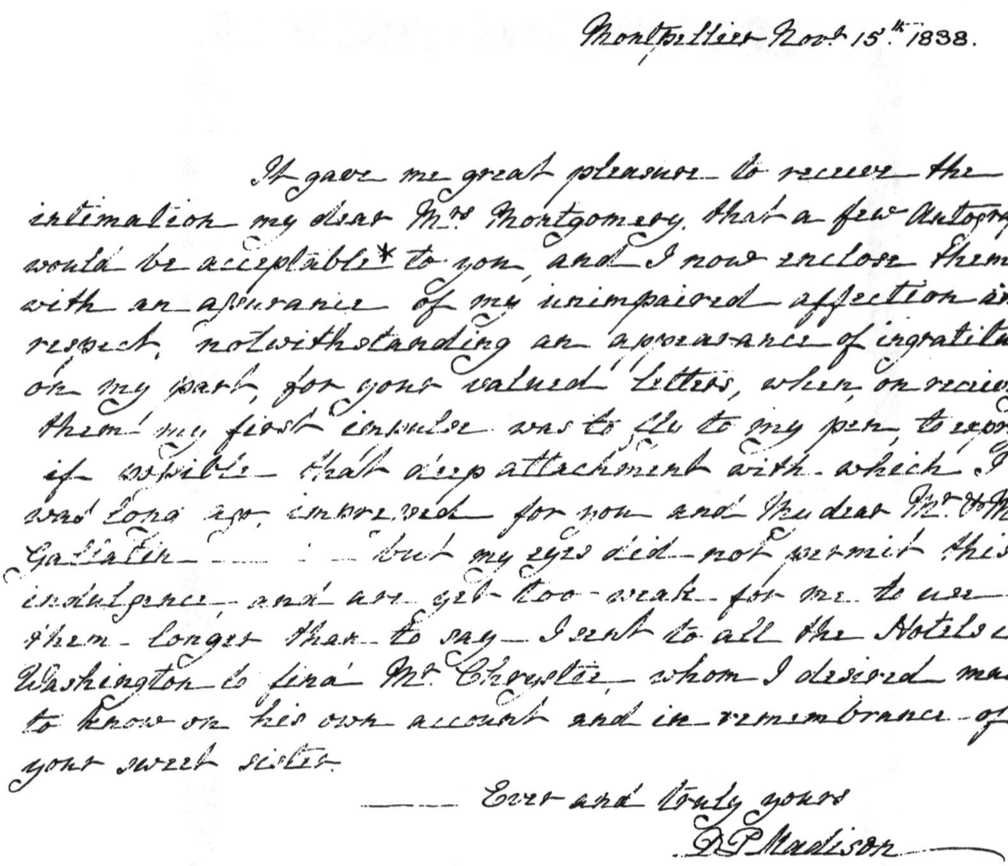

Montpellier Novr 15th 1838.

It gave me great pleasure to receive the intimation my dear Mrs Montgomery, that a few Autographs would be acceptable* to you, and I now enclose them, with an assurance of my unimpaired affection and respect, notwithstanding an appearance of ingratitude on my part, for your valued letters, when, on receiving them my first impulse was to fly to my pen, to express if possible that deep attachment with which I was long ago impressed for you and the dear Mr & Mrs Gallatin --- but my eyes did not permit this indulgence, and are yet too weak for me to use them longer than to say I sent to all the Hotels in Washington to find Mr Chrystie, whom I desired much to know on his own account and in remembrance of your sweet sister.

--- Ever and truly yours

D P Madison

718. MADISON, DOLLY. 1768-1849. First Lady; wife of James Madison; famous Washington hostess; sold her husband's papers to the government after his death. Autograph Letter Signed. 1 page 4to. Montpellier [Virginia], November 15, 1838. [To Mrs. Marvin Montgomery, New York]. She has been informed that the receipt of "a few autographs would be acceptable to you, and I now enclose them, with an assurance of my unimpaired affection and respect, notwithstanding an appearance of ingratitude on my part, for your valued letters, when, on receiving them my first impulse was to fly to my pen, to express...that deep attachment...for you and my dear Mr. & Mrs. Gallatin --- but my eyes did not permit this indulgence, and are yet too weak for me to use them longer than to say I sent to all the Hotels in Washington to find Mr. Chrysler, whom I desired much to know...." A note at the bottom of the page in another hand indicates that the autographs sent were Washington's, John Q. Adams' etc. Attractive letter, and rather scarce in full holograph. With engraved portrait. 975.00

719. ROOSEVELT, FRANKLIN D. President. Typed Letter Signed, as Assistant Secretary of the Navy, on imprinted social stationery of that office. 1 page, 4to. Washington, February 10, 1917. To Hon. Clayton L. Wheeler, Hancock, New York. FDR writes that he has just returned from an inspection trip to Haiti and Santo Domingo to find his correspondent's letter regarding the appointment of a postmaster at Grand Gorge. He continues: "The Postmaster General has taken the position that where post offices of the fourth class are raised to third class the fourth class postmasters should be retained, provided their services have been satisfactory and no charges have been preferred against them and substantiated...." Fine example. 195.00

LEGAL BRIEF BY THE YOUNG ILLINOIS ATTORNEY

720. LINCOLN, ABRAHAM. President. Autograph Document Signed, with the name of his law partnership "Logan & Lincoln p.g.". 1 1/5 pages, legal folio. March Term of the Circuit Court of Sangamon County, Illinois, A.D. 1842. Brief in the suit of William Porter & Co. against Frederick A. Patterson for the non-payment of $200 for building materials. A fine legal document dating from Lincoln's second law partnership, completely in his hand, and very boldly penned in dark ink. Originally broken at several folds, the document has been expertly laminated with tissue on the verso. Once fairly plentiful, Lincoln's legal briefs are now quite scarce, and much in demand by those in the legal profession. 2500.00

SIGNED COPY OF COOLIDGE'S ARMISTICE DAY SPEECH

721. COOLIDGE, CALVIN. President and Vice President. Printed ADDRESS "At the observance of the tenth anniversary of the armistice, under the auspices of the American Legion, in the Washington Auditorium, November 11, 1928...[by] President Coolidge. Large octavo. 10 pp. (back leaf blank). Signed by Coolidge on page nine at the conclusion of his remarks. Fine. 325.00

"I EXPECT TO SAIL FOR LONDON ON BOARD THE SHIP ALFRED..."

722. ADAMS, JOHN QUINCY. President; Secretary of State. Autograph Letter Signed "John Q. Adams" 2 1/4 pages, 4to. Boston, September 12, 1794. To his Harvard classmate Nathanael Freeman, Attorney at Law, Barnstable. Integral address-leaf bearing a straight-line BOSTON postmark, also a "Bishop" mark, and "Paid"; addressed by Adams and docketed by Freeman. Writing just before his departure for his first public office, that of U.S. Minister to Holland, the 27 year old Adams takes leave of his friend: "...On Sunday...I expect to sail for London on board the Ship Alfred...I earnestly solicit the favour of your correspondence... it will now become of more importance to me than ever...Supply me with political intelligence, and if you think that a reciprocation of this commerce would be agreeable or useful to you, I think you may depend on having a punctual correspondent. I have great hopes, that in a very short time your sphere of public action will be enlarged, and shall be highly gratified to see your name among the returns of Members at the next Election for Congress. If not then, I consider it as almost...a certainty that the election subsequent will carry you into the Legislature of the Union, and it is not improbable that I shall still be in Europe at that Time. Whatever our respective situations may be, I am sure your correspondence will always be valuable and precious to me..." Adams also informs Freeman that he has placed his law business with their classmate Beales, and mentions an action pending before the State Supreme Court. Freeman was in fact sent to Congress in both the elections mentioned here by Adams. But before Adams returned to America in 1801 his friend had died, in 1800, at the age of 34. There is some marginal wear and paper repairs to fold breaks, mostly on the address-leaf, and one large seal tear in the blank area of the address-leaf. The letter is boldly penned, and is a fine example of the future President. 2000.00

FROM THE GERALD R. FORD PHILATELIC COLLECTION

723. FORD, GERALD R. President and Vice President. Presentation folder from the United States Postal Service, gilt-lettered on the front leatherette cover: "D. W. Griffith / Commemorative / U. S. Postage Stamp / May 27, 1975 / Gerald R. Ford / President of the United States". Contained inside is a complete sheet of fifty Griffith stamps, boldly signed in ink by Ford on the side selvage. This is the actual sheet of stamps and special lettered case that was presented to President Ford by the Postal Service. Pristine condition, and a wonderful philatelic item! 225.00

724. CLEVELAND, GROVER. President; Governor of New York. Proof engraving of Cleveland's profile bust portrait by the Bureau or Engraving and Printing, mounted on an octavo white mat. Boldly signed and dated as President , Feb. 27, 1889, on the mount beneath his likeness. Signed in the final week of Cleveland's first presidential term, as Benjamin Harrison was sworn in on March 4, 1889. Choice specimen, and rare in this format. 450.00

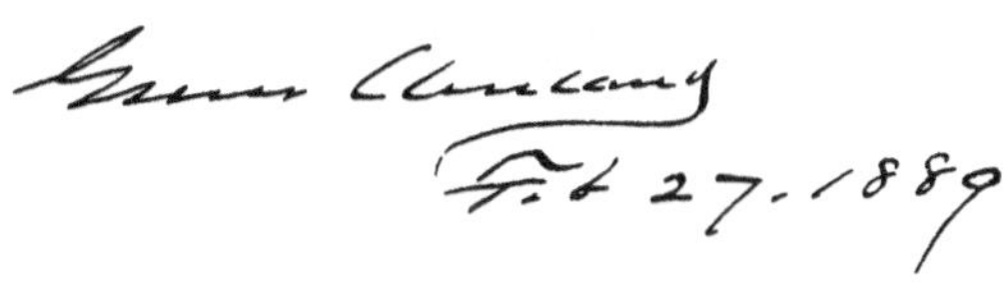

GROVER CLEVELAND - AS PRESIDENT

725. TYLER, JOHN. President and Vice President. Autograph Letter Signed, as a member of the U. S. Senate from Virginia. 1 page, 4to. Senate Chamber [Washington] December 13, 1827. To Samuel L. Southard, Secretary of the Navy, enclosing a letter from Mr. Minor which will "...present to your notice Mr. John P. Rogers of Virginia who is desirous of procuring a commission in the U.S. Marine Corps...In substance it was a strong recommendation of Mr. Rogers...Messrs Minor and Branton are gentlemen of standing and their recommendation may fully be relied on. I have no personal acquaintance with Mr. Rogers...." Fine condition. With portrait. 450.00

726. COOLIDGE, GRACE. First Lady. Handsome engraved vignette of the front approach and entrance to the White House, signed by Mrs. Coolidge on the lower margin, probably as First Lady. Oblong 8vo. Uncommon in this format. Choice specimen. 95.00

Springfield, Ills. July 27th 1849

Hon: Secretary of the Interior

Dear Sir

Yours of the 18th in answer to my inquiries concerning the letters of Messrs Thompson & Embree is received, and for which I thank you.

You are deceived — to some extent at least — Mr Ewing did not inform me at the time he gave me the bundle, or at any time, that any letters, filed in my favor, had been retained — He did not give me the bundle in person; but it was sent to my lodgings, accompanied by a letter from yourself, which letter, now before me, contains no intimation that any of the letters had been retained — On the contrary it speaks of the papers as an unbroken series, "numbered from 75 to 183 inclusive, with a small package filed at a late hour on yesterday"

Again, if the letters of Messrs. Thompson & Embree, were retained under the rule you state, then that rule was applied with a strange partiality in this case; for I have now under my eye, taken from the bundle mentioned, each with the brief upon it made in your office eight letters falling completely within that rule — Five of them are addressed to the President, one to a third person, & two to yourself; all speak of Mr B. in the same tone as Messrs. Thompson & Embree, and none of them was ever in my possession, till they came to me in the bundle referred to. But the strangest of all is, that one of these eight letters, now before me, is the the identical letter of A. G. Henry, which you expressly state in your letter, has been retained by you, or by Mr Ewing, under the rule — Because of these things, I have ventured to say you are deceived —

Your Obt Servt

A. Lincoln

[Item No. 727]

"YOU ARE DECEIVED -- TO SOME EXTENT AT LEAST..."

727. LINCOLN, ABRAHAM. Autograph Letter Signed. 1 1/5 pages, 4to. Springfield, Ills. July 27, 1849. To Hon. Secretary of the Interior [Thomas Ewing]. Lincoln responds to Ewing's reply of the 18th instant. "You are deceived -- to some extent at least. Mr. Caffee did not inform me at the time he gave me the bundle, or at any time, that any letters, filed in my favor, had been retained. He did not give me the bundle in person; but it was sent to my lodgings, accompanied by a letter from yourself, which letter, now before me, contains no intimation that any of the letters had been retained. On the contrary it speaks of the papers as an unbroken series, numbered from 75 to 183 inclusive...Again, if the letters of Messrs Thompson & Embree, were retained under the rule you state, then that rule was applied with a strange partiality in this case; for I have now under my eye, taken from the bundle mentioned...eight letters falling completely within that rule. Five of them addressed to the President, one to a third person, & two to yourself. All speak of Mr. B. in the same tone as Messrs. Thompson & Embree, and none of them was ever in my possession... But the strangest of all is, that one of these eight letters, now before me, is the identical letter of A. G. Henry, which you expressly state in your letter, has been retained by you, or by Mr. Caffee, under the rule. Because of these things, I have ventured to say you are deceived..." Excellent, save for one corner being neatly repaired. An important letter, dealing as it does with possible deceit within President Taylor's cabinet over the highly controversial appointment of Commissioner of the General Land Office. Lincoln unsuccessfully sought this position after serving his single term in Congress. Unpublished. A superb, early Lincoln letter! 9,500.00

728. MC KINLEY, WILLIAM. President; assassinated. Handsome sepia bust cabinet photograph of Mc Kinley by Sarony, New York. Boldly signed, probably as President, against the light background area above the image. Photographer's imprint on lower mount. Extremely fine condition, and a gorgeous photograph. 850.00

729. TAFT, WILLIAM H. President; Chief Justice, U.S. Supreme Court. Typed Letter Signed, as Chief Justice, on imprinted Supreme Court stationery. ½ page, 4to. Washington, October 29, 1922. To Frank A. Holden, Athens, Georgia, thanking him for sending a copy of his book, War Memories. "I shall hope to read it with great pleasure...." Fine example. 150.00

730. FILLMORE, MILLARD. President and Vice President. Partly printed Document Signed, as President. 1 page, 4to. Washington, October 8, 1850. Authorizes and directs the Secretary of State to affix the Seal of the United States to "the pardon granted to Charles Botsford." Fillmore's signature is fine, but some of the other writing is on the light side. Fine condition. With steel-engraved portrait. Fillmore is relatively scarce as President. 450.00

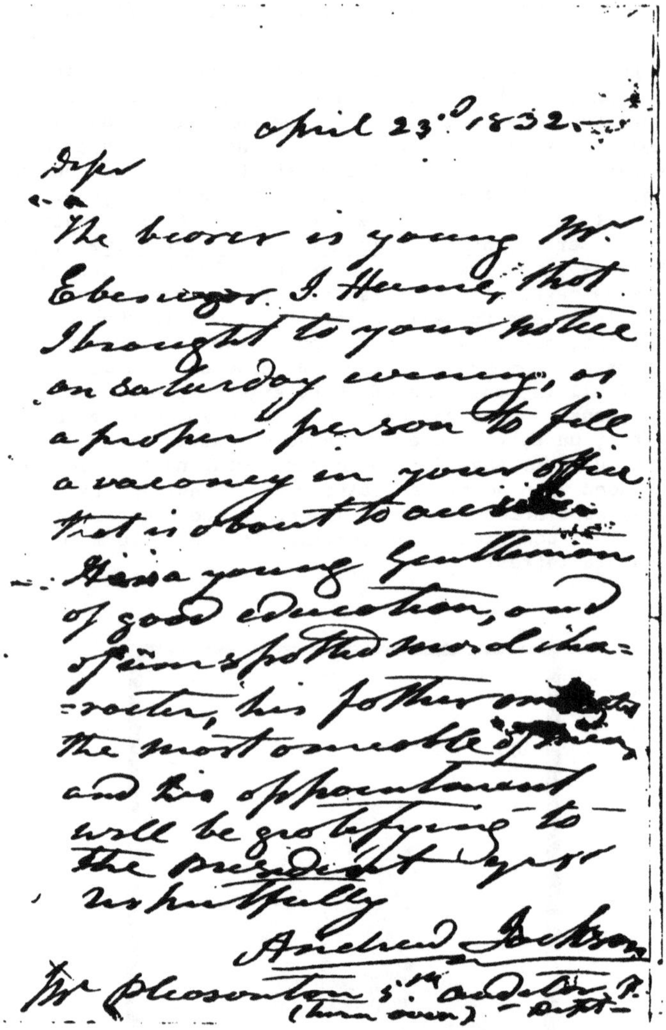

April 23d 1832

Dear Sir

The bearer is young Mr Ebenezer J. Hume, that I brought to your notice on saturday evening, as a proper person to fill a vacancy in your office that is about to occur. He is a young Gentleman of good education, and of unspotted moral character, his father amongst the most amiable of men, and his appointment will be gratifying to the President. yours respectfully

Andrew Jackson

Mr Pleasonton 5th auditor P. Dept.
(turn over)

SCARCE HOLOGRAPH LETTER SIGNED AS PRESIDENT

731. JACKSON, ANDREW. President and General. Choice Autograph Letter Signed, as President. Full page, large 8vo. [Washington] April 23, 1832. To Mr. Pleasanton, 5th Auditor P[ost Office] Department. Jackson writes: "The bearer is young Mr. Ebenezer J. Hume, that I brought to your notice on Saturday evening, as a proper person to fill a vacancy in your office that is about to occur. He is a young gentleman of good education, and of unspotted moral character, his father amongst the most amiable of men, and his appointment will be gratifying to the President...." On the verso, Jackson has also penned the following initialed postscript: "I have mentioned the subject to the Secy. of Treasury who sanctions the appointment. A.J." Fine condition, save for several minor ink blots (probably done by Jackson himself). With a striking steel-engraved portrait. 2950.00

732. EISENHOWER, MAMIE D. First Lady. Typed Letter Signed, on her imprinted stationery. 1 page, 4to. New York, January 16, 1953. To Doris Sousa, Middleboro, Mass. Original envelope. Writing just four days before her husband was inaugurated President, the future First Lady says: "...I am most happy to send you a copy of one of the General's favorite recipes. We hope you will like it. Thank you for your note of faith and confidence in the General. You have no idea how much it means to us to learn of the sincere support of so many millions of Americans ...." On a separate sheet is the typed recipe for <u>Chili By Willi</u>. Fine. 45.00

733. ADAMS, JOHN QUINCY. President. Autograph Manuscript Resolve, unsigned, penned by Adams after his presidential term while representing his district in the Congress of the United States. 1 page, small 4to. No place or date. Draft of a Resolve of the House of Representatives calling on the Secretaries of Treasury, War and Navy to report to the House the names of those appointed as agents for the payment of Pensions, as well as the banks with which they are connected. This interesting and unusual financial document probably dates from the period President Andrew Jackson was having his fight with Nicholas Biddle and the Bank of the United States. With a fine engraved portrait of Adams. 350.00

RARE PRESIDENTIAL LETTER BY WILSON WHILE IN PARIS

734. WILSON, WOODROW. President. Splendid Typed Letter Signed, as President, on stationery embossed "THE PRESIDENT OF THE UNITED STATES OF AMERICA" at top right, and at top left the Presidential Seal is embossed (this type of presidential stationery was used only by Wilson while in Paris for the Versailles Peace Treaty negotiations). 1 page, 4to. Paris, January 11, 1919. To Cannon H. B. Rawnsley, The Abbey, Carlisle, England. Original addressed envelope bearing a French postage stamp (uncancelled). Wilson writes: "It was very gratifying and refreshing to catch a glimpse of you and Mrs. Rawnsley when I was in Carlisle and I thank you warmly for your thoughtfulness in sending me your book Past and Present at the English Lakes. Will you not also thank my Quaker friend in Easedale for the telegram? Mrs. Wilson joins me in friendly greetings. Cordially and sincerely yours..." Very rare from this period. Pristine condition, with a bold signature. 575.00

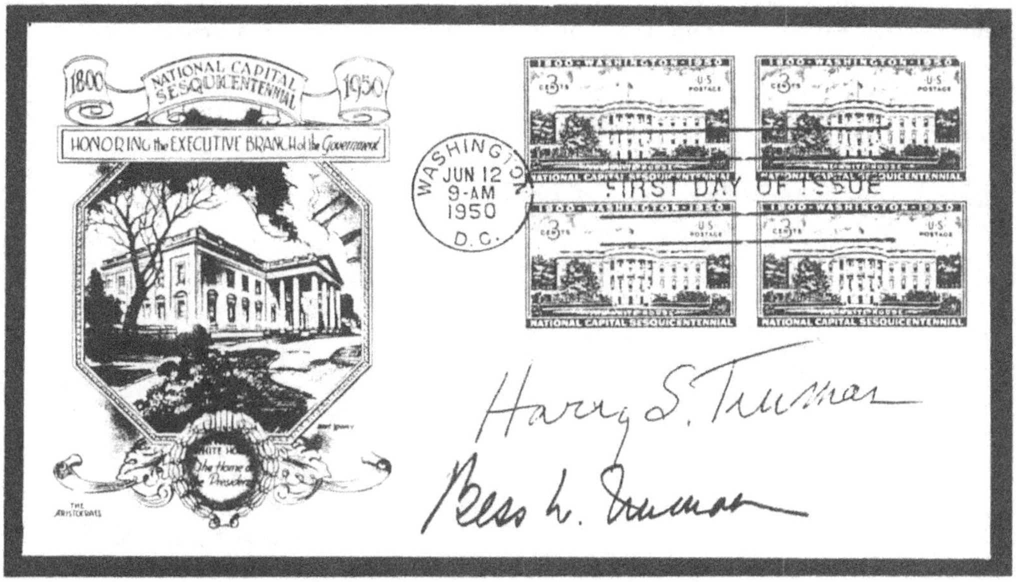

735. TRUMAN, HARRY S. AND BESS W. President and First Lady. Ornate cacheted (The Aristocrats) U.S. First Day Cover honoring the Executive Branch of the Government and featuring a bloc of four green commemorative stamps depicting the White House. Washington, June 12, 1950. Boldly signed by the Trumans to the right of the cachet beneath the stamps. Truman's signature was penned late in life with a ball-point pen, hence the capital "S" and the difference from his earlier signatures. Excellent condition. 250.00

CREDENCE FOR GENERAL SICKLES TO SPAIN

736. GRANT, ULYSSES S. President. Attractive partly printed Document Signed, as President. One page, 4to. Washington, June 28, 1869. President Grant authorizes the Secretary of State to affix the Seal of the United States to "the envelope of a letter addressed to the Regent of Spain (Gen'l Sickles' Credence)..." Union General Daniel E. Sickles (1825-1914), served as U.S. Minister to Spain from 1869 to 1873. Choice association!! Excellent. 500.00

NAVAL BOOK INSCRIBED BY MC KINLEY

737. MC KINLEY, WILLIAM. President. Book entitled: Decatur and Somers. By M. Eliot Seawell. Pictorial cloth. New York, 1894. First edition. Inscribed in Governor McKinley's hand on early flyleaf: "For Harrold Taylor Knowles / With the good wishes of / Mr. & Mrs. Mc Kinley / Dec. 25, 94". This book was designed for young readers, and apparently it was a Christmas gift from the Mc Kinleys to a young lad. Binding slightly worn and inner hinges cracked. Still a very good copy bearing an unusual presentation inscription. 450.00

738. COOLIDGE, CALVIN. President and Vice President. Typed Letter Signed, as President, on imprinted White House stationery. 1 page, 4to. Washington, November 15, 1924. To Hon. Walter L. McMenimen, U.S. Railroad Labor Board, Chicago, Illinois. Writing some ten days after his campaign victory in seeking re-election to the Presidency, Coolidge thanks his correspondent "...for your kind letter of felicitation on the outcome of the election...." Brief, but attractive presidential example. Fine condition. 350.00

739. MADISON, JAMES. President. Manuscript Letter Signed, as Secretary of State. Full page, 4to. Department of State [Washington], no date [April 7, 1808]. Headed Circular. Madison writes: "Agreeably to an Act of Congress, entitled An Act for the more general promulgation of the laws of the U. States...I have transmitted to the Collector of the Customs at Philadelphia 1026 copies of the laws of the United States...being the proportion for the State of Pennsylvania with the request that he would forward them to your Excellency...." Probably written to the Governor of Pennsylvania, who was at this time Thomas McKean. Fine. 950.00

RARE LETTER OF PRESIDENTIAL DATE

739A. MC KINLEY, WILLIAM. President; Governor of Ohio; assassinated in office. Typed Letter Signed, as President, on imprinted Executive Mansion stationery. 1 page, 4to. Washington, November 12, 1900. To Major General William R. Shafter, U.S.A., Retired, Bakersfield, California. Fine letter written several days after McKinley was elected to his second presidential term. He writes: "General Corbin has brought to my attention your courteous message of congratulation. Thanking you for your kindly comment on the subject of the recent election..." Presidential letters of McKinley are seldom encountered. Fine example. 750.00

RARE SIGNED CABINET PHOTOGRAPH OF BENJAMIN HARRISON

739B. HARRISON, BENJAMIN. President of the United States; Senator from Indiana. Handsome cabinet photograph showing a dignified formal bust profile likeness of the bearded President. Signed on the lower mount beneath his likeness. Pencil note on verso states that the photograph was taken by W. H. Potter in 1888, the year Harrison was elected President. Fine! 1500.00

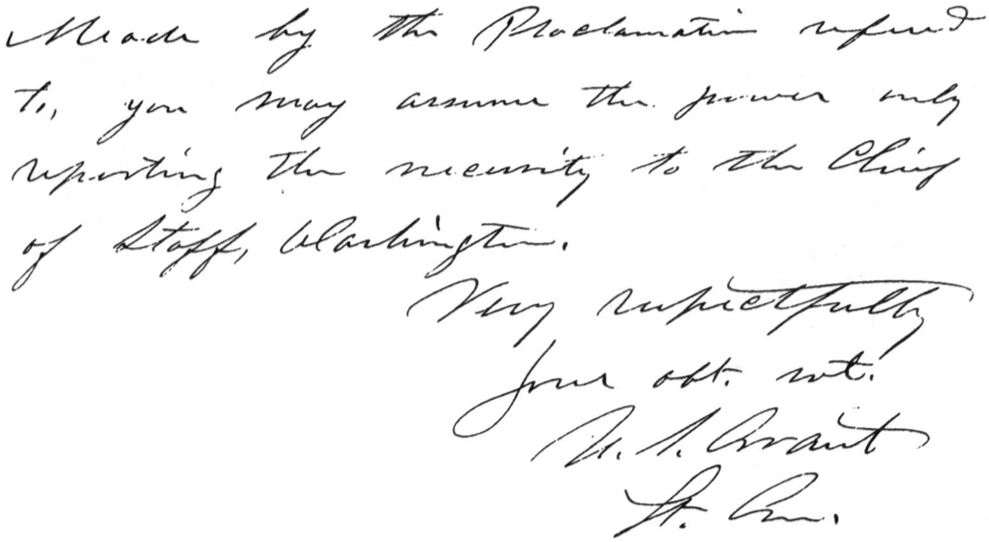
Meade by the Proclamation referred
to, you may assume the power only
reporting the necessity to the Chief
of Staff, Washington.
Very respectfully
Your obt. svt.
U. S. Grant
Lt. Gen.

"THE OBJECT IS TO SEE THAT UNITED STATES LAWS ARE NOT VIOLATED..."

740. GRANT, ULYSSES S. President; Union General in Civil War; accepted Lee's surrender. Important Autograph Letter Signed "U. S. Grant / Lt/ Gen." 2 pages, 4to. St. Louis, Missouri, June 7, 1866. To Major General E. O. C. Ord, Commanding Department of the Ohio.

> "Under the Presidents proclamation of yesterday in support of the neutrality laws of the United States you may use all power necessary to carry it out within your Department. If the Civil Authorities are taking the matter in hand it may not be necessary for you to do more than to give them such aid as they may call on you for. Of this you are the best judge. The object is to see that United States laws are not violated and if it becomes necessary for you to have the same powers, that of using the Military and Naval power of the United States, and the Militia of the States, same as extended to Gen. Meade by the proclamation referred to, you may assume the power only [by] reporting the necessity to the Chief of Staff, Washington...."

The docket on the integral leaf indicates this letter was received at Detroit on June 11th 1866. A fine letter showing that Grant was strongly in favor of President Johnson's proclamation. Excellent condition. 2500.00

741. BUCHANAN, JAMES. President; Senator from Pennsylvania; Secretary of State; Minister to England. Autograph Letter Signed, as Ambassador to the Court of St. James's, on stationery imprinted "Legation of The United States. Full page, 4to. London, December 19, 1853. To Lady Stafford, upon learning of the "melancholy announcement of the death of your Sister, the Marchioness of Wellesley." Buchanan continues: "Most sincerely & deeply do I sympathise with the Duchess & yourself on this irreparable loss. She has gone to her rest; but she has left behind her a character which diserves to be held in perpetual & grateful remembrance. For my own part, -- the elegance & suavity of her manners, the goodness of her heart, the Christian virtues which she displayed under the assaults of a mortal disease, & her kindness to myself have left an impression on my grateful memory which time can never efface...." Fine example. With handsome steel-engraved portrait. 500.00

742. COOLIDGE, CALVIN. President and Vice President. His book: The Price of Freedom / Speeches and Addresses. Gilt-lettered blue cloth. New York, 1924. First edition. Inscribed on the front endpaper: "To Mrs. Annie Murray Hannay / With best wishes / Calvin Coolidge". Dated in another hand at bottom left "April 9, 1926". Fine copy of a relatively scarce presidential book, issued as campaign literature for the 1924 presidential election. 250.00

743. ADAMS, JOHN QUINCY. President; Secretary of State. Autograph Letter Signed, in full, while a young attorney practicing in Boston. 1 page, small 4to. Boston, April 6, 1802. Recipient not identified. Adams writes: "I am directed by James Buckley and Sons to put in suit two notes of hand given to them by you, dated the 1st of October last, payable in 150 days, for 188 dollars 64 cents, and the other in ninety days, for 150 dollars, -- unless the same should be settled within fifteen days....My office is in State Street, under the Centinel printing office..." Fine example. With a fine steel-engraved portrait. 750.00

744. COOLIDGE, GRACE. First Lady. Autograph Letter Signed, as the wife of the Governor of Mass. and the Republican nominee for Vice President. 3 1/2 pages, 8vo. Burlington, Vermont, October 18, 1920. To her Northampton neighbours, Misses Mary and Maud Hammond. Stamped, postmarked envelope addressed by Mrs. Coolidge. After expressing belated thanks for some roses, she writes: "...I have been having a grand time here but haven't had as much spare time as I anticipated having. I have not been at home when college was open since I graduated and I have enjoyed a little fraternity life again. I expect to leave tomorrow for Boston. Tell Mrs. Hammond that I think her Republican day was a great success in every detail. I wish she could be in Boston for the one they are planning there for the 27th. The foliage up here is just grand...." Fine condition, and written at an interesting time in her husband's political career. 125.00

745. TRUMAN, HARRY S. President and Vice President. Typed Letter Signed, on his imprinted letterhead. 2/3 page, 4to. Independence, Missouri, February 8, 1961. To John K. Gott, J.E.B. Stuart High School, Falls Church, Virginia. Truman acknowledges the gift of an Electoral Ticket of Horace Greeley and B. Gratz Brown, commenting: "I more than appreciate it and it will go into my collection for exhibition here in the Library." The "Ticket" referred to was from the presidential election of 1872. Nice political association. Fine. 150.00

WHISKEY FOR A NORTHWEST TERRITORY BARGE CREW

746. HARRISON, WILLIAM HENRY. President; General in War of 1812. Early Manuscript Document Signed "Wm. H. Harrison / A.D.C." Oblong 8vo. Greenville, November 14, 1794. Orders that the Quarter Master issue twelve rations of whiskey for a Barge Crew. Irregularly trimmed at top, else fine. With engraved portrait. 475.00

747. HARDING, FLORENCE KLING. First Lady. Handsome engraved vignette of the White House, oblong 12mo., boldly inscribed: "To ____ _____ with greetings and abiding faith in our America. Florence Kling Harding". Striking exhibition piece! 150.00

748. ROOSEVELT, FRANKLIN D. President. Typed Letter Signed, as Assistant Secretary of the Navy, on the blue-crested imprinted social stationery of that office. 1 page, 4to. Washington, April 16, 1915. To Hon. Clayton L. Wheeler, Hancock, New York. Roosevelt writes: "I am just back from the Pacific Coast and have been delighted to find the pail of maple sugar. The whole family is enjoying it and say it is the most delightful thing they get to eat. I have not yet had a chance to see the Attorney General but expect to do so in a few days. Nothing has been done about appointments and, frankly, I do not know when any action will be taken, but I will keep you posted...." Attractive letter. 225.00

Personal

Washington, D.C.

December 24, 1925.

My dear Bishop McDowell:

On this Christmas Eve I wish to send you my best wishes for a Happy Day for you and all who are dear to you and all who in your long career have come within the influence of your work. Mrs Coolidge joins in best wishes to your dear wife.

Cordially

Calvin Coolidge

Rt. Rev. William F. McDowell

Washington, D.C.

[Item No. 749]

CHRISTMAS GREETINGS TO THE BISHOP
RARE HOLOGRAPH LETTER AS PRESIDENT

749. COOLIDGE, CALVIN. President and Vice President. Extremely rare Autograph Letter Signed, as President. 2 separate pages, 4to. Washington, December 24, 1928. To the Rt. Rev. William F. McDowell, Washington, D.C. Writing Bishop McDowell on Christmas Eve, Coolidge pens: "On this Christmas Eve I wish to send you my best wishes for a Happy day for you and all who are dear to you, and all who in your long career have come within the influence of your work. Mrs. Coolidge joins me in best wishes to your dear wife. Cordially / Calvin Coolidge..." Headed "Personal" in Coolidge's hand. Extremely rare, being only one of a handful of holograph Coolidge letters of presidential date in private hands. Choice condition. 3500.00

750. BUCHANAN, JAMES. President. Handsome partly printed Document Signed, as Secretary of State. 1 page, tall folio. Department of State, Washington, March 6, 1849. Choice eagle vignette at top center. Passport for one Luke Lincoln, giving his physical description, and bearing his signature. Excellent condition, with choice signature of Buchanan. Ornate!! 325.00

751. EISENHOWER, DWIGHT D. President and General. Typed Letter Signed, on his imprinted five-star stationery. 1 page, 4to. No place, December 30, 1947. To Mrs. I. Eisenhower Connor, Ocean City, N.J., acknowledging receipt of her Christmas card. "It was splendid of you to remember Mrs. Eisenhower and me at Christmastime, and we are grateful for your good wishes. We hope the New Year will bring to you the fullest measure of health and happiness...." Attractive example. 250.00

752. COOLIDGE, GRACE. First Lady. Blue-imprinted White House card bearing her full signature, as First Lady. Washington, no date. Choice specimen. 65.00

753. COOLIDGE, GRACE. First Lady. Fine signature on a plain white card. 25.00

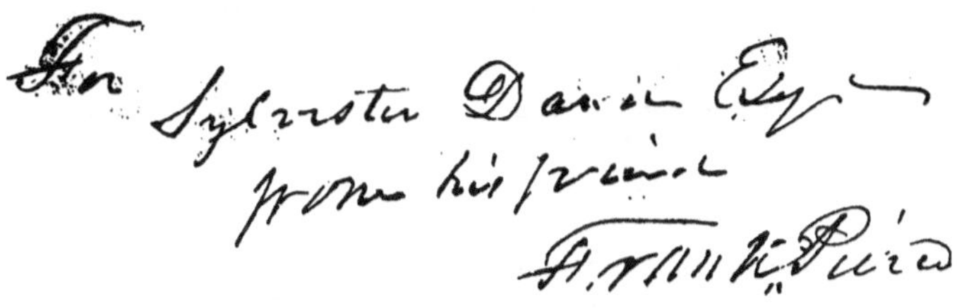

SIGNED PRESENTATION FROM FRANKLIN PIERCE

754. PIERCE, FRANKLIN. President; General in Mexican War; Congressman from New Hampshire. Book: Notes of a Military Reconnaissance, from Fort Leavenworth, in Missouri, to San Diego, in California, including Parts of the Arkansas, Del Norte, and Gila Rivers....Made in 1846-7, with the Advanced Guard of the "Army of the West", by William Emory. 30th Congress, 1st Session, Senate Executive [Doc.] No. 7. Wendell and Van Benthuysen: Washington, 1848. Orginal brown cloth. First edition. With 26 plates of scenery, 14 plates of botany, and 3 plans; lacking the folding pocket map. Inscribed on the front endpaper: "For Sylvester Dana Esq. / from his friend / Frank Pierce". An important volume in the western exploration of the United States, but more important from our standpoint, it bears the very rare presentation inscription of Pierce. Sabin 22536; Howes E-145; Cowan, p. 145; Wagner-Camp 148. Basically in fine condition, showing only moderate wear. 1950.00

755. HOOVER, HERBERT. President. Typed Letter Signed, on his imprinted stationery. 1 page, 4to. New York City, May 31, 1945. To Mrs. A. F. Murray, Bridgeton, New Jersey, saying that her delightful letter recalls many pleasant memories. He continues: "...Certainly all Americans can be most grateful to your boys and those other American boys who are serving their country with such magnificent courage...." Nice war-date letter. Fine. 150.00

756. GRANT, ULYSSES S. President and Union General. Fine signature. With portrait. 100.00

757. TRUMAN, HARRY S. President and Vice President. Attractive engraved 12mo card expressing thanks for Holiday Greetings and extending best wishes for the New Year. Signed and dated "1-5-68" by Truman in the lower margin. Pristine specimen. 75.00

HOLOGRAPH LETTER AS FIRST LADY WITH ENVELOPE FRANKED BY PRESIDENT PIERCE

758. PIERCE, JANE MEANS APPLETON. 1806-1863. First Lady. Autograph Letter Signed "J. M. Pierce", as First Lady, on narrow black-bordered stationery. 6 full closely written pages, 8vo. Washington, July 31, 1855. To her sister, Mrs. John Aiken, Andover, Mass. Original postmarked

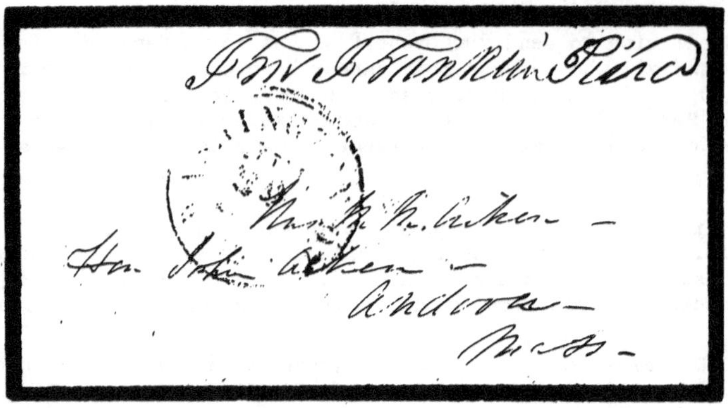

envelope addressed by Mrs. Pierce and franked "Free Franklin Pierce" in the upper right corner by the President. Circular black WASHINGTON postmark. Lengthy personal family letter, from which we can quote only a small part: "If it is as warm with you as it is here, you are hardly feeling like meeting the duties of this busy week....Yesterday I was able to go out only half the day and therefore -- attended in the afternoon Communion....I am not equal to much, although the difficulty which troubled me for the second time, is better now -- but this excessive general weakness appears in many ways....Mr. Pierce is very desirous of my going away, but does not promise to stay with me, and I do not like the thought of separation either on his account or my own....My husband is very busy this hot day. He professes to be well... Monday is always his most perplexing and busy day, when all sorts of things seem to have been gathering themselves to roll down en masse, after the pleasant rest of the Sabbath...He in fact needs entire rest -- the doctor says he must, he says, he cannot take. Gov. Marcy is at Point Comfort, his family in the North. Judge Campbell and his away for the rest of the season. Mr. Dobbin...at the Red Sulphur Springs. Mr. Davis is staying at the Soldiers Retreat... Most of people out of the city...but it never looked more beautifully here in the summer than it now does...." The persons referred to above were members of Pierce's cabinet. Excellent condition, interesting content, and with a choice franked envelope. 975.00

759. TRUMAN, HARRY S. President and Vice President. Typed Letter Signed, as President, on imprinted White House stationery. 1 page, 4to. Washington, November 30, 1948. To Miss Colleen Jenkins, Editor-in-Chief, The Sentinel, Spaulding High School, Barre, Vermont. Writing three weeks after his re-election victory over Thomas E. Dewey, Truman states: "I was indeed pleased to get your letter telling of the friendly attitude of the Spaulding High School Sentinel toward my candidacy. It is particularly gratifying to have this expression of good will from the Republican state of Vermont. My cordial thanks to you all...." Fine. 375.00

THE SAINT LAWRENCE POWER COMMISSION

AN ORIGINAL MESSAGE TO THE NEW YORK LEGISLATURE

760. ROOSEVELT, FRANKLIN D. President. Highly important Typewritten Message Signed, as Governor of New York, on ornate imprinted stationery bearing the State Seal. Executive Chamber [Albany], January 19, 1931. Headed TO THE LEGISLATURE. 7 1/2 separate pages, large legal folio. In this unusual and important message the future President seeks to "clarify and simplify the questions involved in the voluminous and necessarily technical reports of the St. Lawrence Power Commission...." He continues: "On March 12, 1929...I laid down these general principles 'In making use of this potential energy on the St. Lawrence owned by the people of the State, the objective of the problem is essentially this: 1. The physical transforming of falling water into electrical current. 2.The transmission and distribution of this current from the plant where it is developed to the industries and homes of the people of the State.' The first objective was seriously opposed by many people who insisted for varying motives that the physical building of a dam was fraught with danger; that the cost would be prohibitive and that generation by steam had become as cheap as by water power...." FDR quotes extensively from the report of the Power Commission, answering in detail the objections that had been raised, and calls for immediate legislative authority to commence this public project. Actually, the St. Lawrence Power Project was a forerunner of the Tennessee Valley and other rural electrification projects Roosevelt inaugurated during the early years of his presidency. This is the copy of the message that was sent to the State Printer and has several printing instructions in pencil. The concluding page is reduced in size. Choice! 1500.00

LENGTHY ALS WRITTEN AS PRESIDENT

761. **HAYES, RUTHERFORD B.** President; Governor of Ohio; Union officer in Civil War. Autograph Letter Signed, as President, on imprinted Executive Mansion stationery. 3 full pages, large 8vo. Washington, August 23, 1880. To Hon. James M. Dalzell, the famous "Private Dalzell" of Civil War fame, then serving in the U.S. Congress from Ohio.

Dear Sir:

The Soldiers Reunion at Columbus on the 10th 11th and 12th of this month impressed me as one of the most enjoyable and notable gatherings of veterans of the War that I have ever attended. Perhaps it was, taking it all in all, the most satisfactory affair of the kind that has yet been held.

Its casting features well the great number of old soldiers who were present, the encampment in tents for several days, the interest taken in it by the citizens of Columbus and their beautiful and abundant decorations of their Streets, dwellings, places of business etc., the procession of veteran Soldiers with their old flags tattered and torn by storm and battle, and the large and enthusiastic meetings of veterans, especially the deeply affecting and interesting meeting of the Survivors of the Rebel Prisons.

I think this was the seventh, of the general Reunions of the Private soldiers of Ohio. The first I remember to have heard of, was called, as I now recollect, by Private Dalzell and was held at Caldwell in Noble County. The first of these Reunions which I attended was at Marietta in 1877. Gen. Devens of Massachusetts, and Gen. Carroll of Maryland, with many other well known Union Soldiers were present.

I trust that there is no doubt of the permanency of this institution, and that the annual meetings of the Ohio Soldiers and Sailors of the Union will continue to grow in interest and numbers.

Sincerely

R. B. Hayes

Unusually lengthy and quite fine Presidential letter. Some small expert repairs and very light soiling, else fine. Excellent content, and scarce while in office. 1750.00

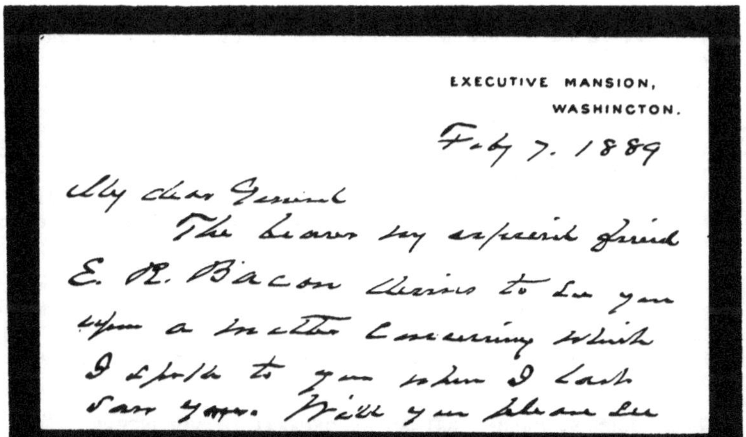

EXECUTIVE MANSION,
WASHINGTON.

Feby 7. 1889

My dear General

The bearer my especial friend E. R. Bacon desires to see you upon a matter concerning which I spoke to you when I last saw you. Will you please see

762. **CLEVELAND, GROVER.** President. Autograph Letter Signed, as President, on imprinted Executive Mansion Card. 2 pages, 16mo. Washington, February 7, 1889. To Major General John M. Schofield. "The bearer my especial friend E. R. Bacon desires to see you upon a matter concerning which I spoke to you when I last saw you. Will you please see him? Yours truly..." Pristine condition, and scarce in this format, as Presidents seldom used autograph cards for writing notes. 500.00

INSCRIBED TO CYRUS W. FIELD

763. GARFIELD, JAMES A. President. Handsome cabinet photograph depicting the profile bust of Garfield, probably while a member of Congress, but approaching the time of his candidacy for the presidency. Inscribed on the lower area of the photographic surface and running on to the lower mount: "Cyrus W. Field / With the kind regards of / J. A. Garfield". Photo is by Brady, with his imprint on the verso. Field is known today for his promotion of the Atlantic Cable; he was also a pioneer in organizing New York's subway system. A handsome photograph of the ill-fated Garfield, bearing an inscription of great association and interest. Choice condition. 2500.00

764. TAYLOR, ZACHARY. President. Manuscript Document Signed "Z. Taylor, Col. / 1st Regt. U.S. Infy / Comdg". 1 page, oblong 8vo. Fort Crawford, Prairie du Chien [Michigan Territory, now in Wisconsin], January 1833. Headed "Requisition for Fuel, for the Office of the Comdg. Officer at Fort Crawford, for the month of January 1833". Taylor, as Commanding Officer, certifies to the correctness of the requisition. Fine condition. With engraved portrait. 650.00

765. HOOVER, HERBERT. President. Typed Letter Signed, as President, on imprinted White House letterhead. 1 page, 4to. Washington, April 26, 1930. To Hon. C. Bascom Slemp, Washington. In this brief letter, Hoover writes: "I have your note of April 25th about Mr. Andrew Jackson. I am taking it up with the Department of Agriculture...." Fine example. 350.00

JOHN S. MASON, BRIGADIER GENERAL OF VOLUNTEERS

766. LINCOLN, ABRAHAM. 1809-1865. President. Handsome ornate partly engraved Document Signed "Abraham Lincoln", as President. Folio, vellum. Washington, April 15, 1863. Countersigned by EDWIN M. STANTON, Secretary of War. Blue wafer War Department seal. Spread-eagle vignette at top center; vignette of battle flags, canon, drum, swords, spears, shot and other military accoutrements at bottom. Lincoln commissions JOHN S. MASON to the rank of Brigadier General of Volunteers. Mason was born in Steubenville, Ohio (1824), and graduated from West Point in 1847. He served in the artillery during the Mexican War. During the Civil War he was breveted for gallantry at the battle of Fredericksburg. Following the war he was engaged in duty on the frontier. This commission is in excellent condition, and bears a choice full signature of Lincoln. Commissions for such high-ranking officers are seldom offered. 2750.00

"YOU MUST NOT PERMIT THAT HYPOCRITICAL SCAMP CROCKETT TO BE ELECTED"

767. JACKSON, ANDREW. President; General in War of 1812, and hero of Battle of New Orleans; Senator from Tennessee. Magnificent Autograph Letter Signed. 3 very full pages, 4to. Hermitage, June 16, 1839. To General Samuel A. Hays, Jackson, Madison County, West Tennessee. Integral address-leaf franked "Free Andrew Jackson", bearing a blue circular NASHVILLE postmark.

> "...I cannot convey to you that grateful sensation your statement of the result of your trial has inspired. Altho I knew malice and perjury had produced the charge, ...there was nothing but those proceedings that are now on record could have shielded you and your dear children from the malignant tongue of Slander of your enemies... There is no Virtue and honesty however pure, can Shield one now adays from the slander of Modern Whigism, and I have no doubt but this attempt at your character has originated from that source, to prostrate you, and prevent your promotion and rising fame. However base and unworthy the tool employed in this wicked attempt...you will find it originated from higher influence and Whig sources. But thank god the record pronouncing it frivolous and malicious, and the court taxing the prosecutor with the costs in an everlasting shield to your character... Truth is mighty and will always ultimately prevail -- it is the atribute of duty....
>
> I have been much benefited by one bottle of the Matchless Laxative, and had I had another bottle...I believe it would have restored me to such health and strength as would have enabled me to have travelled and visited all my friends....It would be a great comfort and pleasure to me to be able to travel and see and mix with our friends, but I am in the hands of that allwise providence who does all things well for the best, and to his will I implicitly submit....I am now labouring under a severe affliction of my head and ears -- but which is yielding to medicine and I hope in a few days will, as usual, have a temporary relief from it.
>
> My little White family are all now in good health...
>
> PS. The democratic republican cause is brightening with us and in the Eastern part of the State. Polk is sure of a majority in east Tennessee and from all accounts I can gather Burton is gaining fast and will beat Bell in Wilson and obtain a Majority in Davidson. You must not permit that hypocritical scamp Crockett to be elected. He is the mere tool of Bell and J. Q. Adams, without principle or talents and has become a good Whig by learning the art of lying and slandering good and honest men. Virginia has done well. I received the returns last night. The Legislature on joint ballott will have a majority of two. Rives is consigned to that fate which is allotted all unprincipled apostates -- contempt of all honest men...."

An outstanding post-presidential letter! The "Crockett" referred to by Jackson was undoubtedly a relative of Davy Crockett, formerly a Congressman from Tennessee, who had been killed three years earlier at the Alamo. The Jacksons and Crocketts were constantly at political odds. John Quincy Adams defeated Jackson in 1824 when he made his first run for the presidency, and Jackson, in turn, defeated Adams in 1828. Some weakness at the folds, else in fine condition. Very boldly penned. 6500.00

768. ROOSEVELT, FRANKLIN D. President. Typed Letter Signed, as Assistant Secretary of the Navy, on the attractive blue-imprinted social stationery of that office. Full page, 4to. Washington, November 22, 1915. To Hon. Clayton L. Wheeler, Hancock, New York. Roosevelt writes: "The Post Office Department will hold up the appointments at Hobart and Stamford until they hear from me. When you have all the data ready on these two places just send it along...and I shall be glad to take the matter up with the Post Office Department. I have taken pleasure in sending you two copies of the President's photograph which I have had autographed by him, and I am also sending you one of my own autographed...." Pristine condition! 225.00

769. HOOVER, LOU HENRY. First Lady. Handsome formal portrait studio photograph by Bachrach, showing Mrs. Hoover in half-length profile. Inscribed in her hand on the lower white margin: "To Mr. George Fox, with much gratitude for his many kindnesses to Herbert Jr. and others of our family and friends. Lou Henry Hoover". Scarce in this format. Striking pose! 225.00

RARE ALS OF PRESIDENTIAL DATE

770. FILLMORE, MILLARD. President and Vice President. Autograph Letter Signed, as President. Full page, 4to. Washington, February 26, 1851. To A. Merwin, New York. Fillmore acknowledges Merwin's letter "...informing me of the fact of my election as an Honorary Member of the American Board of Commissioners for Foreign Missions, and the donation for the purpose was given by Mr. Anson G. Phelps of your City. For this act of kindness on the part of Mr. Phelps, I beg to return him through you, my warmest acknowledgements. With assurances of deep interest in the success of the Board in the holy enterprise in which it is engaged...." Broken center horizontal fold professionally repaired on verso. Some light staining in blank top margin, not affecting text. Fillmore was President for only three years, and his holograph letters dated while in office are quite scarce. Fine appearance, and a rarity! 1750.00

771. COOLIDGE, CALVIN. President and Vice President. Typed Letter Signed, as President, on imprinted White House stationery. 1 page, 4to. Washington, March 1, 1929. To Rufus N. Hemenway, The Fafnir Bearing Co., New Britain, Conn. Fine letter written by Coolidge three days before leaving the presidential office. In part: "...The many friendly messages of good will and sincere appreciation, coming to me at this time are most gratifying. I am hoping to see more of Vermont in the future than I have for some years past...." Original stamped envelope. Excellent condition. 350.00

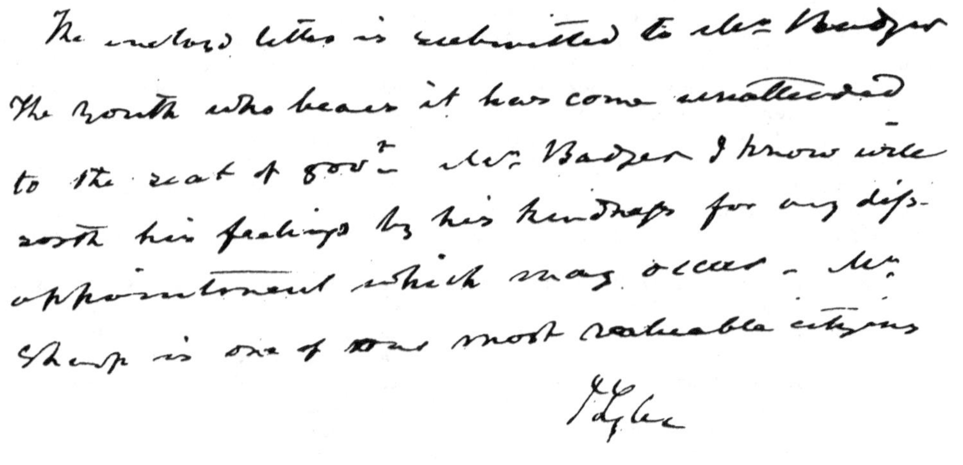
The enclosed letter is submitted to Mr Badger
The youth who bears it has come unattended
to the seat of govt. Mr. Badger I know will
sooth his feelings by his kindness for any dis-
appointment which may occur. Mr.
Sharp is one of our most valuable citizens
J Tyler

772. TYLER, JOHN. President and Vice President; Governor of Virginia. Autograph Message Signed, as President. 1/2 page, 4to. No place or date. To Hon. Mr. Badger / Secretary of the Navy. Docketed integral address-leaf, with address-panel in Tyler's hand, and bearing Badger's docket "The President". Tyler writes: "The enclosed letter (not present) is submitted to Mr. Badger. The youth who bears it has come unattended to the seat of gov't. Mr. Badger I know will sooth his feelings by his kindness for any disappointment which may occur. Mr. Sharp is one of our most valuable citizens. J. Tyler" A most unusual showing of presidential thoughtfulness for a young job seeker who was able to personally talk with President Tyler about his concern for being employed, and apparently had made a highly favorable impression. Fine condition. With handsome steel-engraved portrait. 750.00

773. EISENHOWER, DWIGHT D. President and General. Strikingly handsome quarto photograph depicting Ike in civilian dress, unquestionably as President, seated in a leather chair looking straight at the camera. On the wide, white lower margin a secretary has neatly lettered "For Norman R. Hostler", and Eisenhower has boldly penned: "with best wishes from / Dwight D. Eisenhower". U.S. Army photograph. Pristine condition, and a stunning pose. 250.00

774. TRUMAN, HARRY S. President and Vice President. His account of life after leaving the high office of President: Mr. Citizen. Blue and white cloth. New York, 1960. First edition. Signed by Truman on the half-title page. Very fine copy. 150.00

775. TAFT, WILLIAM H. President; Chief Justice, U.S. Supreme Court. Typed Letter Signed, as Chief Justice, on imprinted Supreme Court stationery. 1/2 page, 4to. Washington, November 30, 1927. To Walter Prichard Eaton, Sheffield, Mass. In part: "...I don't remember distinctly Dr. Snow. I think he wrote a book in some way connected with the Philippines, but I never had to do with him, and I am afraid that my knowledge of him isn't such that I can make a personal recommendation to the Committee on Admissions of the Century Association. Perhaps if you would advise me further about him I could recollect something of him...." Original envelops. 225.00

776. BUCHANAN, JAMES. President; Secretary of State. Partly printed Document Signed, as President. 1 page, 4to. Washington, February 19, 1861. President Buchanan authorizes the Secretary of State to affix the Seal of the United States to a Warrant for the pardon of John C. Stanford. With handsome steel-engraved portrait. Nice pair for framing or display. 450.00

777. JOHNSON, LADY BIRD. [MRS. LYNDON B.] First Lady. Handsome engraved vignette of the White House by the Bureau of Engraving and Printing. Large oblong 8vo. Boldly signed in full by President Johnson's widow on the wide lower white margin. Pristine condition. 45.00

778. COOLIDGE, GRACE. First Lady. Full signature, and "February 8, 1946". 12mo. 25.00

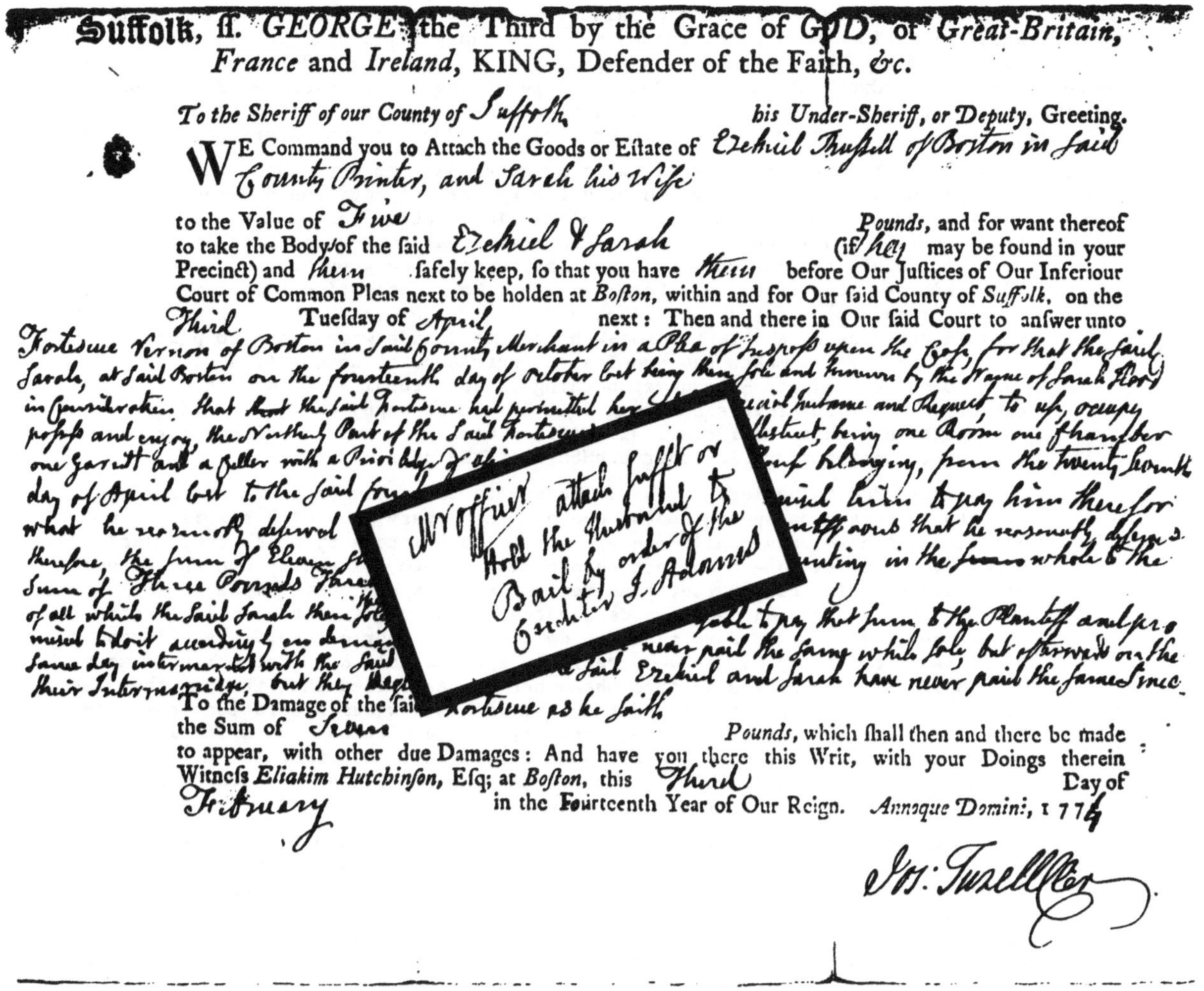

Suffolk, ss. GEORGE the Third by the Grace of GOD, of Great-Britain, France and Ireland, KING, Defender of the Faith, &c.

To the Sheriff of our County of Suffolk his Under-Sheriff, or Deputy, Greeting.

WE Command you to Attach the Goods or Estate of Ezekiel Russell of Boston in said County Printer, and Sarah his Wife to the Value of Five Pounds, and for want thereof to take the Body of the said Ezekiel & Sarah (if they may be found in your Precinct) and them safely keep, so that you have them before Our Justices of Our Inferiour Court of Common Pleas next to be holden at Boston, within and for Our said County of Suffolk, on the Third Tuesday of April next: Then and there in Our said Court to answer unto Fortesque Vernon of Boston in said County, Merchant in a Plea of trespass upon the Case, for that the said Sarah, at said Boston on the fourteenth day of October last ...

To the Damage of the said Fortesque as he saith, the Sum of Seven Pounds, which shall then and there be made to appear, with other due Damages: And have you there this Writ, with your Doings therein. Witness Eliakim Hutchinson, Esq; at Boston, this Third Day of February in the Fourteenth Year of Our Reign. Annoque Domini, 1774

Jo: Tudor Cler

Mr officer attach suff't or Hold the Husband to Bail by order of the Creditor J. Adams

779. ADAMS, JOHN. President and Vice President. Autograph Note Signed, penned on the verso of a partly-printed writ-of-attachment accomplished in Adams' hand. Small oblong 4to. Boston, February 3, 1774. This Suffolk County document authorizes the Sheriff to "Attach the Goods or Estate of Exekiel Russell of Boston...Printer, and Sarah his Wife..." The reason for this action is given in detail and is in Adams' hand. On the verso (see inset above) Adams has penned a signed note to a Court Officer concerning the attachment saying that the husband should be held to Bail. Fascinating legal document involving the future President at the time when he was beginning to emerge as a Revolutionary leader. Fine condition. 950.00

780. FORD, BETTY. First Lady. Her autobiography: The Times of My Life. With Chris Chase. Cloth. New York, 1978. First edition. Signed and dated "July 4, 1980" by the former First Lady on the front endpaper. Pictorial dust-jacket. Mint. 65.00

781. CLEVELAND, GROVER. President. Handsome, ornately engraved Document Signed, as President. Tall folio, vellum. Washington, August 20, 1888. Countersigned by R. MACFEELY, Acting Secretary of War. Embossed blue wafer seal of the War Department at lower center. Appointment of Samuel M. Mansfield to serve as Lieutenant Colonel in the Corps of Engineers. Engraved and printed by the Bureau of Engraving & Printing. Lovely vignettes of a spread-eagle at top center, and another of flags and military accoutrements at bottom. Handsome, clean document, well suited for framing or display. 450.00

782. GRANT, ULYSSES S. President; Union General. Handsome signature: "U. S. Grant / Lt. Gen. U.S. A." penned on a plain visiting card. With small engraved portrait. Pristine! 125.00

PRESIDENTIAL LETTER WITH INITIALED HOLOGRAPH POSTSCRIPT

783. COOLIDGE, CALVIN. President and Vice President. Typed Letter Signed, as President, on imprinted White House stationery. Full page, 4to. Washington, October 8, 1925. To Hon. Myron T. Herrick, Cleveland, Ohio. Coolidge informs Ambassador Herrick that "It was kind of you to remember us and to send your good wishes and congratulations on our anniversary. It was a pleasure to see you while you were here..." In a holograph postscript penned at the bottom of this letter, Coolidge inquires: "When are you coming to visit us? / C." Pristine condition and rare with the holograph postscript. Herrick was Ambassador to France. 650.00

784. VAN BUREN, MARTIN. President and Vice President. Super, magnificent Autograph Letter Signed. 9 full pages, 4to. Lindenwald [Kinderhook, N.Y.]. January 17, 1843. To His Excellency Wm. C. Bouck, Governor of New York. Docketed integral address-leaf. Van Buren begins this lengthy letter by offering advice to Governor Bouck for resolving a scandelous mess in Albany involv-int the state's printing and then launches into a fascinating philosophical discussion of how to conduct the executive branch of government, citing from his own experience as President.

"...Although I have not admitted it in my conversations with those who are given to croaking...I have...witnessed with the keenest regret, the distractions among our friends at Albany; & more particularly in relation to the State printing. It is certainly a lamentable winding up of a great contest, admirably conducted, ...& gloriously terminated....I cannot but experience great pain from the raging of so bitter a controversy....Permit me to make a suggestion & that relates to the importance of a speedy decision, one way or the other. Nothing is so injurious in such cases as delay. It is almost better to decide wrong than to protract the contest. Every day makes new enemies, & increases the animosities...& extends them to other subjects -- and yet nothing is so natural as to desire to put off the decision of controversies among friends. Most happy would I be to find that you had been able to mitigate...all difficulties by providing places for one or more of the competitors in other branches of the public service...

It has afforded me undisguised satisfaction to learn...that you keep your own secrets in regard to appointments, & don't feed every body with promises...a practice which so many public men are apt to fall into & by which they make themselves more trouble & subject themselves to more discredit than they dream of. Persevere in that course, consider carefully every one, & make the selection which your own unbiased judgment designates as the best, & above all, let the people see, as clear as day, that you do not yield yourself to...any cliques or sections of the party....The Democratic is a reasonable & a just party, & more than half of the business is done when they are satisfied that the man they have elected means to do right. The difficulty with a new administration is in the beginning. At the start little matters may create distrust which it will take a series of good acts to remove. But when once a favorable impression is made, & the people become satisfied that the right thing is intended, it takes great errors often repeated to create a counter current.

Will you excuse me if...I go further & touch upon matters not political, or at least not wholly so. Your situation...incites envy & jealousy on the part of some; it is impossible from the character of man that it should be otherwise... There will be people who will make ill natured remarks & there will be still more who will make it their business...to bring you exaggerated accounts of what is said, & if they lack materials, they will tell you, & if they find that you like to listen to such things, a great deal that never has been said. It is my deliberate opinion that these mischievous gossips cause public men more vex-ation, yes ten fold, than all the cares & anxieties of office taken together. I have been perhaps as much of this as any man of my age & claim to be a competent judge of the evil & its remedy. The greatest fault I ever saw in our excellent friend General Jackson was the facility with which (in carrying out his general principle that it was the duty of the President to hear all) he leant his ear, though not in confidence, to such people. Though very sagacious, & very apt to put the right construction upon all such revelations, it was still evident that he was every day more or less annoyed by them. I endeavoured to satisfy him of the expediency of shutting their mouths but did not succeed...If truth could be known...he experienced more annoyance from such sources than from all the severe trials through which he had to pass & did pass with such unfading glory.

Having his case before me & determined to profit by the experience I had acquired in so good a school, I had no sooner taken possession of the White House than I was beset by these harpies. The way in which I treated the whole crew with var-iations of course owing to circumstances, will appear from the following dialogue ... The celebrated Dr. Mayo called upon me & in his stuttering & mysterious way commenced by asking when he could have a few minutes very private consultation with me. Knowing the man, I anticipated his business & told him now, I will hear you now. He then told me he discovered a conspiracy to destroy me politically, the particulars of which he felt it to be his duty to lay before me. I replied instantly & somewhat sternly, Dr. I do not wish to hear them. I have irrefutable proof he replied. I don't care was the response. It is in writing, Sir, said he -- I won't look at it Sir. What, said he, don't you want to see it if it is in writing & genuine. An emphatic No, Sir, closed the conversation. The Dr. raised his eyes and hands as if he thought me demented, & making a low bow...retreated for the door. The story about the Dr. got out partly by me...and alarmed all the story tellers who heard it of it...[and] impressed the whole crew with a convict-ion that nothing was to be gained by bringing such reports to me. The consequence was that although Washington is perhaps the most gossiping place in the world, I escaped its contamination altogether, had no trouble accept such as unavoidably grew out of my public duties, and although I had perhaps a more vexatious time than any of my predecessors in most respects, I was the only man, they all say, who grew fat in that office...."

Handsomely preserved, and the finest content Van Buren letter he have ever had!! 7500.00

Eng^d by A.B. Hall, New York

D. Appleton & Co

PRESIDENTIAL PORTRAITS SUITABLE FOR MOUNTING WITH AUTOGRAPHS

We carry a large stock of portraits of the Presidents and First Ladies. Most of the Nineteenth Century presidents are represented by handsome steel-engraved portraits, similar to the one of Thos. Jefferson illustrated above. Many of these are contemporary of the president depicted. The Twentieth Century presidents are represented by both steel-engraved and colored printed portraits. Our price for all portraits is $9.50 each, regardless of subject, age or style. This constitutes a service charge and does not reflect the actual value of the portrait (which may be higher or lower). Portraits are supplied without charge to those who order autographs of the subject, and make their request at the time of placing the order.

THE PRESIDENTS OF THE UNITED STATES OF AMERICA

AUTOGRAPH LETTERS
HISTORICAL DOCUMENTS

PAUL C. RICHARDS — AUTOGRAPHS

FIVE DOLLARS

www.ingramcontent.com/pod-product-compliance
Lightning Source LLC
LaVergne TN
LVHW061335060426
835511LV00014B/1931